YOU ARE
AN INTRODUCTION TO
PROPHETIC LITERATURE

LOUIS STULMAN
AND
HYUN CHUL PAUL KIM

Abingdon Press
Nashville

YOU ARE MY PEOPLE
AN INTRODUCTION TO PROPHETIC LITERATURE

Copyright © 2010 by Abingdon Press

All rights reserved.

This book is printed on acid-free paper.

Library of Congress Cataloging-in-Publication Data

Stulman, Louis, 1953–
  You are my people : an introduction to prophetic literature / Louis Stulman and Hyun Chul Paul Kim.
      p. cm.
  Includes bibliographical references and index.
  ISBN 978-0-687-46565-1 (binding: book-printed/pbk. with lay-flat binding : alk. paper) 1. Bible. O.T. Prophets—Introductions.   I. Kim, Hyun Chul Paul, 1965–   II. Title.
  BS1505.52.S78 2010
  224'.061—dc22

                                                                                              2010005996

All scripture quotations, unless noted otherwise, are taken from the New Revised Standard Version of the Bible, copyright 1989, Division of Christian Education of the National Council of the Churches of Christ in the United States of America. Used by permission. All rights reserved.

Scripture quotations marked NJPS are taken from *TANAKH: The New JPS Translation According to the Traditional Hebrew Text.* Copyright 1985 by the Jewish Publication Society. Used by permission.

Scripture quotations marked NIV are taken from the Holy Bible, NEW INTERNATIONAL VERSION®. Copyright © 1973, 1978, 1984 by International Bible Society. All rights reserved throughout the world. Used by permission of International Bible Society.

Scripture quotations marked NASB are taken from the New American Standard Bible®. Copyright © 1960, 1962, 1963, 1968, 1971, 1972, 1973, 1975, 1977, 1995 by The Lockman Foundation. Used by permission. (www.Lockman.org)

The lyrics on pages vii and 4 include select verses from "Anthem" published in *Stranger Music: Selected Poems and Songs by Leonard Cohen* © 1993. Published in Canada by McClelland & Stewart Ltd in the USA by Vintage. Used with permission of McClelland & Stewart Ltd.

The lyrics on pages 3–4 are from "Magic" by Bruce Springsteen. Copyright © 2007 Bruce Springsteen. Reprinted by permission. International copyright secured. All rights reserved.

The lyrics on page 4 are from "Devil's Arcade" by Bruce Springsteen. Copyright © 2007 Bruce Springsteen. Reprinted by permission. International copyright secured. All rights reserved.

The lyrics on page 9 are copyright © 2006 Paul Simon. Used by permission of the Publisher: Paul Simon Music.

The poem on page 27 by Carl B. Westmoreland appears courtesy of the National Underground Railroad Freedom Center, Cincinnati, OH.

10 11 12 13 14 15 16 17 18 19—10 9 8 7 6 5 4 3 2 1

MANUFACTURED IN THE UNITED STATES OF AMERICA

For Pete Diamond, who has been busy hatching plots

and interpretive strategies for the rest of us,

in grateful friendship

Ah the wars they will

be fought again

The holy dove

She will be caught again

bought and sold

and bought again

the dove is never free

Ring the bells that still can ring

Forget your perfect offering

There is a crack in everything

That's how the light gets in

—Leonard Cohen, "Anthem"

Hope is what the world needs most

—Thomas Merton,

October 20, 1961

CONTENTS

ACKNOWLEDGMENTS

As the saying goes, "Two heads are better than one." Working collaboratively is not always easy, but it is often rewarding. We have quite candidly struggled with this venture, but at the same time enjoyed it immensely. Often encouraging and prodding each other to rethink and rewrite, we have learned much and discovered how much more there is to learn about the prophetic corpus in the Hebrew Bible.

We joyfully confess that this book is not merely the work of two but so many. Although space does not permit a full recital of all the contributing voices, we wish to express a special debt of thanks to Robert Cecire, Barbara Dick, Jeannine Grimm, Sara Hingson, M. Fulgence Nyengele, Kathleen M. O'Connor, Amy Stulman, and Marvin A. Sweeney. Each has been kind enough to read through our work, at various stages, and offer critical comments.

We express our gratitude to Leonard Cohen, Bruce Springsteen, and Paul Simon for permission to reprint select verses from their work. We thank Westminster John Knox Press for letting us reprint a revised form of chapter 6, "Conflicting Paths to Hope in Jeremiah," in *Shaking Heaven and Earth: Essays in Honor of Walter Brueggemann and Charles B. Cousar* (ed. C. R. Yoder et al.; Louisville: Westminster John Knox, 2005), 43–57; as well as Continuum Books for permission to use a revised version of chapter 5, originally published in *Inspired Speech: Prophecy in the Ancient Near East. Essays in Honour of Herbert B. Huffmon* (JSOTSup 378; ed. J. Kaltner and L. Stulman; New York: T&T Clark, 2004), 302–18.

We are indebted to the Methodist Theological School in Ohio and the University of Findlay for providing the institutional support that helped bring this project to fruition. We are grateful to Deutscher Akademischer Austausch Dienst (German Academic Exchange Service) for providing a faculty research visit grant and to Reinhard G. Kratz and Universität Goettingen for hospitality during the sabbatical research. We also wish to express our appreciation to Kathy Armistead and Katie Johnston of Abingdon Press for their timely cheers and sage advice all along.

And finally we thank our students for their enthusiasm and insights and our families for their very tangible love and support.

ABBREVIATIONS

General Abbreviations

B.C.E.	Before the Common Era
ch(s).	chapter(s)
v(v).	verse(s)

Biblical Texts

Gen	Genesis	Dan	Daniel
Exod	Exodus	Hos	Hosea
Lev	Leviticus	Joel	Joel
Num	Numbers	Amos	Amos
Deut	Deuteronomy	Obad	Obadiah
Josh	Joshua	Jonah	Jonah
Judg	Judges	Mic	Micah
Ruth	Ruth	Nah	Nahum
1 Sam	1 Samuel	Hab	Habakkuk
2 Sam	2 Samuel	Zeph	Zephaniah
1 Kgs	1 Kings	Hag	Haggai
2 Kgs	2 Kings	Zech	Zechariah
1 Chr	1 Chronicles	Mal	Malachi
2 Chr	2 Chronicles	Matt	Matthew
Ezra	Ezra	Mark	Mark
Neh	Nehemiah	Luke	Luke
Esth	Esther	John	John
Job	Job	Acts	Acts of the Apostles
Pss	Psalms	Rom	Romans
Prov	Proverbs	1 Cor	1 Corinthians
Eccl	Ecclesiastes	2 Cor	2 Corinthians
Song	Song of Solomon	Gal	Galatians
Isa	Isaiah	Eph	Ephesians
Jer	Jeremiah	Phil	Philippians
Lam	Lamentations	Col	Colossians
Ezek	Ezekiel	1 Thess	1 Thessalonians

2 Thess	2 Thessalonians	1 Pet	1 Peter
1 Tim	1 Timothy	2 Pet	2 Peter
2 Tim	2 Timothy	1 John	1 John
Titus	Titus	2 John	2 John
Phlm	Philemon	3 John	3 John
Heb	Hebrews	Jude	Jude
Jas	James	Rev	Revelation

Apocrypha

1–2 Macc	1–2 Maccabees
Sir	Sirach/Ecclesiasticus
Tob	Tobit

Bible Versions and Translations

LXX	Septuagint
MT	Masoretic Text
NASB	New American Standard Bible
NIV	New International Version of the Bible
NJPS	*Tanakh: The Holy Scriptures: The New JPS Translation according to the Traditional Hebrew Text*
NRSV	New Revised Standard Version of the Bible
OAN	Oracles against the Nations

Second Resources: Journals, Periodicals, Major Reference Works, and Series

AB	Anchor Bible
AnBib	Analecta biblica
AOAT	Alter Orient und Altes Testament
AOTC	Abingdon Old Testament Commentaries
BETL	Bibliotheca ephemeridum theologicarum lovaniensium
Bib	*Biblica*
BibInt	*Biblical Interpretation*
BTB	*Biblical Theological Bulletin*
BZAW	Beihefte zur Zeitschrift für die alttestamentliche Wissenschaft

CBQ	*Catholic Biblical Quarterly*
CC	Continental Commentaries
CBR	*Currents in Biblical Research*
CurBS	*Currents in Research: Biblical Studies*
FAT	Forschungen zum Alten Testament
FOTL	Forms of the Old Testament Literature
FS	Festschrift
HThKAT	Herders Theologischer Kommentar zum Alten Testament
IBT	Interpreting Biblical Texts
ICC	International Critical Commentary
Int	*Interpretation*
ITC	International Theological Commentary
JBL	*Journal of Biblical Literature*
JSOT	*Journal for the Study of the Old Testament*
JSOTSup	Journal for the Study of the Old Testament Supplement Series
JTS	*Journal of Theological Studies*
LHBOTS	Library of Hebrew Bible/Old Testament Studies
NCB	New Century Bible
NIBC	New International Biblical Commentary
NICOT	New International Commentary of the Old Testament
OBO	Orbis biblicus et orientalis
OBT	Overtures to Biblical Theology
OTG	Old Testament Guides
OTL	Old Testament Library
OTS	Old Testament Studies
OTT	Old Testament Theology
PBS	Public Broadcasting Service
SBLAIIL	Society of Biblical Literature Ancient Israel and Its Literature
SBLDS	Society of Biblical Literature Dissertation Series
SBLMS	Society of Biblical Literature Monograph Series
SBLSP	*Society of Biblical Literature Seminar Papers*
SBLSymS	Society of Biblical Literature Symposium Series
SBS	Stuttgarter Bibelstudien
SJOT	*Scandinavian Journal of the Old Testament*
VT	*Vetus Testamentum*
VTSup	Supplements to Vetus Testamentum
WBC	Word Biblical Commentary
ZAW	*Zeitschrift für die alttestamentliche*

The Divine Name

YHWH   In keeping with the biblical tradition of not pronouncing the Tetragrammaton, we employ this term in literal translation of the Hebrew יהוה.

INTRODUCTION

The present study is not an introduction to the Prophets in any traditional sense. Rather, it seeks—to use Walter Brueggemann's language—to "make the interface of ancient text and contemporary community more poignant and palpable."[1] As will be apparent from the outset, this exercise is far more intuitive and artistic than systematic and scientific. While building on recent developments in the field of biblical studies, this book does not employ a consistent and controlling methodology. What holds the chapters together is an attempt to read the prophetic literature as war-torn artifacts, disturbing cultural expressions of disaster and tapestries of hope intended to help devastated communities survive massive loss. The enduring contribution of written prophecy, we argue, lies in its (1) trenchant truth-telling and dogged refusal to deny the unspeakable *and* in its (2) audacity to imagine a future for defeated and captive people who live in a world in which violence and death are more tangible than coherence and meaning.

> In lonely cities, in starved villages,
> To look at all evil, at the decay of bodies[2]

The prophetic corpus is ultimately survival literature for exiles of old and exiles today.

Here, a few caveats are in order. First, it is our premise that the prophetic literature is the product of a long and complex oral and written tradition spanning many centuries—from as early as the eighth century B.C.E. to well into the Persian period—indeed, with redactions likely in the Greco-Roman period. To deny this long and complex history is problematic. To trace it with any precision is no less daunting. Hence, our focus will be on the synchronic level or final form of the Hebrew Bible, although hopefully our study will always exhibit *diachronic* (historical) sensibilities. We proceed with the awareness that the sacred text before us (in the Hebrew Bible and in Greek translations) is in large measure the only form of the text that is available to us.

At the same time, we attempt to identify or imagine the various communities that first encountered the prophetic scrolls as a formative part of congregational life. We often use the term "interpretive community" to refer to these readers.[3] When we employ this term, we are primarily speaking of exilic and postexilic settings. In contrast to those who actually heard the *oral* words of the prophets, the later interpretive communities of the exilic and postexilic periods enjoyed access only to the written form of the text, at its various stages. Scholars have described these post-587 B.C.E.

settings in different ways. Ehud Ben Zvi, for instance, has coined the term "post-monarchic" to allude to them. Jill Middlemas has introduced the term "templeless" to refer to the period between 587 and 515 B.C.E. in particular.[4] Many new and innovative theories are currently emerging regarding the role and function of the prophetic literature in the Persian period. Taking the lead from recent interpretive perspectives, we attempt to be attentive to the implied or imagined audiences of this era. At the same time, we cannot be certain whether the writers and readers were located in the provinces of Egypt, Babylon, Persia, or Yehud. Were these "implied readers" Yehudites (whether remainees or returnees), diaspora Israelites, or both? One thing does seem certain: even though *written* prophecy is more indicative of the postexilic period, exile—or rather, colonization—never ended for Jewish communities that endured Babylonian, Persian, Greek, and Roman occupations (except perhaps during the time of the Hasmonean period). Accordingly, the term "interpretive community" denotes these diverse groups of readers and audiences living with a deep-seated awareness of war, displacement, captivity, and danger.

Our focus on the text's social and symbolic worlds, and the impact of war and captivity in particular, employs *multiple* interpretive approaches. Our reading will be not only synchronic but also sequential—that is, it will take into account the place and function of each book as it is arranged in its present shape. We will pay attention to the literature's poetic force, its use of metaphor and imagination, to contemporary trauma studies, as well as to other social-scientific and cultural-anthropological research. Ultimately, it is our desire to introduce these prophetic texts as texts that are pregnant with theological and hermeneutical significance, both in their understanding of radical suffering and in their quest for meaning and hope.

At the end of the day, we would be delighted if this book contributes to the growing body of literature on hope. Critical scholarship for many years has justifiably focused on the prophets as envoys of God. It is customary to call these divine messengers preachers of judgment and repentance. Christl Maier has recently noted that prophets are often viewed today as social reformers or moral teachers.[5] Decades ago Abraham Heschel made a strong case for reading the prophets as iconoclasts who had a keen sense of morality and pathos.[6] Building on these varied understandings of the prophetic persona, we would suggest that by the time the prophets were honored in texts that bear their names they had become harbingers of hope amid worlds ravaged by war and violence. And they continue this work of hope-telling today. Biblical prophets map out paths that lead to survival and healing for war-torn and colonized communities, as well as for those of us living in a world on the brink of extinction. These meaning-making figures and their enduring literary legacy help us entertain the possibility of hope in the face of a ruptured and chaotic world.

Art and Atrocity and the Voices of Hope

In the PBS documentary *Peter, Paul and Mary: Carry It On*, Paul Stookey states: "When something as catastrophic or cataclysmic comes as war . . . where lives are lost or [are] in jeopardy, the music steps forward to make the statement."[7] So, after witnessing the horrific suffering in El Salvador firsthand, Paul Stookey wrote a song—a song that helped bring to light the disastrous consequences of U.S. foreign policy in Central America in the 1980s.

In the same important documentary, Mary Travers makes an assertion that is nothing less than a stunning declaration of hope: "A lullaby is in its own way equal to a song of peace."[8] Children's songs say no to our addiction to war, to our investment in the technology of violence, and to the prospect of our own annihilation. As songs of resistance, they affirm that the forces of death will not prevail despite the powers and principalities of this age. Lullabies insist that all God's children must survive and be given the opportunity to flourish. They say yes to life.

In a different though related vein, one could hardly fail to notice the disturbing intersection of art and atrocity in the exhibit "Barcelona and Modernity" at New York's Metropolitan Museum of Art (March 7, 2007–June 3, 2007). In particular, the paintings of Salvador Dalí and Joan Miró, the disturbing sculptures by Julio González, and, most forcefully, Pablo Picasso's studies for *Guernica* expose the horrors of the Spanish Civil War (1936–1939). Indeed, their works grow out of atrocity; they absorb it, interpret it, and survive it.[9]

The Whitney Museum's *American Effect: Global Perspectives on the United States, 1990–2003* takes a penetrating look at the United States from the perspective of artists from around the world.[10] The concentration of pain—including an evocative portrait by Alfredo Esquillo Jr. entitled *MaMcKinley* and a life-size sculptural tableau of old and decrepit American superheroes by French artist Gilles Barbier—tells the often devastating story of U.S. hegemony as well as the ever-increasing signs of U.S. vulnerability, especially in light of 9/11.

With a subtle hand Bruce Springsteen's 2007 CD *Magic* reflects on America's time-honored values. Springsteen's nostalgia, however, is almost completely eclipsed by his cynical commentary on the current state of affairs. In the title track, the "magic" of which he speaks is the smoke and mirrors politicians use to play on our fears and dupe a nation into war.

> I got shackles on my wrists
> Soon I'll slip and I'll be gone
> Chain me in a box in the river
> And rising in the sun

3

> Trust none of what you hear
> And less of what you see
> This is what will be

In the climactic "Devil's Arcade," Springsteen's cynicism gives way to melancholy as he reflects on the tragic war in Iraq.

> Remember the morning we dug up your gun
> The worms in the barrel, the hanging sun

In Leonard Cohen's famous "Anthem," fractured hope trumps melancholy:

> There is a crack in everything
> That's how the light gets in

To add to this litany, minimalist dance, neighborhood graffiti, discordant prose, angry rap, and disturbing war literature all reflect our contemporary cacophony of pain. All represent daring artistic immersions in a world on the brink of the unthinkable. No doubt beauty lingers, but now in broken and distorted forms. Coherent and symmetrical prerogatives of old no longer monopolize the cultural or artistic landscape.

Sometimes art, music, and poetry must "step forward to make a statement." Put more concretely, artistic engagement cannot ignore the nightmare of war and horrific suffering. Moments of unspeakable pain interrupt ordinary aesthetic expressions.

Ours is no doubt one such moment. Many have taken note of our contemporary crisis of meaning and our culture of violence. Many have drawn attention to widespread palpable disease and an escalating disillusionment with dominant economic, religious, and geopolitical systems. No longer confined to the words of poets or social activists, even those at the center have come to recognize the daunting challenges of our present moment: preemptive wars, a growing tolerance for genocide, mounting economic disparities, substandard health care, massive hunger, dwindling natural resources, and an endangered planet. From ravaging starvation in Africa to the increasing numbers of refugees in war-torn Pakistan, from the horrific accounts of genocide in Darfur to the proliferation of weapons of mass destruction, we find demonstrable evidence that our planet is in grave danger.

As Henri Nouwen has observed, "History is filled with violence, cruelties and atrocities committed by people against other people. . . . But never before has it been possible for humanity to commit collective suicide, to destroy the whole planet and put an end to all history."[11] The potential for global devastation has shattered conventional renderings of hope, beauty, and meaning. It has violated our sense of self and morality, and it has created a chasm deep enough to engulf political and civic discourse, as well as art, literature, music, and film. But what is perhaps even more disturbing is that the surplus of violence exceeds our capacity to imagine. It shuts down our ability to feel, it exacerbates our loss of control, and it results in debilitating fear— fear that we are less human than intended.

Reading the Prophetic Literature as Art

What might all this imply for those of us who are committed to the study of scripture—whether out of devotion or dissent? Some would suggest that critical interpretation functions best as a dispassionate historical enterprise. To an extent, this has been the governing theoretical assumption of biblical studies since the inception of the modern period. Notwithstanding the force of this argument and its venerable history, one must still ask: how can scripture study in the initial years of the twenty-first century proceed with business as usual in a world at risk and in the grip of death and disaster? A case can surely be made that the biblical exegesis this side of historicist paradigms must participate fully in critical junctures of the contemporary world, especially when they are suffused in radical human suffering.

Robert P. Carroll has argued that biblical interpretation must begin "where *we are now*."[12] His seemingly innocuous statement would have scandalized generations of scholars whose principal aim was to "'hear' the words of the prophets as they would have sounded to [their] original hearers."[13] Carroll, however, is not dismissing the historical character of biblical exegesis, nor is he suggesting that critical methods should be abandoned. Rather he is merely acknowledging that biblical texts are never read innocently or in a vacuum, which even a perusal of the history of interpretation corroborates. Referring specifically to the book of Jeremiah, Carroll asserts that one can hardly read this text

> as if it were still set in the sixth century B.C.E. *for us*, without also possessing a long reception history . . . taking us from the trope of the lost children of Rachel in Jer 31.15 to the reality of the lost children of Rachel in the death camps . . . of the Third Reich. . . . At the end of such a reception history, the theology of the book of Jeremiah takes on a very different hue.[14]

His point is almost self-evident.

Carroll does not speak in an interpretive vacuum. During the last quarter of the twentieth century, biblical studies has undergone major shifts in interpretive perspective.[15] It is not an exaggeration to say that there has been an explosion of new interdisciplinary approaches to the Bible.[16] These studies are by and large postmodernist and postpositivist in orientation; they are skeptical of the domain assumptions, objectives, claims, and epistemological controls of historicism. Many acknowledge that our methods and approaches to the text must be thoroughly immersed in this world—that so-called scientific inquiry or historical-critical approaches cannot silence contemporary engagement. Reflecting these seismic shifts, participants in "The Scripture Project" concluded that "reading Scripture is an *art*—a creative discipline that requires engagement and imagination, in contrast to the Enlightenment's ideal of detached objectivity."[17]

As an artistic enterprise, informed by historical and ideological sensibilities, biblical interpretation must take into full account our fissured and disconcerting moment in time. Exegetes cannot avert their eyes from unspeakable acts of violence and our planetary emergency any more than Federico García Lorca could ignore the horrors in his homeland, or Picasso the destruction of Guernica. And so perhaps the most urgent challenge for the study of the prophetic literature in the initial years of the new millennium is, again, to "make the interface of ancient text and contemporary community more poignant and palpable."[18] Rather than only describing a world of old, the study of the prophetic literature calls for social immersion and ethical formation. It demands intersecting lines of inquiry: attention to the world of the text with its own networks of meaning *and* the dangerous world we inhabit. Or to use Carroll's terms, we must read this ancient text "where we are now."

Disaster Literature *and* Survival Literature

Oddly, it is not an interpretive stretch to situate the modern reader in the ancient prophetic tradition and place that tradition with the modern reader.[19] To do so is to encounter a montage of harsh and discordant voices, sometimes fractured beyond recognition and almost always immersed in pain, at risk, and on the margins. Such dissonance should not be surprising given the excess of violence and centrality of war. It may not be an overstatement to describe written prophecy in the Hebrew Bible as ancient war literature. More specifically, it is the disaster literature of those who survived the onslaught of three great world powers—Assyria, Babylon, and Persia—and their highly efficient imperialistic designs. If there is a center (*Mitte*) of this literary tradition, it may be war itself.

Written prophecy is a meditation on the horror of war and its devastating repercussions. Not unlike contemporary art, it dares to broach the abyss with candor and fractured beauty. It courageously comes face-to-face with a world in disarray and fraught with moral ambiguity. And it refuses to retreat into denial; otherwise its social and symbolic constructions would scarcely resonate with disenfranchised communities eking out life on the edge of time and space.

Isaiah 1–39 is laden with fear of Assyrian aggression. The prophet from Jerusalem reads the abyss as military defeat and the humiliating loss of autonomy and faith. Isaiah 40–66 deals with the painful aftermath of war and the harsh realities of captivity. This lyrical tradition reads the abyss as loss of memory and the denial of hope. As a result of Babylonian hegemony, Jeremiah's plethora of voices drives home the reality of a dismantled world and the end of culture. The wounded prophet reads the abyss as chaos and cosmic crumbling. Ezekiel addresses a colonized community in jeopardy of losing its core identity. The prisoner of war reads the abyss as absence and alienation. Located on the edge of time, the Book of the Twelve is likewise defined by the wreckage of violence—violence inflicted by the so-called great empires and violence inflicted by Israel's own leaders on the poor and vulnerable. Sometimes anticipating war or questioning its morality, at other times attempting to make sense of it or wondering what went wrong in its aftermath, this rich and diverse literary tradition seeks to survive its brutal assaults from within and without. The Twelve read the abyss as the meltdown of faith in God and one another.

It is quite remarkable that written prophecy in the Hebrew Bible represents the legacy of the losers—the victims of war. Rarely do we find such an artifact preserved for posterity. Even more rarely does the literary tradition of the defeated come to play a pivotal (canonical) role in subsequent cultural history and faith formation. While modern history books are still very much enamored of the great superpowers of the ancient Near East—the winners—the literary legacy of the weak and vulnerable has ironically survived the onslaught of these major brokers to enjoy the more enduring contribution. In some sense, the God of this vulnerable and war-torn community is a survivor as well. As J. H. Hexter put it: whereas the gods of the great empires in Egypt and Mesopotamia are dead, the God of Israel, the God of the abused and humiliated, survives and is still worshiped in churches and synagogues today.[20] This divine alignment with those crushed and conquered no doubt complicates our conventional Western reading strategies. This is why liberation theologians have taught us to read the text from below.

The prophetic literature, however, is more than war literature; it survives as a meaning-making map of hope for "casualties" of war and exile. In this capacity it looks the politics of violence in the eye without flinching and refuses to let death and destruction have the final say. Most astonishingly, it deploys language of hope to imagine a future when none seems possible. First Isaiah insists that reliance on YHWH subverts Assyrian geopolitical power. Second Isaiah heralds a grand homecoming for disoriented refugees. Jeremiah proclaims that God will sculpt new beginnings out of the wreckage of a war-torn community. Ezekiel envisions God's own exile from the temple in Jerusalem, which ironically leads to solidarity with the banished people of

God and the re-creation of the world. When God becomes an outcast, God takes up residence in the borderlands with other displaced persons. The Twelve Prophets eventually transform harbingers of doom into heralds of salvation. By the end of almost every "book" of the Twelve, the prophetic hero morphs into a messenger of hope.

Written prophecy attempts to find meaning in radical suffering—when survival is in doubt and when life appears to end at an impasse. Its literary performance of war and captivity is refracted through the lenses of hope and moral courage. As such, the multiple expressions of hope within the corpus cannot be wrenched from it any more than those emanating from disaster. The two are inextricably linked. They belong together and give this literature its distinctive character. Consequently, written prophecy is at the same time disaster literature *and* survival literature. It functions simultaneously as a disturbing cultural expression of lament and as a complex theological response to massive human wreckage. It pulsates with the pain of war while it fosters hope for survival in those living through crisis—often during or after the collapse of long-standing symbolic, cultural, and geopolitical structures. The cumulative result is a thick meaning-making map—a tapestry of hope—for exiles living on the edge of time.

In sweeping terms, biblical prophecy seeks to foster hope in disaster communities. While this complex literary artifact is polyphonic and wide-ranging, it often seeks one overarching purpose: to subvert the empire's monolithic constructions of reality. In particular, it rejects dominant interpretations of power, loss, and displacement. Prophecy reads the community's debilitating circumstances in a rich variety of expressions and so resists monoliths and finality. Such audacity still rings true because violence—whether erupting in the ancient Near East or in the twenty-first century—is too unwieldy to control. It can rarely be reduced to singularity or certainty. As resistance literature, biblical prophecy thus says no to the empire's unilateral renderings and yes to hope, healing, and embrace.

CHAPTER ONE

READING THE PROPHETS AS MEANING-MAKING LITERATURE FOR COMMUNITIES UNDER SIEGE

Wartime prayers, wartime prayers in every language spoken,
For every family scattered and broken
                                                —*Paul Simon*

O
ne of the sure results of twentieth-century Near Eastern scholarship is that prophecy is an oral phenomenon. Prophets in ancient Israel were primarily spokespersons and intermediaries, not writers; the essence of their enterprise was the spoken word, perhaps even the brief poetic utterance. At the same time, we have become increasingly aware of the difficulty in exhuming ancient prophets (or for that matter in locating contemporary ones!). As Martti Nissinen recently put it: "No videotapes or sound recordings are available to authenticate the oral messages of the prophets."[1] Instead, we have access to this oral phenomenon only in written sources.[2]

Although this observation may seem self-evident, it is neither incidental nor merely a matter of *modus operandi*.[3] Contemporary studies of language have made us well aware that the transition from spoken to written prophecy involves more than a mimetic transposition. Writing does not preserve meaning with externalized precision; rather, it restructures and reconfigures thought. Robert P. Carroll noted: "When the spoken oracle becomes a written document, that is, transcribed from the sphere of uttered word to that of written documentation, changes and even transformations take place. The precise nature of such changes may be debatable, but that change does take place should not be a matter of dispute."[4] Similarly, Ronald E. Clements observes that "written prophecy is necessarily different from oral prophecy precisely because it is written and is thereby made subject to the gains and losses that written fixation entails."[5] The point is this: when the spoken word of the prophet is transcribed, some degree of "metamorphosis" occurs.[6]

In the most modest of terms, written prophecy has fewer geographic and temporal limitations than its counterpart. Whereas oral prophecy functions within well-defined spatial and temporal categories, written prophecy moves about freely in diaspora, both figuratively and literally (for example, Jer 29:1-14). Accordingly, prophetic texts can *do* what prophets cannot; and they can *go* where prophets are forbidden. Scrolls have access to insolent kings who are intent on silencing disturbing prophets. And even though brazen acts of political force can destroy scrolls, others can be produced, demonstrating their resilient character. As Regina Schwartz states, despite royal disdain for the text, "the text persists."[7] Walter Brueggemann suggests that "God will generate as many scrolls as necessary to override the king's [i.e., Jehoiakim's] zeal for autonomy."[8] In spite of its liabilities, the scroll—as symbol, literary artifact, and potent presence—compensates for the vanquished prophet.

Written prophecy, however, is more than a liberated surrogate of the spoken word. Prophetic speech and prophetic writing represent two different though complementary enterprises. Prophecy as oral communication is raw, iconoclastic, immediate, and exacting. It seeks to bring about fundamental changes in social arrangements, often before the collapse of long-standing and cherished structures—political, religious, economic, and symbolic. Prophecy as written communication attends to the survivors. It takes shape during and after the frightful events; all the while it engages in artful *re*interpretation and *re*enactment. This complex literary activity in ancient Israel—which no doubt involves a degree of "routinisation" (coined by Max Weber)—strives to find meaning and reform values during times of war and social dislocation. To be sure, the shift from orality to writing involves a realignment of intentionality, setting, and audience.[9]

Written prophecy converts prewar *oracles* into postwar *texts*. It transforms prophets of doom into prophets of salvation.[10] Written prophecy marches to the beat of "scroll time" rather than to the directives of ordinary (chronological) time. It is governed by a *Sitz im Buch* rather than a *Sitz im Leben*. And eventually written prophecy comes to enjoy an authoritative role that eclipses its oral counterpart, not only in the postbiblical world but also in the evolving biblical tradition itself. In some embryonic form the prophetic text wields the power to dismantle entrenched social and mythic structures.[11] It serves as the basis to judge the legitimacy of oral prophecy.[12] And it seeks to generate hope and a sense of identity in people whose world has collapsed, whose cherished forms of life have been confounded and whose conceptual universe has been shattered.[13]

Building on these observations as well as on other recent developments in the interpretation of the Latter Prophets, we would suggest that written prophecy is survival literature for communities under siege and at risk of symbolic and cultural collapse. In large measure this literary artifact shows marked signs of liminality and danger because of hegemonic constraints; written prophecy is a rich and varied symbolic response to these devastating forces. More specifically, it functions as a meaning-making map intended to help war-torn communities and conquered societies endure decimating loss. While this symbolic map is diverse and wide-ranging, and at times even cacophonic, it is not formless. By being attentive to distinguishing characteristics and overarching structures, one can identify an anatomy of hope amid the literary chaos.

These wide-ranging claims are clearly predisposed—and probably doomed—to formalistic fallacies. Our only defense is that they are intended not to be definitive but only suggestive and, it is hoped, generative. In that spirit, we offer a series of brief statements on the character of written prophecy in the Bible.

The prophetic literature is survival literature for postwar communities living through monstrous events. Coarse language of violence together with penetrating images of cultural ruin run through the literary terrain. Shocking scenes of brutality give the corpus its erratic and discontinuous quality. Put concretely, written prophecy bears witness to unmanageable social and symbolic dissonance as a result of colonizing forces located on the Tigris and Euphrates. As Donald E. Gowan has said, the two focal points of the prophetic literature are the fall of Samaria in the eighth century (by the Assyrian military machine) and the collapse of Jerusalem in the sixth century (by the neo-Babylonian armies).[14] We would suggest that community survival within the Persian Empire is also a focal concern of this literature. Primarily because of imperial constraints—imposed by Assyria, Babylonia, and Persia, and their designs toward absolute power—the prophetic corpus is a literary artifact of terror and vulnerability, a disturbing cultural expression of lament and chaos. Its multiple voices are often raw, unpredictable, and violent because savage forces perceived as both human and divine have devastated symbolic and social worlds.

From the testimony of survivors, both ancient and contemporary, we know that such wreckage not only causes physical and emotional havoc, but it also evokes probing questions about meaning: the meaning of atrocity; the meaning of moral chaos; the meaning of divine silence. The prophetic corpus, like many contemporary expressions of art that are informed by war atrocities,[15] are penetrating responses to multifaceted configurations of evil, hegemony, and cosmic inertia. When detonated, these real and symbolic configurations explode into unthinkable violence and horror.

Bubbling beneath the surface of Isaiah, Jeremiah, Ezekiel, and the Twelve are marked signs of liminality, danger, and palpable disease. The ravages of war and forced deportation are never far from the purview of the Isaian tradition. The collapse of trusted belief systems and long-standing institutions gives Jeremiah its distinctive character. The loss of shrine and the resultant dislocation of God are central concerns in Ezekiel, and these concerns fuel the prophet's insistence that the refugee community should recognize the divine presence in a wide range of arenas of their marginal life (more than forty times, "that you shall know that I am YHWH"). The implied readers of the Twelve, who are also located at the edge of time, must manage their way through profound disorientation as a national narrative unravels. Amos addresses a state on the eve of destruction. Hosea's deathbed musings—for example, *How did it all go so wrong?* (9:15)—reveal late-stage communal trauma. Using the imagery of ravenous locusts, Joel warns of a dreadful military invasion. Zechariah 1–8 pulsates with the pain of demographic dislocation and pining for "the holy land" (Zech 2:12).

Accordingly, written prophecy is eschatological.[16] It addresses communities in the throes of upheaval and disjunction, communities that are living with an acute sense of liminality. The breakdown of cherished social realities and understandings of life is apparent not only in the devastating events and oracles of doom but also in the language itself—language that pulsates with pain, staggers in darkness, and rages in raw emotion. Attempts by later interpretive communities to tone down this incendiary speech do little to mute its renderings of a God who implodes in anguish and lashes out in wrath.

Prophetic literature dares to address the realities of war in particular. It speaks of annihilated worlds and traumatized communities. While its constructions are certainly open to criticism—especially its tendency to scapegoat and trade in wholesale blame (see below)—this corpus refuses to close down the senses and banish memory. W. G. Sebald's thesis in his work *On the Natural History of Destruction* reminds us that postwar Germany did exactly that: it demonstrated well "people's ability to forget what they do not want to know . . . and carry on as if nothing had happened."[17] Written prophecy resists this propensity, at least for its implied audience. Admittedly, prophetic memory can be quite selective; it is capable of "disappearing acts," as in the case of the Judean community that remained "in the land" after the sixth-century B.C.E. Babylonian invasions. Nonetheless, a sustained determination to deal with paralyzing loss defines biblical prophecy.

This literary tradition not only gives speech to disaster; it also functions as a rich and complex response to massive disjunction. More specifically, it serves as a meaning-making map, a tapestry of hope, which strives to sustain those suffering a cascade of direct traumas such as military invasion, occupation, the loss of homeland and family, shaming, torture, forced displacement and resettlement, as well as secondary or historical trauma. And trauma, whether direct or secondary, diminishes agency, numbs the senses, and destroys one's sense of identity; it reduces the world to silence.[18] In prophecy the voice returns!

Although prophetic constructions of meaning are elusive and unwieldy, they are not amorphous. Similar to biological survival, which depends on certain microorganisms as well as complex physical and chemical reactions, *written prophecy enjoys its own anatomy of meaning.* In the broadest of terms, this literature addresses the basic needs of survivors for hope, dignity, agency, acceptance, and forgiveness. It attempts to help displaced communities "make sense" of a world in which death and despair are more demonstrable than moral symmetry. As Gordon W. Allport notes in the foreword to Victor Frankl's *Man's Search for Meaning*, "To live is to suffer, to survive is to find meaning in this suffering."[19] It seems to us that written prophecy is in some measure an attempt to find meaning in events that defy ordinary categories, events that are beyond communal recognition. Put negatively, the "literarization" of prophecy is spurred by the collapse of coherent networks of meaning, including revered social structures, cultural identities, and theological maps. Put positively, written prophecy attends to the symbolic, psychological, and emotional effects of the wreckage and strives to help survivors cope with their dangerous place within the empire.[20]

Attentive to the text itself and its distinguishing indices, patterns, and macrostructures, especially the overarching judgment-salvation schema, one can identify threads of this tapestry of hope, markers of this meaning-making map. Whichever metaphor one employs, the *telos* of written prophecy is communal survival.

Prophetic meaning-making grows within the tumultuous particularities of life. As superscriptions suggest from the outset, configurations of meaning in the prophetic corpus are neither abstractions nor unfettered imagination, but like the faith of Israel are shaped by memory and physicality. In other words, the divine message is rooted in particular moments in the communal life experience of Israel.[21] To "genericize" the realities of community life, to deny its human face, to extricate it from the fissured world is to read against the grain of written prophecy.

Prophetic meaning-making is candid about the deep ruptures of life. It names and breaks a surplus of denials, and it exposes assumptions and values that would anesthetize the community to its true condition. Amos, for instance, announces that the end has come for Israel (8:2). Micah weeps over Judah's incurable wound (1:8-9). While addressing hybrid social realities, Ezekiel attempts to repair the huge breach in the theological world of the Babylonian exiles. Hosea insists that Israel's fascination with other deities will lead to imminent disaster. Jeremiah bears witness to the failure of both venerated institutions and understandings of reality associated with the dynasty and temple. Although certain voices eagerly proclaim, "Peace, peace" (Jer 6:14; 8:11; see also Mic 3:5), the prophetic chorus overwhelmingly contends that *all is not well!* Such engagement may appear to have little to do with hope. But recovery—communal and individual—begins by telling the truth. Indeed, facing life's particularities head-on and relinquishing false hopes and detrimental securities are the principal resources of "collective healing," a term used by psychiatrist and human rights advocate Jean-Marie Lemaire.[22]

Prophetic meaning-making moves beyond candor to critique. As survival literature for war-torn communities, written prophecy not only discerns what others fail to see, it also renders incisive cultural and ethical commentary on existing structures and "first principles." In this capacity, it puts virtually every facet of national life under scrutiny and contends, in large measure, that cardinal infractions have been committed. As long recognized, the prophetic word uncovers the social and symbolic patterns that foster exploitation, injustice, idolatry, and other falsehoods, including unfounded assurances for the future.

Prophetic meaning-making destabilizes and deconstructs (as a starting point for reconstruction and realignment). Written prophecy not only exposes communal acts of injustice—which Abraham Heschel calls a "deathblow to existence, a threat to the world"[23]—it also *authorizes* the dismantling of cultural arrangements and institutions, dogmas, and traditions that perpetuate such wrongdoing. It does so by deploying a rhetorical arsenal, including accusation, disputation, covenant lawsuit, Deuteronomistic alternative speech, sermon, prophetic story and symbolic action, liturgy, dirge, and of course indictment and judgment oracles. When written prophecy takes on perpetrators of injustice and the systems that support them, it vies for congruent ethical arrangements in the face of moral chaos. A corollary of this interpretive move is the capacity to make sense of the nonsense of radical suffering.[24]

Prophetic meaning-making places disjunction and disaster within a context of meaning. In her study "Refugee Women's Psychological Response to Forced Migration," Elzbieta Gozdziak argues that viable explanations of suffering are crucial to individual and community survival.[25] On some primal level, written prophecy functions as a complex theodicy, which is little more than an attempt to help survivors cope with massive devastation and imagine new life springing forth from the ruins of war and exile. To this end, the corpus garners a rich array of metaphorical constructions to harness symbolic, cultural, and emotional chaos. Ezekiel constructs a retributive and morally exacting universe in which disaster and dislocation neither impugn God's character (name) nor compromise God's power. Drawing in part on conventional wisdom norms, Amos argues for a meaningful correlation between Israel's conduct and its imminent demise. Informed by Deuteronomistic categories, the Jeremianic prose sermons articulate symmetrical moral arrangements, which attend to the construction of orderly *Weltanschauung* (comprehension of the world). Complex asymmetrical understandings of suffering in Second Isaiah serve to highlight ethical anomie (see, for example, the "Servant songs"; see also the so-called confessions in the book of Jeremiah).

Prophetic meaning-making—whether symmetrical or asymmetrical—is often informed by the counterimperial claim that YHWH reigns. Written prophecy envisions the fractured world and its ravaging geopolitical and natural forces under YHWH's sovereignty. Consequently, one of its principal claims is that (one's) suffering is neither arbitrary nor gratuitous. Communal disaster is no fluke of world historical forces;

neither is it life spiraling out of God's control. Despite national disaster and social upheaval, God still orders the world with the intention of accomplishing God's purposes. In the midst of great international turmoil, Second Isaiah heralds:

> I form light and create darkness,
> I make weal and create woe;
> I the LORD do all these things. (45:7)

The claim that YHWH reigns does little to diminish human responsibility. The Latter Prophets in fact assert that YHWH holds all people accountable for their actions (see, for example, Amos 1–2; Isa 13–23; Jer 46–51), especially the household of God. In this way, prophetic meaning-making involves the restoration of agency, which is crucial to the survival of trauma victims.[26] When written prophecy reestablishes a sense of agency, it empowers colonized communities to act and choose life in the face of abject despair. It restores a deep sense of identity and hope to those deprived of power and dignity. At the same time, this principal ingredient of prophetic meaning-making— the reestablishment of agency—is deeply strained by the proclivity to blame victims of violence and exonerate responsible geopolitical agents.[27] Deploying categories of culpability, it should be noted, is to some degree teleological: it serves in the construction of an alternative script to *Realpolitik*, a counterstory that facilitates coping with communal disaster.

Prophetic meaning-making refuses to flatten the world into static and uniform categories. Instead, it honors complexity, delights in ambiguity, and relishes *heteroglossia* (Mikhail Bakhtin's term)—that is, a rich diversity of voices and points of view. These qualities are perhaps most evident in the plurality of theologies and multiple voices of written prophecy. They are also present in the rich array of divine images. YHWH is warrior and peacemaker, judge and savior, inscrutable and accessible, confidant and deceiver, hidden and present, approachable and elusive, healer and destroyer. Prophetic renderings of the deity are entirely too polyvalent to be subsumed under any single heading (even the metaphor of king or antiking). The same could be said of the literary portrayals of the prophets themselves. Even though prophets are divine messengers whose lives are to some degree eclipsed by the words they proclaim, they are rarely flat characters.[28] As Abraham Heschel noted years ago, prophets are far more than mere mouthpieces. They are complex figures who are at times conflicted, eccentric, fluid, and iconoclastic. Prophets are YHWH's partners as well as community advocates. As YHWH's messengers, they indict Israel for infidelity, injustice, and hardness of heart; as guardians of the community, they are capable of taking YHWH to task for seemingly harsh and indiscriminate actions. Prophets are emissaries, poets, cynics, performers, intercessors, social reformers, covenant mediators, harbingers of violence, and harbingers of hope—to name only a few of their roles and functions. Interpretive communities resist domesticating their "heroes," even by the voice of YHWH or by the allure to control the fractures and contradictions. The resultant dissonance can be a source of consternation for those interested in linear speech and historical exactitude; yet it is this robust polyphony that leaves the reader disconcerted but also hopeful: hopeful because it rejects reductionist renderings of life; hopeful because it respects a range of human responses to disaster; hopeful because it provides language when ordinary speech fails.

Prophetic meaning-making is sustained by engagement and disputation. Written prophecy reflects a daring, disputatious spirituality that does not shrink from engagement and combative dialogue. To use Walter Brueggemann's theological categories, this corpus not only echoes Israel's core testimony about YHWH, it also gives voice to countertestimony, which is vital to communities under siege.[29] This lively and generative tension—a dynamic interplay within the intergenerational interpretive community—defines written prophecy, especially as it attempts to come to grips with the devastation of war and diaspora. While the dominant voice of written prophecy asserts that the moral workings of the universe are symmetrical and coherent—that a sustained correlation exists between conduct and condition—it is not difficult to discern spirited countertraditions that question the ethical structures of the cosmos and even the character of God (although not theology itself). Habakkuk ponders the moral sanity of the divine instrumentality of Babylon against helpless Judah. Second Isaiah questions the value of the prophetic task in light of the frailty of life and the massive disruption of exile (Isa 40:1-8). Amos intercedes: "O Lord GOD, forgive, I beg you! / How can Jacob stand? / He is so small!" (Amos 7:2). Jonah is angry that YHWH spares Nineveh. Ezekiel voices the community's despair: "The way of the Lord is not just" (Ezek 33:17). Jeremiah protests, rages, and accuses God of covenant infidelity. This quintessential countervoice claims to inhabit a morally strained world in which the innocent suffer while perpetrators of violence get away with murder (Jer 12:1-4). These defiant figures refuse to acquiesce easily; they will not fall in line and submit, even to God! And yet their disputatious speech does little to scandalize the deity. In fact, their cries of distress and protests of innocence become "a modicum of hope,"[30] especially for communities silenced by war. Although the God of the prophets does not often grant reprieves from historical extremities, this God is still approachable and promises to be present during the deluge. Such understandings reflect a rugged piety that is at home with raw emotion and ethical uncertainty.

Prophetic meaning-making calls for action rather than resignation or passivity. Admittedly, the empire may restrict and monitor this action. Nonetheless, the restoration of agency is a crucial ingredient of resilience both in terms of assuming responsibility for past failures as well as in terms of creating a means of enacting funda-mental changes in the ongoing life of the community. Whereas the fate of the first par-ticipants in the oral performance had already been sealed, written prophecy opens the door for subsequent generations to (1) see beyond their own painful realities of exile, and (2) accept or reject the word. Accordingly, it "re-presents" the missed opportuni-ties as new opportunities: divine mandates once rejected are now viable options for the reading or listening community. In this way victims of disaster and their children are empowered to take back their lives and carve out a future when none seems possible.

This dynamic reperformance and recontextualization is in no way extraneous to the developing sacred text; it is in fact an essential part of written prophecy. As James A. Sanders puts it: "Adaptation and stability. That is canon. Each generation reads its authoritative tradition in light of its own place in life, its own questions, its own neces-sary hermeneutics."[31] Like the book of Deuteronomy, written prophecy affords subsequent generations access to the "original events of revelation."[32] And through this liturgical window, communities detect islands of hope and new networks of meaning. Put differ-ently, the prophetic scroll provides a script of "second chances" for beleaguered refugees.

Prophetic meaning-making imagines a better life in the future. Without the prospect of a future, life becomes unbearable and survival nearly impossible. "For surely I know the plans I have for you, says the LORD, plans for your welfare and not for harm, to give you a future with hope" (Jer 29:11). "There is hope for your future, / says the LORD: / your children shall come back to their own country" (Jer 31:17). While this language seeks to dispel despair, it also thwarts the desire of ancient read-ers for a reprieve from cultural, economic, and political subjugation. Consequently, prophetic hope can be as disturbing as prophetic judgment. At the same time, it is audacious enough to reject war and the end of culture as the final word.

Perhaps the most daring and invasive way that written prophecy articulates a buoyant script of hope is by transforming prophets of doom into harbingers of hope. Ronald E. Clements observes that prophetic figures in their present canonical set-ting—and as they are remembered in Jewish and Christian tradition—are messengers of coming salvation.[33] Interpretive communities accomplish this remarkable feat by closing virtually every prophetic "book" with words of assurance and hope. This *Tendenz* may be one of the most distinctive features of the prophetic corpus. Salvific endings are as tenacious as the superscriptions that introduce written prophecy.

Amos announces the demise of Israel, and yet the prophet of justice concludes with a surprising message of restoration: the fallen booth of David will be repaired and the people of God will be replanted in their land, never again to be plucked up (Amos 9:11-15). Joel foresees looming bloodshed when the terrible Day of YHWH arrives; however, the prophetic text concludes with a promise of renewal and restoration:

In that day
the mountains shall drip sweet wine,
  the hills shall flow with milk,
and all the stream beds of Judah
  shall flow with water;
a fountain shall come forth from the house of the LORD
  and water the Wadi Shittim . . .
  for the LORD dwells in Zion. (Joel 3:18, 21b [MT 4:18, 21])

The indiscriminate suffering of God's people torments Habakkuk. Despite his misgivings regarding divine justice, the troubled poet concludes:

Though the fig tree does not blossom,
  and no fruit is on the vines;
though the produce of the olive fails,
  and the fields yield no food . . .
yet I will rejoice in the LORD;
  I will exult in the God of my salvation. (Hab 3:17-18)

Zephaniah has almost nothing but scathing words for God's people and yet the final words of the book allude to joy and dancing:

Sing aloud, O daughter Zion;
  shout O Israel!
Rejoice and exult with all your heart,
  O daughter Jerusalem!
The LORD has taken away the judgments against you,
  [and] has turned away your enemies.
The king of Israel, the LORD, is in your midst;
  you shall fear disaster no more. . . .
Do not fear, O Zion;
  do not let your hands grow weak. (Zeph 3:14-16)

This extraordinary portrait of hope centers on a God who rejoices with gladness and renews Israel in love:

At that time I will bring you home,
  at the time when I gather you;
for I will make you renowned and praised . . .
  when I restore your fortunes
  before your eyes, says the LORD. (Zeph 3:20)

Punctuating the often harsh words of Micah are stunning images of forgiveness (Mic 7:18-20). Micah's litany of divine mercy celebrates a God who pardons sin, passes over transgression, relinquishes anger, delights in letting people off the hook, shows warm compassion, treads iniquities underfoot, casts sins into the depth of the sea, and—if that were not enough—is unwavering in loyalty. The book of Ezekiel ends more succinctly with the triumphant note that God is present even in the most unexpected places: "The LORD is There" (Ezek 48:35). Zechariah concludes with a vision of purity and holiness. And Malachi closes with a promise that the prophet Elijah will come, turning the hearts of parents to their children and the hearts of children to their parents. Isaiah's final chapters imagine a new heaven and earth in which prey and predator coexist in peace (Isa 65–66; see, however, 66:24).

Even the book of Jeremiah, arguably the most tumultuous of the prophetic corpus, concludes with the promise of salvation. While signs of hope are muted in Jeremiah's oracle to Baruch (Jer 45:1-5) and in the closing vignette of Jehoiachin's humane treatment in Babylon (Jer 52:31-34), they are in full bloom in the Oracles against the Nations (OAN in Jer 46–51). In the placement and arrangement of these prophecies in the Hebrew text, we encounter a robust assertion of divine sovereignty. That the Masoretic Text (MT) locates the OAN at the end of the book rather than in the middle, as in the Septuagint (LXX), signals hope for displaced readers. That the collection concludes with a mammoth indictment of Babylon (Jer 50–51) only reinforces its salvific intent for victims of the empire. By concluding the OAN with the defeat of brazen Babylon—the nation that holds the key to the future of an oppressed and demoralized community of exiles—the text both celebrates YHWH's reign and opens a door of hope for the refugees residing there. Through written utterance and liturgical reenactment, the protracted oracle against the *Überpower* affords suffering people lenses of hope to see beyond their shattered world. Though their lives have been turned upside down, the text is still adamant that YHWH reigns and will one day deliver the exiles from their oppressor. The interpretive community punctuates the scroll with the prospect of better times, thus conforming to the prophetic corpus as a whole.

To propose that endings of hope are significant features of the prophetic corpus is far from a novel idea. However, under the influence of historicism and its sustained interest in authorial intention, prophetic endings have often been written off as "secondary" and "untrustworthy"; their exegetical worth is deemed negligible because their referential or historical character is dubious. Such judgments, however, miss the point: while closing words of restoration may well be foreign to the factual datum of oral prophecy and the original networks of meanings, they are part and parcel of written prophecy. That these vibrant words derive from later interpretative communities (rather than the prophets themselves) does little to impugn their poetic and

theological integrity. Quite the contrary, they exemplify one of the most distinguishing characteristics of written prophecy.

From the standpoint of the text itself, prophetic endings are intentionally arranged
and replete with meaning. In this regard it is important to remember that final words
often play a special role in the stories of biblical heroes. The last words of epic narratives
commonly seek to ensure the well-being of God's people. Abraham charges his chief servant to search for a wife for his son Isaac so that the promise of progeny may not be jeopardized (Gen 24:1-9). Isaac urges Jacob not to marry one of the Canaanite women (Gen
28:1-5). Jacob gathers together his sons to bestow on them his blessing for the future
(Gen 49:1-33). Moses, the prophet *par excellence*, gives several parting speeches (Deut
31:1-29; 31:30–32:43; 33:1-29), the last of which invokes blessings on the children of
Israel. Joshua's final speech warns the tribes of Israel to renew the covenant with YHWH
so that they may have a future. Near the end of his life, Samuel reminds the community
of YHWH's great acts of mercy on their behalf, imploring them to follow YHWH faithfully
(1 Sam 12:1-25). On his deathbed, David urges Solomon to govern the nation according to Mosaic instructions so that the dynasty may continue (1 Kgs 2:1-9). In each case,
the hero's final words reveal a profound concern for the future of the community.
Similarly, prophetic figures, as portrayed by their interpretive communities, are defined
by an overwhelming concern for the survival of the community.

Although prophetic endings of hope are diverse and wide-ranging—some speak of a
future ingathering of exiles, a grand homecoming, and an ecological renewal; others
imagine a time of forgiveness as well as the end of subjugation; still others envisage
Israel's deliverance and vindication, the reconfiguration of the Davidic dynasty, the
exaltation of Jerusalem and its temple, and the advent of the Day of YHWH—the rich
diversity of images and utterances can be subsumed under the heading "the assurance of
a future." Prophetic assurances of salvation empower war-torn and colonized communities to look beyond their devastating historical circumstances to "a future of hope."

The dynamic endings of hope open the door to subsequent reenactments of the
prophetic word—beyond concrete particularity. By the force of their message, their
sheer tenacity, and their translucent quality they move beyond the boundaries of their
"original" network of meanings—the one defined by the first generation—to encourage survivors of war and survivors' children. Such reenactments not only comfort suffering people, they also provide the community a script of nonviolent resistance that
rejects cruel power structures as normative and says no to systems of oppression and
humiliation. In such settings—likely in "protosynagogues"—the world is realigned and
hope is born.

**Prophetic meaning-making is tempered and contextualized by the harsh realities
of fallen worlds.** It is crucial to note that prophetic endings of salvation do not exist

in isolation. In the final form of the Hebrew text, hope is never divorced from disaster, or reconstruction from the dangerous work of dismantling. Hope is tempered and contextualized by the harsh realities of fallen worlds. As a rule, networks of hope punctuate pronouncements of judgment; the text juxtaposes tragedy and hope. The putative effect is a schema that frames written prophecy and gives it a distinctive character. Ronald E. Clements has made the case that the macrostructure of the prophetic corpus is the "threat of doom" followed by "the word of salvation,"[34] or "the death and rebirth of Israel, interpreted theologically as acts of divine judgment and salvation."[35] Similarly, Walter Brueggemann notes that "the Latter Prophets have been more or less programmatically shaped and edited into a twofold assertion of *God's judgment* that brings Israel to exile and death, and *God's promise* that brings Israel to a future that it cannot envision or sense for itself."[36] Following these lines of thought, Marvin A. Sweeney suggests that "prophetic books tend to focus on the punishment and restoration of Israel/Judah, with the emphasis on the latter."[37] There is a growing consensus today that the "literarization of prophecy" involves organizing discrete prophetic oracles into an all-embracing "judgment-salvation" design.

This disaster-salvation arrangement has far-reaching literary, theological, pastoral, and praxis implications. From a *literary* perspective, the emphasis on salvation after judgment introduces literary coherence to a jumbled and chaotic poetic world. The resultant formal coherence, even though superimposed by later communities, is a monumental literary achievement. This organizing matrix of death and newness, disaster and salvation, and loss and hope may be the most enduring literary feature of the prophetic genre.[38] It looms so large that it is difficult to read the prophets outside its reach. The judgment-salvation schema enjoys *theological* import as well. It refuses to let divine judgment have the final say. It asserts that hope ultimately triumphs. And it defines compassion as the most enduring facet of the divine character. Although the promise of salvation does not nullify the threat of judgment—especially for perpetrators of injustice—its very presence makes the case that judgment can no longer be construed apart from the gracious workings of YHWH. The juxtaposition of judgment and salvation also plays a *healing* role in the life of the reading community. For at-risk communities, for those who can barely endure the weight of their suffering, it makes the case that hope is possible even in the worst of circumstances.

Of course, the all-embracing judgment-salvation pattern neither domesticates the wild character of prophetic books nor mitigates the social and emotional wreckage of military invasion, occupation, and forced deportation. Written prophecy is still riddled with disturbing and violent images as well as coarse and visceral voices. It still throbs with pain and reads as a cultural commentary on the terror of hegemony and state violence. But at the same time, written prophecy will not accept disaster as the final word and the collapse of the world as the death of community. And this daring stance argues well for reading the prophetic literature as survival literature for troubled times.

Conclusion

The "literarization" of prophecy, or prophetic scroll production, involves seismic shifts in social and symbolic worlds: from ("factual") oral performance to a tapestry of textual constructions "refracted through scribal interpretive intentionality."[39] This artful reenactment departs from a safe homeland for dangerous uprooted diaspora. Along the way, it traffics in symbolic transformations for communities under siege from within and without. Indeed, written prophecy is a resilient script, a meaning-making map of hope for disoriented and dislocated people at risk of losing their bearings. No wonder Philip interprets the prophetic scroll (of Isaiah) as a sure sign of "good news" (Acts 8:35) for a newly formed community struggling to forge a counteridentity existence within the empire.

Still lurking in the background is a disturbing interpretive question for many of us: how can contemporary communities of faith in the United States read the literary legacy of the captured and conquered, the vulnerable and wounded? Undoubtedly we in the United States approach this corpus not "as Israel," "so small a people" (Butterfield), but as citizens of a superpower, with all the attendant rights and privileges.[40] This hermeneutical disjunction is made all the more serious by the alignment of large factions of the church with the state. To be sure, most Christian communities in North America can no longer claim to be strangers to mainstream power arrangements. Instead they represent a dominant political force in American politics. While such an alignment undoubtedly has benefits, it also has tangible disadvantages, including serious interpretive quandaries: how can "citizens of the empire" appreciate the subversive script of a subject people? How are those located at the center able to understand the counterstories of those in the borderlands? Respective worlds and renderings of reality are so fundamentally at odds that the canonical text is at risk of becoming indecipherable. Admittedly, contemporary communities of faith have deployed this literature in the service of the state; but such a reading by and large runs counter to the grain of the text—a text which, at least as we have argued, is disaster literature of communities traumatized by war and forced dislocation. Sadly and ironically, Iraqis and Palestinians living under siege and in exile can appreciate this script all too well.[41]

One could certainly make the case that there is nothing new here, that the hermeneutic dilemma is in fact timeworn. While this is to some extent true, contemporary U.S. foreign policy (especially during the years 2000–2008), and its designs toward unrivaled power, has made the hermeneutical divide far more profound, as has the collusion of large segments of the church with this state. The subsequent chapters do not attempt to address this problem in any detail; instead they seek to explore the character of biblical prophecy and as a sidebar expose the many interpretive (and ethical) challenges that this remarkable corpus poses to contemporary people of faith, especially those in the United States.

PART ONE

THE BOOK OF ISAIAH

CHAPTER TWO

ISAIAH AS MESSENGER OF FAITH AMID DOUBT

Isaiah 1–39: "Swords into Plowshares, Spears into Pruning Hooks"

> *Tell my mother to pray for me*
> *Tell my wife don't cry*
> *Tell my girl be brave for me*
> *Tell my son become a man for me*
> *And, pass on my name*
> *Tell the historian*
> *Tell the ugly truth*
> *Of why they*
> *Brought us here*
> *Tell the rulers of this land*
> *Don't let it happen again*[1]

Prophets are unwelcome by many, especially by those who benefit from the status quo. They are minority voices who sternly oppose the ways of the majority. Prophets tend to be straight talkers rather than smooth talkers (for example, Isa 30:10). Though they are anchored to a particular time and place, their visions and messages traverse temporal boundaries—traveling from past to present, from present to future, and from future back to past. Prophets view sociopolitical establishments from topsy-turvy and upside-down angles. This unique perspective allows them to solemnly dismiss what others consider to be monumental human achievements while at the same time publicly exposing injustices wrought against the powerless. Prophets represent God—or at least the voice, the perspective, and the heart of God. Every moment, known or hidden, matters to them. Every action counts. Indeed, all creation is consequential to prophets. And so they fearlessly upbraid violent and inhumane acts, demanding redress for victims of violence. Although they are no match for empires or even for national or institutional regimes, the oracles of prophets speak truth to power, penetrating the depths of the wounded and instilling hope in those whose world has spiraled out of control.

Isaiah was one such prophet whose voice and vision connected past to present, present to future, and future back to past. While calling for mercy and justice for the nation's widows and orphans, Isaiah condemned the abuse of wealth and power by Judah's elite. He boldly affirmed YHWH to be God of all creation and of all nations and institutions. Isaiah's manifold oracles aligned the powerful and the powerless, the local and the international, the rich and the poor. All wrongdoings and frailties were publicly exposed regardless of socioeconomic status or political rank, although, in keeping with the prophetic tradition, Isaiah reserved his severest criticism for political and religious leaders.

To the casual reader, the book of Isaiah appears to be a depressing book. Despite many popular motifs, such as the Immanuel passages, the so-called Servant Songs, and those included in Handel's *Messiah*, this prophetic book draws readers into the darkest valleys of destruction. The first half of the book, Isaiah 1–39 (hereafter "First Isaiah"), is particularly filled with oracles that pummel its audiences with images of human corruption and horrific warnings of impending doom.[2] When arriving at an explicit passage of hope and restoration in Isaiah 35, after reading through chapters 13–34 filled with harsh oracles of judgment (albeit dotted with oracles of healing and hope in chapters 1; 4; 11–12), a student in one Isaiah class responded, "Finally, a text of hope to hang our hats on!"

To the interpretive community of Isaiah, those for whom the warnings had become an unbearable reality vis-à-vis the catastrophe of the exile, the prophet's harsh oracles offer a reality check.[3] Revisiting these oracles must have been painful; yet the community cherished them. They unrolled, read, reread, and rolled them again, hearing and reflecting on their meaning for subsequent generations: messages concerning God's word to nations, empires, and institutions; messages concerning justice and injustice, suffering and humiliation, survival and glimpses of hope and faith; messages that called multiple audiences to "participate imaginatively in the Isaianic symbolic world in order to be transformed profoundly by that prophetic book."[4]

In this chapter we will explore the various ways in which First Isaiah offers overtones of faith and hope in the midst of sociopolitical turmoil. Focusing on subtle thematic tensions, we will ask, How does it function as a survival text and a meaning-making text of hope amid crisis?

Reading First Isaiah as a survival text demands sensitivity to literary and thematic tensions. One must take into account tensions existing between failing and seemingly sure systems, faith and doubt, order and chaos, and victory and defeat. A once thriving monarchy suffers devastating blows, and consequently doubt and shame supplant Judah's confidence and esteem.

First Isaiah addresses the crucial issues related to God's presence and pathos, human frailty and haughtiness, and the monarchy and neighboring empires. Its interpretive community grapples with divine forgiveness, reversals of fortune, regrets of the past, and prospects of hope for the future.

Monarchy's Final Destiny: Its Glory and Demise

Already well before the destruction of the city and its temple, the monarchic people witnessed their capital besieged as seemingly invincible troops surrounded Jerusalem's fragile walls. Even prior to the siege, the capital city had suffered the consequences of a joint military campaign by Israel and Aram. During these years, moments of relative peace and stability were few and far between. Any geopolitical maneuver created fear and uncertainty. Jerusalem's fate was in large measure vulnerable to the whims of Damascus and Samaria as well as Assyria and Egypt. The Judean people, including the political and religious leaders, needed to react swiftly and wisely. Kings and leaders had to make a choice: whether to ally with or rebel against Assyria vis-à-vis Egypt. According to First Isaiah, rarely did these leaders consider making alliances with YHWH. Even in the brief moments of calm, they shut their ears to the prophetic voice and turned their eyes from the prophetic scroll. Only when faced with the demolition of their temple and monarchy, with the long train of chain-bound captives already in exile, did the urgency of the prophetic word infiltrate their hearts. Only then did the interpretive community reach back and try to come to grips with the loss. It was as though this community called out to its maternal caregiver, yearning to return to its roots. And during this fragile and vulnerable moment, the scroll of Isaiah was unrolled and the readers heard the voice of God.

"Hear, O heavens, and listen, O earth"

The scroll of Isaiah guides the readers back to the voice of YHWH during Judah's military, political, and economic crisis. It was the voice that the besieged Judeans needed to heed in order to survive. First, the divine voice reminds the readers of the enduring *presence of God*. Before shame and guilt infuse the literary landscape, the scroll of Isaiah declares that YHWH is there (cf. Ezek 48:35).[5] During moments of radical suffering, God's presence and power are difficult to recognize. Yet even then—and especially then—the prophet insists that God is to be acknowledged in heaven and earth.

And so the scroll of Isaiah opens with an appeal to listen up: "Hear, O heavens, and listen, O earth; / for the LORD has spoken" (1:2).

Throughout the book, Isaiah utilizes sensory and auditory imagery to convey God's presence. The ability to see and hear serves as the fundamental means of experiencing and knowing God (6:9-10). Put another way, the audibility of God leads to the visibility of God, and both lead to the acknowledgment of God. The initial call to "hear," which continues throughout the prophetic drama, reminds God's people to discern God's presence and perceive God's action. Whereas the demoralizing experience of exile had created a world of eerie silence, the book of Isaiah breaks the silence and urges the people of God to recognize God's presence and hear God's word. Amid the wreckage of life Isaiah affirms that God is present and Israel is reminded of being God's children: "I reared children and brought them up" (1:2b). Out of the depths God's people must cry out, affirming trust in the fundamental premise that the God who is present has already cried out to them, still calling them "my people" (1:3b; cf. 3:12).

Second, the divine voice, as heard by Isaiah, reminds Isaiah's readers of the simple yet profound *principles of God*. Not only do God's people fail to discern God's voice and recognize God's presence, they also disregard God's message. So the initial oracle draws a stark contrast between animals that acknowledge their master and God's people who deny their Maker:

> The ox knows its owner,
>   and the donkey its master's crib;
> but Israel does not know,
>   my people do not understand. (1:3)

What does it mean to "know YHWH"? Knowing YHWH involves living justly and righteously. The call for justice is central in Isaiah and throughout the prophetic traditions. The exilic community looks to the prophetic scrolls to organize its life around such principles. And they discover that God expects justice and righteousness in community life more than venerable religious rituals (1:21, 27; 5:7). Listen to Isaiah proclaim the word of YHWH: "I have had enough of burnt offerings of rams. . . . / Your new moons and your appointed festivals / my soul hates" (1:11b-14). YHWH expects acceptable sacrifices; but first and foremost YHWH expects justice.

Daniel Smith-Christopher aptly points out tendencies among many of the postexilic prophets to favor behavioral values over ritual values: "To be 'pure' of 'abominations' was, at a later point, also a matter of how one engaged one's life activities as well as conducted ritual actions of faith."[6] This emphasis occurs not only in the latter part of Isaiah (cf. 58:5-6) but also in the opening oracle. Hearing the divine voice, the readers would also recall the overriding expectation for a just and righteous life:

Remove the evil of your doings from before my eyes;
cease to do evil,
learn to do good;
seek justice,
rescue the oppressed. (1:16-17)

Jeremiah puts it as such: "If you truly reform your ways and your actions, if you treat each other justly, if you stop taking advantage of the foreigner, the fatherless, or the widow and do not shed innocent blood in this place, and if you do not follow other gods to your own harm, then I will let you live in this place, in the land I gave your ancestors for all time" (Jer 7:5-7, authors' translation). Micah says it this way: "[God] has shown all you people what is good. And what does the YHWH require of you? To act justly and to love mercy and to walk humbly with your God" (Mic 6:8, authors' translation).

Third, the divine voice reminds the readers of the eruptive and indefatigable *pathos of God*. The announcement of the indictment includes YHWH's wrath. Abraham Heschel explains divine anger as a facet of divine care, especially in the form of sustained *hesed*[7] and divine justice. God's pathos implies that prophetic oracles are not static, detached, and legalistic, but rather are passionate and relational. Accordingly, Isaiah perceives YHWH's voice not only as a master but also as a parent with deep emotional affection. It is as though God struggles with human stubbornness as much as human pain. Throughout the book of Isaiah, God frequently declares the divine intention not to hear human prayers:

When you stretch out your hands,
I will hide my eyes from you;
even though you make many prayers,
I will not listen;
your hands are full of blood. (1:15)

Divine anger in the form of parental pathos becomes explicit in the divine "name calling" toward God's people—"sinful nation," "people laden with iniquity," "offspring who do evil," "children who deal corruptly" (1:4a); "you rulers of Sodom," "you people of Gomorrah" (1:10). And yet the pathos of God, as demonstrated in God's responses and reactions in Isaiah's prophetic announcements, is always dynamic and open-ended. Amid the remains of the temple, city walls, houses, and farms, as well as a shattered sense of purpose and pride, the people can barely cry out to God. Like their city, they feel utterly desolate and destroyed. It is in the depth of this agony that the divine voice in Isaiah opens the door to a new dimension—that is, God's cries directed to God's own people: "Therefore the LORD waits to be gracious to you" (30:18). The

31

very yearning of the communities in anguish is met with the divine yearning for a restored relationship; God's yearning is revealed through dynamic pathos. Thus, in the course of the harsh litigation of the covenant lawsuit, "Come now, let us argue it out," contrary to the expected condemnation, YHWH yearns to grant mercy:

> though your sins are like scarlet,
> > they shall be like snow;
> though they are red like crimson,
> > they shall become like wool. (1:18)

"How long, O Lord? . . . We don't understand"

While God's presence and pathos are detectable at the very start of the book of Isaiah, so is the possibility of divine absence or abandonment. Just as the book of Jeremiah contains oracles of chaos alongside order, the book of Isaiah contains oracles that are seemingly internally contradictory, such as messages of judgment and restoration, divine anger and divine mercy, and universalism and particularism. Accordingly, in the call of the prophet (Isa 6), which, unlike in Jeremiah or Ezekiel, does not launch the book of Isaiah, readers encounter the disturbing "reality" of divine absence. It is as though the majestic God who creates humanity in the divine image (in Gen 1) is eclipsed by the meek YHWH who leaves Adam and Eve on their own in the garden (in Gen 2–3).

Indeed, the divine presence is implied in Isaiah 6, where the prophet witnesses the divine council in the temple. The chant of the seraphs, "Holy, holy, holy is the LORD of hosts; / the whole earth is full of his glory" (6:3), points to the imposing presence of God's holiness, against whom the prophet must only confess, "Woe is me! I am lost, for I am a man of unclean lips" (6:5). Yet at the same time the divine charge expresses the mysterious absence of God. The divine inquiry that occasions the prophet's obedient response—"Whom shall I send, and who will go for us?" (6:8)—is reminiscent of a similar inquiry of the divine council in 1 Kings 22, "Who will entice Ahab . . . ?" (1 Kgs 22:20). Clearly, this call narrative is one of the most difficult passages in the prophetic literature: the prophet is directed not only to warn the people but also to "harden" their hearts so that the plan of divine judgment is executed: "Make the mind of this people dull, / and stop their ears, / and shut their eyes" (6:10). Contrary to the Masoretic Text, which does not soften this troubling concept, other ancient manuscripts shift the blame to the people rather than to God:

- Qumran (1QIsaᵃ):   "Keep on listening, *because* you may understand; keep on looking, *because* you may perceive!" (6:9).

- Septuagint (LXX):   "For this people's heart has grown dull,
                         and their ears are heavy of hearing,
                         and their eyes they have closed" (6:10).
- Syriac (Peshitta):   "For the heart of this people has become dull,
                         and their ears are heavy,
                         and their eyes are closed" (6:10).[8]

These modifications indicate that other ancient reading or writing communities must have struggled with a disturbing text before them. It is no surprise that some rabbinic commentaries similarly changed the imperative verbs into future tense.

This call narrative thus suggests that the people's hearts are too hardened to escape the terrible consequence of destruction (6:9-12) and that only a remnant will survive to preserve the seed of hope (6:13). And God implements these destructive and salvific programs via the prophet.

How then are we to understand and interpret the divine command? How did the prophet react to this plan? How would the interpretive community after the exile—that is, "until cities lie waste without inhabitant" (6:11)—comprehend this troubling claim recorded in the call narrative? It seems evident that this passage, among many, invites readers to focus on the central themes of *seeing* and *hearing*, which will occur throughout the book of Isaiah (compare the theme "to pluck up and to pull down, to destroy and to overthrow, to build and to plant" in the call narrative of Jeremiah), and the related themes of *understanding* and *knowing*.

We do not claim to understand this difficult concept, especially when reading in light of the exilic community. The harsh realities of exile cast as many questions as answers on divine presence and divine absence. Isaiah's own query, "How long, O Lord?" (6:11), demonstrates that even this prophet did not grasp it fully; in fact, unlike other prophets, Isaiah fails to confront God and intercede for God's people in light of God's judgment.[9] Or, alternatively, this query may be the prophet's own lament and complaint toward God, as the phrase occurs commonly in many lament psalms; for example, "How long, O LORD? Will you forget [us] forever? / How long will you hide your face from [us]?" (Ps 13:1; cf. Pss 6:3; 79:5; 89:46).

In the aftermath of recent tragedies—including tsunamis, hurricanes, earthquakes, and massacres—we too must honestly and humbly admit, "We don't understand."[10] Exile in the biblical times and a litany of tragedies in our own time share this one common denominator: they leave survivors with more questions than answers. The divine command in the call narrative may subtly hint that God was in some sense a part of the devastation. With no ready answer to the disaster, the notion that YHWH was involved may be comforting news to some: better YHWH than Marduk! Yet to absolutize or normalize this traditional notion, as is so often done, is both cruel and inappropriate. It does little more than blame the victim.

These traumatic events both in ancient and modern times challenge us to acknowledge the following conundrum: many things occurring in this world are unjust, as God seems to be absent, *and* there are miracles in this world, as God seems to be present. When considering the massive suffering in the world—from an individual's diagnosis of terminal cancer to widespread starvation in the two-thirds world—the interpretive claim that life is orderly and morally coherent, rotating on an "action-consequence" axis, is certainly inadequate. In the aftermath of the exile (Isa 6:11), for instance, the symmetrical moral claims of Deuteronomic theology cannot be read apart from the observations of Wisdom's theodicy; nor can voices of assent be heard aside from voices of dissent in the prophetic corpus. In fact, when we disregard the voices and perspectives of the victims, then those of the well-placed—the victors—become all the more dangerous. Hence, we should neither blindly follow nor naively ignore the "misunderstanding" of Job's three friends, as Norman Whybray trenchantly delineates:

> The author has already expressed his own theology through the mouth of [YHWH] in chs. 38–41; this was totally contrary to that of the friends, who had constantly maintained that God always and without fail favours the righteous and punishes the wicked, and had even drawn the further conclusion that a person who had to endure misfortune and suffering was *ipso facto* a wicked person. To the author of the book this was not only untrue; it was blasphemy.[11]

Therefore, inasmuch as we hear the prophetic reminder of the divine presence with divine pathos (Isa 1), we are also reminded of the limitations in our "understanding" of the divine absence or departure (Isa 6). The text hints that not only the people but also the prophet may not understand. Perhaps God also does not understand—that is, as to how events will shape up in light of human actions. In consequence, we should note from the literary flow and rhetorical nuance of this text that the imperative verbs followed by the emphatic infinitive absolute form in Isaiah 6:9 may signify the saddened affairs in which those who hear and see do not get it at all: "Really listen and do not understand; really see and know not" (authors' translation). If so, these phrases may have much in common with the Exodus narrative in which the hardening of the pharaoh is said to be the result of both divine *and* human agency (for example, Exod 4:21; 7:3, 13, 14, 22; cf. Deut 29:1-3; Jer 5:21-23; Ezek 12:2-3; Zech 7:11-12).[12] As such, Isaiah's call narrative may diagnose that insensitivity escalates toward inhumanity. People's certitude of knowledge is thus another critical reason for their misunderstanding, which is narrated in the remaining chapters of First Isaiah.

"Trample my courts no more"

Although both Isaiah and Jeremiah draw attention to the nation's calamity, they portray this sad reality from different perspectives. Whereas Jeremiah addresses the national disaster from the perspective of the prophet's own experiences of agony, Isaiah paints images of the wealth and power of monarchic Jerusalem. In doing so, Isaiah recaptures a sense of the city's once-glorious status, thus inviting the readers and listeners to reexperience the terrible shock that accompanied the city's destruction. Isaiah's tactic is like the movie *Titanic*, in which the viewers are drawn back into the banquet and embarking scenes only to experience again the agony of the catastrophe. Who would have fathomed the dreadful shipwreck of such an awesome piece of machinery! Similarly, who would have fathomed the dreadful destruction of such an awesome city (Lam 1:1)!

This musing on the once-glorious past would help the readers revisit the turbulent times of their own past, including successful and failed leaders of the old dynasty. The glorious dynasty would now serve only as backdrop for reflection. The messages of the prophet and the mockery of the rulers are recorded dialogues for the interpretive community to read and to hear. The tales of the visions of the oppressed and the ever-renewed dissensions of corrupt leaders are together recounted, albeit with pain. In this literary reenactment, human pride—especially of the elite leaders—is exposed. How the mighty have fallen (cf. Isa 2:11-17; 26:5)! How the greedy have lost! How the disease of the corrupt leadership has infected the whole community!

Isaiah's indictments are troubling to hear and comprehend. But we should keep in mind that in most cases his ruthless accusations are directed against those who wield enormous power and control. The prophet tackles specific cases concerning the ruling class. YHWH's scathing lawsuit can thus be found in the opening chapters, "The LORD enters into judgment / with the elders and princes of his people. . . . / What do you mean by crushing my people, / by grinding the face of the poor?" (Isa 3:14-15). In this light, the glorious regimes of the Davidic-Solomonic dynasty would appear replete with self-destructive poisons and vain pride.

First Isaiah has two sections that are commonly referred to as "woe-oracles" (ch. 5 and chs. 28–33).[13] In each section, the word *woe* (*hôy*) occurs six times (5:8, 11, 18, 20, 21, 22 and 28:1; 29:1, 15; 30:1; 31:1; 33:1).[14] These woe-oracles are frequently directed against the royals and leaders, a privileged class of people who were held in the highest esteem in their society. In chapter 5, following the Song of the Vineyard (5:1-7; cf. 27:2-5), the leaders are solemnly accused—or rather, accursed—as if hearing a dirge in the middle of their extravagant feast (cf. Amos 5). They are warned of the essence of God's desire: to uphold justice and righteousness (Isa 5:7). Because of their obduracy

(6:9-10) and arrogance (32:9-11), even the vehement announcements of judgment sound like gibberish to them, the divine oracles sound only as "blah, blah, blahs":

> For it is precept upon precept, precept upon precept,
> line upon line, line upon line,
> here a little, there a little. (28:13; cf. 28:10)

Why is it so? Detailed accusations can be found in chapters 28–33: because they are "drunkards" not only through liquor (28:1) but also through mockery (28:14). Indeed, they are the priests and prophets who "err in vision" (28:7). The prophet insists that these leaders have become so intoxicated with injustice that their refuge is falsehood and their covenant is with death (28:15). How tragic that these—"the proud garland of the drunkards of Ephraim" (28:1) and "scoffers who rule this people in Jerusalem" (28:14)—fatally infect the entire community with mortal diseases such as tyrannical abuse, evil schemes, internal dissension, and incessant corruption. There is an old saying in Asia: "When the upstream water is pure, then the downstream water will be pure." What the top decides has consequences for the whole people.

Considering the immense gap between the ancient Israelite society and the current setting, it is astonishing how forcefully these texts resonate. It requires little imagination to view today's global world as a large community suffering from socioeconomic hardships caused by the monstrous greed of the "superaffluent" and "elite nations." Then, listen to the accusations in light of this social parallel:

> Woe to those who add house to house and join field to field, till there is room for none but you to dwell in the land. . . . Woe to those who haul sin with cords of falsehood and iniquity as with cart ropes. . . . Woe to those who call evil good and good evil. . . . Woe to those who are so wise in their own opinion. . . . Woe . . . to those who vindicate one who is in the wrong in return for a bribe and withhold vindication from another who is in the right. (5:8, 18, 20-23, authors' translation)

Woe to nations and institutions that add house to house, money to money, and power to power when fellow human beings remain homeless, lacking basic sustenance for daily survival and deprived of dignity or a voice of their own. We can hear and see. But will we understand; will we comprehend (6:9)?

As a result, the whole community is addressed with sharp criticism. The whole community is depicted to be incurably infected: "From the sole of the foot even to the head, / there is no soundness in it, / but bruises and sores / and bleeding wounds" (1:6).

In the midst of the ruins the community considers Isaiah's litany of Judah's wrongs and misfortunes, recounting how the nation became almost completely impervious to

YHWH's warnings about social injustice, unrighteousness, and oppression. The people are addressed as YHWH's own vineyard in the Song of the Vineyard. Such an affectionate description, however, concludes with the declaration that the society is laden with "bloodshed" rather than "justice," and "iniquity" rather than "equity" (5:7). The opening oracle of the entire scroll even makes the stinging accusation that faithful Zion has become a harlot (1:21-23). This name-calling of the beloved city is all the more disturbing in an honor-shame culture: "For you shall be ashamed . . . and you shall blush" (1:29). With little warning, the divide between corrupt leaders and tainted people is blurred, presumably in their mutual moral contamination and their collective numbness to injustice: "You rulers of Sodom! . . . You people of Gomorrah!" (1:10). All the negative ills and societal evils are seen as uncontrolled ingredients of Israel's collective guilt, resulting in their renunciation of God, "You have forgotten the God of your salvation" (17:10).

Like the cracks in a wall that widen until they reach the point of a total collapse, the communal intransigence develops into social dissension and distrust. Such a process of social decay is trenchantly diagnosed in Isaiah 8–10, as if each chapter escalates with overwhelming force. In each movement, divine indignation against arrogance (9:8-9) is pronounced: "For all this his anger has not turned away; / his hand is stretched out still" (9:12, 17, 21 [MT 9:11, 16, 20]; 10:4; cf. 5:25). The pleas of the righteous few are stamped over (32:7), and wrongful blame and accusation become a common practice even among kinfolk: "They devoured the flesh of their own kindred" (9:20). How tragic it is when people no longer care for one another, let alone their God!

Isaiah's Debates with the Kings

We have observed that the call narrative does not occur in the first chapter but rather in chapter 6 of the book of Isaiah. This call narrative with its profound and controversial claims is sandwiched between the woe-oracles in chapter 5 and the illustrative account of the obdurate King Ahaz in chapter 7. Interestingly, just as the woe-oracles of chapter 5 recur in chapters 28–33 with the similar themes of the solemn accusation against the obdurate religious and political leaders, so the depiction of a faithless King Ahaz in chapter 7 is contrasted with that of a faithful King Hezekiah in chapters 36–39. To this latter connection and contrast we now turn.

Isaiah's confrontation with the kings is significant not only for its literary function in First Isaiah but also for its thematic implications for the rest of the book of Isaiah. Similarly, Isaiah's confrontation can be seen not only by his relationships with the two kings of Judah, Ahaz and Hezekiah, but also by the intertextual correlations between Isaiah 36–39 and 2 Kings 18–20 (cf. 2 Chr 32).

First of all, readers encounter the prophet's debates with the *two kings*—first Ahaz (chs. 7–8) and then his son Hezekiah (chs. 36–39), respectively. These two accounts make up virtually the only extensive "historical" narratives in the entire book. Scholars have noted that these accounts function as two pillars that support the whole structure of Isaiah. In chapters 7–8, the Ahaz story introduces oracles that are primarily connected to the events and aftermath of the Syro-Ephraimite War (735–732 B.C.E.). In chapters 36–39, the Hezekiah story alludes to the anti-Assyrian rebellion led by the Babylonian ruler Merodach-baladan and the Assyrian king Sennacherib's subsequent assault, resulting in the siege of Jerusalem (705–701 B.C.E.).[15] Both texts deal with the foreign policy determined by the Judean kings in the middle of a national crisis. Isaiah meets both kings in the same location: "at the end of the conduit of the upper pool on the highway to the Fuller's Field" (7:3; cf. 36:2). Yet these two kings make very different choices.

By presenting these two comparable accounts in contrasting outcomes, First Isaiah plays the sage and invites students to learn from two object lessons: a bad king and a good king. Despite the prophet's challenge not to fear the threat from the Syro-Ephraimite coalition but instead to trust in YHWH (7:4-9), Ahaz opts to trust in the Assyrian army.[16] Second Kings 16 describes King Ahaz removing the treasuries of the temple and palace, offering them as tribute to the king of Assyria and erecting an altar after the pagan custom. In contrast, Hezekiah acts faithfully by repenting and trusting in YHWH, who in turn astoundingly rescues Judah from the 185,000-man army in the Assyrian camp (37:36-38). Complicating this traditional rendering of Hezekiah as a pious model king, scholars have conjectured that Hezekiah might have actually joined the Egyptian (19:1-15; 28:14-22; 30:1-7; 31:1-3) or Babylonian coalition (39:1-8) before "repenting."

Then how would the exilic interpretive community read and interpret these portrayals? Here the book of Isaiah's debate with the book of Kings can offer further insights. Though most passages of 2 Kings 18–20 recur verbatim in Isaiah 36–39, there are a few noticeable differences. One obvious difference is the omission of 2 Kings 18:14-16, in which Hezekiah is said to have paid heavy tribute to the king of Assyria, presumably as a subservient vassal, not unlike his father Ahaz.[17] Although Hezekiah is not without blemish (cf. Isa 39), by the omission of this story readers encounter an ideal king of the past and the future. The pivotal issue in these religiopolitical confrontations is not only "Zion's final destiny" but also "David's dynastic destiny."[18] The interpretive community of shattered and shamed identity would discover that the ideal king, announced a long time ago (cf. Isa 9:6-7 [MT 9:5-6]; 11:1-10; 32:1-8), was already exemplified in Hezekiah and would someday arrive again. Thus, the memory of a model king creates hope for the future.

Another crucial element in Isaiah's intertextual dialogue with 2 Kings 18–20 is the addition of Hezekiah's psalm of thanksgiving (Isa 38:9-20). Here the readers learn of the religiopolitical conversion of a devout king who offered a prayer of contrition and thanksgiving, presumably in the temple. That Hezekiah's piety is located in the temple is significant: it echoes the cleansing and commissioning of the prophet Isaiah in the temple (Isa 6). The location of this model king's repentance coincides with the divine promise to the Davidic dynasty (2 Sam 7), for the people would rekindle their hope in YHWH's restoration of Zion (Isa 2:2-4).[19] Likewise, the symbolic meaning of the name Hezekiah (literally meaning "YHWH has strengthened him") would remind the fearful community not to despair but to have faith in YHWH, just as the name Isaiah (literally meaning "YHWH has saved him") would remind them of the source and promise of salvation in YHWH.

Finally, Hezekiah's faith and fate function on the individual level *and* as representatives of the nation. That is to say, the dramatic rescue of Jerusalem (Isa 36–37) and the prophet's dramatic healing of Hezekiah from mortal illness (Isa 38) enable the interpretive community to preserve faith and pursue hope. Joseph Blenkinsopp insightfully expounds the meaning-making possibility of this story read after the exile:

> The story of Hezekiah's sickness, near-death experience, recovery, and subsequent liturgical celebration may well have been read in the post-destruction period as foreshadowing the experience of the people, and we saw that the parallelism between the fate of Hezekiah and that of the Judean people was an aspect, if not of the explicit literary strategy that dictated the inclusion of chs. 36–39 in the book, then at least of the implicit content of the incident. Also implicit but nearer the surface is the contrast between the death of the Assyrian king and the recovery from death of the Judean king as foreshadowing the respective destinies of their peoples in a proximate future.[20]

In summary, the Hezekiah account, in contrast with the Ahaz story, portrays a model king of devout and defiant faith. Readers could revel in their pious king who would participate in YHWH's glorious restoration in the future. Located at a central place in the entire book of Isaiah, this comparative portrayal of Hezekiah (Isa 36–39) serves to inspire the dispirited interpretive community.

This typological reading of "good king–bad king" is not without its theological problems. The simplistic dichotomy does little justice to the complexities in political affairs, especially with the memoirs of the divine absence in the aftermath of the exile. To those who experienced the pain of exile firsthand, a miraculous resolution might seem too fantastic for their everyday struggles. While not discounting the portrayal and possibility of the extraordinary victory in the model of Hezekiah, perhaps the exilic community would also pursue hope inspired by Hezekiah's courageous actions.

In his interpretation of the Ahaz-Hezekiah narratives, Rodney R. Hutton offers this perceptive insight:

> Soon after it became apparent that the Assyrians were about to lay siege to Jerusalem, Hezekiah initiated a massive engineering project to tunnel through the mountain on which Jerusalem was built in order to bring water from its source at the Gihon Spring into a major reservoir inside the city walls, so that the city's water supply could be ensured and the Assyrian army deprived of easy access to water (2 Chr 32:2-4). . . . Trust is not the adoption of unrealistic hope in divine intervention that leads to human inaction and passivity. Trust brings with it a willingness to enter the fray and to participate as an active agent in securing one's own vision of the future.[21]

Beyond Exile: Visions into the Future

Isaiah wrestled with historical circumstances that were as bleak as those Jeremiah encountered (see, for example, Jer 4:23-28):

> The city of chaos is broken down,
> every house is shut up so that no one can enter. . . .
> The earth is utterly broken,
> the earth is torn asunder,
> the earth is violently shaken. (Isa 24:10, 19)

With the palace demolished, so was the symbol of Judah's glorious monarchy. The royal lineage was on the verge of extinction, as was the dynasty itself. The interpretive community would read the prophetic oracles and acknowledge its own frailty and ignominy. In the face of hurt and humiliation, memoirs would be recounted and remembered. Yet no degree of introspection or courage to engage seemingly insurmountable theological questions would mitigate the pain of YHWH's chastised people.

The national disaster virtually overshadowed any rays of hope. And yet First Isaiah does in fact include configurations of hope in the very midst of havoc and chaos. They are intermittent, often subtle, staccato, and never far from the reach of defeat and disaster. However, these various expressions supported the surviving community against the crushing odds.

First Isaiah's messages of healing and visions of peace are often located on the margins, although we encounter them at the outset in chapters 1-2.[22] These texts are never far from harsh warnings of judgment. The cumulative effect is a script that alternates poetically between warning and hope, disaster and survival. To put it another way, amid texts from the abyss we read of survival and meaning-making with hypnotic hope interspersed throughout. It is hypnotic because it has not yet come true. It is hypnotic because it comes and goes like guerilla warfare.[23] It does not operate so in exchange for an end to suffering. Instead, it is hope, resilient to the point of being inane, that prevents total collapse. This is not a cheap hope that denies the harsh realities of the past debacle and present pains. Rather, it grows out of defeat and despair and is daring enough to confront them directly. While acknowledging their lingering impressions, hope does not succumb to violence and fear; it is courageous enough to look into the future:

> Most important for a pastoral theology of hope, this future dimension of our time-consciousness is the staging area for hope and despair. Human beings experience worry, fear, anxiety, and dread in this realm of anticipatory consciousness. The future direction of our narrative ["future stories"] is the arena for possibility—the space in which we can plan action, solve problems, change directions, and mature.[24]

Isaiah's configurations of hope give readers new lenses through which to glimpse the future. No longer paralyzed by fear or shame, they can face a future in which survival is possible and move on. Likewise, we can confront our own "dysfunctional future stories" and construct "hopeful future stories."[25]

Forgiving and Surviving Hope

> What makes hope possible? . . . Hope for Israel not only means hope for God or hope in God; it means first of all hope from God, in that humans have the fundamental chance, right, and freedom to hope which no power in this world can take away from them.[26]

Hope comes from God, who has already shown enduring patience. First and foremost, it is through God and not through political power structures that survival is possible and meaning is constructed. That is to say, hope and vision—and faith as well—are not generated by human ingenuity, financial regrouping, or militaristic aggregates (what is sometimes referred to as "horses and chariots" in the Bible). Rather, hope is far more elusive, buoyant, and subversive; it looks beyond one's own resources and is ultimately rooted in the character of God. Hope is the ability to remember and acknowledge not only God's unmistaken warnings but also God's gratuitous love that wills forgiveness and healing. Hope believes and pronounces "Immanuel," "God is with us," amid the clearer evidence of divine absence (7:14; 8:8, 10). It is willingness to look into the future, "on that day" (2:17, 20; 4:2; 11:10-11; 17:7, 9; 19:16-25; 25:9; 27:1, 2, 6), when past wrongdoings and present hardships will be washed away; on that day, "in which [YHWH's] judgment [will] be in Israel's past and in which the only continuing relationship [will] be God's [*hesed*]."[27]

Accordingly, hope is rooted deeply in God's *hesed*: faithfulness, loyalty, and steadfast love. The prophet had already promised divine forgiveness at the outset of the prophetic drama, even though its broader context may have been a lawsuit oracle against Israel (1:18-20). God's people are provided with the possibility of hope, rooted in their embrace of divine mercy and forgiveness. God pledges to wash "away the filth of the daughters of Zion" and cleanse "the bloodstains of Jerusalem from its midst" and protect God's people as in days of old (4:4-6).

This promise is rooted in the divine pathos. It is God's (com)passion—hidden but sensible and noticeable. So the announcement of punishment against Jerusalem starts with the duplicate calling of the city's own name, "Ariel, Ariel" (29:1). In fact, in these series of woe-oracles, God calls them God's children, albeit stubborn ones: "Woe to rebellious children" (30:1, authors' translation; cf. 30:9).

One wonders whether even in these harsh accusations the implicit anguish—or grieving—of God may be detected. In the context of trauma, there can be no hope without grief, which involves an array of emotions including numbness, denial, anger, bargaining, sadness, and ultimately acceptance. And one might even sense the sorrowful anguish of God beneath the abject numbness, denial, and anger. It is as if the inner grief of God finds expression through those harsh tones of solemn warning.[28] What is crucial to note is that grief—as manifest in its harsh and bleak expressions—is an essential component of hope. In this sense, God the griever emerges as God the forgiver. In other words, here we encounter the notion of "forgrieving"—forgiveness accompanied by deep sorrow.[29] First Isaiah presents God as being torn inside, unable to forgive but grieving with pathos and compassion.

Thus hope may be disrupted or obscured but cannot be detached from the divine promise rooted in the divine pathos. Placed in the deep middle section of the six woe-oracles (chs. 28–33), the interpretive community could see and hear God's enduring presence in God's anxious waiting to be gracious to God's own people:

> Therefore the LORD waits to be gracious to you;
> > therefore he will rise up to show mercy to you.
> For the LORD is a God of justice;
> > blessed are all those who wait for him. (30:18; cf. 25:9; 28:16)

Hope, however, looks not only beyond present realities but also straight into the very harsh realities of suffering. In a way, this outlook toward the future is intricately connected to and dependent upon the present. Instead of denying or turning away from apparent defeat and humiliation, hope directly confronts, somehow mysteriously, the sorrows and agonies in which another starting point then can be found. It is not self-denial; rather it is self-acceptance that can gradually lead toward the regaining of self-worth and self-confidence.

> Traumatic feelings and perceptions, then, come not only from the originating event but from the anxiety of keeping it repressed. Trauma will be resolved, not only by setting things right in the world, but by setting things right in the self. According to this perspective, the truth can be recovered, and psychological equanimity restored, only, as the Holocaust historian Saul Friedlander once put it, "when memory comes."[30]

Decayed scars require enduring patience to be cleansed, disinfected, and transformed with the new skin. To deny this long, painful process would be to deny the present reality and hardship in the interpretive community. Hope that is envisioned, therefore, must anticipate and accompany a gradual progress of long waiting in darkness on the way to light (2:5; 9:2 [MT 9:1]), of long waiting in sorrow on the way to possible joy (12:1-6). Unlike the abrupt interruption of evil, the rebuilding of good requires long-term care and practice: "*Stop* doing evil; *learn* to do good" (1:16-17, authors' translation).

Thus, this hope finds a renewed generation in the very survivors—the remnant. The very existence of survivors can generate a viable resource, empowering the remnant to have hope and to see the positive even in the midst of widespread negativity. At the end of the movie *The Mission*, when westerners have brutally massacred an entire indigenous village, the film portrays young children around the quiet streams of the empty towns, rising one by one and gathering the debris.[31] It would be a long shot by any measure, yet hope cannot deny those vibrant glimpses of survival. Hence, in Isaiah's message, references to remnants imply not only the colossal disaster that will leave only a few survivors in the forward-looking warning, but also the sustaining mercy that will accompany the indomitable signs of hope. In this way, the remnants are the interpretive community. They have the burden to keep hope alive. They must look beyond undeniable defeat and pain, finding and making hope together with God who *forgrieves* and forgives: "The holy seed is its stump" (6:13); "On that day the remnant of Israel and the survivors of the house of Jacob will no more lean on the one who struck them, but will lean on the LORD, the Holy One of Israel, in truth" (10:20); "So there shall be a highway from Assyria / for the remnant that is left of his people, / as there was for Israel / when they came up from the land of Egypt" (11:16); "In that day, the LORD of hosts will be a garland of glory, / and a diadem of beauty, to the remnant of his people" (28:5).

Reversal of Fortune

Although aggression is hardly the monopoly of the human species, humans alone have developed the higher-order neocortical capacities—the very capacities that separate us from other species in the animal kingdom—for efficient, systematized, and over-determined acts of collective violence. In the eternal words of Freud, "Man is a wolf to man. Who in the face of all his experience of life and of history will have the courage to dispute this assertion?"[32]

Hope sees, hears, and imagines a future that is startlingly different from the bleak circumstances of the present. This hope-searching process is deeply rooted in YHWH's promise and fidelity (1:2; 2:3; 34:16; cf. 40:8).

First, Isaiah's radical reversal of fortunes involves *the negation of the negative*—that is, doing away with that which is harsh and oppressive in the present. It is not a denial per se but a deconstruction of the present defeat and humiliation. The Oracles about and against the Nations (OAN) in chapters 13–23 repeatedly express this concrete reversal motif. It is noteworthy through an intertextual comparison that while the main purpose of the OAN in Amos 1–2 is to accuse Israel for its rejection of YHWH's laws and the leaders' oppression of the poor (Amos 2:4-16), the main intention in Isaiah 13–23 is to instill hope in Israel by declaring the demise of Babylon (Isa 13:1-22; cf. 23:13).[33] It is significant to note that in light of the book's present form, the interpretive community would have heard and read harsh condemnations of doom against Israel and Judah—the people of YHWH—in chapters 1–10, and then afterward encountered those oracles concerning the nations in chapters 13–23. Unlike those of Jeremiah (MT), the readers or writers of Isaiah apparently could not wait until the end of the scroll to inaugurate God's vindication over enemy nations.[34] It had to immediately follow the first major section of chapters 1–12. The effect is more than random or coincidental. To the interpretive community, the foreshadowing of the downfall of enemy nations and superpowers resonated loudly. For them, envisioning the humiliation of enemy nations and superpowers vindicated the suffering and humiliation of their own ancestors. It is for this reason that these OAN must have been addressed first and foremost to "little Israel/Judah." The interpretive community of Isaiah—and not the Babylonians—would hear and read these oracles that empowered disenfranchised folk eking out a life in which they would seek maps for survival and texts for restoration, even if they offered a cathartic hope at best.

The OAN thus provide new insight and meaning to those who may have felt besieged by their ongoing exilic and postexilic environments. Already in chapter 10, the downfall of the haughty ruler of the Assyrian empire, once depicted as YHWH's own "rod" and "staff" (10:5), is assertively pronounced: "O my people, who live in Zion, do not be afraid of the Assyrians when they beat you with a rod and lift up their staff against you as the Egyptians did. . . . The LORD of hosts will wield a whip against them, as when he struck Midian at the rock of Oreb; his staff will be over the sea, and he will lift it as he did in Egypt" (10:24-26). This overture to the subsequent OAN is significant, as it introduces against a thesis (can anyone dare to challenge such a formidable superpower?) an antithesis (yes, YHWH will not let them arrogantly oppress forever but instead will trample them down). The reversal of fortune motif can be noted in the way the text uses the same words. Whereas the people of Israel were depicted as "briers and thorns" devoured by fire (9:17-20), now Assyria is met with the fate of being "thorns and briers" devoured by fire (10:16-19). In a rough allusion, the Assyrian king is graphically illustrated as being a simpleminded animal, like an ox or ass, who should acknowledge its Owner:

> Because you have raged against me
> and your arrogance has come to my ears,
> I will put my hook in your nose
> and my bit in your mouth. (37:29; cf. 1:3)

These role reversals become even more distinctive and expansive in the OAN. Hopeful envisioning involves this reversal of misfortune and erasure of hurt. For example, YHWH's anger against YHWH's own people (5:25; 9:11, 17, 20; 10:4) is superseded by YHWH's wrath against Babylon (13:3). Because the forces of Babylon are so overwhelming, YHWH is said to be "mustering an army for battle . . . from a distant land, from the end of the heavens" (13:4-5), as if the celestial army will arrive to deliver a decisive victory—reminiscent of the culminating war in the film trilogy *Lord of the Rings*. Israel, which was called "Sodom" and "Gomorrah" (1:9-10), now learns that "Babylon, the glory of kingdoms, . . . / will be like Sodom and Gomorrah / when God overthrew them" (13:19). Likewise, the shouts of Moab's pride and haughtiness will turn to howling and moaning (16:6-7), just as "the fields of Heshbon languish. . . . / Joy and gladness are taken away / from the fruitful field" (16:8-10; cf. 5:1-7; 27:2-6). The reversal of Judah's humiliation during the Syro-Ephraimite War indicates that "Damascus will cease to be a city" (17:1). Here the reversal motif is so pronounced that the phrase "pruning hooks" involves the defeat of the enemy nation: "He will cut off the shoots with pruning hooks" (18:5; cf. 2:4). The oracle against Babylon then comes back as if its condemnation needs to be repeated: "Fallen, fallen is Babylon" (21:9; cf. ch. 13).[35]

Second, this positive hope involves *reformation of the people's mentality and attitude*. It involves more than deconstruction of hardship. It is also reconstruction for healing and prosperity. Isaiah 11 displays a unique place, preceding a song of thanksgiving (ch. 12) and following the first major section of the accusations and announcements of

Israel's punishment (chs. 1–10). This chapter in the present form provides a culmi-nating statement that reverses earlier condemnations through the use of precisely sim-ilar phrases, and presents perspectives of hope. In a way, chapter 11 can be read as a *Fortschreibung* (expansion) or midrash of previous chapters, by way of summarizing the foregoing notions and presenting a reconstructed vision and meaning.[36]

Accordingly, the "shoot" and "branch" out of the stump of Jesse (11:1) regenerate the hope for a time of peace and prosperity with a Davidic heir. This heir will not be like those who walked in sinful ways but rather will be guided by "the spirit of the LORD . . . / the spirit of wisdom and understanding" (11:2). The Davidic ruler shall judge not by what is perceived with "eyes" and "ears" (11:3; cf. 6:10), but rather by equity and jus-tice (11:4; cf. 10:2). The "rod" that often denoted the tool for Israel's chastisement (10:5) is now depicted positively, since the righteous ruler will "strike the earth with the rod of his mouth" (11:4; cf. 30:31-32). Righteousness and truth, once suppressed by bloodshed and outcry (5:7), will be the symbols of the new dynasty (11:5). Contrary to the times of chaos when little children were forced to govern in anarchy (3:4), they will now gently guide the flocks and play unharmed with dangerous animals (11:6, 8). In this rebuilt era, in a "peaceable kingdom," the cow and ox will not only acknowledge their master (1:3) but also peacefully graze together with a bear and a lion (11:7; cf. 30:24; 32:20).[37] On YHWH's sacred mountain there will no longer be anything evil or corrupt (11:9; cf. 1:16; 5:20; 10:1; 65:25). Furthermore, the relationship between Ephraim (North) and Judah (South) that was filled with enmity and hatred (9:20) will be resolved peacefully (11:13). YHWH's hand that was stretched out against YHWH's people (1:25) will now be turned against the Euphrates (11:15). Isaiah's vision of new-ness thus includes not only the downfall of the enemy nations but also the restoration of YHWH's people (11:11-12): "In days to come . . . all the nations will stream to . . . the mountain of YHWH's house" (2:2, authors' translation).

Third, this hope of reformation leads to *a transformation that reaches beyond the set boundaries of past experiences or perspectives.* It is not merely an antithesis of a thesis but a synthesis of a transformed community and relationship. Hope emerges from survival and extends to shalom. The reconstructed well-being through reversals of fortune can-not remain a repetition of the old society, old temple, and old dynasty. It does not hope for a return of the old world; it anticipates a startlingly new and magnificent future. This understanding of shalom in a transformed future points to a complete, once-and-for-all victory of YHWH's people. Israel will be vindicated with its honor and fortune restored. And even the nations will participate in this kingdom of shalom (2:2-4).

People who struggle to survive colonial oppression often hope for such a utopian age, when war ends and peace prevails. How sick and tired of war—with its incessant inva-sions of superior empires—they are! It is not unusual for their constructions of peace to include the longing for the demise of their oppressors. But even more stunning, utopian arrangements also include expressions of mutual trust and peace.[38] Such perspectives are exhibited in Isaiah, as already hinted at in chapter 11, where broken or war-torn relationships between humanity and nature, and between nation and nation, will be healed and transformed. This transformation provides hope for dispirited people, enabling them not only to persevere against the suffocating sorrow in their midst but also to envision a higher and greater joy: "O dwellers in the dust, awake and sing for joy! / For your dew is a radiant dew, / and the earth will give birth to those long dead" (26.19).

The so-called Isaiah Apocalypse (chs. 24–27), which follows the OAN (chs. 13–23), offers such visions of transformation.[39] Repeatedly, the motif of war and vindication emerges. Yet the enemy nations are no longer identified: "And he will destroy on this mountain / the shroud that is cast over all peoples. . . . / He will swallow up death forever" (25:7-8). In a way, God conquers new enemies such as cruelty (25:3), tyranny (25:5), and pride (25:11). Again, this is less a form of denial than a subversive act of defiance against the harsh realities that continue to haunt survivors. Surviving hope looks beyond oppressors, despite their desire for retribution. This hope enables the survivors to envision a greater sense of purpose for themselves.

Such a surviving hope may have generated the visions of the peaceable kingdom with God's ultimate victory:

> Many peoples shall come and say,
>   "Come, let us go up to the mountain of the LORD,
> to the house of the God of Jacob;
>   that he may teach us his ways
> and that we may walk in his paths." . . .
>   They shall beat their swords into plowshares,
> and their spears into pruning hooks;
>   nation shall not lift up sword against nation,
> neither shall they learn war any more. (2:3-4)

This hope is rooted in faith that God can conquer death (25:8).[40] This hope is rooted in a God who will not let the tears of the most vulnerable go unnoticed: "The Lord GOD will wipe away the tears from all faces" (25:8). Thus, military counterattack is not excluded as the vision declares the trampling of the haughty by "the feet of the poor, the steps of the needy" (26:4-6; 34:1-2). But YHWH has already won the victory and will punish Leviathan and slay the dragon (27:1). Now the people of God are to be strong, trusting in God's ultimate salvation, even with joy amid sorrow (28:16; 30:15; 35:4, 10), because all threatening forces—including illness, beasts, and heartache itself—will disappear soon.

> Then the eyes of the blind shall be opened,
> and the ears of the deaf unstopped;
> then the lame shall leap like a deer,
> and the tongue of the speechless sing for joy. . . .
> no traveler, not even fools, shall go astray.
> No lion shall be there,
> nor shall any ravenous beast come up on it; . . .
> they shall obtain joy and gladness,
> and sorrow and sighing shall flee away. (35:5-6, 8-10)

Answers Found in the Past

The hope-building process includes retrieving records from history. As Henri Nouwen has noted, hope requires "remembering."[41] Although looking into the future is vital, looking to the past is equally significant.[42] Answers for the future can be found in the past. Records of the past—when reviewed, revisited, and reinterpreted—can provide evidence of a country's rich history—its strengths and weaknesses, successes and failures. This evidence can then regenerate hope and create a strong sense of coherence. Although traditionalism can lead to misguided nostalgia, reflecting on the past can provide invaluable wisdom for the present and the future.

Records of the past can help subsequent generations reflect on their generation's shortcomings and failures. And such documents can help a community avoid those same missteps. Isaiah's interpretive community would have learned of such written records. Throughout the scroll there are, for instance, key allusions to sealed documents: "Take a large tablet and write on it in common characters, 'Belonging to Maher-shalal-hash-baz,' and have it attested for me by reliable witnesses" (8:1-2; cf. 30:8); "bind up the testimony, seal the teaching among my disciples" (8:16). These documents, along with long-transmitted oracles, offer additional witnesses to YHWH's enduring presence and expectation for faith.[43] They function somewhat like a cosigned contract with endorsement of benefits. It was not the lack of records but rather the lack of people's understanding of them, even though the people kept hearing and seeing:

> Pangs have seized me,
> like the pangs of a woman in labor;
> I am bowed down so that I cannot hear,
> I am dismayed so that I cannot see. (21:3-4)

Precisely because of the greed or arrogance of key leaders (29:9-10), the whole population could not truly comprehend and follow the instructions of YHWH: "The vision

48

of all this has become for you like the words of a sealed document" (29:11). And yet, there is a secret for comprehension—that is, the humble and needy, not the tyrant or scoffer, would truly learn the teaching:

> On that day the deaf shall hear
>> the words of a scroll,
>> and out of their gloom and darkness
>> the eyes of the blind shall see.
> The meek shall obtain fresh joy in the LORD,
>> and the neediest people shall exult in the Holy One of Israel. (29:18-21)

Records of the past could also help the people find direction and regain a vision of the future. Even through the shortcomings of their dynasty, later generations could find a sign of pride and honor. In Zion, they would discover a symbol of YHWH's enduring promises of presence and protection. The interpretive community would learn how futile it was to hold on to human power (8:21) and thus would put their trust in YHWH: "I will wait for the LORD, who is hiding his face from the house of Jacob, and I will hope in him" (8:17; cf. 33:2). Moreover, through records of the past (30:8-17), future generations would come to understand that YHWH desires to show grace and pardon transgression (30:18-19).

Indeed, ultimately God's people would learn that YHWH was no longer absent, nor were they deaf and blind: "Yet your Teacher will not hide himself any more, but your eyes shall see your Teacher. And when you turn to the right or when you turn to the left, your ears shall hear a word behind you" (30:20-21).

Every nation claims its own sovereignty in connection with major founding myths or legends. Israel's birth as a nation and covenant relationship with YHWH played a significant role in this regard. The prophetic oracles, placed in the written and sealed documents, likewise offered evidence of deep roots that the people of YHWH could rediscover. For subsequent generations, the word of YHWH and its constancy provided bedrock upon which they could stand (2:1, 3; cf. 40:8). Hence, chapter 34, one of the culminating sections of First Isaiah and a literary bridge between the two halves of Isaiah, recalls the addresses of the witnesses, "heaven" and "earth" (1:2):

> Draw near, O nations, to hear;
>> O peoples, give heed!
> Let the earth hear, and all that fills it;
>> the world, and all that comes from it. (34:1)

At the same time, these addressees echo the nations encountered in the OAN (chs. 13–23). Here then YHWH's promise of vindication against the unrighteous (34:8) is reiterated with the stamp of the surety of YHWH's word: "Seek and read from the book of the LORD: Not one of these shall be missing" (34:16). The promise encompasses drastic renewal and rebirth, as if the people were given a second chance to start anew and build afresh in the Eden-like place:

> The wilderness and the dry land shall be glad,
>> the desert shall rejoice and blossom;
> like the crocus it shall blossom abundantly,
>> and rejoice with joy and singing. . . .
> They shall see the glory of the LORD,
>> the majesty of our God. (35:1-2)

A New Leader for a New Era

Just as the Isaiah scroll depicts national disaster in the most tangible of terms, so also it envisions the epoch to come. One of the key motifs of First Isaiah is the reign of God; but rather than imagining a pure theocracy, the text anticipates God using an actual human agent. This expectation creates literary and symbolic symmetry: just as the Assyrian ruler is described as an instrument of the divine judgment (10:5), so a human agent is employed for divine salvation. In Second Isaiah, we will encounter various candidates for this agency. Here in First Isaiah, we find preliminary depictions of those candidates, especially from the internal domestic realm.

First Isaiah alludes in numerous ways to the qualifications of a new leader. The hope for an ideal ruler is compared to the dawn of a bright light amid darkness (9:2 [MT 9:1]; cf. 2:5; 42:6; 49:6; 60:1). This ruler will have the qualities of "Wonderful Counselor, Mighty God, Everlasting Father, Prince of Peace" (9:6 [MT 9:5]). He will be filled with the "spirit of the LORD"—a spirit of wisdom, insight, counsel, valor, devotion, and "fear of the LORD" (11:2). This leader will enjoy the core values of justice and righteousness (32:1). Analogous to the parallel narratives of King Ahaz and King Hezekiah, the king will put the utmost trust in YHWH (7:9) and be willing to come to genuine repentance and courageous actions for the sake of the people and the country (37:21; 38:5).

First Isaiah underscores another crucial quality of this ideal ruler: communal solidarity, which many Israelite kings had outright neglected and destroyed. For Isaiah, genuine power should manifest itself in care for the powerless, just as God passionately takes the side of the powerless (3:15). A righteous ruler must uphold the cause of the most vulnerable—the orphans and widows—in ancient society (1:23; 10:2; cf. 3:16-23). Indeed, justice is defined as knowing the pathos of YHWH whose concern reaches out to the oppressed and downtrodden: "The LORD has founded Zion, / and the needy among his people / will find refuge in her" (14:32;

cf. 10:2; 11:4). In a larger scope, chapters 24–27 accentuate YHWH's concerns for the needy and poor (25:4; 26:6), whereas chapters 28–33 highlight the divine accusation against the priests and prophets who "err in vision" and "stumble in giving judgment" (28:7) so as "to ruin the poor with lying words, / even when the plea of the needy is right" (32:7).

Indeed, the monarchy had demonstrated time and again the human tendency to abuse power at the expense of the weak. Foreign monarchies had demonstrated the same propensity, whether it was Assyrian and Babylonian or eventually Persian and Greek. The solemn curse is invoked on those crushing rulers:

> All the kings of the nations lie in glory,
> > each in his own tomb;
> but you are cast out, away from your grave,
> > like loathsome carrion,
> clothed with the dead, those pierced by the sword,
> > who go down to the stones of the Pit,
> like a corpse trampled underfoot. (14:18-19)

Yet, in utter contrast, First Isaiah announces that the ideal ruler in the coming age shall execute "endless peace" in faithfulness, justice, and equity (9:7 [MT 9:6]; 16:5) and shall utilize power to defend the needy (1:17). Equally significant, this righteous heir is not named (cf. chs. 9, 11, 32), so that the ongoing generations—the disciples of Isaiah and the remnants of Israel—can continue to cherish hope.

At the same time, the scroll of Isaiah points out that the divine king will govern the new era. The interpretive community will acknowledge that unlike failed human kings, YHWH remains the trustworthy ruler:

> For you have been a refuge to the poor,
> > a refuge to the needy in their distress,
> > a shelter from the rainstorm and a shade from the heat. (25:4)

Hence, the prophetic oracles warn of "those who go down to Egypt for help . . . who trust in chariots" (31:1), seeking "refuge" and "shelter" in Pharaoh (30:2-3). Whereas human leaders build up falsehood as "refuge" and treachery as "shelter" (28:15), the anonymous anointed one will provide a true "hiding place" and "shade" (32:2). In the climactic oracle toward the end of Isaiah 28–33, the people acknowledge their God as the true king:

> For the LORD is our judge, the LORD is our ruler,
> > the LORD is our king; he will save us. (33:22)

Conclusion

First Isaiah depicts the abyss as the defeat of the nation Israel, the demise of the dynasty, and the deprivation of purpose for a war-torn people. Such wreckage gave rise to tormenting questions and abject despair. And yet, in the reading of this scroll, the dejected people of God would hear the resounding assertion of YHWH's presence and pathos as proclaimed through the prophet Isaiah. In reflecting, they would read two similar but contrary stories of past kings, Ahaz and Hezekiah—one king representing the common tendency to trust in "horses and chariots" and the other embodying the rare quality of genuine faith in God. And they would recall the menacing power of the giant empires, both in the past and in the present, and revel in the incomparable power of God, which would ultimately undermine these bullying superpowers.

When reading the scroll, God's people would be able to connect the dots of hope and breathe sighs of justice amid the ongoing realities of doubt, defeat, and despair. The pompous superpowers would not remain formidable forever, especially if they continued their oppressive policies. Why is it so? Because the superpowers are not gods but merely ephemeral creatures. YHWH is the true "King, YHWH of hosts" (6:5). And so, in and beyond exile there *is* hope. The promises of hope are planted among the prophetic oracles of judgment, sporadically but distinctly. Hope is available through faith in the divine forgiveness, the reversals of misfortune and fortune, the records of the divine *hesed* in the past, and the anticipation of the righteous leader, culminating in the dawn of the kingdom of the divine king. While such hopeful configurations buoy survivors, they neither deny nor neglect their arduous journey of faith, as the prophet intimates in his call: "How long, O Lord?" (6:11).

CHAPTER THREE

VISION OF HOMECOMING AMID DIASPORA

Isaiah 40–66: "I Will Uphold You with My Victorious Right Hand"

brupt transitions, shifts of tone, and different settings inaugurate the second half of the book of Isaiah (Isa 40–66; hereafter "Second Isaiah").[1] Harsh accusations virtually disappear—at least at the beginning of the prophetic drama—and words of consolation and hope replace them. There are now few specific chronological or sociopolitical allusions; only poetic oracles addressed to downtrodden refugees. Second Isaiah throbs with the pain of defeat, displacement, and humiliation. Against this desolate background, the prophetic text speaks of homecoming, survival, and hope.

Second Isaiah is indeed a message of hope. It combats the loss of faith and the escalation of cynicism. Rather than calling attention to persecutors or traitors, it admonishes the people of God to recognize their unnamed heroines and unsung heroes in the courageous servant(s) of YHWH and the defiant daughters of Zion. Rather than submitting to despair, it elevates these heroes and heroines who never give up in the face of tormenting persecution and colonization. Rather than letting captivity have the final say, it invites the displaced community to return home, even though such a vision might seem implausible. And even when the community eventually encounters the ordeal of returning and rebuilding, and must deal with the disillusionment, Second Isaiah pleads with the faithful not to submit to fear or animosity. In solidarity with their sisters and brothers of every diasporic community, the defiant daughters of Zion and the courageous servant(s) of YHWH bear witness to resilience and faith.

In this chapter, we will examine Second Isaiah's visions of hope for a displaced community. Put differently, we will explore how this prophetic tradition functions as a survival text amid diasporic realities. To read Second Isaiah in this way is to imagine it growing out of the ashes and ruins in hometowns, the tempest and mirage in the wilderness, and the disappointment and frustration in faraway colonies. In such trying circumstances, the prophetic text generates hope for the wounded daughters of Zion and the humiliated servant(s) of YHWH, challenging their offspring to look beyond their bleak settings to the possibility of restoration and renewal. If First Isaiah presents the abyss as the defeat of the monarchy, pride, and faith, Second Isaiah presents the abyss as amnesia, despair, and injustice. In the aftermath of national calamity and during the hard days of captivity, Second Isaiah addresses Judah's unwieldy loss with candor and artistic force. And as such, the prophet joins a myriad of others in the struggle for hope and justice.

Memoirs of Exilic Realities and Survival of Hope

Doubt, Lamentation, and Denial

As opposed to psychological or physical trauma, which involves a wound and the experience of great emotional anguish by an individual, cultural trauma refers to a dramatic loss of identity and meaning, a tear in the social fabric, affecting a group of people that has achieved some degree of cohesion.[2]

Second Isaiah is well known for its uplifting messages of comfort and powerful metaphors of hope. It is no coincidence that many of the beautiful choruses and arias in Handel's Messiah derive from this prophetic tradition. Readers clearly encounter in this literary legacy an inspiring symphony of hopeful voices. However, it would be reductionist to hear only voices of consolation and renewal. No doubt such voices are present and likely give Second Isaiah its distinctive character. Yet bubbling beneath the surface of the text are equally important voices—voices of outrage and doubt, pain and humiliation.[3] Consequently, the prophet's lyrical words of assurance can never be divorced from the suffering of forced relocation. In other words, Second Isaiah attends to the exilic realities of subjugation and hopelessness.[4] Our primary task as readers then is to hear those voices of pain and acknowledge the wreckage of dejected communities stripped of power, prestige, and purpose.

First of all, one encounters throughout Second Isaiah explicit voices of doubt and complaint—especially expressed by YHWH's servant Jacob/Israel (ch. 40) and by YHWH's Daughter Zion/Jerusalem (ch. 49). Numerous times the prophet responds to probing questions: "Why?" "To whom?" "Have you not . . . ?" Listen to one such complaint muttered by Jacob/Israel: "Why do you say, O Jacob, and speak, O Israel, 'My road is hidden from the LORD, my justice is passed over from my God'?" (40:27, authors' translation). Despair and dislocation have apparently so shrouded the exiles' vision that they feel abandoned and deprived of justice. The metaphor employed in this text heightens the vivid memory of defeat. The words "road" (*derek*) and "passed over" (*'ābar*) echo the

Exodus tradition, except that here the speakers cry out as if they are experiencing a perverse reversal of the great recitals of old. No longer can they see a cloud by day or a pillar of fire by night. No longer can they hear the outcry of the enemy in the Passover (cf. Exod 12:11-12), for they are back in the wilderness and in captivity.

A similar complaint of abject despair can be found in Zion's lament, "The LORD has forsaken me, / my Lord has forgotten me" (Isa 49:14). The complaint made by YHWH's servant Jacob/Israel (cf. 40:27-31) is matched by that of YHWH's Daughter Zion/Jerusalem. Together they comprise the collective community of Israel—one masculine and the other feminine. In the previous text, the servant Israel complains that God has ignored his right and petition. Here Daughter Zion goes further in declaring that YHWH has forgotten her. A strong sense of neglect and abandonment unites these laments, although the active verbal construction of Zion's complaint perhaps intensifies the language: Israel raises a complaint while Zion makes a trenchant accusation against God. How could you forget us, Lord? How could you abandon us? Yes, we are all too prone to forget. But how can God forget, especially, God's own children?

Daughter Zion does not beat around the bush. Instead she confronts God directly and levels a distressing charge. She speaks out of her maternal instinct:

> Who has borne me these?
> I was bereaved and barren,
>   exiled and put away—
>   so who has reared these?
> I was left all alone—
>   where then have these come from? (49:21)

Her agony, which is detectable in her later recollection, represents all those who have lost kinfolk during the exile. Her sorrow points to the sorrow of fathers, mothers, husbands, wives, brothers, sisters, sons, and daughters. Much like Mother Rachel's grief (Jer 31:15-22) or Naomi's bitterness of heart (Ruth 1:20-21), Zion is inconsolable. Whereas some may talk of mere casualties of war, this is not so for mothers! For them, the loss of a family member—whether abducted or massacred—is never abstract or quantifiable. It is a disaster beyond words, and so it is for Daughter Zion.

Second, the voices of victims of war and violence fill the silence between chapter 39 and chapter 40. From the outset, the prophet's proclamation of "comfort, comfort" to the people of YHWH (40:1) implies the absence of consolation. Likewise, the divine call to "not fear" (43:1) addresses the rampant fear of the exiled people of God. A glimpse of the war-torn community can be discerned in the graphic oracle against Daughter Babylon. The troubling violence and humiliation inflicted upon Daughter Chaldea (47:1) is likely a mirror image of Daughter Jerusalem's defeat and captivity:

> Come down and sit in the dust. . . .
> For you shall no more be called
>> tender and delicate. . . .
>> remove your veil,
> strip off your robe, uncover your legs,
>> pass through the rivers.
> Your nakedness shall be uncovered,
>> and your shame shall be seen. (47:1-3)

These depictions are too graphic to expand on.[5] Yet the brutal violence of exile must not be diminished. A foreign city or distant population may be attacked and violated without evoking empathy, but never a daughter! Thus, the outcry of "daughter" Zion and her suffering strikes home, as does the sorrow and weeping of all women in war and violence—mothers, sisters, and daughters.

In chapter 52, YHWH addresses Jerusalem directly and pledges to reverse Zion's bad fortune. The imagery echoes what is forecast for Babylon in chapter 47. Jerusalem lies in the dust after suffering indescribable violence:

> For the uncircumcised and the unclean
>> shall enter you no more.
> Shake yourself from the dust, rise up,
>> O captive Jerusalem;
> loose the bonds from your neck,
>> O captive daughter Zion! (52:1-2)

The text opens a window into the utter vulnerability and despair of the Judean refugees. Jerusalem has been violated, and the poetry gives voice to this trauma and horror.[6] The "ruins of Jerusalem" (52:9) are silenced except for cries of dejection. Yet these sounds of sorrow and tears tell the story of exilic suffering.

Third, Second Isaiah broadens the scope of the outcry by focusing on the communal voice. The sharp contrast between individual and community can be noted in the shift from chapter 39 to chapter 40. In chapter 39, King Hezekiah replies to Isaiah, "There will be peace and security in my days" (39:8; emphasis added). His concern is primarily about himself. That is how the Hezekiah narrative ends, abruptly and anticlimactically. In contrast, and immediately following, the oracle in chapter 40 is addressed to the collective people: "Comfort, O comfort my people" (40:1). The divine concern covers the whole people. The Judean refugees who identify with Jacob/Israel and Zion/Jerusalem are the ones who experienced the national calamity, and together they are the ones who must endure and survive its ongoing difficulties in diaspora. Hence, the transition from singular to plural is noteworthy, much the same way we find the transition from the singular "servant of the LORD" (chs. 40–53) to the plural "servants of the LORD" (chs. 54–66).

After the national catastrophe, the people of Israel in exile are addressed as the "faint" and the "powerless" (40:29; 50:4). They are too weary to gain strength and too fearful to search for hope. Yet those who "wait" for YHWH will renew their strength, no matter how long that waiting may take (40:30-31). The people in exile are also identified as the "poor" and the "needy" (41:17; 49:13; cf. 10:2; 14:30; 25:4; 26:6; 32:7). Whether noble or common during the time of monarchy, they are now the poor and needy—terms used to describe the most vulnerable classes in society (Deut 15:11; 24:14; Pss 35:10; 37:14; 74:21; Prov 31:20). To them, YHWH's assurance is all the more resounding, "I the LORD will answer them, / I the God of Israel will not forsake them" (Isa 41:17). Furthermore, Israel in exile is referred to as the "blind" and the "deaf" (42:16, 18-19; 43:8; 48:6-8; cf. 29:18; 35:5). Although the prophet at the outset of his mission must expose and even exacerbate the people's inability to see and hear YHWH's message (6:9-10; 43:8), now God promises to guide and protect them (48:4):

> I will lead the blind
>> by a road they do not know,
> by paths they have not known
>> I will guide them.
> I will turn the darkness before them into light,
>> the rough places into level ground.
> These are the things I will do,
>> and I will not forsake them. (42:16)

Exile as the Wilderness Life

After Auschwitz, Theodor Adorno had written that no more poems could now be written. And he was wrong. Had he read the Scroll of Lamentations, he might have realized that after destruction there must be an opportunity to express anguish and pain, that there must be the reassertion of the self, the rediscovery of hope.[7]

Second Isaiah uses the metaphor and motif of "wilderness" to describe the multifaceted experiences of exile. The wilderness is a place of vulnerability and wandering. It is an arid terrain in which survival is always in question. Indeed, the wilderness is a place of danger, testing, and scarcity. And it inevitably evokes the memory of the old Exodus story in which the first generation of Israelites escaped the captivity of Egypt only to confront the hardships and wonders of the wilderness. The desert tempted this first generation to return to Egypt, to rebel against Moses, and to give up on its faith altogether. Indeed, it consumed that generation before giving birth to a new community that would eventually enter the land of promise.

It is no coincidence that Second Isaiah repeatedly uses the language and metaphor of the wilderness and its full arsenal of images. Wilderness captures the austere experience of forced deportation and internment. It is intriguing that the psalmist in the Babylonian captivity calls the place where the exiles sat or resided "there" ("By the rivers of Babylon— / *there* we sat down," Ps 137:1; emphasis added), denoting that even though the psalmist was physically "here" in Babylon, the place was emotionally "there" to this psalmist.[8] Similarly, Second Isaiah employs with multiple meanings the metaphors for wilderness: first and foremost, the metaphors represent the sorrow and agony of captivity in Babylon, as if the exilic community were neither physically nor emotionally "there," in a place far from home; and yet at the same time, these metaphors anticipate homecoming out of Babylon—that is, through the wilderness on the way back to Jerusalem. How would this wilderness language serve readers in the aftermath of the exile?

First, exile as the wilderness life symbolizes an intentional denial of imperial dominance. Admittedly, Babylon had its impressive metropolitan cities along the Tigris and Euphrates rivers, nothing short of the magnificent temples and palaces of Egypt.[9] Their glitz and glamour, however, do not seduce Second Isaiah. The prophetic text does not even mention the Ziggurat or Marduk temples, except in polemical discourses (for example, when disparaging Babylonian temples and their statues). Instead, Second Isaiah leads readers away from the splendor of Babylonian culture and into the parched wilderness terrain. To the exilic prophet and his community, the glories of Mesopotamian civilization are nothing more than a desert mirage. To them Babylon is wilderness. It is an arid and uninhabitable topography, a place of loss and vulnerability:

> All people are grass,
>   their constancy is like the flower of the field.
> The grass withers, the flower fades,
>   when the breath of the LORD blows upon it. (Isa 40:6-7; cf. 44:23; 51:12; 55:10)

Or as the psalmist laments: "How could we sing the LORD's song / in a foreign land?" (Ps 137:4). The city's splendors do little to dispel the painful realities of colonization. Babylon is nothing more than a dangerous and undomesticated wasteland.

Wilderness serves as a metaphor for the many hardships of captivity. During the initial stage of captivity, many exiles may have been forced to live in the least arable and inhabitable desert locales.[10] To them, this foreign soil was not an exotic oasis but literally a parched and suffocating desert. Similarly, to those placed into the labor camps as imperial slaves, any goods or luxury of this imperial civilization would look like a mere wilderness, an endless tunnel of suffering and humiliation:

Some of the captives, joining other conquered groups, likely were put into forced labor in Babylonia as imperial slaves. Indeed, even those who settled into their own ethnic communities likely did not possess any rights of citizens. The language of imprisonment and metaphors of slavery are numerous in texts likely dating from this period (Isa 43:6; 45:14; 52:2).[11]

Thus, the language of exile as wilderness seeks to encourage Judean refugees to avert their eyes—both physically and emotionally—from the imperial splendor, since such splendor was the very cause of their hard labor and pain.

Second, wilderness represents the physical or psychological place for the somber work of grief, reflection, and reclamation. A city full of human pride and violence is no place to encounter the God of Israel; nor is it where the community can reclaim its identity. The wilderness, in contrast, is exactly such a place. In this parched and dangerous terrain, in this liminal space, one can find God *and* oneself. It is no wonder that Moses discovers God in the wilderness of Sinai rather than in the royal temples of the Pharaoh (Exod 3:1-12). It is no happenstance that Elijah is recommissioned in the sheer silence of the lonely wilderness, not at the site of the momentous victory over the Baal and Asherah prophets (1 Kgs 18–19). Although the desert is clearly no place for attraction or habitation, it is, paradoxically, an utterly fitting place for solitude and reflection.

The significance of wilderness for the "soul" is thus noteworthy. How would the exiles reclaim their identity and their relationship with God in the wilderness? Trauma theorists suggest that healing takes place when victims of war and abuse face their excruciating wounds and the impact on their lives. Thus, trauma awareness is the key to recovery and transformation. To be healed, to reclaim one's life and move on, one must do grief work, which involves telling the truth and facing the cluster of feelings and emotions occasioned by grief, including fear, anxiety, anger, and guilt.[12] Walter Brueggemann addresses the exilic community's practice of grief:

> The practice of grief is an exercise in truth-telling. It is, as evidenced in Psalm 137 and Lamentations, an exercise in massive sadness that acknowledges, with no denial or deception, where and how Israel is. But the grief is not resignation, for in the end, Israel is incapable of resignation. Resignation would be to give up finally on [YHWH] and on [YHWH's] commitment to Israel. This Israel will not do, even if [YHWH] gives hints of such abandonment.[13]

While living in the barren and uninhabitable wilderness, perhaps figuratively and topographically, the exiles can lament and grieve. In the rugged hills and parched plains (Isa 40:4; 41:17), disconsolate refugees can reclaim their lives and reinvest their energy in meaning- and mission-making. In the desert, the exiles can behold the stars, hear the tempest, and learn the constancy of their God. The valleys and rough terrain are stark reminders of how ephemeral human power structures actually are; and in the desert the exiles can rediscover their true identity as God's children.

Third, the image and experience of exile as wilderness revives a paradoxical vision of hope amid despair. It is paradoxical because such configurations of hope are so implausible. For example, compare the Greek (Septuagint) and Hebrew (Masoretic) versions of 40:3: LXX (Greek): "The voice of the one who cries out in the wilderness: 'Prepare the way of the LORD, make straight the paths of our God' "; MT (Hebrew): "A voice cries out: 'In the wilderness prepare the way of the LORD, make straight in the desert a highway for our God.' " The LXX uses the wilderness as a modifier—that is, the one who proclaims is located in the wilderness. In this call for building the way of YHWH, the notion of the wilderness is missing, as if building a way in the wilderness would seem nonsensical. In contrast, the MT takes up the paradoxical claim that the highway is indeed to be made in the wilderness. While text-critical issues should not be discounted, we can detect emphatic language in each text tradition. From the LXX, readers would learn of a prophetic figure who will appear nowhere else but in the wilderness to proclaim such good news (cf. Matt 3:3; Mark 1:3; Luke 3:4; John 1:23). To those living hopelessly in life's wilderness, such an announcement would bring great hope (cf. Isa 52:7). From the MT, readers are not informed as to the identity of the voice, but they are invited to envision that which seems paradoxical: to build a highway in the desert, which is full of valleys, hills, crooked ways, and rough places (40:4; cf. 11:16; 35:8). To the exiles, such a message would have kindled a spark of hope, at best, and yet a spark that would grow stronger within the hearts of God's people.

Thus, the desert can become a place of revelation. Put differently, inspiring vision and voice emerge from the wilderness and in spite of it. In the movie *The Shawshank Redemption*, based on a best-selling novel by Stephen King, the inmates in a maximum-security penitentiary chat about an incident in which the protagonist, Andy Dufresne, defiantly plays a beautiful Mozart aria through the prison speakers. At the dining hall, Andy describes the power of music and hope. "That's the beauty of music. They can't get that from you. . . . Here's where it makes the most sense. You need it so you don't forget. . . . There's something inside that they can't get to, that they can't touch. That's yours. . . . Hope." The others, however, just don't get it. Red, another inmate, challenges Andy: "What are you talking about? . . . Hope is a dangerous thing. Hope can drive a [person] insane. It's got no use on the inside. You'd better get used to that idea." Eventually Red begins to grasp the importance of hope, and so Andy reiterates: "Remember, Red, hope is a good thing, maybe the best of things. And no good thing ever dies."[14]

The prisoners view hope as dangerous because it might foster a false expectation for freedom. Hope demands trust, vulnerability, and openness. As such, it might "dupe" the prisoners into forgetting the harsh reality of their prison life and lead to further disappointment. And yet without hope survival is nearly impossible. Joseph Barndt describes a compelling illustration of the invincible power of hope and vision even inside the prison walls:

> The witnesses to this truth abound. St. Paul's great dissertations on freedom were written from a jail cell. Mahatma Ghandi and Martin Luther King Jr. taught and demonstrated that being in prison can even be a means of promoting freedom. Nelson Mandela, after twenty-seven years in prison, emerged to demonstrate that his identity as a free person had been strengthened in prison. And, during 300 years of enslavement, Africans in the United States never lost sight of freedom, and proclaimed in their spirituals that their slavemasters could "kill the body but not the soul."[15]

Hope is paradoxical by virtue of generating newness out of the bleakest of circumstances. Second Isaiah is replete with motifs and metaphors of paradoxical hope, announcing and inviting "prisoners" (42:7; 49:9) to imagine the marvelous amid the miserable and freedom while incarcerated. How does the prophet express such possibilities? Largely it is in and through the imagery of wilderness: where people feel not only the desert soil and scorching heat but they also imagine highways leading home and springs of water in an oasis. Whereas Ezekiel envisions dry bones becoming wholesome flesh in the valley (Ezek 37:1-14), Second Isaiah leads the readers through the dangerous wilderness where travelers encounter seeds of life sprouting in the most unlikely places. Looking at the desert, they imagine the possibility of homecoming, as announced and envisioned by the prophetic exhortations. In the wilderness, they can smell anew the flowers of freedom and breathe afresh the mighty winds that once split the Red Sea; and this wilderness will soon become a highway for a new exodus. Although many see nothing but death and despair in the desert, the prophet discerns the steadfast love and fidelity of YHWH.

Second Isaiah often underscores this paradoxical hope by employing wilderness metaphors, often in conjunction with contrasting word pairs. For example, just as the prophet heard the divine intention to commission a messenger to make the people obdurate (6:8-12), now the prophet hears the divine command to turn the wilderness into a highway, the desert into a road, the valley into a level, and the ridges into a plain (40:3-4). Furthermore, God promises to pour out "rivers on the bare heights, / and fountains in the midst of the valleys" and make the "wilderness a pool of water, / and the dry land springs of water" (41:18). The same God who "makes a way in the sea, / a path in the mighty waters" (43:16; cf. Exod 14:21-22) is to "make a way in the wilderness / and rivers in the desert" (43:19).[16] In the dry terrain of wilderness, the exilic people will be renewed by flowing water and gushing rain (44:3-4; 48:21). The exilic community can anticipate pastures on bare heights and springs of water against hot desert wind (49:9-10). And the oasis in the desert is not a mere mirage or fleeting sight; it is the garden of Eden (51:3) and a great banquet of water, wine, and milk, with an invitation extended to all who are thirsty and poor (55:1). YHWH sets in the desert

> the cypress,
>> the plane and the pine together,
> so that all may see and know,
>> all may consider and understand,
> that the hand of the LORD has done this,
>> the Holy One of Israel has created it. (41:19-20)

And so through images from "nature's temple," Second Isaiah inspires dispirited Judean refugees to soar beyond the daily grind to that which is grand. Through the metaphor of the wilderness, Second Isaiah enables exiles to anticipate newness against all odds. In the wilderness they can grasp anew God's promise to be with them even through water and fire (43:2). And in the wilderness they can encounter the constancy of the divine word in contrast with the ephemeral grass and flowers of the field (40:8). Perhaps it is desert hope that enables God's people to "mount up with wings like eagles / . . . [to] run and not be weary / . . . [and] walk and not faint" (40:31).

"Remember Not . . . Remember"

> *And as one looks down into the Casentino, far beneath, the Valley Enclosed itself becomes a thought, a memory. The past grows more vivid than the present, and the course of the river below symbolises itself into an image of the strong currents of life and passion which once coursed through the Valley.*[17]

Out of sight, out of mind. Abandoned in the wilderness of parched soil and immense hardship, Judean refugees in Babylon survived with few supports from their former world. The old world of temples and palaces, land occupation, and political autonomy was now only a distant dream. Captivity created fear and hostility as well as the tendency for some to forget the past. The exilic psalmist defies this powerful temptation to forget:

> If I forget you, O Jerusalem,
>> let my right hand wither!
> Let my tongue cling to the roof of my mouth,
>> if I do not remember you. (Ps 137:5-6)

Second Isaiah's plea to "remember" more than suggests the onslaught of communal amnesia.

Equally traumatic is the experience of being forgotten. To be forgotten is perhaps the greatest show of disdain. Every moment and event in life is annulled. Every feeling of joy and alienation, wonder and loneliness, gratitude and anxiety, is taken. The past vanishes and one essentially disappears. When Elie Wiesel realized that the people of the Hungarian town of Sighet had forgotten the Jews who only decades earlier had been rounded up and sent to concentration camps, he was not angry with them for driving "out their neighbors of yesterday." "If I was angry at all," he recalls, "it was for having forgotten them. So quickly, so completely . . . Jews have been driven not only out of town but out of time as well."[18] Second Isaiah addresses a community that feels forgotten and abandoned by God. "Zion said, 'The LORD has forsaken me, / my Lord has forgotten me' " (49:14). At the same time, the prophet accuses this community of acting in kind: "You have forgotten the LORD, your Maker, / who stretched out the heavens / and laid the foundations of the earth" (51:13).

How does the exilic prophet instill hope in those suffering the pangs of rejection and divine abandonment? How does Second Isaiah seek to heal the emotional and psychological scars of the refugee community? The prophet obviously does not provide a handbook for psychological counseling or a manual for therapy. Rather, Second Isaiah urges the people of God to take two decisive courses of action: to relinquish what is destructive (i.e., to *forget* what needs to be forgotten) and to embrace what is essential to survival (i.e., to *remember* what is crucial). These two dynamic and dialogic tasks are expressed in two seemingly contradictory phrases:[19]

> Do not remember the former things,
>> or consider the things of old.
> I am about to do a new thing;
>> now it springs forth, do you not perceive it? (43:18-19; emphasis added)

> Remember the former things of old;
> for I am God, and there is no other;
>> I am God, and there is no one like me. (46:9; emphasis added)[20]

Second Isaiah admonishes the community to "not remember" the "former things," as YHWH is about to do a "new thing." What then are they to forget? In the first place, the exiles are to forget "a wide-ranging complex of traditions, not restricted to the book of Isaiah,"[21] including the wondrous exodus traditions.[22] Oddly, the imperative "Do not remember" is linked to YHWH's victory over Egypt in the old exodus:

Thus says the LORD,
>who makes a way in the sea,
>a path in the mighty waters,
who brings out chariot and horse,
>army and warrior;
they lie down, they cannot rise,
>they are extinguished, quenched like a wick. (43:16-17; cf. Exod 14:26-29; 15:19, 21)

The exiles are not to anticipate a replica of age-old acts of God; they are to imagine something startlingly new that will totally eclipse "the former things," however glorious. YHWH will "make a way in the wilderness and rivers in the desert" (43:19).

The exiles are also to forget—or rather, "not remember"—the undeniable struggles and shame they have had to endure. It is noteworthy that the "former things" in Isaiah may also allude to the messages of warning and judgment, occurring predominantly in the first half of the book of Isaiah, which involve divine absence or abandonment and Israel's defeat and humiliation (cf. 41:22; 42:9; 43:9; 48:3; 65:16-17). Christopher R. Seitz elucidates: "The older wilderness tradition also included a highly complex, far from uniform depiction of complaint, scarce resources, divine absence, and the judgment of death over an entire generation."[23] Here it is important to note that the prophetic appeal is not to forget the evil inflicted on the exiles or the pain they have endured. Communities ravaged by evil cannot merely forget their suffering. Nor can individuals disregard the deep scars of abuse. On the contrary, acts of brutality, whether communal or personal, must be faced and exposed. Perhaps this is why Second Isaiah confronts the seemingly unrivaled deities of Babylon (for example, 46:1) and disparages daughter Chaldea (47:5, 11). The choice of negation, "Do not remember" (especially stated in the initial chapters of Isaiah 40–66, for example, 43:18, as opposed to the imperative "forget"), may suggest that the exiles are to relinquish those social, emotional, and psychological forces that hold them captive to the past. Walter Brueggemann alludes to this point in Beverly J. Shamana's powerful sermon "Letting Go," in which the preacher "understands the 'former things' to be 'let go' as the 'old baggage of slavery,' or more precisely 'a slave mentality.'"[24]

Interestingly, the people of God are not left on their own to do the work of "letting go": YHWH leads the way. Second Isaiah asserts that YHWH will "forget" Israel's wrong and wronged past: "I, I am He / who blots out your transgressions for my own sake, / and I will *not remember* your sins" (43:25; emphasis added). YHWH reassures bereaved Zion by pledging to help her "forget" the disgrace she has suffered:

> Do not fear, for you will not be ashamed;
>> do not be discouraged, for you will not suffer disgrace;
> for you will *forget* the shame of your youth,
>> and the disgrace of your widowhood you will
>>> *remember no more.* (54:4; cf. 49:14-21; emphasis added)

> For I am about to create new heavens
>> and a new earth;
> the former things shall *not be remembered*
>> or come to mind. (65:17; emphasis added)

"Letting go" is only one facet of the dynamic reciprocity of hope: the community is also to "remember" the "former things." What exactly are the exiles to keep in mind? First, the community must remember the *unspeakable* crimes committed against them. Henri Nouwen observes that we have an enormous propensity "to forget the pains of the past—our personal, communal, and national traumas—and live as if they did not really happen. But by not remembering them we allow the forgotten memories to become independent forces that can exert a crippling effect on our functioning as human beings."[25] The exiles' struggle to move beyond their shame and guilt is intractably bound to telling the truth about the trauma they have endured. Such truth-telling makes survival possible. The post-*Shoah* world has taught us all too well that victims of trauma cannot mask or deny the many distorted postures of evil; atrocities must be confronted and perpetrators of such acts must be taken to task.[26] This is not merely a stance against the victimizer; it is a redemptive act on behalf of the victim, who is often imprisoned in false guilt and humiliation. And when shame is not processed appropriately, it turns inward against the self. That is to say, a major casualty of shame is the self, so severely wounded that any sense of esteem or worth is crushed. And shame distorts identity and quells hope.

> Just as traditions that attempt to continue the past require rituals of commemoration, so ruptures between past and present, too, require rituals of repentance and cultures of memory. Neither can persist if we recall the events only occasionally, incidentally, and individually. Cultivating memories by rituals and memorials creates a collective identity that is protected against doubts and objections.[27]

Representing the work of Jewish refugees in Babylon, Second Isaiah dares to attend to the evil committed against Israel by its oppressors.[28] In the middle section of Isaiah 40–55—for example, chapters 46–47—the reader encounters oracles that are similar to the Oracles against the Nations (chs. 13–23). Here the prophet depicts the seemingly unrivaled deities of Babylon, Marduk and his son Nabu, crouching in utter shame and impotence: "Bel bows down, Nebo stoops" (46:1). The ridicule Judah felt is now turned into a curse against Babylon. The shame Daughter Zion endured is turned into lamentation against Daughter Chaldea:

> Sit in silence, and go into darkness,
>> daughter Chaldea!
> For you shall no more be called
>> the mistress of kingdoms. . . .
> But evil shall come upon you,
>> which you cannot charm away;
> disaster shall fall upon you,
>> which you will not be able to ward off. (47:5, 11)[29]

These prophetic accusations may sound harsh to modern readers, who might expect more amicable words. However, for victims of deportation to overcome their indescribable pain and humiliation, they must remember the deeds of violence committed against them. Such remembrance and ridicule—for example, telling and performing the story of trauma, perhaps in liturgical settings—represents a vital stage of healing and hope.

Second, and in apparent contradiction to an earlier directive, Second Isaiah exhorts the exiles to remember the past history that narrates God's creation, deliverance, and covenant traditions. Recalling these time-honored testimonies no doubt carries the risk of anesthetizing God's people to the pressing concerns of the present or relegating the object of hope to the past. It can also function as a mechanism for regret or con-gratulations. Nonetheless, the process of building hope depends on reembracing the past, not forgetting it.

> Remember this and consider,
>> recall it to mind, you transgressors,
>> *remember the former things of old;*
> for I am God, and there is no other;
>> I am God, and there is no one like me,
> declaring the end from the beginning
>> and from ancient times things not yet done,
> saying, "My purpose shall stand,
>> and I will fulfill my intention,"
> calling a bird of prey from the east,
>> the man for my purpose from a far country.
> I have spoken, and I will bring it to pass;
>> I have planned, and I will do it. (46:8-11; emphasis added)

The former things, long past, include the old exodus tradition, echoing the motifs of wilderness, homecoming, and reunion. The exile-scarred community is thus to remember its covenant relationship with God:

> I am the LORD your God,
>> the Holy One of Israel, your Savior.
> I give Egypt as your ransom,
>> Ethiopia and Seba in exchange for you. (43:3; cf. 43:16-17; 52:4)

In order not to lose their bearings, sever their religious ties, and shift their elemental loyalties, the Judean exiles must take into account their roots—where they came from and to whom they belong. Walter Brueggemann forcefully points out the importance of remembering the past for the sake of the future:

> When we have completely forgotten our past, we will absolutize the present and we will be like contented cows in Bashan who want nothing more than the best of today. People like that can never remember who they are, cannot remember their status as exiles or that home is somewhere else. It takes a powerful articulation of memory to maintain a sense of identity in the midst of exile.[30]

Memory is crucial to the survival of each generation, especially those suffering the emotional and psychological wreckage of exile. But memory is more than mere recollection; it is reperformance and recontextualization. Each successive community of faith struggles with and appropriates anew the demands and promises of the *traditum*. Each successive generation reenacts and reclaims the testimonies of old ("I am God, and there is no other," 46:9). Accordingly, the past is not simply past; it is a powerful force in the present and the future. It sustains the community through the morass of the present and it informs imagination to light the way forward. And so Second Isaiah urges the interpretive community of exiles:

> Look to the rock from which you were hewn,
>> and to the quarry from which you were dug.
> Look to Abraham your father
>> and to Sarah who bore you;
> for he was but one when I called him,
>> but I blessed him and made him many. (51:1)

Recount God's covenant promises to the forebears and reenact them in continuous memory-making:

> For the coastlands shall wait for me,
>> the ships of Tarshish first,

> to bring your children from far away,
>   their silver and gold with them,
> for the name of the LORD your God,
>   and for the Holy One of Israel,
>   because he has glorified you. (60:9)

If the exiles engage in such work, they will serve as YHWH's collective witness among the nations: "You are my witnesses, says the LORD" (43:10; cf. 44:8).

Third, and perhaps most important, the exiles are to remember their true identity: they are God's precious children, as noted in YHWH's emphatic utterance, "I love you" (43:4). The prophet repeatedly refutes the assertion that YHWH has forgotten or forsaken them. No doubt the exiles could hardly cast off their sense of shame and fear; but Second Isaiah's message of consolation is potent enough to mitigate its sting. In fact, the divine testimony, in the I/Thou and We/Thou term, that Israel (still) belongs to God and is God's beloved, facilitates healing and recovery:

> I have called you by name, *you are mine.* (43:1; emphasis added)

> *Remember* these things, O Jacob,
>   and Israel, for you are my servant;
> I formed you, you are my servant;
>   O Israel, you will *not be forgotten* by me. (44:21; emhasis added)

> *You are my people.* (51:16; emphasis added)

These words of assurance further indicate that YHWH is not oblivious to Zion's deep sorrow:

> Whereas you have been forsaken and hated,
>   with no one passing through,
> I will make you majestic forever,
>   a joy from age to age. (60:15)

> You shall no more be termed Forsaken, . . .
> but you shall be called My Delight Is in Her. (62:4)

> And you shall be called, "Sought Out, A City Not Forsaken." (62:12)

Although such language may not eradicate the taunting forces of fear and palpable despair, it empowers the disheartened community to see beyond its wounded condition. When exile-laden Israel remembers the divine voice of affection, shattered faith and broken trust can be restored.

Metaphors of God

Second Isaiah also seeks to restore shattered faith and broken trust through a rich array of metaphors for God. As such, the divine utterance "You are my people" (51:16) is further delineated. Here, prophet meets poet most forcefully and most intimately, although the two are never actually estranged from each other. More specifically, this poet-prophet plays the tutor and instructs with concrete illustrations rather than with vague and abstract language. Who is our God? Why should we trust and hope in this God? How can we grasp the promise that God will comfort, redeem, and bring us home? Second Isaiah responds to these focal concerns by directing the community's attention to two relational realms: the public sphere (where God is depicted as the creator and divine king or warrior) and the domestic sphere (where God emerges as husband and father or mother).

The prophet-poet first leads the reader to the dangerous public arena, which includes Babylon's deities and the political leaders. In this realm, Second Isaiah depicts YHWH as the sole creator who dwarfs all Babylonian would-be deities, whether Marduk, Nebo, or any other foreign god. Such a claim is one facet of an all-encompassing monotheizing tendency to honor YHWH as the true and living God while disparaging the Babylonian pantheon.[31] For those living under Babylonian rule, this interpretive perspective was anything but incidental. In situations of captivity, there is a powerful inclination to bond with the perpetrator. As Judith Herman notes: "The perpetrator becomes the most powerful person in the life of the victim, and the psychology of the victim is shaped by the actions and beliefs of the perpetrator."[32] While Herman focuses on the psychological effects of domination on individuals, many of her observations clarify the consequences for larger social units as well—including prisoners of war and communities under siege. And so it is no coincidence that readers find numerous passages of anti-idol polemics throughout Second Isaiah. The community under the duress of Babylonian control faced an entirely foreign symbol system—one that challenged the domain assumptions of Israel's understanding of reality and at the same time held enormous appeal. In response to a myriad of social, cultural, and religious pressures, Second Isaiah delivers a contrasting polemic:

Have you not known? Have you not heard?
The LORD is the everlasting God,
    the Creator of the ends of the earth. (40:28; cf. 42:5; 44:24; 45:12; 65:17)

Throughout Second Isaiah, readers encounter an armory of rhetorical polemics against idol fabrication. In a culture entrenched in polytheism, the prophet-poet contends that the empire's idols are nothing but "a delusion; their works are nothing; their images are empty wind" (41:29; 40:19-20). The one who produces idols is likened to a clown reenacting a street performance: "Part of it he takes and warms himself; he kindles a fire and bakes bread. Then he makes a god and worships it, makes it a carved image and bows down before it" (44:15; cf. 45:9, 20, 24; 46:6-7). In a stark contrast, although using similar language and metaphors, the prophet depicts YHWH as creator of heaven and earth and all that belongs within them. In fact, this God creates the cosmos by the divine utterance (Gen 1:1-3) and fashions human beings as an artisan's skill (Gen 2:7, 22; cf. Isa 45:9-13).[33] This same God provides a tent for the sun, commonly venerated as the sun-god Shamash: "In the heavens he has set a tent for the sun" (Ps 19:4 [MT 19:5]), which echoes in Second Isaiah:

> It is he who sits above the circle of the earth,
>   and its inhabitants are like grasshoppers;
> who stretches out the heavens like a curtain,
>   and spreads them like a tent to live in. (Isa 40:22)

YHWH, not Marduk, the text asserts, controls the whole course of world history events:

> I form light and create darkness,
>   I make weal and create woe;
>   I the LORD do all these things. (45:7)

Still in the public arena, the prophet-poet draws on ordinary political metaphors to portray this God. YHWH is a righteous king who supports the powerless against their oppressors. The Holy One of Israel, the incomparable God, is divine ruler: "I am the LORD, your Holy One, / the Creator of Israel, your King" (43:15; 44:6). Hope in God, for Isaiah, is expressed as hope in the true king (see 6:1-5), over against the empires and emperors to whom the exiles had to pay due obeisance. So the herald of good news proclaims to Zion, "Your God is King" (52:7, authors' translation). Likewise, this divine king is a mighty warrior and vindicator, the reliable protector of the people: "See, the Lord GOD comes with might, / and his arm rules for him" (40:10). The arm of YHWH represents the sway of the divine warrior over the chaotic forces of nature and world historical events:

> The LORD is a warrior;
>   the LORD is his name. . . .
> Your right hand, O LORD, glorious in power—
>   your right hand, O LORD, shattered the enemy.
> (Exod 15:3, 6; cf. Deut 4:34; Isa 48:14; 51:5, 9; 62:8)

Into the deep and dark abyss of colonization comes the divine ruler-warrior who defends those disfigured by humiliation and affliction, stripped of hope and purpose:

> Do not fear, for I am with you,
>> do not be afraid, for I am your God;
> I will strengthen you, I will help you,
>> I will uphold you with my victorious right hand. (Isa 41:10)

The downcast community can thus identify with the servant who claims, "He who vindicates me is near. / Who will contend with me?" (50:8).

The claim that God is the righteous king and triumphant warrior leaves little room for compromise or neutrality. The gods of Babylon are mere imposters; and so the prophet-poet mocks them fiercely and announces their doom:

> You felt secure in your wickedness;
>> you said, "No one sees me."
> Your wisdom and your knowledge
>> led you astray,
> and you said in your heart,
>> "*I am, and there is no one besides me.*" (47:10; cf. 47:14-15; emphasis added)

The counterclaims against the idols highlight the true source of hope—YHWH—who will not let oppressors go unpunished but who grants salvation to those who hope in God:

> For thus says the LORD . . .
>> *I am the LORD, and there is no other.* (45:18; emphasis added)

> Even the nations are like a drop from a bucket,
>> and are accounted as dust on the scales;
>> see, he takes up the isles like fine dust. . . .
> It is he . . . who brings princes to naught,
>> and makes the rulers of the earth as nothing. (40:15, 22-23)

Alongside metaphors from the public domain, Second Isaiah deploys images from the domestic realm. The prophet-poet personifies YHWH as a trustworthy husband who embraces his disgraced and forlorn spouse Zion. Such imagery is reminiscent of Hosea 1–2 and Jeremiah 2–3, as well as Ezekiel 16. In fact, the phrase "You are my people" in Isaiah 51:16 may be an echo of the same phrase in Hosea 2:23 (MT 2:25).[34] In each case, the turbulent strife between husband and wife is approximated in divine wrath and abandonment. In Second Isaiah, however, the intent of the language is distinctive.

71

Rather than focusing on the (abusive) punishment of the wife, the prophet-poet highlights divine compassion toward her and even dares to accord to YHWH a degree of blame for the marital discord (see, for example, Isa 54:4-8). The negative portrayal of wife and mother Zion still lurks in the background (cf. Isa 1:21); indignation and chastisement are still within the purview of the text. But now the promise of Zion's restoration takes precedence and her complaint (49:14) is heard.[35] For example, in an unconventional disputation, YHWH insists that Zion's divorce is void and thus she and her children still belong to God: "Where is your mother's bill of divorce / with which I put her away?" (50:1; cf. Jer 3:1, 8). YHWH is the one who redeems the abandoned woman, just as Boaz the faithful kinsman redeems Ruth (Ruth 4). YHWH is Zion's husband, her redeemer: "For your Maker is your husband / . . . the Holy One of Israel is your Redeemer" (Isa 54:5; cf. 52:9). Dejected and brokenhearted, the exiles are reminded of the divine fidelity: "For the LORD has called you / like a wife forsaken and grieved in spirit" (54:6). With great care and affection, YHWH promises to turn Zion's shame into honor (43:1-7). Therefore, the metaphor of YHWH as husband now underscores God's love and commitment to the exiles:

> For a brief moment I abandoned you,
> but with great compassion I will gather you.
> In overflowing wrath for a moment
> I hid my face from you,
> but with everlasting love I will have compassion on you,
> says the LORD, your Redeemer. (54:7-8)

This expression of love (and regret) is no mere whim. God makes an eternal covenant with Jerusalem—as firm as the oath made to Noah—never again to disregard Israel (54:9; cf. 54:11-12).

The prophet-poet also personifies YHWH as a compassionate parent who will safely bring Zion's offspring home. God assumes the role of the father and mother for distraught refugees orphaned in defeat and sorrow. God's paternal love flows unconditionally and unboundedly to the children who are living in distress:

> For you are our father,
> though Abraham does not know us
> and Israel does not acknowledge us;
> you, O LORD, are our father;
> our Redeemer from of old is your name. (63:16)

YHWH as the father is the potter who shapes the clay:

> Yet, O LORD, you are our Father;
>> we are the clay, and you are our potter;
>> we are all the work of your hand. (64:8 [MT 64:7])

God's tender love is heightened in maternal care:

> Listen to me, O house of Jacob,
>> all the remnant of the house of Israel,
> who have been borne by me from your birth,
>> carried from the womb;
> even to your old age I am he,
>> even when you turn gray I will carry you.
> I have made, and I will bear;
>> I will carry and will save. (46:3-4)

YHWH's undying devotion toward Israel is portrayed poignantly in the culminating section of Second Isaiah, where mother YHWH pledges to comfort Zion and her descendants: "As a mother comforts her child, / so I will comfort you; / you shall be comforted in Jerusalem" (66:13).[36] Thus the prophet-poet urges the estranged people of God to discover anew true parental love. Second Isaiah casts a firm reminder that the "fatherless and motherless" Judean refugees do indeed have a Parent, YHWH, who is sure to return, console, and bring them home.

In conclusion, it is noteworthy that the metaphors of God as the creator, king, warrior, husband, father, and mother are frequently and poetically intertwined in terms of their usage and meaning. Just as Zion takes the role of a daughter, wife, and mother, so YHWH appears as the creator who is husband and father, especially in helping Zion beget children.[37] Thus, the prophet describes YHWH as the maker of Zion's offspring, and at the same time describes YHWH as the creator who begot them:

> Woe to anyone who says to a father, "What are you begetting?"
>> or to a woman, "With what are you in labor?"
> Thus says the LORD,
>> the Holy One of Israel, and its Maker:
> Will you question me about my children,
>> or command me concerning the work of my hands? (45:10-11)

Similarly, the warrior imagery of YHWH is paradoxically juxtaposed with the birthing imagery of the mother. This subtle juxtaposition is most evident in 42:8-17:

> The Lord goes forth like a soldier,
>> like a warrior he stirs up his fury;
> he cries out, he shouts aloud,
>> he shows himself mighty against his foes.
> For a long time I have held my peace,
>> I have kept still and restrained myself;
> now I will cry out like a woman in labor,
>> I will gasp and pant. (42:13-14)

Sarah J. Dille interprets the fusion of these two seemingly conflicting metaphors in a trenchant way:

> A warrior is a very masculine figure and destructive. A *yoledah* [a woman in labor] is a very feminine figure, creative and life-giving. Yhwh is both destructive and creative, both masculine and feminine. Yet the warrior is not only destructive; the warrior saves. Birth is not only creative, it is life-threatening. How very apt for the exiles is the ambiguity of destruction and creation, of salvation and bondage.[38]

What readers encounter in Second Isaiah, therefore, is an amalgamation of diverse—and even clashing—renderings of God that converge in a concentrate of hope. This fusion of polarities (majesty and mercy; power and gentleness; transcendence and presence) creates hope because it honors a wide range of human needs and concerns, especially of those whose lives are severely dislocated.

> To whom then will you compare me,
>> or who is my equal? says the Holy One. (40:25)

> Who is like me? Let them proclaim it. (44:7)

> I am the Lord, and there is no other. (45:18)

> Sing for joy, O heavens, and exult, O earth. . . .
> For the Lord has comforted his people,
>> and will have compassion on his suffering ones. (49:13)

Unlike the seemingly formidable gods of their captors, the God of the losers, the Judean refugees, is high above and yet looks far down into the depth of their despair and pain. Their creator-king-warrior is as attentive as a devoted spouse and a doting parent.

Agents of Hope: The Servant of YHWH and Daughter Zion

Hope is rooted deeply in the character and activity of YHWH. Second Isaiah heralds that YHWH is creator, redeemer, king, and warrior as well as husband, mother, and father—all metaphors that intend to instill hope in those struggling through the morass of captivity. The exilic text insists that Zion's consolation and future restoration depend wholly on this God.

> For the LORD will comfort Zion;
>> he will comfort all her waste places,
> and will make her wilderness like Eden,
>> her desert like the garden of the LORD;
> joy and gladness will be found in her,
>> thanksgiving and the voice of song. (51:3)

> I, I am he who comforts you;
>> why then are you afraid of a mere mortal who must die,
> a human being who fades like grass? (51:12)

And as elsewhere in the prophetic literature, Second Isaiah accentuates the sovereign "I," often at the expense of the conditional "if" (of human initiative and responsibility).

> I, I am the LORD,
>> and besides me there is no savior.
> I declared and saved and proclaimed. . . .
> I am God, and also henceforth I am He. . . .
>> I work and who can hinder it? . . .
> I am the LORD . . . who makes a way in the sea,
>> a path in the mighty waters. . . .
> I am about to do a new thing; . . .
> I will make a way in the wilderness. . . .
> I, I am He
>> who blots out your transgressions for my own sake. (43:11-13, 15-16, 19, 25)

> Surely, the people are grass.
>> The grass withers, the flower fades;
> but the word of our God will stand forever. (40:7d-8)

Notwithstanding the force of such claims, human intermediaries play an indispensable role in generating hope. In Isaiah 1–39, God deploys particular people at particular times and places to foster hope, often in the face of human cruelty and injustice.

The prophet himself on occasion assumes that role, although his prophetic mission is too complex to be subsumed under any singular heading (for example, 6:10-13). A Davidic heir from the lineage of Jesse serves as God's instrument of hope. This royal feature, Isaiah declares, will govern with wisdom and understanding, and champion the rights of the poor and needy. And such governance will usher in an epoch of justice, righteousness, peace, and harmony for God's people (11:1-7). The loyal remnant functions as an agent of hope and a symbol of survival. And the persona of faithful King Hezekiah inspires hope in those living under the tyranny of foreign rulers. All are heroes during times of national tragedy.

We all need heroes and heroines, especially in moments of fear and uncertainty. We look to them to sustain us, to inspire us, and to represent the best of ourselves. During the horrific years of apartheid, South Africans looked to imprisoned Nelson Mandela as a symbol of hope and survival. Once labeled "Most Dangerous Negro in America" by FBI director J. Edgar Hoover, Martin Luther King, Jr. still inspires hope and courage in those struggling for justice and equality. And during the September 11, 2001 tragedy in New York, amid chaos and terror, we learned of firefighters who risked their lives to save others. Bruce Springsteen honors these slain heroines and heroes in his 2002 song "Into the Fire":

> But love and duty called you someplace higher
> Somewhere up the stairs, into the fire.

The stories of their sacrifice will be told for years to come.

Judean refugees in Babylon likewise found courage and inspiration through heroic figures. During moments of national tragedy, they identified a number of divine instruments of hope: the unnamed prophet of the exile (Second Isaiah), King Cyrus of Persia, the "Servant of YHWH," and "Daughter Zion." Through these chosen ones, the exiles came to experience God's sustaining care and saving power. And, in each case, they discovered within themselves the strength to become channels of hope to their descendants.

Second Isaiah lifts up heroes and heroines to cultivate hope in God. The prophet himself fulfills that role. Unlike Isaiah of Jerusalem whose call involved dulling the people's minds, stopping their ears, and sealing their eyes so they could not see, hear, understand, and ultimately be healed (6:10), Second Isaiah is responsible for announcing YHWH's imminent arrival as a gentle shepherd (40:1-8). In contrast to his earlier counterpart, the prophet-poet from the exile proclaims unambiguous salvation (in chs. 40–55, especially). And this salvation—particularly manifest in the refugees' return to their land—is not dependent on human initiative or devotion, which is often shaky ground, but on YHWH's word.

King Cyrus emerges in the text as a champion and liberator of Judah. And unlike his counterpart, the king of Assyria (10:5), the Persian ruler is a divine instrument of salvation not only to Israel but also to the whole world (45:1-25). Second Isaiah declares that Cyrus is YHWH's "shepherd" and "anointed" (44:28; 45:1, literally "messiah"; cf. Jer 25:9; 27:6). YHWH summons "that swooping bird from the East" (Isa 46:11a; NJPS), "the man for my purpose from a far country" (46:11b), and charges him with a crucial mission to fulfill. Indeed, YHWH has "spoken and called him, / . . . and he will prosper in his way" (48:15). Through the agency of Cyrus, the people of YHWH will be liberated from their oppressors. And even though some would question such a plan, YHWH's resolve is firm (45:9-13). Israel's very existence is at stake:

> For the sake of my servant Jacob,
>   and Israel my chosen,
> I call you by your name,
>   I surname you, though you do not know me. (45:4)

In some sense, Cyrus assumes the role of a Davidic heir (cf. chs. 9, 11, 32) yet remains only an instrument through which YHWH intends to accomplish the goal of delivering Jacob/Israel out of bondage and slavery.

It is important to note that readers encounter in Second Isaiah a transition from individual agency—often anonymous—to collective agency. For instance, at first the prophet speaks of an unnamed messianic king from the lineage of David who will usher in a epoch of peace and righteousness (11:1-10). This figure is associated with the "shoot . . . out from the stump of Jesse" and "a branch . . . out of his roots" (11:1). Near the end of the book, the "shoot" planted by YHWH is no longer an individual but rather God's people who now enjoy a messianic role in establishing righteousness and glorifying their creator (60:21). Likewise, the "servant of YHWH" (42:1-4; 42:19; 43:10), who is sometimes unidentified and other times referred to as Jacob/Israel (41:8, 9; 44:1, 21; 45:4; 48:20), eventually morphs from the singular into the plural, the "servants of YHWH" (54:17; 56:6; 63:17; 65:9; 65:13-15; 66:14). The passage known as a crux for identifying the servant (49:1-13) draws attention to this metamorphosis. Although we cannot reconstruct the evolution of this process with any certainty, scholars postulate a propensity to democratize in the text—a propensity that shifts from singular (often unnamed) figures—such as Cyrus, a prophet, a voice crying in the wilderness, God's servant, and a Davidic king—to the collective people of Israel. If we follow this line of reasoning, it is the people of Israel, the offspring in diaspora, who, having been inspired by key individuals, are now commissioned to become heroes and heroines themselves. Or in the language of the text, YHWH charges faithful Israel to be "a covenant to the people" and "a light to the nations" (42:6) and to carry out the tasks of opening eyes, rescuing prisoners in exile, and restoring survivors and the land (42:7; 49:6, 8). The people of God are to take the lead and become agents of hope.

The literary construction of the "servant" in Second Isaiah bristles with rich theological import, and Jewish and Christian commentators for millennia have found it a topic of impassioned interpretation. Most have focused on the identity of the servant of YHWH. And a number of commentators have identified the prophet Jeremiah as the prototype for this figure. Whereas inner biblical analyses of citations and motifs lend support to their argument,[39] Second Isaiah not only keeps the servant's identity anonymous (when not referring to him as Jacob/Israel) but also depicts the servant in quite different ways from Jeremiah.[40] Hence, others consider the servant to be the prophet Isaiah, Second Isaiah, a Davidic heir, a later prophet, and a messianic figure— victorious or suffering. Traditionally, Christians identify the servant as Jesus of Nazareth, while most Jewish commentators opt for the collective people of Jacob/Israel.[41]

Recent scholarship often questions an "either-or" interpretation, calling attention to the text's *intentional* lack of clarity. This resultant ambiguity, it is argued, is too overdetermined for any single identity or construal: the servant of YHWH appears as a prophetic figure (44:1-5; 49:1-4) and a royal figure (42:1-4) as well as a priestly figure (53:4-12). The servant of YHWH plays a soteriological role as well as a judicial and geopolitical one. YHWH calls the servant from birth and assures him of help to fulfill his mission (44:1-5; 49:1-3). YHWH empowers the servant with the spirit, even though God's envoy feels that his labor is in vain (49:4). And although he does not cry or lift up his voice, or make it heard in the streets (42:1-2), the servant still succeeds in mediating justice, the word, redemption, and forgiveness. Accordingly, the robust image of servant engages both the individual and the community on multiple levels.

The *suffering* of the servant of YHWH is as important as the figure's identity and role (52:13–53:12). This heroic figure is the paradigmatic survivor. No wonder subsequent generations (quite possibly the disciples of the prophet) honored and found enormous meaning in the suffering and legacy of this servant.[42] They would remember not only the teachings but also the witness of innocent suffering, perhaps even vicarious suffering:

> Surely he has borne our infirmities
>   and carried our diseases;
> yet we accounted him stricken,
>   struck down by God, and afflicted.
> But he was wounded for our transgressions,
>   crushed for our iniquities;
> upon him was the punishment that made us whole,
>   and by his bruises we are healed. (53:4-5)

They would then acknowledge that despite the servant's apparent defeat, this servant's pain and humiliation were not in vain. No matter how appalling and startling the affliction of this servant appeared (52:14-15; 53:3), the disciples would firmly learn that their hero's sacrifice was not futile and his vision not extinguished. The descendants likewise would discover that the hardship their righteous ancestors endured was not to be regarded as meaningless. Rather, such sacrifice would inspire ensuing generations and plant within them seeds of hope.

We might expect raw political power, impressive structures, and intimidating military machines to foster hope and security, but Second Isaiah uses language of defeat and death: "He was cut off from the land of the living" (53:8; cf. 38:11; Jer 11:19). It was not only the servant's disciples but also the surrounding people and later descendants who mourned over the humiliation and suffering forced upon this servant. The issue of theodicy lingers, as if in unending waves.[43] But one thing remains certain, at least to later generations: the vision voiced and exemplified by this servant and the divine promise for upcoming generations were not in vain. They spurred new meanings and interpretations of suffering; they demonstrated in the *bios* of this heroic figure that suffering is not a consequence of wrongdoing but a sign of righteousness. Moreover, they encouraged everyone to participate in the mission to serve as a "light of nations" and a "covenant of people." The present form of this text starts in the future tense (Isa 52:13-15), proceeds into the past tense (53:1-10aα), and ends with the future tense (53:10aβ-12). It is no coincidence that the promise was already foretold at the outset:

> See, my servant shall prosper;
>   he shall be exalted and lifted up,
>   and shall be very high. (52:13)

Toward the conclusion, God's exiled people learn that they, as offspring of the seemingly defeated servant, are a testimony of the promise and vision:

> When you make his life an offering for sin,
>   he shall see his offspring, and shall prolong his days;
> through him the will of the LORD shall prosper.
>   Out of his anguish he shall see light;
> he shall find satisfaction through his knowledge.
>   The righteous one, my servant, shall make many righteous,
>   and he shall bear their iniquities. (53:10-11)

Finally, threatened by diminishing numbers, the interpretive community looks to Daughter Zion and finds hope in the promise of progeny and in progeny's glorious future with God. Zion, personified as a barren woman, cries out over the loss of her children and the crisis of her progeny. Zion now hears the divine assurance of hope for her children, the next generations:

> Enlarge the site of your tent,
>> and let the curtains of your habitations be stretched out;
> do not hold back; lengthen your cords
>> and strengthen your stakes.
> For you will spread out to the right and to the left,
>> and your descendants will possess the nations
>> and will settle the desolate towns. (54:2-3; cf. 66:8)[44]

Daughter Zion is reminded of the promise so that Zion can continue Sarah's legacy of hope for progeny. Daughter Zion reconnects with the matriarchs of the Torah so she can cherish and rekindle the divine promise for a great nation and kingdom:

> Look to Abraham your father
>> and to Sarah who bore you;
> for he was but one when I called him,
>> but I blessed him and made him many. (51:2; cf. Gen 12:1-3)

The interpretive community finds hope in this promise of progeny. People often say that children are the future of our world. And indeed the defeated and devastated Judean community could see a spark of hope in the prophetic announcement that "In the LORD all the offspring of Israel / shall triumph and glory" (Isa 45:25). Like a pregnant woman who envisions a future for the child in her womb, Zion imagines the survival and prosperity of her offspring: they will be numerous "like the sand" and overpopulated "like its grains" (48:18-19).

> The children born in the time of your bereavement
>> will yet say in your hearing:
> "The place is too crowded for me;
>> make room for me to settle." (49:20)

Moreover, Zion's descendants will return home triumphantly:

> Thus says the Lord GOD:
> I will soon lift up my hand to the nations,
>> and raise my signal to the peoples;
> and they shall bring your sons in their bosom,
>> and your daughters shall be carried on their shoulders.

> Kings shall be your foster fathers,
>> and their queens your nursing mothers. (49:22-23; cf. 60:4, 9)

This glorious homecoming involves the promise of transformation as well. Just as YHWH endows the righteous leader with the "spirit" (11:2; 42:1; 61:1; cf. 32:15), so now all the descendants of Zion will receive the spirit:

> For I will pour water on the thirsty land,
>> and streams on the dry ground;
> I will pour my spirit upon your descendants,
>> and my blessing on your offspring. (44:3; cf. 59:21; 61:9; 65:9, 23; Jer 31:33-34)

Thus, the interpretive community, Zion's offspring, discovers joy and hope in the promise of progeny. The reenactment of the stories of the matriarchs and patriarchs validates the survival of the traumatized community.

Messages of Hope amid Postexilic Struggles

Imagination fuels hope. Without it injustice and despair often prevail. Walter Brueggemann notes that by the power of imagination prophet-poets "not only *discerned* the new actions of God that others did not discern, but they *wrought* the new actions of God."[45] Isaiah's exquisite language of homecoming is a striking example of the power of poetic imagination:

> And the LORD will utterly destroy
>> the tongue of the sea of Egypt;
> and will wave his hand over the River
>> with his scorching wind;
> and will split it into seven channels,
>> and make a way to cross on foot;
> so there shall be a highway from Assyria
>> for the remnant that is left of his people,
> as there was for Israel
>> when they came up from the land of Egypt. (11:15-16)

> For you shall go out in joy,
>> and be led back in peace;
> the mountains and the hills before you
>> shall burst into song,
>> and all the trees of the field shall clap their hands.

> Instead of the thorn shall come up the cypress;
>> instead of the brier shall come up the myrtle;
> and it shall be to the LORD for a memorial,
>> for an everlasting sign that shall not be cut off. (55:12-13)

Such lyrical utterances both envision new possibilities and set them in motion. The power of prophetic imagination inaugurates the grand return of Judean refugees to their homeland.

Although such speech is capable of spurring hope in action, it can also breed resentment and cynicism, especially when social realities do not measure up. "Hope deferred makes the heart sick" (Prov 13:12). And, in fact, rebuilding would be long and arduous; it would demand tenacity and commitment, labor and sacrifice. History is full of stories that illustrate how difficult it is to rebuild people's lives and navigate the processes of recovery. The returnees within the Yehud would thus need a good measure of encouragement. The poetic word that sustained them in exile and propelled them to return would now need to prod them to confront the challenges before them: "Build up, build up, prepare the way, / remove every obstruction from my people's way" (57:14). And not only are the returnees to face these challenges; they are to get it right: "Thus says the LORD: / Maintain justice, and do what is right" (56:1). The ensuing generation is to practice hospitality and justice (56:1-8; 59:1-21), resist evil detractors (57:1-13), and attend to the needs of the hungry and homeless, the afflicted and dispossessed (58:1-14; 61:1-11). At the same time, the prophet-poet does not fail to remind YHWH of the divine promise to restore Zion:

> For Zion's sake I will not keep silent,
>> and for Jerusalem's sake I will not rest,
> until her vindication shines out like the dawn,
>> and her salvation like a burning torch.
> The nations shall see your vindication,
>> and all the kings your glory;
> and you shall be called by a new name
>> that the mouth of the LORD will give.
> You shall be a crown of beauty in the hand of the LORD,
>> and a royal diadem in the hand of your God. (62:1-3)

The people of God no doubt had more than their quota of suffering—in Jerusalem, Babylon, and now back in Jerusalem (whether in the Persian or Hellenistic period). They had lived through the strain of plucking up and pulling down. Now it was time to plant and build (to use Jeremiah's motto); but restoration would turn out far more grueling than some ever imagined.

Tension and Turmoil in Transitions

In Second Isaiah, readers can detect formal and thematic transitions. Regarding form, on the one hand, a unique phrase—"'There is no peace,' says YHWH, 'for the wicked'"—occurs in two places, in 48:22 and 57:21. Akin to doxological refrains found in the Psalms (Pss 41:13 [MT 41:14]; 72:19; 89:52 [MT 89:53]; 106:48; 150), this phrase functions as a marker that subdivides Isaiah 40–66 into three sections: chapters 40–48, 49–57, and 58 66.[46] (Interestingly, each section respectively has nine chapters, though these chapter divisions derive from the rabbinic era.) It may have functioned for bookkeeping purposes in the bulky scrolls. On the other hand, as noted above, commentators have long pointed out another formal transition—from the singular to the plural form of the servant(s) of YHWH. In chapters 40–53 the term is consistently in the singular form, whereas in chapters 54–66 the term is attested in the plural. It should be noted that both formal indices bring to light the inadequacy of the hard and fast divisions between First Isaiah (chs. 1–39), Second Isaiah (chs. 40–55), and what is sometimes called Third Isaiah (chs. 56–66). Joseph Blenkinsopp astutely summarizes the current scholarship on Isaiah 40–66 as follows: "In subject matter, tone, and emphasis, chs. 56–66 are distinct enough to warrant separate treatment, yet they belong on the same textual and exegetical continuum as chs. 40–55."[47]

At the same time, there are a number of thematic shifts, as Bernhard W. Duhm astutely delineated at the end of the nineteenth century, that support the conventional categories, even when approaching the book synchronically. Readers discover a transition in mood in chapters 40–66 from messages of divine consolation to messages of divine accusation[48]—that is, from the divine announcement to pardon the sins of the people to the divine admonition for the people to turn away from their sins. This transition apparently grows out of different implied settings: from exilic devastation to postexilic return and rebuilding. In the early chapters of Second Isaiah, readers find situations of immense suffering and humiliation among the exiles in the texts of consolation vis-à-vis complaints and laments. Now they detect tension and strife in the course of postexilic rebuilding. And so beyond comfort (in chs. 40–55) comes chastisement for covenant infractions that have resurfaced among those engaged in the work of rebuilding (in chs. 56–66):

> Shout out, do not hold back!
> Lift up your voice like a trumpet!
> Announce to my people their rebellion,
> to the house of Jacob their sins. (58:1)

YHWH's people are taken to task for their sins. What are their transgressions? Second Isaiah sharply points to the community's failure to bar oppression and injustice from its gates.

The redeployment of key terms underscores these thematic shifts. For instance, the word *justice* is often associated with divine indictment in First Isaiah, with salvation in chapters 40–55, and with divine indictment (for the dearth of justice) in the latter chapters of the book. Other lexical indices used to console dispirited exiles in chapters 40–55, such as *iniquities, clothing, highways,* and *roads,* now bring to light resurgent corruption, disregard of the poor, and works of injustice:

> No one brings suit justly,
>   no one goes to law honestly;
> they rely on empty pleas, they speak lies,
>   conceiving mischief and begetting iniquity. . . .
> Their webs cannot serve as clothing;
>   they cannot cover themselves with what they make.
> Their works are works of iniquity,
>   and deeds of violence are in their hands.
> Their feet run to evil,
>   and they rush to shed innocent blood;
> their thoughts are thoughts of iniquity,
>   desolation and destruction are in their highways.
> The way of peace they do not know,
>   and there is no justice in their paths.
> Their roads they have made crooked;
>   no one who walks in them knows peace.
>   (59:4-8; cf. 40:3; 41:29; 42:16; 49:11; 50:9; 51:6, 8; 52:1)[49]

Altogether, the text claims that covenant infractions and strife among the various parties have not gone away. The harsh realities of disappointment and failure have cast a dark shadow over previous visions of homecoming and new beginnings.

Conflicts of one sort or another permeate the turbulent transitional eras. Earlier the readers learned of the hostility between Israel and the imperial superpowers, such as Assyria, Egypt, and Babylon. In a subsequent era they learn of another tension, no longer in the arena of international politics but within the very community of Israel: between the righteous and the wicked.[50] Strictly speaking, this tension is not entirely new: from the outset of Isaiah, corrupt rulers are charged with oppressing the suffering poor.[51] Even in exile the prophet alludes to the wicked versus the righteous:

> Let the wicked forsake their way,
>   and the unrighteous their thoughts;

> let them return to the LORD, that he may have mercy on them,
> and to our God, for he will abundantly pardon. (55:7)[52]

But now the problem is far more endemic. The wicked are everywhere (57:20, 21; 58:4), as are the righteous, though fewer in number (57:1-2). Apparently the process of democratization is at work here as well!

Second Isaiah is clearly a text of hope. But hope not only comforts and consoles the afflicted; it also afflicts the comfortable. The prophetic texts make the case that God will not tolerate economic injustice, exclusion, and oppression. To forge an identity as the covenant people of God, the democratized postexilic community must confront the harsh realities of ongoing corruption within its own borders. Prophetic visions of renewal in diaspora expose such wrongdoing and at the same time challenge the community, amid hardships and turmoil, to "keep justice and do righteousness" (56:1, authors' translation).

Radical Reversals

Is the suffering of others also our own? In thinking that it might in fact be, societies expand the circle of the we.[53]

For hope to be more than a word, it must find concrete expression in access, acceptance, economic justice, and hospitality. Second Isaiah's language of hope includes visions of a glorious future as well as a transformation of present conditions. For both of these, the prophet-poet deploys what Michael Fishbane calls "lay exegesis" and what Mark G. Brett describes as a "subversive" resistance literature to call for a reconception of community life.[54] When community strife increases, Second Isaiah does not demand a mere easing of the tensions but rather a radical inversion of categories. The first involves the status of *insiders and outsiders*. And here the prophet addresses *socioethnic tensions*. Second Isaiah exposes corrupt insiders while offering righteous outsiders the assurance of divine acceptance. The outsiders here are foreigners and eunuchs who are excluded from the community (56:3; cf. Deut 23:1-8; Neh 13:1-3).[55] The insiders are the sentinels and shepherds, figuratively alluding to the prophets and rulers, respectively (56:10-11). The prophet dares to make the case that the most profound threat to the community's quality of life lies with insiders who distort justice and compromise covenant observance, not with outsiders who live in the hinterlands. Thus, outsiders are not to be disparaged and excluded but welcomed and incorporated into the life of the community. No doubt, their elevation to the status of "a monument and a name" (*yād wašēm*, 56:5),[56] "as priests and as Levites" (66:21), would have scandalized some, as would their opportunity to observe the Sabbath and hold fast to the covenant. For outsiders to enjoy the blessings of familial honor ("I will give them an everlasting name," 56:5) and priestly honor ("Their burnt offerings and their sacrifices / will be accepted on my altar," 56:7) was an audacious claim. Yet Second Isaiah's configurations of hope shatter conventional boundaries and envision the possibility of honor and blessings for those previously excluded. The prophet's vision of inclusive hope involves a far-reaching shift in perspective, embracing options perhaps otherwise unthinkable.

No doubt other texts speak on behalf of the disenfranchised. The Deuteronomic law code, for instance, demands communal protection for aliens, orphans, and widows (Deut 14:29; 24:14; 26:12; see also Jer 7:5-7).[57] It even draws the conclusion that "bad insiders"—more than outsiders who reside beyond the borders—pose the most serious threat to the social order and community survival.[58] Yet, here in Second Isaiah, the disregarded and abandoned are not only protected; they are also given a chance, indeed, a divine grant.[59]

Second Isaiah's radical hope not only takes into account the status of insiders and outsiders; it also inverts *top and bottom* categories. This top-bottom dichotomy speaks to *religiopolitical tensions* (Isa 57:1-21). The prophet depicts those who practice the idolatrous sacrifices of the powerful imperial religions as arrogant and self-inflated: "Upon a high and lofty mountain / you have set your bed, / and there you went up to offer sacrifice" (57:7). In contrast, the devout are "contrite and humble in spirit" (57:15), and will indeed be revived and protected. Here chapter 57 paints a picture of these contrasts through chiasm:

57:1-2	The righteous and pious seem vanished.
57:3-13a	Children of sorcery and idolatry will not be saved.
57:13b-19	Children lowly in spirit will be revived and healed.
57:20-21	The wicked will have no rest.

The offspring of sorcery and religious adultery (57:3), as well as the children of iniquity and treachery (57:4), will ultimately be brought low without any sure foundation: "The wind will carry them off, / a breath will take them away" (57:13a; cf. Ps 1:4). Only those who take "refuge in me"—those contrite and lowly—declares YHWH, shall be taken up to possess "my holy mountain" (Isa 57:13b). Hope has to involve humility—not in succumbing to coercion but in resolutely seeking to maintain justice and righteousness.

Second Isaiah's radical reconceptualization not only inverts insider-outsider and top-bottom categories; it also confronts the disparity between the *rich* and the *poor*—or more specifically, with those who are hungry and those who presumably have enough. This third dichotomy thus addresses *economic tensions*, exemplified in the ritual of fasting (58:1–59:21).[60] The prophet contends that the "righteous" practice Israel's rituals but still miss the mark. They starve their bodies in fasting (58:3) but do not comprehend the need "to share [their] bread with the hungry" (58:7). They put on sackcloth and ashes (58:5) but do not understand the importance of clothing the "naked" (58:7). Indeed, they show little solidarity with their kin who are hungry and in dire need.[61] Hence, the prophetic voice registers an inventory of complaints, including "rebellion" (58:1), "evil" (58:9), "wickedness" (59:3), "lies" (59:4), "violence" (59:6), "iniquity" (59:7), and "oppression and revolt" (59:13). God does not respond favorably to those who observe festival rituals for self-interest, to exploit their laborers and "to fight and to strike" (58:4). Once again the divine pathos resounds forcefully with the call for genuine solidarity with the poor and needy.[62] Justice and righteousness must prevail so that the hungry are fed and the thirsty are given water. Then they too will have hope:

> Is not this the fast that I choose:
>> to loose the bonds of injustice,
>> to undo the thongs of the yoke,
> to let the oppressed go free,
>> and to break every yoke?
> Is it not to share your bread with the hungry,
>> and bring the homeless poor into your house;
> when you see the naked, to cover them,
>> and not to hide yourself from your own kin? (58:6-7)

Second Isaiah's radical reversals do not dispose of the old covenant traditions. On the contrary, they seek to foster ancient equalitarian arrangements. The prophet's constructions of hope are nothing more than a demand for inclusion, humility, and generosity. The interpretive community might recognize this vision in chapter 55. Located immediately after the divine assurance to abundantly provide for barren and abandoned Zion (54:1-17), as if she too were a lowly outsider, the divine invitation is offered to "*everyone* who thirsts" without money (55:1; emphasis added). Those who hear the initial call *hôy* (55:1) might anticipate judgment like that found in the woe-oracles in chapter 5 and chapters 28–33. But here the call *hôy* is no indictment; it is instead an invitation to all—yes, including outsiders, lowly and poor—to feast on the riches of God's banquet: a banquet offered as an "everlasting covenant" (55:3), "everlasting sign" (55:13), and "everlasting name" (56:5; cf. 60:15, 19).

Hope for a Glorious Future

Without the prospect of a future, struggling communities within the Yehud and in diaspora could barely go on. Without the prospect of a future, despair would trump hope. Admittedly for some, prophetic hope might seem too distant to grasp, too elusive to fathom. It might even trigger resentment and cynicism in light of trying circumstances. Yet hope for a future is essential for survival, individually and communally. No wonder Isaiah 60–66 is replete with language of hope—lyrical hope that envisions a glorious homecoming and reunion, the restoration of justice and honor, and a long-awaited reconciliation with God. It is noteworthy that these splendid visions of newness do not stand on their own; they are interspersed with words of judgment and admonition. As is the case for the prophetic corpus as a whole, promissory language is rarely, if ever, divorced from the painful realities of community life. Grand visions of a new era are built on the "ancient ruins" (61:4).

Second Isaiah's vision of a glorious future involves the gathering of the dispersed to Jerusalem. We have already heard the prophet herald the good news of homecoming (chs. 40–55). Now this message is articulated in even more grandiose, almost eschatological terms (not unlike the New Jerusalem and Temple in Ezekiel).[63] The prophet envisions those scattered to the far ends of the earth finally coming *home* to family, kin, and peace. The refugees had experienced the pain and paradoxical value of the wilderness. They had learned the importance of remembering their ancestral legacy. They had gained strength and inspiration from their heroes and heroines. And they had survived the empire's fierce military and socioeconomic assault. Now, after years in the hinterlands, their deepest yearning is fulfilled: they can come home to return to their roots and reunite with family and kinfolk.

> Lift up your eyes and look around;
>> they all gather together, they come to you;
> your sons shall come from far away,
>> and your daughters shall be carried on their nurses' arms. (Isa 60:4)

Second Isaiah portrays this homecoming as a triumphant entry: the refugees return not in sorrow or regret but in festive procession (cf. 40:1-5). Dwarfing even the magnificent exodus of old, the prophet performs the event as a royal pageant in which they arrive as princes and princesses marching to Zion. In a stunning inversion, the very kings and queens of the menacing nations now serve their former subjects, constructing their walls, gates, and temple:

> Foreigners shall build up your walls,
>> and their kings shall minister to you. . . .
> Your gates shall always be open;
>> day and night they shall not be shut,
> so that nations shall bring you their wealth,
>> with their kings led in procession. (60:10, 11; cf. 60:18, 21; 62:6)

Such adulation is already anticipated in chapters 49 and 60:

> Kings shall see and stand up,
>> princes, and they shall prostrate themselves,
> because of the LORD, who is faithful,
>> the Holy One of Israel, who has chosen you. . . .
> A multitude of camels shall cover you,
>> the young camels of Midian and Ephah;
>> all those from Sheba shall come.
> They shall bring gold and frankincense,
>> and shall proclaim the praise of the LORD. (49:7; 60:6; cf. 60:16; Exod 19:6)

How wonderful to imagine a safe and secure home for all God's children to dwell in! How much more when the royal principalities bring their cedars, riches, and forces to build the city of YHWH (cf. Exod 12:35-36)!

In this glorious new world in which "nations . . . come to your light, / and kings to the brightness of your dawn" (Isa 60:3), Zion's *honor* is fully restored. There could be no grand homecoming, no joyous repatriation of diaspora Jews, without the restoration of honor. In the ancient world, honor (versus shame) was one of life's most cherished values, treasured far beyond riches or success.[64] To experience military defeat, forced displacement, and captivity, as Judah did, was to suffer abject shame. Zion's (as well as YHWH's!) honor was severely damaged. That the humiliation took place in public before the nations only exacerbated the disgrace. To restore community (and divine) honor, the prophet-poet will not keep silent until Jerusalem's vindication "shines out like the dawn, / and her salvation like a burning torch" (62:1). Her vindication demands reprisals: divine retribution for crimes against God's people. The brutal nations that abused her must receive their due (63:1-6). In addition, her vindication requires the restoration of moral and social symmetry, the reversal of fortunes:

> The descendants of those who oppressed you
>> shall come bending low to you,
> and all who despised you

89

> shall bow down at your feet;
> they shall call you the City of the LORD,
> the Zion of the Holy One of Israel. (60:14)

Retribution and reversals, however, are only two facets of Zion's restored honor. YHWH also lavishes upon Zion great affection and unparalleled abundance—all in the presence of her oppressors. The nations witness (and participate in) the magnificent homecoming of Jerusalem's children; they recognize Zion's joy and favored status (60:1-22). They come to see her dignity repaired:

> The nations shall see your vindication,
> and all the kings your glory;
> and you shall be called by a new name
> that the mouth of the LORD will give. (62:2)

No longer is Zion known by the old humiliating terms "Forsaken" and "Desolate"; now she is called "My Delight Is in Her":

> For the LORD delights in you,
> and your land shall be married.
> For as a young man marries a young woman,
> so shall your builder marry you,
> and as the bridegroom rejoices over the bride,
> so shall your God rejoice over you. (62:4-5)

No longer is Zion subject to violence or ruin (60:18; 62:12); now her attendants are peace and righteousness. Although once judged for her wrongdoing, now she is robed in righteousness. Indeed, the prophet imagines all God's people as "righteous" (60:21): "They will be called oaks of righteousness" (61:3); Zion's "righteousness" will "spring up before all the nations" (61:11). Though once spurned and abused, now Zion is the glad recipient of divine favor and compassion (60:10; 61:7). Instead of sorrow and grief (60:1, 19-20; 61:3), she "greatly rejoice[s] in the LORD" (61:10). Instead of disgrace, Zion is clothed in praise and basks in the light of God's glory. It is not incidental that the word *glory* (or *honor*) occurs fairly often in chapters 60–62 (60:1, 2, 13; 61:6; 62:2; see also 60:19; 61:3). The prophet assures God's captive people that they will no longer suffer shame and that their honor will be fully restored (62:4-5; see also 50:7; 54:4). This promise is sealed in love and the certainty of God's word: "I am the LORD; / in its time I will accomplish it quickly" (60:22).

Second Isaiah's glorious vision of the future involves not only Zion's return to land and kin but also her return to God. Homecoming first and foremost involves reunion with YHWH. To convey the extraordinary character of this reunion, the prophet deploys a rich array of metaphors: the dawning of God's light upon Jerusalem (60:1, 19-20); the return of an abandoned wife (62:4-5); a reception of a new name given by YHWH (i.e., re-creation; 62:2); a joyous wedding celebration (61:10); the return of prodigal children to beloved parents (63:16; see also 66:7-9). All convey the depth of divine love and all make it clear that the Judean refugees are indeed God's beloved. Such claims are of course not new. Earlier the prophet spoke of the intimate nature of God's love for Israel:

> Do not fear, for I have redeemed you;
>> I have called you by name, you are mine. . . .
> Because you are precious in my sight,
>> and honored, and I love you,
> I give people in return for you,
>> nations in exchange for your life. . . .
> Do not fear, for I am with you. (43:1, 4, 5)

Now the prophet fills out the details, and God's people respond with gratitude: they celebrate God's intimate love.

> I will greatly rejoice in the LORD,
>> my whole being shall exult in my God;
> for he has clothed me with the garments of salvation,
>> he has covered me with the robe of righteousness,
> as a bridegroom decks himself with a garland,
>> and as a bride adorns herself with her jewels. (61:10; cf. 59:17; 61:3; 63:3)

They tell of God's great acts of love:

> I will recount the gracious deeds of the LORD,
>> the praiseworthy acts of the LORD,
> because of all that the LORD has done for us,
>> and the great favor to the house of Israel
> that he has shown them according to his mercy,
>> according to the abundance of his steadfast love. (63:7)

Mingled with this gratitude, however, are sure indications of continued strife. God's children beg for divine compassion:

> Look down from heaven and see,
>> from your holy and glorious habitation.

> Where are your zeal and your might?
> The yearning of your heart and your compassion?
> They are withheld from me. (63:15; see also 63:16-19)

They implore God to intervene as in days of old (64:1-5). They mourn over their present hardships (63:17-19; 64:9-11; 65:11-12); all the while they are aware of their own failings (63:7-14; 64:4-6; 65:1-7). Not unlike the sufferer Job, they confront YHWH: "After all this, will you restrain yourself, O LORD? / Will you keep silent, and punish us so severely?" (64:12).

The divine reply is mixed. In the first place, YHWH has never been aloof and inaccessible. YHWH has been as inclined to Israel as Isaiah was to the divine call. Indeed, YHWH has always longed to act on behalf of Israel: " 'Here I am, here I am,' . . . / I held out my hands all day long" (65:1-2). But God's people do not respond in kind. They rebel and continue to engage in sinful practices; thus they must brace themselves for further judgment (65:1-12). But not all are guilty. As suggested earlier in the book, the prophet identifies both the righteous and the unjust within Israel. Whereas apostates are threatened with judgment, YHWH promises to save the righteous remnant:

> Therefore thus says the Lord GOD:
> My *servants* shall eat,
>   but *you* shall be hungry;
> my *servants* shall drink,
>   but *you* shall be thirsty;
> my *servants* shall rejoice,
>   but *you* shall be put to shame;
> my *servants* shall sing for gladness of heart,
>   but *you* shall cry out for pain of heart,
>   and shall wail for anguish of spirit. (65:13-14; emphasis added)

> For my servants' sake I will not destroy them all. (65:8 authors' translation)

YHWH will expose the disloyal (66:3-6) and comfort those who truly hope in God's saving acts. In reply to their cries, YHWH is adamant: "As a mother comforts her child, / so I will comfort you; / you shall be comforted in Jerusalem" (66:13).

The Israel that emerges in the final chapters of Isaiah is clearly riddled with conflict. It continues to struggle with its core values and allegiances. Some within the community rebel against YHWH—as evident in their participation in pagan rituals (65:3-5; cf. Deut 14:8; 18:11-12)—while others seek to fulfill their mission as God's servants. Moreover, the community still lives in liminal space betwixt and between worlds: they are burdened by the harsh circumstances in the return while they await the fulfillment of God's promises for a future full of hope. In this long and arduous in-between period, they must remain faithful to YHWH's covenant, confident that the God "who has promised is faithful" (Heb 10:23). They may recall that the Torah does not conclude with the fulfillment of the promise of the land but with open-ended anticipation grounded in hope. Like their ancestors who lived as aliens within the empire, they too are few in number and poor in stature; yet they hope to become "a great nation, mighty and populous" (Deut 26:5). Although the scroll concludes rather anticlimactically, acknowledging profound tensions (Isa 66:24), it still follows the resounding visions of a new era and a grand homecoming, even a home away from home:

> For I am about to create new heavens and a new earth;
> the former things shall not be remembered or come to mind.
> But be glad and rejoice forever
>   in what I am creating;
> for I am about to create Jerusalem as a joy,
>   and its people as a delight. . . .
> They shall build houses and inhabit them;
>   they shall plant vineyards and eat their fruit. . . .
> Before they call I will answer,
>   while they are yet speaking I will hear.
> The wolf and the lamb shall feed together,
>   the lion shall eat straw like the ox;
>   but the serpent—its food shall be dust!
> They shall not hurt or destroy
>   on all my holy mountain,
>   says the LORD. (65:17-25)

Conclusion

Just as pain and warning are juxtaposed with hope and promise in First Isaiah, so resounding voices of consolation and renewal are intertwined with the haunting depictions of hardship and disappointment in Second Isaiah. The interpretive community well understands exilic humiliation and postexilic strife. The wreckage of war, exile, and colonization—whether because of firsthand or historical trauma—left an indelible mark on social and symbolic structures. Jewish communities within the Yehud as well as those in diaspora would continue their struggle for survival.

Likewise, the community that emerges in the book of Isaiah finds itself banished to a dangerous, faraway country. Though crushed and despondent there, it hears the prophetic voice of comfort. In exile, it is invited to journey home and imagine a bright future. It hopes for a reversal of fortune, a time and place when God provides water for the thirsty, food for the hungry, freedom for the oppressed, joy for the brokenhearted, and hope for the hopeless. In the interim, it recalls the mighty acts of God through the legacy of the devout servant of YHWH, just as the descendants of Daughter Zion testify to the wondrous fulfillment of YHWH's divine promises. Eventually, this entire community—the offspring of the servant and the descendants of Zion—would become instruments of hope, YHWH's heroes and heroines of justice and righteousness.

Notwithstanding the force of this striking vision, pressing social realities of dissension and distrust linger in the postexilic diaspora provinces. It would take great effort to rebuild unity and gather fruit despite the perseverance and defiant sacrifices of their exilic heroes and heroines. Their seeds of hope would take time to flourish. Their vision of inclusion, hospitality, justice, and compassion would require radical reform. To elevate communal solidarity and mutual honor over older, well-established forms of power would no doubt confound and disturb, as would embracing Torah obligations over syncretistic practices. The text's realism thus precludes a retreat to a fanciful utopian world; the harsh realities of displacement and captivity are just too massive.

Nonetheless, the interpretive community would not relinquish hope, because they had buoyant faith in a God who sculpts new beginnings out of the wreckage of fallen worlds:

> Sing, O barren one who did not bear;
>> burst into song and shout,
>> you who have not been in labor!
> For the children of the desolate woman will be more
>> than the children of her that is married, says the LORD. (54:1)

PART TWO

THE BOOK OF JEREMIAH

CHAPTER FOUR

JEREMIAH AS A MESSENGER OF HOPE IN CRISIS

Jeremiah is an artifact of terror. . . .
Jeremiah is an artifact of hope.

N early forty years ago, William L. Holladay, one of the leading historical critical scholars of our time, made an intriguing case for reading Jeremiah as a
"spokesman out of time." While insisting that the prophet was firmly grounded
in "a very particular and unique historical situation,"[1] Holladay dared to assert that
Jeremiah "speaks to us in [a] *more* special and direct way *than* [he did] *to his own time.*"[2]
Following Holladay's lead, we would suggest that this strange sense of immediacy is even
more palpable today. And it is not difficult to garner support for such a contention.

Jeremiah's[3] coarse language of violence and alarm together with penetrating images
of cultural ruin, emotional malaise, and symbolic "disease" resonate in a world where
"optimism has given way to a sense of ambiguity."[4] Jeremiah's horrifying accounts of
death and destruction—often in the form of siege, military occupation, and forced
relocation—are curiously not unlike those that cover the front page of the *New York
Times.*[5] The prophetic testimony to the breakdown of meaning and civility as well as
to the crumbling of trusted social systems and venerable institutions all sound remarkably familiar. Even the eerie vision of the order of creation returning to primeval chaos
(4:23-28) is no longer merely the stuff of science fiction, especially in view of the
torrent of early-twenty-first-century ills:

- Cities in crisis
- Schools in disarray
- A burgeoning national debt that threatens future generations and whittles away
  at already dwindling funds for basic human services
- Preemptive military doctrines that destabilize large regions and erode interna-
  tional morale and morality
- New technologies that result in alienation and dehumanization
- Consumerist values that anesthetize us to our true selves
- Immigration legislation rooted in xenophobia and garbed in evangelical piety

- Global economic policies that breed resentment, rage, and abject despair
- Rapid depletion of nonreplaceable natural (and cultural) resources
- Limited access to basic health care, adequate food, and safe water among the world's most vulnerable communities
- Mounting indifference to savage acts of violence, including torture and the systematic killing of civilians
- Children exploited as sexual commodities

Notwithstanding the ever-increasing threat of nuclear, biological, and chemical terrorism, such a list has cumulative force. No wonder the prophet's haunting scenarios and poignant utterances of anger and despair ring true to many today!

Taken in totality, the book of Jeremiah is a literary artifact of terror, a disturbing cultural expression of lament and chaos. Danger, disjunction, and distress bubble beneath the surface of virtually every text. Sometimes in denial, sometimes in despair, and sometimes in defiance, the implied readers of this literature find themselves located at the edge of time. As such, Jeremiah is "eschatological" in that it addresses dispossessed people who have suffered unmanageable loss and are eking out life on the margins of the empire. Put differently, the book is *war literature*: it speaks of annihilated worlds, shattered communities, and the collapse of cherished institutions and understandings of life, before viable alternatives emerge to fill the chasm. This ethos of liminality is apparent not only in the barrage of devastating events and in the anguish of the major characters of the book—Judah, Jeremiah, and YHWH—but also in the jumbled and erratic poetry itself. There we encounter language that throbs with pain, staggers in confusion, and rages in disappointment. Attempts to order the chaos and tone down the incendiary texture—often through Deuteronomistic prose discourses—do little to mute the text's raw emotion.[6]

The book of Jeremiah not only gives speech to the disaster; it also functions as a complex theological response. The text's judgment-salvation schema[7] *and* its embedded cacophony of voices and countervoices create a thick meaning-making map, a *tapestry of hope*, designed to help displaced people survive a world in which irrationality, violence, and loss are more tangible than moral coherence and meaning. In large measure, Jeremiah attempts to find meaning in events that defy ordinary categories, events that are beyond communal recognition.[8]

Jeremianic Hope Unfolds along Canonical Lines and with Narrative Force

The interpretive community (MT)[9] presents Jeremiah as a messenger of hope and his book as a meaning-making map. It does so by organizing the polyvalent tradition as a two-part prophetic drama with Jeremiah (and of course YHWH) as the major player(s): the first act performs the collapse of Judah's once stable and reliable world (Jer 1–25); the second articulates a survival script in the face of social and symbolic mayhem (Jer 26–52). In Act 1, Jeremiah takes dead aim at the nation's sturdy pillars of faith and venerated institutions: the temple and its systems of worship (7:1-15), covenant arrangements (11:1-17), and insider status of privilege (18:1-12), as well as ancestral land claims and the Davidic dynasty as traditionally understood (21:1-10). YHWH's iconoclastic spokesperson deconstructs these defining beliefs and institutions, which long served as a bulwark against dangers from inside and outside the borders. With uncompromising force, Jeremiah insists that the securities of the old world will not save Judah from loss and dislocation.

Once these hopes are dashed, Act 2 of the prophetic drama seizes almost every opportunity to demonstrate that the implied readers, the Jewish refugees in Babylon, will survive the dismantling of their once stable culture. In other words, the end of the old world is not the end of the line for Judah! Clearly the horrors of war still loom large, as do the emotional scars and symbolic debris, but amid the devastation Jeremiah emerges as a wounded harbinger of hope announcing the advent of God's program of "building and planting." The prophet first takes on powerful representatives of the royal-temple establishment who are absolutely sure that the embattled systems will remain intact despite Babylon's onslaught. Jeremiah rejects their optimism, arguing that authentic hope must bear the scars of disaster and embrace the harsh realities of the shattered world (Jer 27–29). Adamant that returning to the past is no longer possible, Jeremiah outlines the contours of God's fresh initiative: the Judean refugees will survive the ravages of war and the travail of a shattered world, albeit without many of the old support systems. The exiles will be bound by the memory of suffering and the experience of dislocation, although ever mindful of God's gracious acts of salvation (Jer 30–33).

No sooner does Jeremiah complete this resilient script than the prophet and his countrymen plunge into the abyss. Landowners renege on their covenantal obligation to the poor (Jer 34), Jehoiakim shows "cutting" disdain for the prophetic scroll (Jer 36), and the nation violently refuses to "listen to" YHWH, all of which set in motion a series of shocking events (Jer 37–44). Yet even during this dark hour, when Jerusalem falls and Judah plunges into civil war, when coups, massacres, and duplicity saturate the landscape and Jeremiah is led off to Egypt, modest signs of hope are visible. Perhaps the most significant of these is Jeremiah's own survival: despite torture and imprisonment, his life is spared and the voice of God is not silenced. Faithful supporters come to his aid at the royal palace (36:11-19, 26) and at the cistern of Malchiah (38:7-13), as well as during the siege of Jerusalem (39:11-18; 40:1-6).

Thanks to the courage of these faithful few, Jeremiah, who comes to symbolize the war-torn people of God, endures personal assaults and national devastation. And eventually the prophet heralds the downfall of Babylon and the liberation of the beleaguered exiles (Jer 50–51). The performance concludes with an intentionally ambiguous vignette in which Judah's captive king, Jehoiachin, is released from prison and afforded a place of honor at the royal palace in Babylon (52:31-34; see also 2 Kgs 25:27-30). The cryptic allusion to the kind treatment of Jehoiachin, literally the lifting of his head (in Jer 52:31, which is strangely reminiscent of Gen 40:13 and 40:19), may signal the restoration of the Davidic dynasty or, more broadly, God's continuing work among the Judean refugees in Babylon.

As a whole, the prophetic drama appears as a diptych of sorts; on the one hand it is governed by "plucking up and pulling down" (Jer 1–25) and on the other by "building and planting" (Jer 26–52). It is not unusual for readers to interpret only sections of the latter as hopeful, in large measure because of an almost intuitive correlation of judgment with divine wrath and salvation with divine love. Such a view, however, is reductionistic. Whereas oracles of judgment must be distinguished from oracles of salvation *formally*, the two are not mutually exclusive in Jeremiah's formulation of hope. The first makes healing and survival possible by looking massive loss straight in the eye and breaking various forms of denial. The second moves beyond denials and despair to meaning-making constructions (especially in chs. 30–33 and 46–51). Accordingly, the text's motto (1:10) is not a dualistic formula that divorces plucking up and pulling down from building and planting but rather language that belongs together and translates into an anatomy of hope in crisis.

Within these canonical boundaries, meaning-making arrangements—a taxonomy of hope—emerge for exiles of old and those on pilgrimage today.

Jeremianic Hope Is Born out of the Crucible of Local Contexts

Almost without exception, the interpretive communities of the Latter Prophets situate their "heroes" in a particular time and place. Likewise, the book of Jeremiah opens with an apparently innocuous superscription (1:1-3) that anchors "the words [or 'affairs'] of Jeremiah" as well as "the word of YHWH" in spatial and temporal categories.[10] Henceforth, "divine revelation" is pinned down and defined by a particular corner of the world. It is neither an abstraction nor an unfettered imagination, but like the faith of Israel is tied to and shaped by memory and physicality. The word of YHWH spoken through Jeremiah is concretely existential, community based, and rooted in a particular world historical context. Specifically, the first words of the prophetic drama establish the "chronological" boundaries of this disorderly and discontinuous book: the unfolding events take place from the thirteenth year of King Josiah's reign (627 B.C.E.) to the fifth month of the captivity of Jerusalem (587/6 B.C.E.). It is important to note that these turbulent years culminate in the disorienting memory of "the captivity of Jerusalem," which represents the defining *kairos* of the book.

At first, this ominous framework seems to have little to do with hope. However, the same text that establishes the alarming "historical" circumstances also affirms that YHWH enters the fray of this "history" to lament and liberate, to judge and save, to disrupt and embrace, and to subvert and sustain.[11] To generalize the particular, then—to divorce "the words of Jeremiah and the word of YHWH" from the realities of community life, to deny its human face, and to extricate it from the actual world of human posturing and power plays—is to read against the grain of the text. Although generic language may create fewer epistemic problems, it does not sustain careful scrutiny, especially for suffering communities. Any notion of hope worthy of its name must grow out of the crucible of local contexts—even if those contexts are the ovens of Auschwitz or the killing fields of Cambodia, Kosovo, Rwanda, Baghdad, or Darfur. And so, while Jeremiah may well be a "spokesperson out of time," he nonetheless speaks out of his own peculiar corner of the world. Jeremianic hope is rooted deeply in a particular social reality, the disturbing reality of sixth-century B.C.E. Jewry as a subject community in Babylon.[12]

The movie *Smoke*, starring William Hurt as Paul Benjamin and Harvey Keitel as Auggie Wren, drives home the importance of the contingent character of texts and the situated texture of our lives as well as the mystery of the mundane. In the film, Paul, a writer who can barely cope with the murder of his pregnant wife by random street violence, stops by Auggie Wren's tobacco shop on the corner of Third and Seventh Streets in Brooklyn. Near the register Paul notices a camera, which Auggie explains holds the key to who he is and what he's really about. He shows Benjamin a pile of photo albums with thousands of pictures of the same scene: people passing by the corner of Third and Seventh Streets at 8:00 in the morning every day of the year. "It's my corner after all. I mean, it's just one little part of the world, but things happen there, too, just like everywhere else. It's a record of my little spot." Paul, however, doesn't get it. He sees only pages and pages of the same thing, until he slows down and looks closely. Then he begins to understand! As Auggie explains,

> They're all the same but each one is different from every other one. You've got your bright mornings and dark mornings. You've got your summer light and autumn light. You've got your weekdays and weekends. You've got people with overcoats and galoshes and . . . people in T-shirts and shorts. Sometimes the same people, sometimes different ones; sometimes the different ones become the same. The same ones disappear . . . every day the light from the sun hits the earth from a different angle.[13]

When Paul slows down and becomes more observant, he even discovers a few photos of his wife Ellen going to work. At first, Auggie's corner store and his more than four thousand pictures of Third and Seventh Streets at 8:00 A.M. appear trite and rather odd. A closer look reveals that his small slice of the world, his concrete particularity, was nothing less than extraordinary.

The opening words of the prophetic drama discourage disengagement from real communities living in particular corners of the world. For the Jeremiah tradition, this world is wounded by war and engulfed in tears. In *this* place of crisis hope takes shape.

Jeremianic Hope Is Candid about Deep Ruptures of Life

An essential ingredient of Jeremiah's meaning-making map, his tapestry of hope, is truth-telling. From the outset, the prophet names and breaks a surplus of denials and deceptions, and he dares to critique social structures, domain assumptions, and prevailing values that anesthetize the community to its true condition. After putting his nation under a prophetic microscope, he is convinced that Judah's world is shattered beyond repair and that its institutional and ideological mainstays will do little to rectify its condition. Impressive sanctuaries, brawny nationalism, urban think tanks, and even trusted doctrines will not avert disaster and fundamental transformations in community life. And so Jeremiah speaks truth to the powerbrokers invested in these systems: prophets and priests who proclaim, " 'Peace, peace,' / when there is no peace" (6:14; 8:11), sages who reject wisdom and "the word of the LORD" (8:8-9), and Judean kings who show utter disdain for opposing positions (see, for example, 36:1-32; 37:17-21; 38:14-28).

The prophetic critique, however, is not restricted to the powerful: Jeremiah places the entire enterprise under biting scrutiny. As YHWH's spokesperson, he exposes the spiritual and moral bankruptcy of the shareholders as well (for example, 2:1-13; 5:1-5, 20-29): "All alike [have] broken the yoke, . . . [all have] burst the bonds" (5:5). Greed is insatiable, apostasy is rampant, neglect of the poor is reprehensible, and liturgy devoid of compassion is an affront to YHWH. Put succinctly, Jeremiah the truth-teller asserts that all is not well! No wonder professional mourners are called upon to lament:

> Death has come up into our windows,
>> it has entered our palaces,
> to cut off the children from the streets
>> and the young men from the squares. (9:21)

The tradition of Jeremiah simply will not trade in prevarication and denial, nor will it close down the senses and banish memory. The text confronts social and symbolic patterns that foster exploitation, idolatry, and specious assurance for the future. And it refuses to conceal the truth of the city's death.

Such scathing commentary again appears to have little to do with hope. But healing—communal and individual—begins with the candor and courage to relinquish false hopes and detrimental securities. YHWH's prophet of hope insists that the refugee community must surrender its old identity in the land and accept its marginal status in diaspora in order to survive and eventually flourish (for example, 21:1-10; 29:4-10).[14] Although his opponents, including Hananiah and Shemaiah, conclude otherwise and so appear to be harbingers of hope, their patriotic fervor only strengthens the grip of despair. Truth-telling is the starting point of hope and the path to communal healing. Or as therapist Linda Centers observes regarding ALS patients, "Real hope cannot thrive in a climate of deception or where truth is being withheld."[15]

Jeremianic Hope Attempts to Make Sense of the Nonsense of Radical Suffering

Cognitive, emotional, and spiritual "understanding" of disaster is a key to resilience and the management of grief among refugees. Viable explanations of suffering are crucial to individual and community hope.[16] The book of Jeremiah is a complex theodicy or, more precisely, a theology of suffering that strives to help survivors cope with the ruins of war and deportation. Virtually every utterance of this meaning-making map is informed by the conviction that YHWH reigns, which is arguably the root metaphor of the book. The prophet envisions the fractured world and its array of vicissitudes under YHWH's sovereignty. Consequently, suffering is not arbitrary. Judah's crisis is not a fluke of world historical forces or the result of strategic geopolitical actions. It signals neither life spiraling out of control nor the impotence of Israel's God. From start to finish, Jeremiah affirms that despite national disaster and social upheaval God is still ordering the world with the intent to accomplish God's purposes. Or to echo the book's refrain, God is plucking up and pulling down, destroying and overthrowing "the whole land" (45:4).

The assertion that YHWH reigns does little to devalue human responsibility. On the contrary, Jeremiah claims that YHWH holds all people accountable for their actions, especially the people of God. "Turn now, all of you from your evil way, and amend your ways and your doings. But they say, 'It is no use! We will follow our own plans'" (18:11, 12). Agency is an essential, albeit disturbing, ingredient of Jeremianic hope. The prophet holds to the belief that Judah's predicament is in large measure a consequence of its own actions. The breakdown of Torah values—especially fidelity, justice, and compassion—results in chaos and destruction. It is hard to deny that this ethical vision on some level blames the victim. To place responsibility on the shoulders of the Judean people is to let off the hook the principal protagonists in the fall of Jerusalem (see, however, Jer 50–51). While this causal argument is no doubt problematic, it serves in part as a survivor's strategy to make sense of inexplicable suffering.[17] For those victimized by geopolitical and natural forces beyond their control, the reestablishment of agency, even through scapegoating and blame, is a core ingredient of hope and resilience. It renders dangerous forces "powerless" and eradicates "mess." In particular, it serves to demonstrate that the community's crisis is far from indiscriminate; rather, it is an outcome of an orderly and morally meaningful universe. And the tradition assembles a rich variety of metaphors, including Deuteronomic and covenant understandings, to harness symbolic, intellectual, and emotional chaos and set it within a coherent context of meaning (see, for example, 11:1-17).

What is rather distinctive about the book of Jeremiah is that the prophetic persona subverts these stable and symmetrical categories.[18] The prophet emerges as one who is faithful yet tortured, obedient yet rejected. For instance, on the heels of the covenant sermon (11:1-14), which draws a direct correlation between Judah's conduct and its condition, Jeremiah laments that though he has faithfully delivered the message of divine judgment, as commanded by YHWH, his countrymen seek to kill him. Like many psalmists, as well as suffering Job, he staunchly maintains his innocence and cries out for justice. In the prose oracle response that follows (11:21-23), YHWH assures Jeremiah that those who seek his life will not get away with their malevolent intentions. But in the meantime, before justice materializes, the prophet finds himself tormented by moral incoherence, failure, and divine inertia. Accordingly, Jeremiah the innocent sufferer becomes a symbol of hope when justice languishes in exile. In the prophetic persona, we discover that suffering is not shameful but rather a mark of faithful service to God.

Jeremianic Hope Refuses to Flatten the World into Monolithic and Rigid Categories

Perhaps more than any other prophetic writing in the Hebrew Bible, the book of Jeremiah is an elaborate tapestry of meaning-making that honors complexity and delights in a multiplicity of perspectives. It dares to grapple with focal concerns and crippling fears that challenge ordinary conventional understandings. This bold literary tradition eschews superficiality and resists the temptation to flatten the world into safe, monolithic categories. We see this interpretive propensity in the text's unstable quality, dissonant voices, plethora of genres, and, perhaps most poignantly, in its penetrating understandings of disaster. The Jeremiah tradition will not reduce the crumbling of Judah's world to a single cause or a unified explanation. Instead, the interpretive community participates in "an ongoing *conversation* . . . concerning the crisis faced by the community of Israel at the demise of Jerusalem."[19]

This conversation includes those who would censure the upper tiers of social hierarchy—hostile kings, inept prophets, and self-serving priests—while others implicate the nation as a whole for systemic wrongdoing. Some speak of communal rebellion and apostasy, covenant and Torah infractions, and unlawful political alliances. Others assert that Sabbath violations led to the unraveling of the universe. Still others conclude that the cessation of offerings to the Queen of Heaven—likely after the Josianic Reform—contributed to their plight (44:15-19). A prose constituency makes a sustained case that Judah's predicament is inextricably linked to its rejection and ill treatment of Jeremiah (Jer 37–44). At the same time, the tradition gives voice to those who accuse YHWH of excessive and indiscriminate force. Like Dostoyevsky's Ivan Karamazov, Jeremiah dares to call God's justice into question (see, for example, 12:1-4).

Amid these clashing voices are those that reject retributive and punitive categories and opt instead for expressions of sorrow, exasperation, pain, and disappointment. It is not incidental that much of the poetry of Jeremiah is cast in the form of a lament. Nor is it inconsequential that the major participants in the drama, YHWH and Jeremiah, are often depicted as fractured figures who participate in the anguish of the community. Their requiem for Israel pulsates with grief. Notwithstanding this painful involvement, the tradition is also capable of disassociating God from human violence and suffering. Notice, in this regard, the divine absence in the narrative of Gedaliah's assassination and the "massacre of the innocents" (40:7–41:18), as well as in the telling of Jerusalem's fall (39:1-10).

In addition to the many interpretations of catastrophe, one can also recognize the rich conversational texture of Jeremiah in the array of divine images, ideological platforms,[20] understandings of empire (cf. 27:1-11 and 50:1–51:58), and renderings of the prophet. The tradition depicts its hero as a complex character who is multidimensional, conflicted, and hard to pin down. He is YHWH's faithful spokesperson as well as the community's advocate. As YHWH's messenger, he indicts Judah for infidelity, injustice, and hardness of heart (for example, 2:1-37; 5:1-5, 20-31); as guardian of the community, he takes YHWH to task for harsh and indiscriminate judgment (for example, 12:1-4; 14:13-18; see also 14:19-22). This same Jeremiah is a survivor, pariah, intercessor, tester, refiner, iconoclast, itinerant preacher, covenant mediator, and political advisor—to name only a few of his many roles. He supports Babylonian imperialism (Jer 27–28) and eventually condemns it (Jer 50–51). He encourages capitulation to Babylon and then tacitly fosters rebellion against the empire.

The interpretive community resists domesticating Jeremiah the prophet or Jeremiah the book, even by a formidable Deuteronomistic propensity to control and organize symbolic disorder. Admittedly, this dissonance has been a source of great consternation for readers interested in linear speech, authorial intent, and historical exactitude.[21] Yet this cacophonous texture leaves the reader not only disconcerted but also engaged and hopeful: hopeful because Jeremianic dissymmetry takes seriously massive and unmanageable loss; hopeful because it honors a range of human responses to the horror of suffering; hopeful because it provides language when ordinary speech fails. The text's labyrinth of voices and countervoices will not settle for simplistic answers to complex questions, and thus it commands an integrity and force that is capable of helping victims cope with the ravages of palpable disease.

Jeremianic Hope Is Sustained by Engagement and Disputation Rather than Resignation and Passivity

If the "confessions" of Jeremiah are more than personal prayers, as Graf Reventlow, Mark Biddle, and others have cogently argued,[22] they represent a daring, disputatious communal spirituality that does not shrink from liturgical engagement, "scandalous" complaint, and combative dialogue. While these laments differ markedly one from another, they share a common ethos and orientation. From the first lament (11:18–12:6) to the final utterance of despair (20:7-18), these prayers reflect a social world fraught with fear and vulnerability. As already noted, Jeremiah, the larger-than-life figure, is not insulated from danger—divine or human—but must live in a fractured and morally problematic universe in which the righteous suffer while God appears indifferent (12:1-4).

Rather than accepting this situation as it is or painting an implausible picture of it, Jeremiah confronts it head-on and seeks recourse through prayer and social pressure. In this dangerous world, the prophet is adamant about his own virtue and the wrongdoing of his adversaries. One looks in vain for confessions of sin or pleas for forgiveness from Jeremiah. Like Job, he is more convinced of his own innocence than he is of the innocence of YHWH. And so he protests, rages, and accuses God of ethical mismanagement and covenant infidelity. Jeremiah even hurls at YHWH a battery of frontal questions concerning his own plight and divine inertia. This language of defiance, this spirituality of candor, refuses to acquiesce easily; it will not fall in line and submit—even to God! Nor will it let God off the hook. In the perilous social world of Jeremiah's laments, God is not scandalized by such dissent. On the contrary, cries of distress and protests of innocence become a source of hope.[23] And even though God offers Jeremiah—and the community he represents—little hope for an immediate reprieve from disorientation, God is still responsive to human suffering and promises to be present during the deluge. Such understandings reflect a rugged spirituality that is comfortable with raw emotion, astonishing boldness, ethical uncertainty, and intense displays of public grief.

Hope Is Impossible without the Prospect of a Better Life and Future

Jeremiah's map of hope involves more than truth-telling and deconstruction, emotional integrity and candor, engagement and disputation; in the tradition of Jeremiah, hope imagines a future when none seems possible. It is no accident that the two primary occurrences of the word *hope* (*tiqvah*) in the book refer to the future of the displaced community (29:11; 31:17; see also the word *tiqvah* as used in 14:8; 17:13; 50:7): "For surely I know the plans I have for you, says the LORD, plans for your welfare and not for harm, to give you *a future with hope*" (29:11; emphasis added); "There is *hope for your future*, / says the LORD: / your children shall come back to their own country" (31:17). Without the prospect of a future, hope is impossible; with little chance of survival and a better future, life becomes unbearable. Jeremiah, God's harbinger of hope, asserts that the collapse of Judah's universe signals neither the end of faith nor the death of the community. Despite overwhelming indications to the contrary (read, for instance, the two verses that immediately precede 31:17), God is still at work mending a broken world and healing lives wracked with pain.

Although Jeremiah's vision of Judah's future is far from unified or systematic, its broad outlines emerge most clearly in the second act of the prophetic drama (chs. 26–52). There we encounter glimmers of hope (for example, 26:24; 38:7-13; 39:15-18; 45:1-5) as well as lush gardens (30:1–33:26). Jeremiah envisions a future in which YHWH consoles and heals, creates and transforms, liberates and restores, builds and plants, and eventually gathers scattered Israel for a grand homecoming (see, for example, 29:10-14; 30:1-3; 32:1-44). In a display of mercy, YHWH promises to act unilaterally in the creation of a new covenant with Israel based on internal renewal and forgiveness (31:31-34). YHWH even resolves to restore the royal leadership of David and the priestly supervision of the Levites (33:14-26, although these are missing from the LXX).

These striking overtures of restoration, however, are never far from the purview of exile and empire. Rarely utopian or Edenic, God's script for newness is replete with reminders of the painful past.

> Thus says the LORD:
> The people who survived the sword

> found grace in the wilderness. . . .
>> With weeping they shall come,
>>> and with consolations I will lead them back. (31:2, 9a; see also 30:4-11)

Such renderings create a hopeful realism that takes seriously the plight of the captured community while affirming that it will survive and eventually thrive. One day—indeed, "the time is surely coming" (for the eschatological formulation, see 23:5, 7; 30:3; 31:27, 31; 33:14; 51:47)—YHWH will restore justice and moral sanity to all people.

In the meantime, before God's wondrous work of renewal is fulfilled, the displaced community must resist the temptation to sit back and do nothing or hastily follow the guidance of those who promise imminent restoration. To do either would result in further suffering. And so Jeremiah challenges the exiles in Babylon to put down roots and work hard at creating a viable communal life in a faraway place. Rather than clinging to an old identity, Jeremiah urges the Jewish refugees to accept their new place on the margins of society (29:4-10):

> Build houses and live in them; plant gardens and eat what they produce. Take wives and have sons and daughters; take wives for your sons, and give your daughters in marriage, that they may bear sons and daughters; multiply there, and do not decrease. But seek the welfare of the city where I have sent you into exile, and pray to the LORD on its behalf, for in its welfare you will find your welfare. (29:5-7)

Such a disenfranchised social position surely looks bleak, but Jeremiah argues to the contrary: accepting this reality and letting go of the past makes room for the new workings of God. As counterintuitive as it may seem, the exiles will find God in their present place of risk. There they will participate in God's new creation, and there they will discover seeds of hope.

Hope Is Buoyed by Resistance

Resistance and hope are partners in meaning-making. Whether it takes the form of a beauty pageant in Kosovo, reading *Lolita* in Tehran, draft-card burnings in the United States, boycotts in South Africa, mass demonstrations on the streets of Paris, or hunger strikes at the U.S. prison in Guantanamo Bay, resistance keeps hope alive and sometimes sets it ablaze. As is often the case in the tradition of Jeremiah, perceptions of resistance and empire coexist in tension. Throughout much of the prophetic drama, Jeremiah opposes insurrection and in fact encourages capitulation to the empire and its king whom he calls "YHWH's servant" (25:9; 27:6; 43:10):

Thus says the LORD: See, I am setting before you the way of life and the way of death. Those who stay in this city shall die by the sword, by famine, and by pestilence; but those who go out and surrender to the Chaldeans who are besieging you shall live and shall have their lives as a prize of war.[24] For I have set my face against this city for evil and not for good, says the LORD: it shall be given into the hands of the king of Babylon, and he shall burn it with fire. (21:8-10)

Similarly, Jeremiah said to Zedekiah, "Thus says the LORD, the God of hosts, the God of Israel, If you will only surrender to the officials of the king of Babylon, then your life shall be spared, and this city shall not be burned with fire, and you and your house shall live" (38:17). From a geopolitical perspective, one could certainly make the case that Jeremiah's "pro-Babylonian" rhetoric pulsates with political realism. Submission to Babylon, in compliance with the word of YHWH, was clearly the only viable option to ensure Judah's survival. Jeremiah's instructions to the Judean exiles reflect the same realism (29:7).

Notwithstanding this political pragmatism, Jeremiah eventually takes on Babylon (50:1–51:58). The final image of Jeremiah presented by the Hebrew text is that of a dissident prophet to the nations who speaks out against the empire and its imperial designs toward absolute power. In this context, Babylon is no longer YHWH's instrument of judgment or even one of many nations that sins against YHWH. Rather, Babylon is "the hammer of the whole earth" (50:23), "a horror among the nations" (50:23), a country that has "challenged" (50:24) and "arrogantly defied the LORD" (50:29), and a "destroying mountain" (51:25); to be sure, Babylon is "the pride of the whole earth" (51:41), the embodiment of insolence (50:31-32).

Once Jeremiah exposes this hubris, he heralds the empire's demise. YHWH disposes of brazen Babylon once and for all:

> Suddenly Babylon has fallen and is shattered. . . .
> How Sheshach is taken. . . .
> How Babylon has become
>   an object of horror among the nations! . . .
> For the LORD is laying Babylon waste,
>   and stilling her loud clamor. (51:8, 41, 55)

This grand realignment not only signals the defeat of Nebuchadnezzar and the powers of Marduk;[25] it also inaugurates an epoch of hope. Now Judean exiles situated on the margins can imagine life without the oppressive regime. Now dispirited refugees have lenses to see that worldly power is not ultimate power, that military technology is fleeting, and that God acts on behalf of those who cannot act on their own. And now those who bear the physical wounds and psychological scars of war and forced displacement can entertain the possibility of their own freedom. By the force of this "hidden transcript" of justice, no doubt deployed under the radar of Babylon, Jeremiah empowers God's people with the will to survive and the resolve to act.

If this script of resistance "emerged in the midst of liturgic celebrations of the sovereignty of [YHWH],"[26] we might do well to reconsider conventional notions of worship. In addition to addressing the deity with language of adoration, this subversive expression of worship dares to address the empire; it refuses to ignore political aggression and monstrous immorality; it rejects cruel power structures as normative; and it says no to systems of oppression and humiliation. This liturgical performance, however, does not employ violence to rectify the empire's offenses.[27] Rather, through holy defiance, it provides sacred space and time that is removed from infected time and space.[28] In such a setting the world is realigned and hope is born. In the end, worship becomes a robust matrix for hope.

Conclusion

Jeremiah is an artifact of hope. Jeremiah is an artifact of terror. This enduring literary tradition neither placates nor pacifies, and certainly does not traffic in entitlements. Jeremianic hope is instead dangerous, disruptive, and disturbing. It subverts long-held beliefs, dismantles trusted social structures, and exposes illusions and trivialities. It does not avert its gaze from hypocrisy and injustice but demands wholehearted obedience. Clearly, Jeremiah's "future of hope" is not what Judah desired! It includes few assurances of victory and even fewer exemptions from suffering. The promised future for God's people is not unlike that pledged to Baruch: "Thus says the LORD: I am going to break down what I have built, and pluck up what I have planted— that is, the whole land. And you, do you seek great things for yourself? Do not seek them; for I am going to bring disaster upon all flesh, says the LORD; but *I will give you your life as a prize of war in every place to which you may go*" (45:4-5; emphasis added). Like faithful Baruch, the community will not triumph (nationally or militarily) but it will survive, and survival is nothing to scoff at during times of war.

This artifact of hope, this artifact of terror, may indeed be as urgent today as it was for a refuge community living under the shadow of the empire in the sixth century B.C.E. It may also be as disconcerting, *especially for citizens of the empire*. With economic systems in jeopardy and long-standing geopolitical and religious institutions under scrutiny, with an increasing awareness of the United States' vulnerability, many of us find ourselves longing for the restoration of the old world and its standard modes of operation. Such inclinations do not bode well for those who take this meaning-making map seriously. While the book of Jeremiah is full of fractures, tensions, and contradictions, it is firm in the conviction that conventional power structures, settled religious categories, and robust geopolitical systems are the wrong places to look for hope and God's blessings. By the end of the book, it becomes clear—if there were ever doubt—that God's place in the world is among the broken and dispossessed, the captured and conquered. Indeed, hope is to be found among the vulnerable and wounded. In this way, the book of Jeremiah unmasks illusions of power and reveals God's solidarity with exiles of old and exiles today.

CHAPTER FIVE

JEREMIAH AS A COMPLEX RESPONSE TO SUFFERING

The rest was death, and death alone. . . .
  At five in the afternoon.
    —"Lament for Ignacio Sanchez Mejias"

Death has come up into our windows,
  it has entered our palaces,
to cut off the children from the streets
  and the young men from the squares. . . .
Human corpses shall fall
  like dung upon the open field,
like sheaves behind the reaper,
  and no one shall gather them.
            —*Jeremiah 9:21-22*

Startling images of death and destruction! The first derives from the modern poet and dramatist Federico García Lorca, who "at five in the afternoon" beheld the death of Ignacio Sanchez Mejias, a death that symbolized the violence that would engulf Spain, the country García Lorca passionately loved. The second is associated with the biblical prophet Jeremiah, who in the late seventh and early sixth centuries B.C.E. witnessed his own country ravaged and occupied by enemy forces. Although García Lorca and Jeremiah lived in entirely different worlds, they stand together in the company of poets, artists, dissidents, saints, and seers whose images of human tragedy have forever seared our minds and hearts. In our modern context, one thinks of the haunting cries from the killing fields of Buchenwald, Dachau, Cambodia, Baghdad, El Salvador, Hiroshima, Nanking, Kosovo, and Rwanda. From survivors' literature, we know that such massive, gratuitous suffering not only causes physical and emotional devastation; it also evokes probing questions about ultimate reality. Where is God? How can such random and obscene acts of violence occur? Does evil go unpunished? Is it possible to live through the darkness and embrace life again? The testimonies of survivors to the multifaceted configurations of evil and the silence of God shatter all neat and cohesive understandings of life.

113

The witness of the book of Jeremiah is no exception. Its fifty-two chapters—comprising the largest writing of the prophetic literature in the Hebrew Bible—come face-to-face with human suffering and moral ambiguity. Jeremiah, or more precisely, the book that bears his name, depicts the unraveling of a culture that many perceived to be indestructible. With graphic imagery and unflinching courage—and often with thick, symbolic language—this prophetic writing "chronicles" the dismantling of Judah's sacred and social world. In a relatively short span of time, the imposing neo-Babylonian military machine under King Nebuchadnezzar (605–562 B.C.E.) delivered three crushing blows to Judah and its capital city Jerusalem. According to the biblical narratives, the first military assault resulted in the loss of Judah's independence and in the deportation of many of its leading citizens (597). The second took the greatest toll on the nation (587). The siege and capture of Jerusalem ended in death, displacement, and the breakdown of Judah's social and political order. The Babylonian army burned to the ground the Jerusalem temple and the royal palace complex. In order to squelch signs of insubordination in the years following the fall of Jerusalem, Babylon attacked again and carried a third wave of Judean citizens to Babylon (582). In less than two decades, long-standing institutions associated with God's blessings and protection, cherished belief systems, and social structures in place for centuries all came to an abrupt halt.

The book of Jeremiah is a complex and multifaceted response to these tragedies. It dares to speak of the horrors of war and of people whose lives are full of pain. The text bears witness to a "moment" so terrible that it defies ordinary categories. Walter Brueggemann calls the crisis the end of Judah's known world.[1] Kathleen M. O'Connor refers to the devastation as the "colossal collapse" of Judah's world.[2] Louis Stulman has used the term "cosmic crumbling" to speak of Judah's undoing.[3] For the Judean people, the fall of Jerusalem and the series of deportations to Babylon represented nothing less than the "end of history," the dissolution of the created order (for example, Jer 4:23-27). Written by and large in the shadow of the wreckage, Jeremiah attempts to make symbolic sense of the upheaval and help survivors cope with the devastation. The book's plurality of voices and claims converge to come to terms with war, invasion, exile, and the accompanying existential dilemmas.

The interpretive community of Jeremiah maintained from the outset that the crisis would permanently change the character of the nation, despite the Jerusalem establishment's insistence that the royal-temple structures would endure the onslaught of invasion. For instance, in the first half of the prophetic drama, chapters 1–25, the text *predicts* the collapse of the temple and its liturgical systems (7:1-15), the covenant relationship between YHWH and Israel (11:1-17), the election tradition (18:1-12), and the Davidic dynasty (21:1–23:40), as well as the capital city and ancient land claims.

The text asserts that the old world and its social and symbolic configurations of reality would go down to destruction. Nothing would remain to prop up its vestiges. The second part of Jeremiah, chapters 26–52, *depicts* the dismantling while sustaining the reader with hope for coming restoration. Together the two "acts"—Jeremiah 1–25 and 26–52—announce the end of Judah's once safe and stable world. Alongside the suffering nation stands the prophet who also experiences unspeakable hardship. The book portrays its hero as one who suffers *with* his fellow citizens and *because of* their impassioned opposition to God's message. Even God is not above the fray in Jeremiah. God is beset by pain. Every divine word and act is entrenched in suffering.[4] Because of the slain people of Judah, God weeps day and night, and is inexorably embroiled in the ordeal (9:1-2). Thus, all three major participants in the prophetic drama—Judah, Jeremiah, and YHWH—are drenched in tears.

In this chapter, we will argue that the book of Jeremiah is a labyrinth of thick theological interpretations of suffering. We will consider three of these claims. The first and perhaps governing assertion in the book is that, despite Judah's ordeal, the world is orderly and congruent, moral and stable. It exacts punishment on wrongdoers and, by implication, promises blessing to the faithful. In support of this reading of reality, a surplus of prose and poetic texts contend that Judah—and especially its leaders— is responsible for its own demise. Judah's infidelity to God, mistreatment of the poor, and royal policies of brutality have brought down the walls of the city. That is to say, insiders—not dangerous outsiders—constitute the principal protagonists in the fall of Judah. Consequently, God's people—not God—are culpable. Although a host of passages in Jeremiah 1–25 reflect such a view, this chapter will focus on Jeremiah 11:1-14, a representative prose sermon with a distinctly Deuteronomic texture.

The second theological response to Judah's plight is far more at home in a dissonant and morally ambiguous universe. In the Joban tradition, this formulation looks to the "innocent" suffering of Jeremiah as a way to work through the devastation. Here we encounter one who is faithful to God and yet is not granted immunity from the sorrow of his country. Like innocent Jerusalemites, Jeremiah endures enormous hardship through no fault of his own. Thus, in the prophetic persona, we discover that suffering is not always punitive. The world bristles with conflict and danger, and clearly defined categories do not do full justice to the scope of human pain. Now permission is granted to grieve the community's profound losses. One can discern this anti-theodicy strand throughout the book, but it is most transparent in the so-called confessions of Jeremiah and in the Baruch narrative (chs. 36–45). Both literary units depict their hero as a tormented and conflicted figure whose suffering is not wholly manageable, at least from a rational standpoint.[5] To highlight Jeremiah's theology of protest, we will briefly consider three of the confessions[6] (11:18–12:6; 15:15-18; 20:7-18).

The third theological interpretation of Judah's crisis—particularly the suffering of the post–587 Judean community—is not as sweeping as the first two but is no less significant. Here the interpretive community of Jeremiah distances, indeed extricates, YHWH and YHWH's spokesperson from the gratuitous violence. As such, divine silence and divine absence play a central role. The most stunning example of this bold overture is found in the account of Gedaliah's failed government (40:7–41:18). Without reference to God or God's envoy Jeremiah, this segment of the Baruch narrative details the brutal death of Gedaliah and the pilgrims en route to Jerusalem.

The First Strategy for Addressing Judah's Plight: Moral Order amid the Chaos

The dominant voice in the book of Jeremiah maintains that Judah is to blame for its troubles, that life is not spiraling out of YHWH's control, and that the world is by and large orderly and morally manageable. Although the prose sermons in Jeremiah do not hold a monopoly on these claims, they articulate them most forcefully; to be sure, they organize a range of poetic and prose texts that make similar and counter assertions.[7] Influenced to a large measure by Deuteronomic theology, the prose sermons affirm that Judah's political and social devastation is a direct outcome of its own actions. YHWH had warned Israel by "his servants the prophets"[8] to turn from its evil ways and keep the commandments; Israel rejected this message and therefore suffered divine judgment (see, for example, 7:25-34; 25:4-11; 26:4-6; 29:17-19; 44:4-6; cf. 2 Kgs 17:13-18). Consequently, Judah's disobedience exonerates God of injustice and mismanagement. The destruction of Jerusalem and the exile to Babylon "make perfect theological sense": YHWH only acts in accordance with the covenant demands.

Jeremiah 11:1-14 is one of many texts that represent such understandings. In the prose sermon Jeremiah indicts Israel and Judah for breaking the covenant. Not unlike the first ten chapters of the book, it asserts that the people of God have been unfaithful and therefore must brace themselves for YHWH's judgment. Jeremiah 11:1-14, however, expresses this motif in the language, style, and theology of Deuteronomy. Similar to Deuteronomy, the language of Jeremiah 11:1-14 is verbose and repetitive. Its prose is parenetic and rhetorical. A number of words and phrases in the text are virtually identical to those found in Deuteronomy.[9] Moreover, the prose sermon reflects the Deuteronomic belief that divine blessing accompanies obedience, whereas disaster results from disobedience (for example, Deut 28). If Israel complies with the stipulations of the covenant, well-being and prosperity will follow. If Israel does not heed YHWH's commandments, judgment will ensue. The structure of Jeremiah 11:1-14 is also strikingly similar to speeches in the Deuteronomistic corpus (for example, Deut 6;

8; 2 Kgs 17:7-18): it includes an introduction (Jer 11:1-2); the word of YHWH in the imperative—that is, the commandments (11:3-6); a statement of disobedience (11:7-10); and the pronouncement of divine judgment (11:11-14).

In the prose sermon YHWH addresses Jeremiah four times with four distinct commands (11:2-5, 6-8, 9-13, 14). Couched in the negative, the first follows the letter of Deuteronomy 27–28 (Jer 11:2-5). "All are cursed who do not obey the terms of this covenant" (11:3, authors' translation). God instructs Jeremiah to summon the people of Judah to obey the terms of the covenant. The demand for obedience grows out of the exodus story—that is, obedience is supposedly the joyous response to God's gracious act of liberation from oppression, "when [God] brought them out of the land of Egypt, from the iron-smelter" (11:4). God freed the Israelites from Egyptian bondage so that they might obey a benevolent suzerain and enjoy a special relationship with this divine king. God's covenant with Israel is a gift and a great privilege, but it does not offer Israel a free ride. Privilege involves responsibility. God expects Israel to obey its covenant obligations, and in large measure Israel's continued status as God's people is dependent upon such fidelity. Obedience is thus in no way ancillary but is the very centerpiece of the covenant relationship. To remain in the land and enjoy the blessings of the covenant, Judah must be a faithful vassal (11:3-5). In other words, the blessings of the covenant are not entitlements: they are dependent on observing the terms of the solemn agreement (11:3-5).

The second admonition (11:6-8) builds on the harsh tone of the previous verses. Jeremiah implores the people of Judah to "hear the words of this covenant and do them" (11:6). Earlier communities had their chance to obey the terms of the covenant but adamantly refused. "They did not obey or incline their ear, but everyone walked in the stubbornness of an evil will" (11:8). YHWH therefore brought upon them "all the words of this covenant." This historical synopsis is another somber warning for the contemporary community. It characterizes Israel's entire history as one of incessant disobedience and infers from this judgment that the present hearers will likely do little to change it. Interestingly, the Septuagint almost entirely omits verses 7-8. The shorter Greek text states succinctly, "The Lord said to me . . . hear the words of this covenant and do them, *but they did not.*" Whereas the Hebrew text uses the ancestors' disobedience as a rhetorical device to coax the contemporary people of God into obedience, the Greek text hones in only on the unwillingness of the contemporary community to heed YHWH's word. Both the Hebrew and Greek texts agree that violating the stipulations of the covenant carries grave consequences.

Next YHWH informs Jeremiah of a "conspiracy" brewing among the people of Judah and the inhabitants of Jerusalem (11:9-13). What makes the conspiracy so dangerous is that it is waged against God. The Judeans have resolved to follow their ancestors' example of disobedience. The first two verbs in verse 10 convey the nature of the "revolt" in stereotyped language: the people of Judah have *turned back* (*šûb*) to the iniquities of their ancestors and have *gone after* (*hlk*) other gods to serve them. The third verb is less common: the house of Israel and the house of Judah have *broken* (*prr*) *the covenant* made with their ancestors. For the first time in the book, Jeremiah *explicitly* accuses the nation of breaking the covenant. The precise language, to "break covenant," occurs five times in Jeremiah (11:10; 14:21; 31:32; 33:20; 33:21), and two of these references identify Judah as the covenant breaker (11:10 and 31:32). Jeremiah 31:32, a principal text for the construction of exilic and postexilic Judaism, states that the establishment of a "new covenant" is necessary since Israel has broken the covenant that God made at Sinai. The reference in Jeremiah 11 is significant because it refers to a breach that places the future of the house of Israel and the house of Judah in grave danger. This text asserts that one cannot write off the covenant demands without suffering grave consequences, even more so since the people's love affair with "many gods" violates the very cornerstone of the covenant relationship: "You shall have no other gods before me." Furthermore, by associating covenant breaking with the conspiracy against YHWH (11:9-10), Jeremiah declares that the people's disobedience is a formal and brazen renunciation that will result in the covenant curses (11:11-13).

Last, YHWH prohibits Jeremiah from interceding on behalf of the community (11:14). The command not to intercede is essentially a repetition of Jeremiah 7:16. The people have "not listened" to YHWH (11:8) and now it is YHWH's turn "not to listen" (11:14). By betraying their covenant obligations, the people of Judah have forfeited their covenant claim upon God and their right to enter YHWH's house (11:15). No prophetic intercession or priestly offerings can thwart God's plans to strip away Judah's world (11:14-15). This final admonition serves to intensify the scope of God's judgment and prevent loopholes.

The covenant sermon accuses Judah of fracturing the ancestral covenant and bringing upon itself inescapable judgment. As such, Jeremiah's diatribe is couched in retributive terms. The prophet predicts that the covenant curses shall befall the nation (such as exile and military defeat) as a penalty for its moral failure and breach of covenant obligations. Just as the ancestral community disobeyed the conditions of the covenant and reaped the consequences of its conduct, so the present nation runs the same risk of suffering the consequences of covenant disloyalty. Such arrangements dispel any trace of ethical ambiguity. The lines that separate good from evil are clear and well-defined. A correlation between conduct and condition is distinctly drawn; acts have prescribed consequences; and thus, life is manageable and predictable. In a universe controlled by a just God who is a faithful covenant partner, evildoers are punished for their wrongdoing, even if they are God's people. In a universe with a meaningful ethical code, suffering is explicable and never beyond the scope of God's just governance. National crisis, disaster, and personal suffering are thus not the products of an arbitrary and chaotic world.

Clearly informed by Deuteronomic categories, Jeremiah 11:1-14 articulates a coherent and symmetrical *Weltanschauung*, which attends to the construction of a morally exacting universe. In this world, blessing and punishment are purposefully meted out according to conduct. The righteous enjoy blessing from God (cf. Deut 28:1-14), while evildoers are punished for their wrongdoing (Deut 28:15-68). In this morally unequivocal universe, Judah's devastating circumstances are not value neutral. The nation brings exile and destruction upon itself by refusing to comply with its covenant obligations. God only holds Judah accountable for its behavior.[10]

This well-proportioned and balanced view of social and symbolic reality is certainly not distinctive to Jeremiah or to the Deuteronomic literature. Scholars have long noted that a number of torah, wisdom, and creation psalms reflect a similar orientation. Psalm 1, for example, speaks of two clearly defined ways of life, each with clearly defined consequences: the way of the righteous, which is blessed, and the way of the wicked, which leads to ruin. In addition, conventional wisdom literature generally construes the world as having straightforward moral categories. Proverbs 4:18-19 says it this way: "The path of the righteous is like the light of dawn. . . . / The way of the wicked is like deep darkness." Also informed by such assumptions are Job's friends, who are absolutely certain that the sufferer has committed some moral failing. For these defenders of conventional wisdom, Job must have done something to bring on his problems or else their relatively unambiguous worldviews would crumple, which, of course, they did. These various sources, including Jeremiah 11:1-14, are for the most part crystal clear about life and its workings.

The Second Strategy for Addressing Judah's Plight: Jeremiah's Suffering and Moral Chaos

The portrayal of Jeremiah's prophetic experience, especially his suffering, calls into question and then shatters stable and congruent categories. The interpretive community of Jeremiah presents the prophet as one who is faithful to God and yet is attacked, ostracized, ridiculed, and rejected. Immediately following the covenant sermon, for instance, Jeremiah cries out to YHWH concerning his own unjust treatment at the hands of evildoers (Jer 11:18–12:6). As we have seen, he has done nothing except obey God, yet he is maligned and persecuted. He sees himself as innocent and naive, as "a gentle lamb / led to the slaughter" (11:19). As a result, he appeals to YHWH for protection and for the punishment of his persecutors. Although YHWH responds to the prophet's complaint with the assurance of eventual retribution (see, for example, 11:21-23), Jeremiah is still caught in the chaotic interim before justice materializes. And so, he accuses YHWH of wrongdoing and collusion with his enemies (12:1-2). During the interim, between the "already and not yet," Jeremiah bears witness to the disturbing reality of undeserved suffering and the apparent indifference of God. In stark contrast to his clear-cut proclamation, Jeremiah *lives* in a social environment in which the righteous are denied justice and the innocent encounter real evil. Jeremiah's first confession describes this dangerous world without offering an explanation or justification for evil. Here there is no cover-up, no denial of the randomness of suffering, and no easy answers that anesthetize people to the deeply fissured universe. Even innocent prophets, who represent a myriad of tormented people, suffer abuse, bitter opposition, and failure. Thus, Jeremiah has only questions, and these reveal his conflicted character as well as his bold courage to confront moral ambiguity without flinching.

In Jeremiah 15:15-18, another of Jeremiah's laments, the battered and tormented prophet again cries out to YHWH. Jeremiah reaffirms his dedication to his prophetic call:

> Your words were found, and I ate them
> and your words became to me a joy
> and delight of my heart;
> for I am called by your name,
> O LORD, God of hosts. (15:16; see also Ezek 3:1-3)

The prophet, who is YHWH's voice, has done all God expects of prophets (Jer 15:17-18). He has internalized the divine message (15:16), avoided "the company of merry-makers" (15:17; cf. Ps 1:1), and "[sat alone] under the weight" of YHWH's hand (Jer 15:17b). Nonetheless, he suffers excruciating pain and persecution. *For the distraught prophet, God has failed.* Thus, he likens the Lord to a "deceitful brook" (15:18), a figure that draws on the image of a desert mirage that tricks a parched wanderer into believing there is water when the wadi is dry. YHWH has sorely disappointed, and such disappointment leaves the prophet deeply wounded (15:18).

Jeremiah 20:7-18 employs perhaps the most scandalous words in the book to depict Jeremiah's address to God. In this passage the prophet accuses God of being unreliable and deceptive. With raw emotion and astonishing boldness, Jeremiah holds YHWH responsible for his abuse. In anguish and anger, he accuses God of "betraying," "enticing," "seducing," and "overpowering" him:[11]

> O Lord, you have *enticed* me
>   and I was enticed;
> you have *overpowered* me,
>   and you have prevailed.
> I have become a laughingstock all day long;
>   everyone mocks me. (20:7; emphasis added)

This language pushes the lament genre to the limits. Although other laments dare to question the reliability of YHWH, none does so in such a frontal manner. The verb "overpower" (*hzq*, the *hipʿil*) in verse 7 has a wide semantic range, which includes seizing, compelling, strengthening, taking hold of, and even raping (Deut 22:25). The Hebrew word translated as "deceive," "entice," or "seduce" (*pth*), depending on the English translation, has a more narrow range. It occurs in about twenty-five texts in the Hebrew Bible and generally means to "trick," "deceive," or "seduce."

With this language Jeremiah 20:7 conveys the idea of being duped and besieged by the power and purposes of God, forces over which Jeremiah has little control (for example, 20:9). At the outset of his prophetic ministry, YHWH had assured him that "kings . . . princes . . . priests, and the people of the land" (1:18-19; cf. 15:20) would not "prevail" (*ykl*) against him. But now it seems that all prevail against him. Priests beat and imprison him; his enemies slander and mock him (20:7c-8); and his "close friends" attack him (20:10). Even YHWH, his ally and covenant partner, has "crushed" him and "prevailed" (20:7b). All this evokes a deep sense of rage and betrayal. And Jeremiah does not hesitate to confront YHWH with his doubts and misgivings. Yet at the very same time he acknowledges YHWH's trustworthiness. The prophet affirms that YHWH is with him "like a dread warrior," and as a result his persecutors "will not prevail" but "will be greatly shamed" (20:11). He declares that YHWH has "delivered the life of the needy / from the hands of evildoers" (20:13), which harkens back to the divine promise at his commissioning (see 1:8, 19). These turbulent responses defy logic but show raw human emotion.

According to the final words of chapter 20 (vv. 14-18), Jeremiah plunges into the depths of despair as his hopelessness reaches its most critical level. Now the term *curse* (*ʾrr*) no longer applies only to disobedient Israel (11:3) or the one who "trust[s] in mere mortals" (17:5). Now Jeremiah, like Job, curses the day of his birth (20:14-17). Now we see what Gerhard von Rad calls the "lowest point in the suffering of Jeremiah."[12] "Night has now completely enveloped the prophet."[13] All hope for equilibrium is gone. Alongside the nation's descent to destruction is a prophet who is not granted immunity.

Jeremiah functions in these texts as an archetypal or representative figure. In the tradition of the righteous sufferer Job, Jeremiah assumes a larger-than-life identity whose experiences and piety transcend his own solitary experience.[14] As such, he speaks not only for himself, articulating his own disappointment and brokenness to God, but also for those living in the aftermath of Jerusalem's demise whose suffering was inexplicable. In this way, Jeremiah's obedience, his devotion to God, and his hardship take on paradigmatic force. His suffering service and surrender to God, in defeat and utter trust, become a model of faithful living.

As an exemplary righteous sufferer, Jeremiah finds himself in a place of extreme vulnerability. His social environment is harsh and dangerous, with few structures in place to protect him. He endures great hardship at the hands of adversaries; he is ridiculed and cries to Yhwh for help. The prophet seeks vengeance on his persecutors and even curses the day of his birth (20:14-18). He faces scorn, humiliation, and reproach. The opponents of the prophet threaten to kill him unless he abandons his prophetic mission (11:18-23). They conspire against him (18:18-23; cf. 11:9) and dig pits to trap him (18:22). Those who pursue Jeremiah attempt to "prevail" over him (20:7-13); they bar him from the temple precincts (36:5) and eventually arrest and imprison him (20:1-6; 37:11-16). This lack of protection and moral symmetry results in anxiety and sorrow, so much so that Jeremiah longs for death (20:14-18). Yet, like Job and the embattled psalmists, in the face of adversity and persecution Jeremiah declares his innocence, maintains his personal and prophetic integrity, and takes an active stance against oppressors and evildoers (11:20; 12:3; 15:15; 17:18; 18:21-22; 20:12).

As one who suffers in solidarity with God and those deprived of justice, Jeremiah gives voice to an alternative understanding of suffering. Suffering is not a shameful consequence of wrongdoing or evidence of divine injustice. On the contrary, suffering is a sign of faithful service to God.[15] Hence, Jeremiah becomes a symbol of hope for those whose distress is borne in obedience to God.

It is important to note that the final form of the text does not privilege the suffering of the prophet over the well-defined arrangements of his prophetic message. Instead, it holds both in abeyance. Wild, explosive, and at times cynical outbursts are located alongside texts that are absolutely sure about the workings of the universe. The portrait of a tormented prophet, which accentuates the failure of rational understandings to account for human evil, does not quash conventional arrangements of divine retribution. Voices that pulsate with internal anxiety and testify to the fractured human condition join the chorus with those that insist that the fall of Judah is a sure consequence of the people's rebellion. Such dissonance creates an engaging cacophony, which at the end of the day proclaims that Judah's wreckage is too massive for any singular explanation.

The Third Strategy for Addressing Judah's Plight: Silence and Divine Absence

Another strategy for dealing with Judah's disaster is buried in a story about the post-war era. It is a response of silence—divine silence. Without reference to Jeremiah or YHWH, the composer of the Baruch narrative (chs. 36–45) tells the story of Gedaliah's failed government (Jer 40:7–41:18). In fact, this narrative is the only one in the book where neither the prophet nor YHWH is present. Until recently, historical categories have governed most explanations of the lacuna. Jeremiah is absent, it is often argued, because he wasn't there. That is to say, the text merely reflects the authorial conviction that Jeremiah does not play a prominent part in the Gedaliah administration, even though an earlier account places him in the custodianship of the governor (40:1-6). In his Old Testament Library commentary, Robert Carroll takes a somewhat different slant, although informed by similar assumptions. Carroll suggests: "The story of Gedaliah's assassination and the break-up of the community is told without reference to Jeremiah *because the editor had it in this form*" (emphasis added).[16] That the material was handed down in this way may be well and good, but it says little about the artistic and theological significance of the missing God and prophet. It may be that the missing God and prophet have less to do with objective presentation than with literary representation, less with history than theology. As such, their absence functions as a meaningful part of the narrative. The missing voice, the silence of God, speaks with eloquence about gratuitous suffering.

In order to determine how this *silence* functions, we turn to the story itself. The central character of Jeremiah 40:7–41:18 is introduced in the preceding text where he is appointed governor of the postwar Judah. Gedaliah, son of Ahikam, is the one on whom the people of Judah come to depend for continued land occupation. The news of his leadership reaches those who have been in hiding since Babylon's victory, and soon Judeans return home and rally around him (40:7-12). The first to arrive at Mizpah, the provincial capital, are "freedom fighters" who had fought against Babylon's incursion and subsequently retreated to the Judean hills. Gedaliah demands loyalty of the commanders for the assurance of welfare and amnesty. They must only stay in the land and submit to the current government and "it shall go well" with them. Like Joseph's kind treatment of his brothers (Gen 50:19-21), Gedaliah encourages the Judean nationalists and provides for their needs. This is no time for reprisals. There has already been enough suffering for a lifetime. Now is the time for rebuilding and restoration, for breaking the vicious cycle of violence. Soon refugees from the Transjordan and elsewhere join the commanders and their units. All are united in the land under the care of Gedaliah. And the governor responds to their needs by inviting them to partake in a bountiful harvest of wine and summer fruits. This portrait of abundance has an idyllic quality (Jer 40:12).

But there is trouble in the air. Johanan and other leading military figures approach Gedaliah with news of a plot on his life (40:13–41:3). According to the report, the king of the Ammonites is behind the conspiracy, and Ishmael, one of their compatriots, is about to execute the plan. The syntax of the interrogative, "Are you at all aware?" (*hyd td*) suggests that the governor should know about the conspiracy (40:14). This is a time of intense political power struggles. There are enemies near and far. Gedaliah must surely be privy to such dangers. Nonetheless, he dismisses the warning as being unfounded. Even after a clandestine meeting in which Johanan volunteers to take matters into his own hands, Gedaliah refuses to act. "You are telling a lie (*šqr*) about Ishmael" (40:16). Gedaliah will have no part in a preemptive strike, and so he forbids Johanan from slaying Ishmael.[17] Before long it becomes apparent that Johanan's concerns are well-founded. Gedaliah's refusal to listen will cost him his life and the remnant of Judah their hopes for a future in the land.

The report of the assassination of Gedaliah is succinct (41:1-3). The narrator relates the actions without dialogue or embellishment. Ishmael, the subject of the previous conversation, shows up at Mizpah with ten men. The reference to his royal ancestry (41:1; cf. 36:12, 20, 21) and Gedaliah's Babylonian loyalties (41:2) suggests that the meeting is laden with political and ideological anxiety. Perhaps Ishmael harbors aspirations for the throne. If so, Gedaliah, a "Babylonian pawn," is the only thing that stands in his way. Even with these signs of trouble and Johanan's previous warning, the parties sit down together. The meal they share represents a gracious act of hospitality. Hospitality, says Henri Nouwen, overcomes hostility and bears the seeds of community.[18] However, not in this case. Under the guise of covenant friendship and the banner of patriotism, Ishmael and his cohorts betray their unsuspecting host. During the meal, they rise up and "with the sword" strike down Gedaliah. To complete their coup, Ishmael murders all the Judeans who are with the governor as well as the Babylonian soldiers stationed at the garrison.

The massacre does not end with the death of Gedaliah and his cadre (41:4-10). Ishmael eyes eighty pilgrims from the northern cities of Shechem, Shiloh, and Samaria en route to Jerusalem. With beards shaved, clothes torn, and bodies gashed as a sign of mourning, presumably over the tragic events of 587, they bear gifts to present to God at the temple. (Apparently, the narrator assumes that some form of worship continued at the temple site after the fall of the city.) Ishmael intercepts the pilgrims, feigns solidarity, persuades them to meet Gedaliah, and then carries on his killing rampage in the middle of the city. He spares only ten men because they had "stores of wheat, barley, oil, and honey hidden in the fields" (41:8). After throwing the corpses into a cistern King Asa built, desecrating a holy spot, Ishmael takes off with hostages in hand.

Johanan and his brigade hear of the bloodbath and set out in pursuit. They eventually overtake Ishmael near the great waters in Gibeon, six miles northwest of Jerusalem (41:11-18). The pool of Gibeon had been the site of an earlier civil war between Israel and Judah (2 Sam 2:12-17). Now, some four hundred years later, it is the field of Ishmael's last stand. But Ishmael does not even engage in battle. Beset by Johanan's forces, he and his men abandon their hostages and escape to Ammon (Jer 41:15). At that point, Johanan gathers the captives and sets out toward Egypt. He resolves to go there because he is afraid of Babylonian reprisals. Before leading the remnant south, Johanan stops at a village near Bethlehem, where Jeremiah reenters the picture (42:1-6).

Jeremiah 40:7–41:18 is probably the most grisly section in the book. It is saturated with violence, brutality, and duplicity. The death of Gedaliah and his company as well as the mass murder of the seventy pilgrims flood the streets of Mizpah with innocent blood. All are victims of cunning and cruelty. Whether fueled by patriotic zeal or sheer madness, the murderous acts are indefensible. One can hardly read of the carnage without shock (see Judg 20–21 for an earlier text set at Mizpah that is equally savage). To make matters worse, the killers go unpunished. They flee unharmed to the Ammonites. Clearly, the text presents to us a historicized world in total disarray (cf. Jer 4:23-27 for a poetic counterpart). As the story of the Judean remnant winds down, communal life falls into a downward moral and religious spiral that reaches its lowest point. The social order is broken down, all forms of civility disappear, evildoers run rampant, and innocent people are butchered. And, perhaps most perplexing, YHWH and Jeremiah are absent! Where is the prophet whom Nebuzaradan had entrusted into Gedaliah's care? And more important, where is YHWH?

Initially, Gedaliah's policies, like those of King Josiah, may have rendered Jeremiah's prophetic speech unnecessary.[19] The text portrays Gedaliah as a hero, a benevolent leader, who accomplishes what the last kings of Judah could not. This Babylonian appointee cares for the vulnerable in the land, "men, women, and children, those of the poorest of the land" (40:7). He attracts Judean survivors "from all the places to which they had been scattered" (40:12). And when the refugees return, he calms their fears, provides for their needs, and serves as their advocate before the Babylonians. Gedaliah wins the hearts of the survivors and creates a sense of optimism for the future of the community in Judah. Here is one who at last complies with Jeremiah's instructions, submits to Babylonian rule, and whose speech to the gathering of the remnant echoes Jeremiah's oracles and program for sustained life in the land.

But then all goes awry. And it is at this critical point, when the postwar community falters and its social world collapses, that the silence of God is most troubling. Why does the narrator exclude YHWH and YHWH's prophet from Judah's darkest hours? Put differently, how does "divine silence" function in the narrative and serve as a response to Judah's wreckage? Although the story provides no direct explanation or commentary, it nonetheless resonates with interpretive possibilities. Only three will be noted below.

First, the absence of the book's two major characters may imply that neither YHWH nor Jeremiah had anything to do with the coup of the nationalists. In particular, YHWH does not figure in the bloodbath of Ishmael, nor belong there! *YHWH has no part in the treachery, betrayal, or brutal fanaticism of the Judean nationalists.* The militants may think YHWH does; they may even act in YHWH's name. But YHWH does not show up and certainly does not sanction the brutality, whether in the guise of patriotism or religion. Thus, there is no divine voice or presence, no divine intrusion or prophetic witness. In a bold and daring literary move, the narrator distances YHWH and Jeremiah from the politics of violence. They are missing because they are not involved in the savage acts.

Admittedly, the book is replete with the rhetoric of violence, indeed with theopolitical violence. It pulsates with the conviction that YHWH is "plucking up and pulling down, destroying and overthrowing" Judah and its capital city. Jeremiah asserts that Babylon is the *divine* instrument charged with executing the dangerous dismantling. And yet, when the armies *actually* pounce on Judah, as described in Jeremiah 39:1-14 and 52:3b-30, the narrators become far more reticent to use God language. Rather than seizing the moment to corroborate the prophetic message (see Deut 18:21-22; cf. Jer 28:17), the tellers merely present a nonintrusive account of the events, without theological commentary or evaluation. As in the Gedaliah fiasco, the description of the fall of Jerusalem is told without explicit reference to God. Consequently, YHWH is neither implicated nor exonerated. YHWH is just missing.

Second, *the absent God (and prophet) helps refute the theodicy argument in the book.* The events surrounding the death of Gedaliah are not only tragic but are also theologically embarrassing. The unimaginable evil flies in the face of principal tenets of the book: that life makes moral sense; that acts have consequences; that the universe is a morally coherent place. As we have seen, these claims are used to make the destruction of Judah rationally manageable. Judah's recalcitrance, as demonstrated in its utter rejection of the word and person of Jeremiah, gives rise to its present predicament. In traditional terms, Judah's woes are divine punishment for sin. Gedaliah's death and God's absence, however, challenge these fundamental assumptions. Again, here is one who obeys YHWH's word and yet dies without cause. Despite being a custodian of Jeremiah and being a part of a pious family—his grandfather Shaphan and father Ahikam both played prominent roles in King Josiah's reform (2 Kgs 22:3-14) and his father was instrumental in saving Jeremiah's life (Jer 26:24)—Gedaliah is slaughtered. His death makes no sense.[20] It contradicts moral logic and exposes holes in the conventional understandings of suffering.

Yet, by facing the ethical chaos head-on, the narrative shows remarkable courage. By refusing to clean up the mess with oracular speech, the story honors moral ambiguity. It courageously rejects easy answers and clear-cut systems. Slain Gedaliah and the massacred worshipers, alongside a hostage prophet, subvert congruent and symmetrical views of suffering. The countertheodicy concedes—perhaps even asserts—that the righteous *do* suffer, that God *is* sometimes silent, and that the world *is* indeed a dangerous place. In a haunting manner, this text mirrors the world in which we live—a world that seems at times to be morally irrational and expressly evil. Gedaliah's death, Ishmael's coup, the slaughter of the innocent, the escape of the murderer, and the silence of God all shatter illusions of moral certitude.

Last, *the silence of God is necessary from a literary and human perspective.* It "speaks" on behalf of the innocent. It allows the voices of the brutalized to be heard. It preserves their story and their memories. Any prophetic utterance would risk trivializing the losses. Divine silence is therefore absolutely essential.[21] In Chaim Potok's *The Chosen*, Reb Sauders says it this way: "You can hear the pain of the world in silence." Kathleen O'Connor recently explored the "missing voice" in Lamentations and concluded that

> Lamentations' haunting power lies in its brutal honesty about the Missing Voice; its brilliance is that it does not speak for God. . . . It prevents us from sliding prematurely over suffering toward happy endings. It gives the book daring power because it honors human speech. God's absence forces us to attend to voices of grief and despair, and it can reflect . . . our own experiences of a silent God. . . . If God spoke, God's words would diminish the voices of pain, wash over them, and crowd them out. Even one word from God would take up too much space in the book.[22]

Similarly, Jeremiah 40:7–41:18 allows the testimony of a slain leader and murdered worshipers to linger and the cruelty of the killers to haunt us. It refuses to clean up the "mess." The cries of the innocent must be heard and embraced before life can go on. No wonder Elie Wiesel remained silent for so many years after the years of darkness at Auschwitz. Words, although essential for testimony, would only diminish the unspeakable horror of the camps. And no wonder Christians see the silence of God in the death of Jesus Christ (see, for example, Matt 27:45-46). Perhaps Christians would do well to linger there, that dreadful Friday and long Saturday, before moving on to Sunday's daybreak.

Conclusion

The three theological responses explored in this chapter cannot by themselves account for the collapse of Judah's world. The wreckage is too massive, complex, and unmanageable. The losses and resultant despair are beyond ordinary patterns of speech. Instead, the three voices expose the inadequacy of monolithic assertions and assured assumptions. They also contribute to the book's cacophony of claims and counterclaims, testimonies and opposing testimonies, arrangements and dissymmetrical arrangements. Since the groundbreaking work of Bernhard Duhm and Sigmund Mowinckel,[23] Jeremiah research has spent enormous energy attempting to tame this complex and chaotic character. To make Jeremiah more "intelligible," countless articles and monographs have privileged one genre, tradition, or source in the book over all others.[24] Such efforts have had mixed results. While they have failed to domesticate Jeremiah's chaos—the book is just too unwieldy to control—they have, unfortunately, been more successful in dismissing marginal voices.[25] Walter Brueggemann has recently proposed an alternative approach to the textual dissonance. Instead of disparaging the chaos, he suggests that we read it as "a meditation upon the abyss, into it and out of it."[26] As such, Jeremiah's ruptured and chaotic literary shape "makes sense" as a window into Judah's profound loss "for which we have no ready categories."[27] If Brueggemann is correct, the book's many undulations, including the three voices examined above, present to us another sign of Judah's unbearable pain.

CHAPTER SIX

CONFLICTING PATHS TO HOPE IN JEREMIAH

We have seen that Jeremiah is a book for our time. Its haunting language of death and destruction resonates with many today, as do Jeremiah's penetrating portrayals of a crumbling world. It seems as though only yesterday such horror was an oddity, another's script but not our own. Only yesterday Jeremiah's dangerous terrain would have seemed altogether alien. Our place in the world was safe and symmetrical, our lives well insulated and predictable, with only a few glitches along the way.

But all that has changed. As of this writing, we are still engaged in a war that tens of millions consider deeply troubling and potentially catastrophic. Our country's foreign policy (especially during the years of 2000–2008) has cast a dark cloud over international law and American credibility. Moreover, we are facing global economic challenges that endanger the survival of countless people. Like no other time in recent history, hard-wrought social programs, especially for the most vulnerable among us, are in grave danger. After careful scrutiny, trusted institutions—political, religious, judicial, and economic—are now more than suspect. Dwindling funds for basic human services and a burgeoning national debt, caused partially by massive military spending, put at great risk generations to come. It seems as though the entire global arena is coming unglued and our nation is in part a protagonist in the undoing.

And so, we are left to ponder the grotesque and unspeakable: waves of darkness and smoke; searing images of "indestructible" buildings dissolving; ferociously "precise" weapons ravaging innocent civilians; military occupation breeding violence and hatred; anarchy leading to riots, abduction, and rape; as well as mounting numbers of hungry, war-torn refugees. The litany of suffering does not seem to end. In stark contrast to Isaiah's vision of peace, we live in a world where plowshares are beaten into

---

A revised form of this chapter was first presented at the 2003 Colloquium, "Shaking Heaven and Earth: Bible, Church, and the Changing Global Order," at Columbia Theological Seminary. It was later published in *Shaking Heaven and Earth: Essays in Honor of Walter Brueggemann and Charles B. Cousar* (ed. C. Roy Yoder et al.; Louisville: Westminster John Knox, 2005), 43–57.

swords and pruning hooks into spears, where nations lift up sword against nation and war is the "mother tongue" (see Isa 2:4). What a collage of horror! Who would have ever thought that crippling fear, cynicism, and loss of confidence would be part of our individual and national narrative?

Jeremiah as a Map of Hope for Shipwrecked Exiles

In this chapter, we argue that the book of Jeremiah is a map of hope for people living on the brink of despair—for exiles in Babylon and exiles today. First of all, the text dares to speak of an experience too painful for most to utter. With candor it testifies to the end of long-standing institutions associated with God's blessings, cherished belief systems, and social structures that for centuries appeared invincible. Initially this brutal honesty may seem to have nothing whatsoever to do with newness; but truth-telling, as we all well know, is the first step to healing and restoration.[1] Beyond this, the interpretive community of Jeremiah organizes the moral and symbolic chaos into shapes that are orderly and rationally manageable. The structure of the book, as we have seen, bears witness to a God who "plucks up and pulls down" in chapters 1–25 *and* who "builds and plants" in chapters 26–52. Accordingly, Jeremiah moves beyond brute geopolitical forces—forces that spell death—to a God whose purposes are ultimately redemptive and salvific. In the end, Jeremiah offers a path to hope that is diametrically at odds with the establishment position. Unlike the prophet Hananiah and others who would insist that the devastating events are merely bumps in the road, Jeremiah asserts that they represent true turning points. That is, the hope that Jeremiah holds is not for a return to the old world but for a new beginning and a new community defined by justice, obedience, and inclusion. This fresh formulation, by the way, in part gave birth to Judaism. And this hope, we believe, is instructive to us in our troubled world.

By and large the book of Jeremiah has not been associated with hope (even though chapters 30–31 are clearly devoted to the topic).[2] When one is cataloging the central themes of Jeremiah, hope is usually last to be mentioned, if at all. Most read Jeremiah as a prophet of doom and gloom. Only rarely, it is maintained, does the "weeping prophet" speak words of hope (for example, the Book of Comfort, chs. 30–33), and when he does, his utterances are obscured by a larger literary context of sin and judgment. Whereas there is little doubt that the book of Jeremiah resounds with such language, it nonetheless also articulates a script for new life and hope beyond disaster. In fact, Brevard Childs finds the key to the canonical shaping of Jeremiah in its "salvation oracles."[3] According to him, "Regardless of the severity of the divine judgment on Israel, the ultimate goal in the divine economy was redemption."[4] Ronald

Clements and Walter Brueggemann have organized their commentaries around the dual role of divine judgment and salvation. Clements goes so far as to suggest that the central message of Jeremiah is that of hope.[5] The subtitle of Brueggemann's commentary, *Exile and Homecoming*, highlights his conviction that the book moves beyond dislocation and disaster to return and restoration.[6] Developing this thought, Brueggemann has recently made the case that the final form of Jeremiah is designed "to walk Jews into, through, and beyond the reality of destruction and exile."[7] Kathleen M. O'Connor has likewise proposed that disaster and survival are the "chief subjects" of the book of Jeremiah.[8] The point of the prophetic text, O'Connor suggests, is to create a world in which survivors can name the disaster, interpret it, and find hope through the persona of Jeremiah, a "survivor of disaster."[9] Following suit, Louis Stulman has argued that the literary architecture of Jeremiah itself, governed by the prose tradition, leads the reader on a path to hope.[10] After the first scroll (Jer 1–25) dismantles the foundations of Judah's social and theological "first principles," the second scroll (Jer 26–52) begins to develop strategies designed to enable refugees to cope with and even thrive in their new setting in Babylon. Thus, the symbolic logic of the book paves the way for profound configurations of hope and new life. Before examining these arrangements, we will again consider the brutal honesty that makes them possible.

Organizing the Chaos into Manageable Shapes

The book of Jeremiah speaks of a world under massive assault and of a people whose lives are riddled with pain. With disturbing images and raw emotion, it bears witness to a tragedy so terrible that it defies ordinary categories. For the Judean nation, the fall of Jerusalem and exile to Babylon represented nothing less than the shaking of heaven and earth. Perhaps the most poignant words to describe this cosmic shaking appear in Jeremiah 4:23-26. The NRSV captures the text's cadence of terror:

> I looked on the earth, and lo, it was waste and void;
> and to the heavens, and they had no light.
> I looked on the mountains, and lo, they were quaking,
> and all the hills moved to and fro.
> I looked, and lo, there was no one at all,
> and all the birds of the air had fled.
> I looked, and lo, the fruitful land was a desert,
> and all its cities were laid in ruins
> before the LORD, before his fierce anger.

Jeremiah envisions the horrors of war. Make no mistake: enemy invasion and occupation are what the text alludes to in haunting, symbolic language. The order of creation collapses and reverts to its primeval state of chaos, "wild and waste" (cf. Gen 1:2); the heavens become dark, mountains and hills tremble, birds take flight, and fertile land turns into uninhabited desert. The earth loses its form and beauty as all is reduced to desolation and hopelessness. Ironically, this vision of chaos is meticulously structured. The parallel construction: "I looked . . . I looked . . . I looked . . . I looked" is followed in each case by the Hebrew predicator of existence (*hinnēh*), "there was . . . there was . . . there was . . . there was," although no life signs can be found. The symmetry and repetition of the prophetic words only heighten the dread.

This text of terror is one of a myriad that speak of unbearable suffering and loss of meaning. We also encounter in Jeremiah a surplus of disturbing metaphors: death sneaking through the windows to do its insidious work (9:21), Daughter Zion being attacked and raped (13:20-27), and a dangerous (mythological) foe from the north poised to pounce on the inhabitants of Judah (for example, 1:14; 6:22). We read of ferocious lions (2:15; 4:7) and venomous snakes (8:17), as well as devouring swords, ravenous wild dogs, and vultures consuming their prey (15:3). As a result, "hands fall helpless" (6:24); sackcloth is donned (4:8; 6:26); and the bereaved of Judah outnumber the sand of the seas (15:8), which is an inversion of the ancestral promise of progeny (Gen 22:17; 32:12). At the sight of ground zero, the tears of God, Jeremiah, and Judah inundate the world:

> O that my head were a spring of water,
>   and my eyes a fountain of tears,
> so that I might weep day and night
>   for the slain of my poor people! (Jer 9:1)

How could profound sadness not accompany the end of life as it was known?

As we have said, the first twenty-five chapters of Jeremiah broadcast the collapse of Judah's once stable world.[11] Organized around prose sermons in chapters 7, 11, 18, 21, and 25, these texts reenact the demise of the nation's sturdiest pillars, its sacred canopy: (1) *the great temple of Solomon and its systems of worship*, Jeremiah contends, will end up like Shiloh—nothing but rubble (7:1-15); (2) the *beloved covenant* between God and Israel testifies to the guilt of God's people rather than to their special place (11:1-17); (3) the *election tradition*, once a source of great confidence, is now in the service of outsiders who enjoy the seat of honor (18:1-11); (4) strangers occupy *the land* Israel once inhabited, and Israel in turn must live far from its home as a disenfranchised people in Babylon (21:1-10); and (5) *the dynasty*, the venerated Davidic dynasty, comes to an abrupt and screeching halt—at least as traditionally conceived

(21:1-10). With Zedekiah's violent death and Jehoiachin's deportation, the kingdom and its long line of kings dies out. God has indeed "plucked up and pulled down, destroyed and overthrown." To drive home this point, by the end of the "first scroll" Jeremiah envisages the people of Judah leading the wayward nations in drinking the cup of divine wrath (25:17-29). And so, the first half of the book portrays the prophet Jeremiah frustrating every argument that God is inextricably tied to Judah's conventional religious and social systems, especially those associated with the temple and the state. Hence, nothing remains to prop up its toppling world.

The prophetic drama holds nothing back. It confronts Judah's national catastrophe without flinching. The Jeremiah tradition courageously tells the truth about the gravity of the moment; it rejects denial and it even claims that in some measure the people of God, especially their leaders, are coconspirators in the collapse. Judah's unfaithfulness to God and mistreatment of the poor in tandem with its royal policies of brutality and unbridled greed have brought down the walls of the city. In all this, Jeremiah, God's messenger, merely does what prophets do best: he sees through facades, shatters illusions, and grasps that such crimes are no mere misdemeanors but catastrophes that threaten the survival of the world.[12]

Not everyone buys this critique. In fact, few do. The Jerusalem establishment contends that Jeremiah is uncompromising and incendiary. It treats Jeremiah as a traitor who must be exiled or executed. His townsmen seek to silence his "eschatological" reading of the moment:

> Let us destroy the tree with its fruit,
>> let us cut him off from the land of the living,
> so that his name will no longer be remembered! (11:19)

Still others write him off as "a madman" to be put "in the stocks and the collar" (29:26). Hardly anyone even entertains the possibility that Jeremiah might be speaking the word of the Lord. His detractors are sure that he is misguided when he nails the coffin shut on Judah's accepted modes of living and construals of reality (for example, 18:18). God would never "uproot and tear down" the nation's public policies and social arrangements! Cosmic upheaval, the shaking of earth and heaven, is simply out of the question. Only time would tell how wrong they were.

Hope through the Wreckage

Does Jeremiah's scathing critique of the old world close the door on the future? Does the text leave any room for hope after the wreckage? The second scroll, chapters 26–52, asserts that Israel's final chapter has not yet been inscribed. Although God "plucks up and pulls down," God also "builds and plants." Amid the destruction, seeds of hope spring forth: God sculpts new beginnings out of the rubble of fallen worlds.

The second half of the prophetic drama asserts that the end has not come for the people of God. For the first time, for instance, individuals emerge who are receptive to the message of Jeremiah. These faithful few come to Jeremiah's aid when his life is on the line in the temple (26:16-19) and the royal court (36:9-19, 26), when he is thrown into a cistern (38:7-13), and during the Babylonian siege of Jerusalem (39:11-18; 40:1-6). In each case, supporters not only rescue Jeremiah from harm's way; they also protect the nation from "bringing innocent blood upon [itself]" (for example, 26:15). Jeremiah's battle with prophets (Jer 27–29), moreover, is essentially waged over the question of which configuration of hope is "true." Whether the nation will survive is not the issue. What is at stake is the developing character of the embattled nation. The most stunning display of hope is found in the Book of Comfort (Jer 30–33). Here God reverses the judgments against Judah and outlines in their place a resilient script for the future. Even the Baruch narrative, which recounts the suffering of Jeremiah and the fall of Jerusalem, makes the case that hope for the future lies with the exiles in Babylon and not with those remaining in the land.[13] That is to say, while the text is describing the end of one world, it is at the same time creating symbolic space for the emergence of another, albeit in a faraway land.

Finally, the three endings of Jeremiah, chapters 45, 46–51, and 52—each representing different points in the development of the book—speak of better times for the suffering people of God. The first is an oracle response to Baruch in which God promises Jeremiah's scribe his "life as a prize of war" (45:5). The Oracles against the Nations (OAN; Jer 46–51), another ending of the Hebrew text of the book, punctuate the book with implicit hope for exiled Judah. Specifically, the announcement of Babylon's defeat signals an epoch of hope and salvation for Judah (Jer 50–51). And the concluding report winds up with the kind treatment of King Jehoiachin in Babylon (52:31-34), apparently whispering that the future of Judah has not come to an irrevocable end.

Despite the fact that Jeremiah's path to hope is neither unified nor systematic (cf. Ezek 40–48), we are still able to discern its broad features. From the literary arrangement of the second scroll and from the text's recurring motifs, the following shapes emerge: **First, hope is rooted in suffering.**

> The people who survived the sword
> found grace in the wilderness. . . .
> With weeping they shall come,
> and with consolations I will lead them back. . . .
> I will turn their mourning into joy,
> I will comfort them, and give them gladness for sorrow. (Jer 31:2, 9a, 13cd)

Please note in these passages that sadness permeates nearly every moment of joy. Indeed, the Book of Comfort (Jer 30–33) unites expressions of hope with suffering and marginality.[14] The first chapter of the Book of Comfort is a case in point. Its oracles of consolation are far from idyllic (for example, 30:5-17). There is no utopian vision of the future, no garden scene, no ideal notion of peace and happiness. Instead, one encounters an assortment of disturbing images of war and invasion juxtaposed with language of embryonic hope:

> Alas! that day is so great
> there is none like it;
> it is a time of distress for Jacob;
> yet he shall be rescued from it. (30:7)

Battle cries, expressions of panic, and excruciating pain pepper the literary landscape. The condition of God's people is deplorable; the prognosis is bleak (30:12-16). Their wound is "grievous," and there is no one to mediate and nowhere to turn for help. All their lovers, or political allies, have forsaken them. Yet, unexpectedly and in a sheer act of grace, God resolves to restore and heal outcast Zion (30:17-22). God promises to redeem Israel from many troubles; but this redemption throbs with pain.

Hope is possible when the community embraces the painful realities of exile. In contrast to prophets who would deny these tragic dimensions and predict a speedy return to business as usual, Jeremiah affirms that there can be no ecstasy without mourning, no homecoming without exile, no salvation without judgment, and no joyous songs without the memories of loss. Any vision of the future that avoids the real world of human suffering makes a travesty of the past and can never deal with the emotional and symbolic pain of exile. It is therefore no accident that the Book of Comfort depicts the people of God as "survivors." They have endured war, amputated hopes, splintered families, and the travail of a shattered world. Now, by the force of the prophetic word, God empowers shipwrecked people to imagine a future when none seemed possible. This is the starting point for hope and recovery.

Second, hope involves letting go of the old world. Jeremiah maintains that the people of God cannot return to the securities of the past. The old social world and its conventional scripts are forever gone. All that remain are ghosts. There is a powerful temptation during times of uncertainty to cling to the familiar and glamorize the ghosts of the past, no matter how destructive they may have been (see, for example, the stories of the wilderness wanderings in Exod 16:1-3; Num 11:1-9). Jeremiah urges the Jewish refugees in Babylon to recognize this temptation for what it is and abandon all expectations of returning to the old world—especially a world defined by a dynasty and a temple. When they relinquish the illusions of the past and its modes of power and orientation, and when they surrender their old identity and accept their marginal status in Babylon, then despair loses its grip and hope is born.[15] Only then are they open to the new things that God has waiting for them. "There is hope for your future. . . . / For the LORD has created a new thing on the earth" (Jer 31:17a, 22c).

In his wonderful book *With Open Hands*, Henri Nouwen describes prayer as letting go and surrendering to God.[16] Nouwen tells a disturbing story of an old woman brought to a psychiatric center clenching her fist and swinging at everything in sight in fear that the doctors might take a penny from her. "It was as though she would lose her very self along with the coin." With this image Nouwen speaks of prayer as opening one's hand and heart to God. To let go of one's "small coins" is to discover the many gifts that God has in store. Indeed, with open hands one discovers God. Nouwen's story illustrates how frightening it is to let go of the "treasures" we cling to. But relinquishment is even more terrifying when the prevailing voices of the time insist that one hold on for dear life.

Jeremiah's prophetic opponent Hananiah represents one of those voices (28:1–17). According to Hananiah, there was little need to let go of the old world, for Judah's crisis was only temporary and in the long run inconsequential. After a few difficult years, life would return to normal. The nation's social structures and embroiled networks of meaning would withstand the upheaval and remain intact. "Be patient, give it some time, and the market will rebound!" With ringing authority Hananiah even gave dates and places. "Within two years [the LORD] will bring back to this place all the vessels of the LORD's house. . . . [The LORD] will also bring back to this place King Jeconiah . . . and all the exiles from Judah who went to Babylon" (28:3–4).

To Jeremiah, his opponent's appeal to traditional categories of continuity, even though grounded in Isaiah's prophecies, was not only dangerous and deceptive but also a demonstration of profound denial. Indeed, Hananiah embodies denial in the narrative account. He rejects the fissured dimension of Judah's experience in favor of unfounded hope. Anesthetized by wishful thinking, he would forget the personal and national traumas and live as if they did not really happen. Hananiah would create a pleasant, comfortable world that conformed to his own daydreams. And we, of course, do the same.[17] Yet fabricating a fictive world, no matter how appealing, cannot bring about healing and newness. Hope involves telling the truth and letting go of the old so that God's newness can break through.

Third, hope exists on the margins. This claim probably caused the most stir and incited the most opposition. And for obvious reasons! We almost instinctively link hope with power and success, with being at the hub of our little universe. It is difficult to imagine otherwise. The rush of adrenalin and the sense of euphoria that accompanies winning bear this out. For Jeremiah, however, hope is not found in triumphant nationalism, hegemony, or the customary military pomp and circumstance—that is, *in the garb of winners.* Hope emerges among the vulnerable and wounded.[18] The first readers of Jeremiah knew this all too well. Those who survived the fall of Jerusalem were no longer privileged in the old ways; they no longer enjoyed the insulation of a safe and reliable world, and they could no longer look to reassuring modes of orientation as a sign of God's blessing.

One can also look to the persona of Jeremiah, the righteous prophet and model of the new community, and his loyal scribe Baruch to see that faithful living is not always rewarded in the traditional ways. There were no trophies for "best prophet" or "best scribe." Instead of receiving the conventional affirmations for obedience, Jeremiah suffers for God's sake. In the confessions, moreover, God repeatedly rejects the prophet's petitions for equilibrium. Likewise, Baruch will not receive the assurances he so desperately desires: "And you [Baruch], do you seek great things for yourself? Do not seek them; for I am going to bring disaster upon all flesh, says the LORD; *but I will give you your life as a prize of war* in every place to which you may go" (45:5; emphasis added). Perhaps God blesses the faithful with "great things" in the best of times. But during the shaking of earth and heaven God promises only that the faithful will survive. And yet survival is no sign of God's rejection or God's impotence. Living on the margins does not mean that God has forsaken suffering people or reneged on past promises. In the midst of all the devastation, God is present and God's purposes prevail. Only now it becomes altogether clear that God's place in the world is among the broken and dispossessed. The importance of this overture of hope cannot be overstated: by unmasking the illusion of power and by subverting conventional modes of orientation, the mystery of incarnation—and perhaps even that of the cross—is broached.

Fourth, hope involves community building.[19] While the new world of exile pulsates with anxiety and vexation, it also presents unique opportunities. Jeremiah encourages the exiles in Babylon to seize the moment to create genuine community. "Build houses and live in them; plant gardens and eat what they produce. . . . Multiply there, and do not decrease. . . . For surely I know the plans I have for you, says the LORD, plans for your [*shalom*] and not for harm, to give you a future with hope" (29:5, 6d, 11). During their time of displacement the people of God might be tempted to sit back and do nothing or hastily follow the guidance of those who promise an imminent return to Jerusalem. So Jeremiah presses the exiles to unpack their bags, put down roots, affirm the bonds of family, and work toward peace and community building in their own neighborhoods—that is, in their own local settings in Babylon. "Seek the [*shalom*] of the city where I have sent you into exile, and pray to the LORD on its behalf, for in its [*shalom*] you will find your [*shalom*]" (29:7). Such instruction would surely not have been welcome. To pray for the welfare of their enemies, to set up homes in Babylon, and to forgo—at least for a long time—their aspirations to return to Jerusalem was anything but good news. Nonetheless, Jeremiah insists that the key to survival and hope is to join God in creating a just and compassionate counterculture, a place of new shapes and social alternatives where violence, exploitation, and idolatry do not reign.

The second scroll in no way delineates the precise character of this "new yet old" community, but it does consider its rough contours. The Book of Comfort, for example, speaks of the exilic community as a place of joy, love, and embrace of the other (31:7-14). It imagines an alternative society in which individuals are accepted regardless of where they have been or what they have done. This war-torn community pays little attention to social position, thus leveling the playing field. Indeed, Jeremiah advocates the notion of community as inclusive and unified. Israel's homecoming is to comprise the northern and southern kingdoms. "At that time, says the LORD, I will be the God of all the families of Israel, and they shall be my people" (31:1). All God's people are invited to the banquet, but above all the most vulnerable and needy among the Jewish refugees (31:7-9). Furthermore, the knowledge of God is available to everyone, often without priestly mediation (31:34); and God showers all who return with blessing (for example, 30:18-19; 31:1-6; 32:36-41). Hierarchical arrangements of community life, while not abandoned, are diminished. For instance, the newly imagined leader does not wield interminable military authority or rule with an iron fist. The promised descendant of David is a just and righteous upholder of the social and judicial order, without the traditional military trappings. He is a royal savior committed to preserving justice and *shalom* (see 30:9, 21; cf. 33:14-26).

Fifth, hope emerges in the form of a new spirituality. The spirituality of the new world enjoys a deeply "personal" texture.[20] Although the book of Jeremiah does not promote a piety that divorces the individual from the group—an idea that is clearly modern—it does envisage a community in which individuals enjoy a close relationship with God, where people's lives and personal affairs matter to God. The "new" relation, described in one place as a "new covenant" (31:31-34) and in another place as an "everlasting covenant" (32:36-44), carries with it the assurance of full acceptance before God (31:34; 33:6-8), divine favor and protection (30:10-11; 32:36-44; 33:1-9), deliverance from captivity (30:10-11, 18-21; 31:7-14, 23-25), joy (30:18-19; 31:3-6), and inner renewal (31:33; 32:39-40).

Unlike the old piety, which stressed human responsibility, this new spirituality depends far more on the extraordinary workings of God. The "if" of the divine-human relation takes a backseat to the sovereign and gracious workings of God.[21] Such a shift is absolutely necessary for people whose treasured theologies, rituals, nationalism, and ready assumptions have all failed. To address these failures, God, in a grand display of mercy, pledges to mend the broken relationship. In a bold and unprecedented move, God promises to inscribe the Torah on the hearts of the women and men who make up Israel (31:31-34). This internalization of divine instruction, this interiorization of religion, empowers victims of exile to love and obey God; and it enables them to break out of a vicious cycle of guilt and failure. The cornerstone of the new spirituality is divine forgiveness. To be sure, the new divine-human relationship hinges on God's resolve to "forgive their iniquity, and remember their sin no more" (31:34). Refugees laden with guilt are granted clemency. Only then can the dispirited find the emotional energy to face the challenges that await them in the new world order.

Sixth, hope is textual. The formation of hope in Jeremiah is integrally related to a scroll—that is, to the written word of God. The prophetic scroll that authorized the undoing of the nation (25:13) now endorses the future of the surviving community of exiles (Jer 26–52). In the second half of the book, written prophecy takes on a life of its own, often independent of the spoken words of Jeremiah. The transition from the spoken word to the written word emerges at critical junctures of the book. At the start of the second scroll, officials come to Jeremiah's defense by citing an oracle of Micah, presumably a written oracle (26:16-19). And their appeal to written prophecy, along with historical precedence, saves the day. At the end of the book, Jeremiah writes on a scroll "the disasters that would come on Babylon" (51:59-64). This symbolic action bears seeds of hope for captive peoples in Babylon—seeds that would eventuate in their liberation.

In the intervening chapters, Jeremiah sends letters to the exiles in Babylon with the intention of dispelling despair and engendering genuine hope in a faraway place (29:1-32). At the command of the Lord, Jeremiah prepares a "book" that takes dead aim at heartache and hopelessness (30:1–31:37). God instructs Jeremiah to preserve written documentation of the transaction between his cousin Hanamel and himself (32:6-44). The written materials, which Baruch places in an earthenware jar, serve as a testimony that God will one day restore the people of God. Perhaps the best-known example of the shift from spoken to written prophecy is the confrontation between King Jehoiakim and Jeremiah (36:1-32). In the narrative account, Jeremiah dictates the word of YHWH to Baruch, who reads it before Jehoiakim. The king in turn destroys the scroll of oracles only to have Jeremiah create another scroll, which contains "all the words of the scroll that King Jehoiakim of Judah had burned in the fire; and many similar words" (36:32). When all is said and done, the story affirms that this seemingly innocuous scroll trumps the king. The word is victorious!

In all, the new epoch of hope rests firmly on YHWH's written word. In lieu of fallen social and theological supports—a temple and its liturgical systems, a king and a strong nation, a land and the old covenant assurances—the word, and ultimately the God who utters it, now forms the foundation for newness. This word matters even when economic systems collapse. This word matters even when rulers conspire to tame its subversive force. YHWH's word matters because it disarms powers and principalities, undermines tyranny, mobilizes the faithful, and generates hope in those suffering from debilitating fear and despair (cf. Isa 40:1-8; 55:10-13).

Finally, hope is found in worship. As noted earlier, a number of scholars have made a plausible case for the liturgical character of sections of Jeremiah.[22] It is now fairly well established, for instance, that the confessions of Jeremiah are more than private prayers. In all likelihood these laments are expressions of some facet of Israel's public worship. Moreover, Mark Biddle has argued cogently that the multiple voices in Jeremiah 7–20 represent various constituencies participating in communal worship.[23] It is also reasonable to suppose that the Oracles against the Nations (OAN; Jeremiah 46–51) emanate from community worship rather than elsewhere in the social world of early diasporic Judaism. Not unlike several royal psalms and hymns in the Psalter (for example, Pss 2, 68, 95–97, 99; see also Pss 83, 94), the OAN both celebrate YHWH's victory over world-destroying nations and make an array of stunning claims regarding YHWH's reign on earth. In strange and unfamiliar garb, the OAN affirm that YHWH, the divine ruler (Jer 46:18; 48:15; 51:57), will defeat nations resorting to the politics of arrogance and exploitation, especially Babylon. YHWH, they declare, will not be foiled by oppressive regimes—and particularly not by rebellious vassals. In the end, the OAN herald that YHWH, not random geopolitical forces, controls Israel's destiny. Thus, the OAN conclude the book of Jeremiah with the triumphant note that YHWH reigns in and through the vicissitudes of life.

Notwithstanding the force of such claims, the OAN do more than make astonishing assertions. When these texts reenact God's rule on earth, they improve the vision of exiles assembled in the synagogues of Babylon to 20/20. Through the lens of worship, beaten-down refugees in Babylon are able to see clearly that worldly power is not ultimate power, that economic and military domination is not the final word, and that God is a strong advocate for those who have been devastated by war. In this way the OAN are nothing less than "guerilla theater," a term that has been used to describe other biblical texts of resistance.[24] Such speech reperforms the fall of the powerful, without resorting to physical violence;[25] it rejects oppressive politics as normative and it says no to despair and inertia. This public expression of faith, this subversive form of worship, sees through sinful social and political systems and in response creates its own matrix of justice and mercy. In doing so, it does not attempt to escape the fractured and troubled world or transform it through violence. Rather, this act of worship, this holy defiance, ennobles the people of God to protest and dissent, to ridicule and revel, and to imagine a counterview and a counter world order. For the exiles in Babylon, such worship was anything but innocuous; it was a dangerous "weapon of hope" that refused to knuckle under to political aggression and military hardware.

Conclusion

Hope is a rare commodity these days. In fact, despair may be one of the most debilitating diseases of our time. It is palpable, and it is everywhere. The book of Jeremiah provides an alternative script to despair for exiles of old and exiles today. It intends to inspire hope in those whose lives have been ransacked by loss—not the kind of hope that imagines a return to the world as it was, but hope that generates faith and courage to live through the shaking of earth and heaven; hope that is rooted in suffering; hope that demands open hands and open hearts; hope that exists on the edge and not at the center; hope in action, building genuine community; hope that emanates from the Scriptures and that comes alive in worship. In sum, the book of Jeremiah is a map of hope for the vulnerable and disenfranchised. It is a word for our troubled time.

PART THREE

THE BOOK OF EZEKIEL

CHAPTER SEVEN

EZEKIEL AS
DISASTER LITERATURE

War ravages and debilitates; it numbs the senses and renders ordinary language useless. It shatters dreams and constructions of self and community. War devastates everyone, but it annihilates the losers; bodies are desecrated and families are splintered, faith is destroyed and voices are shamed into silence. Albert Hourani aptly observes:

> Defeat goes deeper into the human soul than victory. To be in someone else's power is a conscious experience which induces doubts about the ordering of the universe, while those who have power can forget it, or can assume that it is part of the natural order of things and invent or adopt ideas which justify their possession of it.[1]

No wonder we rarely read the stories of the defeated or see a human face on the displaced. Rarely do we tally the number of dead, maimed, and bereaved, except as war trophies. Instead, the inflated narratives of the victors monopolize memory.

The prophetic corpus in the Hebrew Bible is a striking exception to the rule. This "war literature" speaks on behalf of the losers, the dispossessed, the disappeared. It bears witness to their pain. It lines out their abyss in a wide range of expressions. And perhaps most remarkably, it imagines their survival. The book of Ezekiel, more than most, conforms to these contours. It opens a dark shadowy window into the pain of displaced people. This stunning literary artifact refuses to cover up and banish memory. At the same time, it dares to map out a path of hope through the massive debris of loss. As Margaret S. Odell has argued, Ezekiel is a manifesto for war-torn refugees,[2] a survival trajectory for the crushed and conquered; or put more modestly, this diasporic text is literature of resistance in the struggle for community survival.

Although acknowledged for its towering contributions, Ezekiel has by and large been relegated by recent scholarship to secondary status.[3] This tendency may be due to its idiosyncratic character; more likely, it is the result of the book's surplus of violence and unrelenting blame. Donald E. Gowan suggests that the brutal nature of Ezekiel's message and his insistence "on the completeness of the death of the people of God"[4] contribute to the "unenthusiastic, if not negative judgment . . . by some interpreters."[5] The text's harsh portrayal of God does little to foster interest. Its focus on ritual purity is quite foreign, especially for some Protestant readers. Although the tradition addresses issues of morality and social justice, Ezekiel spends far more time on "the politics of cult,"[6] which treats sin as apostasy and defilement.

Even the most influential twentieth-century interpreter of the prophetic literature, Abraham Heschel, only cursorily treats the book of Ezekiel in his seminal book on the prophets. Except for a brief discussion of the prophet's mental illness, Heschel ignores Ezekiel in a work that continues to influence generations of readers.[7] We of course can only speculate as to why he paid so little attention to Ezekiel. Perhaps Heschel discerned too little pathos in the prophetic persona. Perhaps he found the moral sensibilities of other prophets more penetrating. Perhaps he could not reconcile Ezekiel's supposed mental illness with his understanding of prophets as charismatics. It is rather clear that Ezekiel's role as YHWH's mouthpiece and instrument does not conform to his view of the prophet as partner and associate. In any case, Heschel's lack of interest has likely contributed to the current malaise, if only indirectly.[8]

It is not difficult to appreciate this indifference. Ezekiel's stern and even chilling texture poses deep-rooted theological problems. The book portrays the God of Israel as exacting and punitive. Its judgment oracles are beset by brutal, even horrific, imagery. Its internal community boundaries, designed to separate insiders from outsiders and even good insiders from bad insiders, are rigid and insular. Even the tradition's hopeful utterances are rather calculated. Ezekiel's constructions of hope grow out of a priestly piety that honors ritual and purity above emotion and intimacy. As such, it reflects a symbolic universe that is more positional than personal. Unlike Isaiah's lyrical hope or Jeremiah's combative hope, Ezekiel's hope is often detached and uncompromising. It is rooted less in the syntax of love than in declarative speech.

Nonetheless, the full range of constructions in Ezekiel is still quite remarkable given the menacing character of Babylonian hegemony and the marginal status of the Judean refugees. This prophetic text dares to articulate, presumably under the radar of the oppressors, a subversive, nonviolent counterscript to that of the empire. It represents a radical interruption to war and the politics of violence. And eventually it invites a dispirited community of refugees to participate in a literary performance that imagines a new way of living, an alternative to that of established power structures.

Though this tradition is often disparaged and dismissed as bizarre, Walter Brueggemann is correct to suggest that "Ezekiel may be exactly the right text for such a 'bizarre' time as ours."[9] Saying no to the powers of death at any time or circumstance is a stunning act of moral courage.

Ezekiel within the Prophetic Corpus

There are many facets of Ezekiel's world that are difficult to reconcile with the rest of prophetic literature in the Hebrew Bible. First, the book has a markedly priestly texture; priestly mores, taboos, virtues, and vices shape both the prophetic message and persona. Second, its dominant form of divine communication is visionary. Whereas prophetic writings often include visionary reports (for example, Amos 7:1-9), this particular genre organizes Ezekiel as a whole (chs. 1–3, 8–11, 40–48). Third, the oracles in the book are lengthy and dominated by prose (or formal or artistic prose) instead of the customary poetry. Fourth, the text reads as a personal or prophetic diary; first-person speech almost completely monopolizes the rhetoric. Finally, Ezekiel is replete with thick symbolism and cryptic language. Its dominant genre and worldview border on apocalyptic, especially when the text focuses on the distant future. One gets the distinct impression that the book of Ezekiel inhabits a world that has almost as much in common with Daniel as it does with Jeremiah or Isaiah.

Notwithstanding this brief inventory, the book undoubtedly belongs to the prophetic corpus proper because its symbolic actions and speech forms, however eccentric, fall under the category of intermediation; the text is essentially divine-human communication. In fact, Ezekiel conforms to the ancient Near Eastern prototype of prophet as ecstatic visionary more naturally than any of the so-called writing prophets in the Hebrew Bible. Further, the prophecy of Ezekiel is intermediary language *on the edge of time*. It takes shape at a crucial juncture in history when long-standing categories, cultural givens, and cherished institutions are on the verge of collapsing; as such, it is eschatological in orientation—if we take this term to designate written speech that grows out of cultures in crisis.

In addition, Ezekiel's dominant idiom is part and parcel of prophetic discourse. The text employs *oracular judgment* to accuse, indict, and demand obedience, holiness, and repentance. It uses *oracular assurance* to generate hope in the face of bleak historical circumstances. As is typical of prophetic literature in the Bible, these binary forces—the acknowledgment of tragedy and the audacity to name it penultimate—frame the final form of the text. That is to say, the typical disaster-hope or judgment-salvation schema shapes the tradition as a whole, even though Ezekiel actually breaks down into three (or four) major divisions: scathing oracles of judgment against Judah and Jerusalem in chapters 1–24, stylized oracles against foreign nations in chapters 25–32, and oracles of restoration in chapters 33–48 (or 33–39 and 40–48), culminating in the vision of the new temple.[10] As long recognized, these divisions are far from exact; one can find prophecies of salvation in the first section (11:14-21) and announcements of judgment in the latter parts of the book (33:21-22). But in broad strokes they follow the prophetic proclivity to punctuate disaster with salvation and judgment with hope. This structure supports the contention that the prophetic corpus in its present form is far from a montage of discrete voices. It also lends credence to the argument that the prophetic literature serves to sustain communities under enormous pressures from within and without. Written prophecy, including Ezekiel, fosters hope when disaster calls into question basic constructions of self, community, faith, and meaning.

Akin to Isaiah, Jeremiah, and the Twelve, Ezekiel is beset by an empire's designs toward world domination. It deals with the harsh realities of hegemony and the resultant collapse of long-standing national arrangements. In particular, Ezekiel's implied readers cannot elude the menacing maneuvers of Babylon; and so Ezekiel bears poignant witness to the horror of war and the trauma of displacement. Rather than faltering under the weight of the superpower's social arrangements and its symbolic universe, however, Ezekiel constructs its own complex "system" of resistance. This alternative rendering of the universe in the first place involves "the defining reality of YHWH"[11] over and against rival forces—mythic and geopolitical. Indeed, Ezekiel not only refers the whole matrix of geopolitical contingencies to this reality, but the exilic text also interprets "the crisis [of 587 B.C.E.] as one of YHWH's *judgment* that produces the crisis."[12] Ultimately the tradition moves beyond the panorama of judgment to sustaining hope for the future. In this manner Ezekiel joins the prophetic chorus as disaster literature *and* survival literature. It addresses the atrocities of war while uncovering a passage through the horror.

The Anatomy of Trauma

From beginning to end, the book of Ezekiel pulsates with the pain of war and occupation, exile and captivity. It dares to ponder the unthinkable: the loss of land, temple, capital city, and dynastic claims, and even the collapse of Israel's royal theology, which Isaiah had bolstered more than a century earlier when confronted by an aggressive Assyrian military machine. It is not difficult to understand why Ezekiel's contemporaries would have interpreted such tragic circumstances as the nullification of God's promises. Land occupation, the Jerusalem temple, and a strong dynastic government long symbolized divine blessing and favor. Their dismantling threw the entire world into disarray. Ezekiel speaks to the barrage of broken promises and shattered dreams.

Although the book of Ezekiel is only one of many prophetic traditions that addresses these focal concerns, its preoccupation with exile and captivity is clearly distinctive; the lingering social and symbolic damage of war completely dominates the prophetic horizon. No other prophetic writing enters the liminal world of exile more fully and more directly than Ezekiel: exile frames the text; it defines the text; it engulfs the text in pain and leaves an indelible mark on it. Ezekiel can hardly be read apart from the historical realities of military conquest and forced displacement. This is why recent scholarship has employed trauma and disaster studies as a window into this world.[13]

Granted that the precise character of exilic life in sixth-century Babylon is still uncertain, it no doubt involved some form of domination. The term *slavery* may not be appropriate, but the Babylonian exile limited political autonomy and resulted in divestiture of privilege and power. As Walter Brueggemann maintains:

> The exiled Jews of the Old Testament were of course geographically displaced. More than that, however, the exiles experienced a loss of the structured, reliable world that gave them meaning and coherence, and they found themselves in a context where their most treasured symbols of faith were mocked, trivialized or dismissed. That is, exile is not primarily geographical, but it is social, moral and cultural.[14]

Andrew Mein contends that exile presented an "almost unparalleled crisis for the Jewish people."[15] Ralph W. Klein says flatly, "Exile meant death, deportation, destruction, and devastation."[16] Daniel L. Smith-Christopher insists that "we do not 'hear' Ezekiel clearly unless we also 'hear' the imperial voice of Nebuchadnezzar the conqueror."[17] In even more sweeping terms, Oded Lipschits opens his important opus on the fall and rise of Jerusalem by asserting that "the years of the Babylonian Empire constituted the most important turning point in the history of Judah and the Judeans in the first millennium B.C.E."[18] Lipschits concludes that "the destruction of Jerusalem and the forcible deportation of the elite of the nation from their homeland to Babylon effected grave religious, national, and personal crises for the exiles living in Babylon."[19]

The interdisciplinary field of trauma and disaster studies has largely confirmed the profound effects of forced migration and captivity on individuals and communities. In the second half of the twentieth century in particular, researchers began to study the traumatic neuroses of war with scientific scrutiny. Several identified an anatomy of trauma associated with captivity. Although we need not universalize the experience of deported people or reduce the impact of victimization to rigid formal structures, the trauma of exile, like that of grief itself, is manifestly "formful." Focusing on individuals rather than communities, Judith Lewis Herman has argued that captivity or coercive control "seeks to destroy the victim's sense of autonomy."[20] It creates feelings of distrust, fear, and alienation. It causes the loss of will to live as well as "the intrusive symptoms of post-traumatic stress disorder,"[21] including "the hopelessness of depression,"[22] hyperarousal, rage, self-hatred, and the loss of connectivity. Under extreme circumstances, captives shut down "feelings, thoughts, initiative, and judgment."[23] The loss of memory and the capacity to feel is observable in the tragic creation of children soldiers.

Irahim Aref Kira states that survival-threatening experiences such as exile can "shatter . . . assumptions and beliefs about self and objects"; it can undermine "behavioral and emotional independence"; and it is potent enough to dismantle "the schema, the beliefs, the assumptions, and judgments about the self and the world."[24] Put differently, the trauma of exile can destroy faith, coherent networks of meaning, and constructions of communal and individual identity. Interestingly, when describing those responsible for producing the book of Ezekiel—namely, Judean refugees in Babylon—Henry McKeating notes that "their survival [was] at stake because their identity [was] at stake. They [had] lost most of what [had] defined them."[25]

One of the peculiar corollaries of traumatic violence, including the violence of exile and despotic control, is that it often leaves victims guilt laden. R. J. Lifton contends that "no survival experience . . . can occur without severe guilt."[26] Judith Herman observes that feelings of guilt occur in part because "the psychology of the victim is shaped by the actions and beliefs of the perpetrator";[27] it is not unusual for victims to develop a sense of dependence and attachment to their captors. Prisoners of war, hostages, and other victims of violent crimes often cope with an "unsatisfactory resolution of the normal developmental conflicts over initiative and competence," which leaves them "prone to feelings of guilt and inferiority."[28] Herman even suggests that "guilt may be understood as an attempt to draw some useful lesson from disaster and to regain some sense of power and control. To imagine that one could have done better may be more tolerable than to face the reality of utter helplessness."[29] Perhaps these dynamics help explain why guilt plays such a formative role in the book of Ezekiel. At its best, guilt serves as an effective survival mechanism during times of severe crisis. At its worst, it results in self-inflicted violence.

"Survivor's guilt" is only exacerbated by acute social vulnerability: those who are forced to leave their homelands in time of war and military occupation often find themselves in the borderlands without legal rights and protections, adequate food and safe water, medicine, and other basic needs. As a consequence, they survive with debilitating fear and a greater susceptibility to disease and psychological illness. At the same time the displaced often demonstrate a remarkable capacity to construct new narratives and mechanisms for survival.

Recent trauma studies and documented reports of victimization support the interpretive perspective that the sixth-century Judean exile was indeed a catastrophe involving wide-ranging social, economic, political, emotional, and symbolic forces.[30] Drawing upon sociologies of trauma and the biblical testimony, Daniel L. Smith-Christopher argues that "the specific Babylonian exile must be appreciated as both a historical human disaster *and* a disaster that gave rise to a variety of social and religious responses with significant social and religious consequences."[31] Exile, Smith-Christopher notes, "is a form of disaster and trauma that is inseparably connected to human actions related to power, dominance and brutality."[32]

Signs of Trauma in Ezekiel: Exile and Captivity

The Hebrew Bible almost unambiguously interprets the experience of exile as a massive disruption in life. Although the scope of the Judean exile may not have been large in terms of sheer numbers—the total number of deportees may have been as low as three thousand or four thousand (Jer 52:28-30)—the symbolic significance of exile was clearly disproportionate to the actual losses. Exile was a meaning-making event that transformed virtually every facet of life, both for the victims as well as for subsequent communities that had not experienced exile firsthand. It created a great divide in time and space as well as in social and symbolic structures. Exile represented the death of a cherished cultural and religious identity, which felt like the collapse of the created order. Exile—in conjunction with loss of temple and dynasty, city and land—threw into utter jeopardy Israel's national consciousness.[33] A wide cross section of biblical texts reflects a sustained nostalgia for the "preexilic" forms of life, even though one can discern an emerging conviction that the *absence* of land, temple, city, and king is the key to new beginnings for diasporic Judaism.

Ezekiel envisions exile (and the fall of Jerusalem) as the principal social crisis of community life. It not only represents a historical datum but also a metaphor for the end of all that is valued. Exile transforms "insider Israel" into dangerous outsider, an indigenous people into a community of strangers; it limits access to established social structures and power arrangements. Exile catapults Israel into an unclean land. It casts grave doubts on Israel's election tradition. It rocks the very foundations of Israel's identity, especially in its priestly forms. Exile, moreover, poses a serious threat of accommodation and loss of "self." It creates an enormous hole in Israel's symbolic universe. Exile jeopardizes the belief in a meaningful world; it ruptures coherent networks of meaning and it gives birth to a myriad of pressing theological dilemmas, the most important of which is the perceived abrogation of the covenant God. Has the God of Israel failed? Can the God of Jerusalem be worshiped in a foreign land? Is God's presence restricted to familiar places and long-standing institutional structures? How can we survive so far from God's manifest presence? More than any single event in ancient Israel's historical circumstances, exile gave rise to grave symbolic repercussions. It created the dire need for theodicy, for it mirrored the painful memory of slavery in Egypt and mocked the revered recital of liberation.

Exile from homeland, city, temple, and divine presence cuts off the community from all that has meaning and value. It imperils trust in God. It creates a disturbing *absence* from formative symbols and institutions, cultural givens, and beloved structures. And this devastating absence threatens to nullify Israel's long and cherished salvation history and metanarrative. Forced deportation seemingly represents nothing less than the cessation of divine blessing and the unthinkable absence of a God who is by self-decree ever present. It calls into question the very character of the covenant God who is capable of creating newness and hope for captive people.

No wonder exile serves as such a resonant metaphor for many today. Although living with affluence and at the center of power, we find ourselves disoriented, anxious, and dislocated; we are out of sorts with ourselves, with one another, with the larger culture, and with God. Walter Brueggemann notes, "Utilization of the metaphor of 'exile' for the situation of the church in the U.S is not easy or obvious, and for some not compelling. . . . [But] I believe that . . . *(a) loss of a structured, reliable 'world' where (b) treasured symbols of meaning are mocked and dismissed,* is a pertinent point of contact between those ancient texts and our situation."[34] Henri Nouwen notes with prophetic force that "as humanity we have entered a period in which our faith is being stripped of all support systems and defense mechanisms."[35] Interestingly, Nouwen claims that the community of faith that will emerge from "the darkness of our age" is one defined by "total vulnerability," an acute awareness that the world in which we live is unstable and in grave danger.

Exile shapes both the message and messenger in the book of Ezekiel. The portrait of the prophet as captive or refugee is so embedded in the texture of the book that it is hardly possible to imagine the prophet apart from this social location. Ezekiel introduces himself in solidarity with his displaced community: "In the thirtieth year, in the fourth month, on the fifth day of the month, as I was among the exiles by the river Chebar, the heavens were opened, and I saw visions of God" (Ezek 1:1). His inaugural vision of God occurs "in the land of the Chaldeans" during "the fifth year of the exile of King Jehoiachin" (1:2-3). With his fellow Judeans, Ezekiel is a casualty of war, a victim of coercive control and political captivity. He speaks as a displaced person and as a wounded priest-healer whose world has been fractured beyond recognition. Like his compatriots, Ezekiel is caught betwixt and between worlds. He resides in the country of his incarceration and yet lives with a marked sense of nostalgia for his beloved city that lies in ruins. This profound sense of displacement creates dual "citizenships."

Despite conflicted loyalties, the tradition clearly locates its hero among an "enclave of exiles, whom Nebuchadnezzar had deported from Judah to Babylonia in 597 B.C.E."[36]

And it is in Babylon that Ezekiel prophesied from 593 to 571 B.C.E. The precise system of internal dating supports this position. The book's chronological formulas (for example, 1:1-3; 8:1; 20:1; 24:1; 26:1; 29:1, 17; 32:1; 40:1) anchor every oracle, sign, and vision to the harsh realities of captivity in Babylon. With a certain cadence of grief, these indices relentlessly bear witness to war and despotic control. They refuse to wander far from the painful reality of confinement in Babylon, except when Ezekiel takes his prophetic "visionary journeys" to the capital city, Jerusalem.

Ezekiel addresses not only *exiles in Babylon* but exiles who once enjoyed a central role in community life (see, for example, 2 Kgs 24:13-17); the custodians of the old political order now find themselves relegated to a marginal place in a faraway country. The newly formed enclave of refugees—once leading citizens and upper-tiered stakeholders—must deal with forced displacement *and* major shifts in identity and power arrangements.[37] The cumulative force of relinquishing land, control, and prestige creates a massive dialectic of trauma. Evicted from the securities of country and banished to the dangerous hinterlands, this dominated minority must forge a new life as a "guest people" in some measure dependent on the perpetrators of violence.

In sum, forced resettlement exacts an enormous toll on Ezekiel's implied audience; it results in profound sadness, vulnerability, fear, and a protracted sense of disconnection to self, community, the world, and God. Exile reduces the world to despair, as sad voices testify: "Our bones are dried up, and our hope is lost; we are cut off completely" (Ezek 37:11). Indicators of emotional and psychological "dis-ease," however, take the form not only of despair (Ezek 33:10; cf. Pss 73; 77:7-10; 137; Isa 40:27) but also of outrage, cynicism, and apathy (see, for example, Ezek 12:21-23; cf. Jer 12:1-4; 20:7-20). "The way of the Lord is unfair" (Ezek 18:29). "The days are prolonged, and every vision comes to nothing" (Ezek 12:22).[38] Captivity overwhelms the senses and alters fundamental perceptions of reality. It threatens a sense of safety and coherence in the universe. Accordingly, the text is fraught with overt signs of danger as well as covert subnarratives of trauma.

A Traumatized Prophet and God

Life and death, survival and trauma, are always before us on the pages of Ezekiel. Although one can discern these signs throughout the book, its two major characters, Ezekiel and YHWH, exhibit the most profound signs of victimization. As a result of war, exile, and captivity, both show striking symptoms of traumatic violence and dislocation.

The tradition presents its hero as a survivor whose life is inundated in pain. Ezekiel is a person of deep suffering. And like his contemporary Jeremiah, Ezekiel's pain can be encoded in his body as well as in his oracles, symbolic actions, and visionary reports. At the outset of the prophetic drama we learn that Ezekiel must ingest a scroll with "words of lamentation and mourning and woe" to fulfill his calling (Ezek 2:10). This act prepares him to bear witness to death and destruction in word, symbolic action, and in his *bios*.

The impending destruction of Jerusalem and the captivity of Judah monopolize the initial stage of his prophetic performance (chs. 1–24). At this juncture the prophet's language is unmistakably disturbing; his imagery is scathing; his visionary reports and symbolic acts are shocking. Violence dominates much of the symbolic topography, including the portrayal of God. Donald Gowan notes that when Ezekiel employs this language "he is not *imagining* a wrathful, vengeful God, nor expressing his own anger. He speaks of things he and his audience have already seen, and like the other prophets he claims they deserved it."[39] The prophet's rhetoric of disaster, often used in the name of divine judgment, is thus refracted through the lenses of war and the trauma of captivity.

For perpetrators and victims alike, violence is capable of creating its own distinctive dialect. This is in part why victims of abuse sometimes become abusers. Traumatic violence not only deadens the senses; it also reperforms its own horror. A case in point: immersed in a culture of violence, the readers and writers of the book of Jeremiah employ language of sexual violence to depict their own victimization; they then turn this language against Babylon, the geopolitical perpetrator of violence against them (i.e., the text depicts Israel as a ravaged harlot and then Babylon as a plundered whore). The readers and writers of Ezekiel do something similar. Ezekiel's language of terror, although sometimes formulaic, reflects the horrors of war. Ironically, Ezekiel does not primarily deploy this language against dangerous outsiders, the perpetrators of violence and control, but rather against insiders who ostensibly pose a danger to the survival of the community. Although his derisive rhetoric serves in part to rein in those who resist community order, it also reveals signs of trauma and encroachment; that is, the text's harsh and punitive language is indicative of a society that feels itself at risk and in grave danger—a community that has been overexposed to the destructive forces of war.

In addition to proclaiming a terrifying message, Ezekiel carries the pain of war within his own body. The prophet's life serves as a "sign" for the community at large (for example, 12:6; 24:24). The prospect of captivity leaves the prophet "in bitterness, in the heat of [his] spirit" (3:14). Like a prisoner of war, he lives in isolation, restrained and silent (3:22-26). Ezekiel lies on his left side and then on his right side to represent a prolonged period of siege (4:4-8). Also indicative of siege and deportation, he suffers scarcity and defilement (4:9-17) as well as shame and humiliation (5:1-4). To symbolize Judah's captivity, Ezekiel packs his bag for a period of exile (12:1-6). To convey the terrible violence inflicted upon Jerusalem, he eats his "bread with quaking," and drinks his water "with trembling and with fearfulness" (12:17-20). When Ezekiel's wife dies, he is forbidden to find solace through the standard forms of mourning (24:15-27). Yet even this most personal form of grief holds communal import: like the prophet's bereavement, the people of Israel will suffer the loss of their beloved temple, "the delight of [their] eyes," as well as the death of "[their] sons and daughters." Despite these crushing blows, the nation, like the prophet, is banned from conventional mourning rituals. Such symbolic performances convey the end of Judean culture as it was long known (cf. Jer 16:1-9).

The text's portrayal of the prophetic psyche also reflects symptoms of traumatic violence. Early- and mid-twentieth-century studies often subjected Ezekiel's personality to psychological analysis. For instance, drawing on the work of E. C. Broome, Abraham Heschel noted that Ezekiel exhibits "behavioristic abnormalities consistent with paranoid schizophrenia," including "periods of catatonia . . . [and] delusions of persecution and grandeur."[40] More recent interpretive perspectives tend to view Ezekiel's behavior—or rather the literary portrayal of the "disordered" personality—as more indicative of trauma and posttraumatic stress than psychosis or paranoid schizophrenia.[41]

First, like those who suffer unmanageable violence, Ezekiel appears detached and disconnected, often vacillating between worlds. Although Ezekiel resides in Babylon, he takes imaginative journeys to Jerusalem; these alterations in consciousness blur his cultural and symbolic boundaries and leave his loyalties, vested interests, and constructed audience conflicted. Second, Ezekiel manifests a certain fixation with violence and death, even when imagining future hope (37:1-14). Only in the vision of the new temple (chs. 40–48) does the reader enjoy a reprieve from language of war, captivity, and loss. Third, Ezekiel's preoccupation with ritual defilement not only reflects a priestly orientation to life but also an individual and community under siege and in grave danger.[42] In response to such dire conditions, Ezekiel seeks to establish well-defined lines between purity and pollution. At the start of the prophetic drama, we learn that Ezekiel is hypervigilant about such matters (4:13-14).

In addition, it is not difficult to discern in the persona of Ezekiel dissociative episodes, constriction, paralysis, hyperarousal, helplessness, and the loss of control (as perhaps indicated by the phrase "the hand of the LORD"). Even the formulaic expression "son of man" (*ben ʾādām*) (or "mere mortal" or "O mortal" [NRSV]) conveys a sense of vulnerability and disempowerment. This address is a constant reminder of Ezekiel's frailty and mortality. Ezekiel is an earthling whose existence, like that of Adam, is drawn from the earth (*ʾădāmâ*) and sustained by the breath or spirit of God. And God's spirit almost always overpowers and silences the diminutive prophet.

Strangely similar to the exercise of despotic control, YHWH's interaction with Ezekiel is intense and overpowering. The commanding voice of YHWH dominates the landscape; it dwarfs both prophet and people. It is authoritative and assertive. It monopolizes symbolic and discursive space, relegating dissent to the margins. As a result, Ezekiel does not readily challenge the divine perspective, even when it suggests the unthinkable (for example, 20:25). The prophet does not oppose the divine point of view, even when it appears excessively punitive. Nor does Ezekiel readily negotiate with YHWH. The force of YHWH's directives is too powerful, and ultimately Ezekiel is overwhelmed into submission. Because YHWH is exacting, dangerous, and above all holy, neither Ezekiel nor his readers defy this God or attempt to circumvent God's holy resolve. Such a piety honors conformity over engagement and submission over interaction; it is more positional than personal.

This is not to imply that countervoices are absent from the book. Although an all-consuming voice governs Ezekiel's landscape, the text still provides dark windows into the complex and fractured interiority of the prophet and the refugee people. For instance, before he obeys, Ezekiel must be told three times to eat the scroll (2:8–3:3). And when he leaves his initial encounter with YHWH, he is angry or "in bitterness in the heat of . . . spirit" (3:14). When confronted with the wholesale destruction of Jerusalem, the prophet intercedes: "Ah Lord GOD! will you destroy all who remain of Israel as you pour out your wrath upon Jerusalem?" (9:8) At the death of Pelatiah son of Benaiah, Ezekiel falls to the ground and pleads with YHWH for the remnant of Israel (11:13). While the voices of Judean refugees are generally subdued, one can occasionally find expressions of dissent and despair. The Jerusalem elders insist, "The LORD does not see us, the LORD has forsaken the land" (8:12); prophet and people recite the conventional saying "The parents have eaten sour grapes, and the children's teeth are set on edge" (18:2); some contend, "The way of the Lord is unfair" (18:25), and "The way of the Lord is not just" (33:17; see also 37:11). As a rule, however, these dissenting and lamenting voices are few in number and limited in scope. And they are placed in the mouths of others—most often YHWH and Ezekiel—as disputation speeches and then used against those who supposedly uttered them (see 9:9; 11:3; 12:21-25; cf., however, 33:10).

YHWH's overpowering voice is part of a symbolic universe that is largely free of moral inconsistency and ambiguity. Not only is there little tolerance for dissent, resistance, and vexation in this world, there is also little acknowledgment of gratuitous suffering, divine injustice, or ethical slippage; one is hard-pressed to find evidence of anomie. Meaning-making is coherent, symmetrical, and for the most part monologic. If there is *any* moral slippage, it is found in the promissory language where YHWH's unilateral and sovereign speech destabilizes a rigid act-consequence schema.

Constructions of newness are not for Israel's sake or because Israel is deserving, but rather for God's sake and to preserve God's reputation. Otherwise, the book's governing categories are stable, well-defined, and in effect seamless.[43]

Notwithstanding this symbolic symmetry, something strange and unexpected takes place: YHWH eventually becomes fully immersed in Israel's pain and alienation. This metamorphosis is most clearly evident in the three vision reports that organize the book of Ezekiel. There we discover that the sovereign God is susceptible to the anguish of war and displacement. No longer detached and unscathed, YHWH is drawn into Israel's fractured world as a wounded participant. In solidarity with traumatized Israel, YHWH astonishingly becomes a displaced God, and in so doing identifies with the endangered refugee community, even to the point of humiliation. Ultimately this radical displacement becomes a source of healing and newness for suffering Israel. For Christians this abject vulnerability paves the way for the scandal of the passion of Christ. But before hope can blossom, YHWH must feel the full brunt of Israel's pain and alienation.

In the inaugural vision the prophet encounters YHWH arrayed in splendor in the heavenly throne room (Ezek 1). This glimpse into the divine world draws on traditional forms such as fire, light, glory, cloud, spirit, and the bow, several of which are reminiscent of the wilderness tradition—the formative period *before* YHWH takes up residence in the temple. Indeed, the wheels on the divine chariot drive home the point that God's heavenly throne is not tied to the monarchy or the state—whether Judean or Babylonian; and as importantly, God's abode is constructed for transit. YHWH will go wherever YHWH desires! Besides traditional symbols, Mesopotamian traditions and iconography influence the vision. But now the servants and spirits of the Babylonian gods are harnessed to the chariot throne of YHWH and so are subservient to YHWH. Margaret Odell notes that the use of Mesopotamian iconography not only bolsters claims of YHWH's universal rule, but it also subverts hegemonic claims, driving home that YHWH, not Mesopotamian rulers, controls the destiny of Israel.[44]

Whether Ezekiel's first vision signifies judgment or coming salvation is not entirely clear; in either case, it represents a stunning revelation of the otherness of divinity. The mind-bending vision of strange living creatures with four faces, intersecting crystalline wheels with rims full of eyes, awesome crystal domes, and sapphire thrones symbolizes YHWH's boundless power and mobility. The unrivaled God of Israel is sovereign, elusive, and impervious to self-aggrandizing human leaders and impressive military machines. This God stands over and against mighty Babylon *and* captive Israel. As divine ruler YHWH commands *all* forces in the created order—until something unexpectedly occurs.

In the second major vision in the book, however, idolatry, violence, and injustice drive YHWH out of the temple (8:1–10:22 and 11:1-25). The holy one cannot dwell in such a setting. So the glory of YHWH moves "from the cherub to the threshold of the house" (9:3; 10:3-4), leaves the threshold of the house, and hovers over the cherubim at the entrance of the east gate of the house of the Lord (see 10:18-22). Then the divine glory rises above the city, passes by the Kidron Valley, and eventually "heads east, stopping at the Mount of Olives."[45] This move is replete with danger. Departures eastward can be perilous. Humanity is banished east of Eden to a life of conflict, danger, and death (Gen 3:24). At risk and in grave danger, Cain is evicted from the divine presence to live out his life as a vulnerable refugee, east of Eden (Gen 4:16). Angry and despondent, Jonah leaves Nineveh and sits "down east of the city" (Jonah 4:5; see also Isa 2:6; Ezek 25:4, 10). The east represents a faraway place of vulnerability, banishment, and exile, in large measure because menacing superpowers (Babylon in particular)—Israel's tormenters—reside east of Jerusalem.

When YHWH departs from the Jerusalem temple for the eastern regions, YHWH becomes an outcast in solidarity with the diasporic community. YHWH not only takes up residence in the borderlands; YHWH becomes a "displaced person" there. God becomes an exile! Like the community with which the God of Israel identifies, YHWH suffers massive disjunction. It would seem that this God has little choice than to participate in this dangerous setting. Even though YHWH is sovereign and free, YHWH is not insulated from Israel's wreckage. Like the Judean exiles, YHWH is forced to leave the safety of land, city, and temple—driven out by pornography, corruption, and gratuitous violence. And like any other refugee, YHWH is shattered and traumatized beyond words. Terrorized at home and humiliated in exile, YHWH suffers the debilitating loss of reputation (similar to the so-called Jerusalem elite now in exile) as well as the disorienting chaos of a world gone amok in moral insanity. YHWH is shamed by the battery of events and by Israel's misdeeds. And in response YHWH lashes out (1) to restore a damaged reputation, (2) to rectify the wrongs done against him, and (3) to clean up the symbolic mess. These actions are evident in part in the oft-used statement of recognition, "Then you [or they] will know that I am the LORD" (for example, 13:23).

The violence that erupts from YHWH's mouth mirrors the rage of a war-torn people. It also represents a "measured" response to a crumbling world on the brink of destruction. YHWH is angry for good reason! The world is on the verge of collapse. The enemy is at Jerusalem's gates. Judah's leaders have lost their way. Families are splintered; hostages have been taken. And the temple has been desecrated. However, rather than lashing out at Babylon, the geopolitical agent of disaster, YHWH targets Israel. Perhaps the converse would be too dangerous in diaspora, even for YHWH (cf., however, the language against the empire in Jeremiah). Regardless, Israel, not Babylon, is the focus of YHWH's attention.

Ultimately, YHWH's exile from the temple leads to solidarity with the traumatized community—in location, in rage, in suffering, and eventually in hope (11:22-24). As John Kutsko notes, "The divine *kābôd* would be available to Israel in exile, as it was available to Israel in the wilderness."[46] Again landless and in the wilderness, YHWH returns to this liminal place, now as a refugee among dispirited refugees. "Therefore tell the exiles: This is what the sovereign LORD says: Though I exiled them among the nations and scattered them among the countries, yet I will be a sanctuary to them for a little while in the countries where they have gone" (11:16, authors' translation).

In the third and final vision (Ezekiel 40–48), the exiled God returns to the temple. God's "banishment" is over. The "glory of the God of Israel" enters the temple by the east gate and fills the sanctuary (Ezek 43:5; 44:4), not unlike earlier descents of the divine presence into the holy place (for example, 1 Kgs 8:11; cf. 2 Chr 5:14; 7:2). The prophetic drama ends with a consecrated, thoroughly purged, and coherent structure in which God can finally reside (Ezek 43:6-9). The array of religious improprieties, including "vile abominations" (8:9) and temple wall portraits of "all kinds of creeping things, and loathsome animals, and all the idols of the house of Israel" (8:10), are altogether gone. Now the divine residence in the restored temple becomes a source of blessing for the world, although it is still predominantly in the service of a beleaguered Judean community. The location of this vision, however, should not be overlooked: the prophet sees the new temple and the return of YHWH while residing in exile. Thus, it is still born in the maelstrom of war, upheaval, and estrangement.

It is no accident that Ezekiel concludes with a great triumphant note that YHWH is present in the new city of God (48:35). In fact, the name of the city "from that time on shall be, The LORD is There." Such an utterance affirms that nothing can separate God's people from God's presence. It asserts that this God is accessible in the most unlikely places—even in the faraway country of Babylon. The psalmist makes a similar claim when confessing that if one were to make a home in the depths of the earth, God would even be there. If one were to hide in the utter darkness, the "darkness [would be] as light to you" (Ps 139:12). And Paul echoes such audacity when asserting that "neither death, nor life, nor angels, nor rulers, nor things present, nor things to come, nor powers, nor height, nor depth, nor anything else in all creation, will be able to separate us from the love of God in Christ Jesus our Lord" (Rom 8:38-39). When all is said and done, the last two words of Ezekiel—YHWH *shammah*, "YHWH is There"—respond to the danger lurking in the text.

But what exactly is this danger? What threatens faith and jeopardizes the coherent constructions of the universe? What places trust in God at risk? Most concretely, it is the harsh reality of war and captivity. And Ezekiel dares to speak to these destructive realities. This courageous text participates fully in Israel's fractured world and gives this world of loss its own name. Deploying priestly categories, *Ezekiel names the abyss "absence."*[47] From opening vision to concluding doxology, the book of Ezekiel throbs with the pain of divine absence.

More directly, Ezekiel reads the abyss of forced relocation and captivity as absence—the absence of land, temple, king, city, and, most painfully, God. And this tangible absence creates a dreadful sense of abandonment, disconnection, and shattered reality, all of which converge as a raging assault against hope. Yet amid all the wreckage comes YHWH, Judah's displaced God, to fill the absence and repair a ruptured world. "Right in the middle of the tear, the dance of joy can be felt."[48] In the vortex of loss, Ezekiel claims, the traumatized community can discover the mystery that "God is hidden in the pain and suffering of the world."[49]

CHAPTER EIGHT

EZEKIEL AS SURVIVAL LITERATURE

That the book of Ezekiel is disaster literature is almost beyond dispute. It imagines a community ravaged by war and forced deportation, a community that has experienced the humiliation of defeat and the trauma of captivity. In this haunting literature we encounter historical losers whose sense of self and deity has been shattered seemingly beyond repair, a prophet who exhibits many of the classic signs of posttraumatic stress, and a God who fully enters the fray of Judah's fissured world. As a result, Ezekiel throbs with pain from beginning to end. Even its visions of survival are set against a background of violence and death (for example, 37:1-14). Coursing through this tradition are voices of despair and disdain as well as dislocation and disjunction.

Yet this resilient meaning-making map refuses to give in to hopelessness; instead it trades in symbolic construction and community healing. In broad strokes Ezekiel makes the paradoxical claim that life's greatest gifts emerge in the most unlikely places. Who would have ever expected Babylon to become a fulcrum of hope and newness? And yet this literature heralds that the God of Israel is not found in safe and familiar places but in brokenness and at the margins. Ezekiel's opening vision of YHWH's breathtaking throne chariot drives home this point with force. Ezekiel does not—of course cannot—encounter God in the Jerusalem temple, surrounded by the traditional priestly apparatus. The prophet is gripped by God's presence in the faraway place of captivity. Even more scandalous, Ezekiel envisions YHWH leaving the safety of the temple to live as a refugee in Babylon. Such a dangerous move creates an entirely new set of categories, and unexpectedly it fosters hope for the prospect of survival in the face of war and exile.

How does this metamorphosis take shape? How does a failed national-cultic state emerge as a dynamic community bound together by fidelity, holiness, and sacred text? Taken as a whole, Ezekiel, the harbinger of disaster, morphs into a messenger of hope. This radical shift in the prophetic role is most evident in the structure of the book itself, which moves on a linear trajectory from dystopia to utopia. At the outset of the prophetic drama Ezekiel utters almost nothing but scathing denunciations of Israel. By the end he envisages almost nothing but salvation. To be sure, exile envelops the entire prophetic performance; but Ezekiel construes exile as a passage to something startlingly new. Consequently, the book is far more than disaster literature; it is also a daring textual enactment of hope. Like Jeremiah, Isaiah, and the Twelve, Ezekiel sub-verts despair and inspires hope in those located at the edge of time. In unpretentious terms, this refugee text is a survival manual for those suffering from tormenting absence.

Ezekiel's perilous hope counters a culture of violence; it serves as an alternative to hegemonic constraints. And it functions as an antidote to tormenting absence—the community's principal source of despair and inertia. Ezekiel's language of hope affirms that the world is not spiraling out of control, that God is still at work even in the worst of times, and that the covenant God—not despots, raw geopolitics, or superpowers—ultimately rules human destiny. It insists that God is present in dangerous and faraway places and at critical junctures when cherished beliefs, institutions, and symbols have gone down in defeat. It boldly claims that God's people will not only survive but will also eventually thrive and become a conduit of blessing to the world. Israel's salvation, or more precisely the river of life flowing from the new sanctuary in the city of God, will one day bring about wide-reaching healing and renewal (Ezek 47:1-12).

As is the case for much of written prophecy, Ezekiel's rendering of hope *testifies* to the horrors of war and war's dreadful repercussions, it *organizes* lived chaos into montages of meaning, and it *maps out strategies for survival in diaspora*. All three facets of meaning-making require complex literary performances. All engage in forms of theodicy that confront massive loss and disjunction. All seek to restore faith and community identity. All authorize definitive breaks with long-standing precrisis arrangements, including uninterrupted land claims, nationhood, the central shrine, and monarchic forms of governance.

Put succinctly, Ezekiel's calculus of hope involves three defining parts: candor, theodicy, and imagination. First, it tells the truth: the prophetic text bears witness to the collapse of the old world and exposes denials and implausible expectations for a return to precrisis conditions. Second, Ezekiel creates a measure of symbolic coherence and symmetry in the face of unmanageable loss. Third, Ezekiel dares to flesh out God's promise of newness. More concretely than any other prophetic writing, this text creates mosaics of hope and restoration amid a world in disarray.

Testimony and Truth-Telling

The starting point for healing and hope—individual and communal—is the audacity to speak, or as Tod Linafelt notes, to put "the destitution into words."[1] Victims of traumatic violence sometimes conceal their "narrative" as if it were shameful. Tormented by various forms of victimization—be it physical, verbal, or sexual—the wounded live under a dark cloud of silence. "Atrocities, however, refuse to be buried. . . . denial does not work."[2] Testimony, or truth-telling, is an essential component of survival—be it individual or communal. "When the truth is finally recognized, survivors can begin their recovery."[3] Speech breaks the silence, shatters denials, and is nothing less than a stunning act of redemption. Such daring makes films like *The Killing Fields* (1984), *Schindler's List* (1993), *Osama* (2003), and *Hotel Rwanda* (2004) devastatingly powerful. It makes Elie Wiesel's memoir *Night* (1960) and Alexander Solzhenitsyn's *Gulag Archipelago* (1973) disturbingly important. Authentic responses to gratuitous violence can haunt us back to life.

The book of Ezekiel is a written response to Judah's national tragedy. It speaks of the wreckage and it portrays siege and forced deportation in the most graphic of terms (4:1–7:27; see especially 5:1-5; 6:1-14; 7:1-20). This courageous text refuses to sanitize the harsh realities of war or conceal its devastating aftermath (10:1-22). And it does not cower under unmanageable suffering. A world so laden with human debris is difficult to broach. That is in part why one can hardly read Ezekiel without being offended. Yet this speech, however disconcerting, is an important witness to survival.

Ezekiel testifies to a nation on the brink of destruction. Foreshadowing this terrifying fate, the prophet ingests a scroll that contains "words of lamentation and mourning and woe" (2:10). And even though the consumption of the scroll is surprisingly "sweet as honey" (3:3), it nevertheless prepares both prophet and reader for the impending death of a nation. Subsequent oracles and symbolic acts dispel any doubts to the contrary. No sooner does the initial vision end than the text takes up Jerusalem's downfall, often couched in punitive terms. First comes the siege of the city:

> And you, O mortal, take a brick and set it before you. On it portray a city, Jerusalem; and put siegeworks against it, and build a siege wall against it, and cast up a ramp against it; set camps also against it, and plant battering rams against it all around. Then take an iron plate and place it as an iron wall between you and the city; set your face toward it, and let it be in a state of siege, and press the siege against it. This is a sign for the house of Israel. (4:1-3)

Next YHWH vows to bring about its utter ruin (5:14-17):

> I will make you a desolation and an object of mocking among the nations around you, in the sight of all that pass by. You shall be a mockery and a taunt, a warning and a horror, to the nations around you, when I execute judgments on you in anger and fury, and with furious punishments—I, the LORD, have spoken—when I loose against you my deadly arrows of famine, arrows for destruction, which I will let loose to destroy you, and when I bring more and more famine upon you, and break your staff of bread. I will send famine and wild animals against you, and they will rob you of your children; pestilence and

bloodshed shall pass through you; and I will bring the sword upon you. I, the LORD, have spoken. (5:14-17)

The devastation is enormous and complete, bordering on eschatological:

> The word of the LORD came to me: You, O mortal, thus says the Lord GOD
> to the land of Israel:
>> An *end!* The *end* has come
>>> upon the four corners of the land.
>> Now the *end* is upon you,
>>> I will let loose my anger upon you;
>> I will judge you according to your ways,
>>> I will punish you for all your abominations.
>> My eye will not spare you, I will have no pity.
>>> I will punish you for your ways,
>>> while your abominations are among you.
>> Then you shall know that I am the LORD.
>> Thus says the Lord GOD:
>> Disaster after disaster! See, it comes.
>>> An *end* has come, the *end* has come.
>> It has awakened against you; see, it comes!
>> Your doom has come to you,
>>> O inhabitant of the land.
>> The time has come, the day is near—
>>> of tumult, not of reveling on the mountains. (7:1-7; emphasis added)

The ordeal is not only a dreadful geopolitical event; it is also a catastrophe with cosmic import. Repeated five times, the impending disaster represents the *end* for Israel. The wreckage is all the more disturbing because it names YHWH, not Babylon, as Judah's formidable antagonist. As disturbing as this assertion may sound to the contemporary reader, Ezekiel will not (cannot) read the national disaster merely in terms of raw military power. Rather, he interprets Judah's crisis—through the lenses of divine sovereignty—as a pivotal moment fraught with theological and human import. By the conclusion of the first section of the book (chs. 1–24), it becomes altogether apparent that the destruction of Jerusalem is inescapable. The city is beyond repair; all forms of mediation are exhausted; the end has therefore come! "In the ninth year, in the tenth month, on the tenth day of the month, the word of the LORD came to me: Mortal, write down the name of this day, this very day. The king of Babylon has laid siege to Jerusalem this very day" (24:1-2). Even when the tradition begins to imagine the possibility of restoration for the Judean exiles in Babylon, it cannot ignore

Jerusalem's fate; in terse and candid terms the report is broadcast: "The city has fallen" (33:21).

And so this prophetic text leaves little doubt about Judah's predicament. Its candor breaks the silence. Its horror conveys a deep sense of loss. Its testimony exposes any illusion that it might be otherwise. David G. Garber notes that Ezekiel is "a response to . . . Jerusalem's destruction" and "the entire book, and the first twenty-four chapters in particular, attempt to give testimony to this traumatic event that shapes the exilic community's memory."[4] Ezekiel 1–24, argues Garber, "offers the members of the community an avenue through which to articulate their suffering, promoting the community's survival as it defines itself around the central event."[5] This exilic voice is a penetrating witness, assuredly a haunting meditation on the abyss.

Percolating beneath the surface of this performance is a longing for precrisis normality. Fueled in part by patriotic zeal (for example, Ezek 13:1-23), the imagined audience refuses to relinquish its old national identity; it longs for the reestablishment of Jerusalem and the treasured forms of worship and governance. For those ravaged by war and captivity, nostalgia for the predisaster world is nothing more than the natural longing for equilibrium and stability.

All the same, Ezekiel reads these seemingly innocuous expectations as dangerous forms of denial, completely out of sync with the attendant social and symbolic realities. Ezekiel insists that the community must make a clear break from the old forms of institutional life. The tradition is sure that the national crisis is not merely a blip on the radar, a momentary disruption to enduring networks of meaning; it represents a social and symbolic reality that will change virtually every facet of community life. That is to say, military invasion, the razing of the temple, and the exile to Babylon carry monumental import. They result in fundamental shifts in the structures of the world, the end of long-established approaches to reality, and the onslaught of a world at risk. They create major power realignments. And they specifically produce cavernous breaks with the cherished national cultic identity. Any attempt to suggest otherwise, no matter how well-intentioned, creates a barrier to healing and recovery. To proclaim an "innocuous" message of " 'peace,' when there is no peace" (13:10) cannot be more dangerous.

For this reason the book of Ezekiel is uncompromising in its decentering of Jerusalem as the *axis mundi*, the very center of the universe.[6] Jerusalem *must* fall; its king and old guard *must* be toppled; its temple *must* be laid waste; the land *must* be evacuated (if only rhetorically); and the divine presence *must* depart from its idolatrous surroundings to reside in a new, albeit dangerous, setting in diaspora. Yehezkel Kaufmann notes that Ezekiel's purpose is "to persuade the exiles that they must separate their fate from that of Jerusalem, the abode and symbol of sin. . . . Jerusalem must perish; Israel will be regenerated from its exiles."[7] The prophet's mission then is not primarily to call the Jerusalem community to repentance but to declare its unconditional demise. Although this "fierce antipathy toward Jerusalem"[8] is in part a sectarian trope to bolster the status of the exilic community in Babylon (see, for example, Ezek 11:14-21), it is far more than propaganda: it is the impetus for autonomy and survival. For the exilic community to forge a new identity it must extricate itself from Jerusalem's dominant power arrangements. Hence, Ezekiel declares war on the old world. In disturbing and often grotesque ways the prophet dashes any hope that might distract the refugee community from its new cultural realities. The decentralization of Jerusalem and its ancillary values and symbolic structures is necessary for the emergence of diasporic Judaism.

Ezekiel's candor therefore uncovers a web of lies and false expectations. It breaks a monolith of denials and dashes hope for precrisis recovery. It lays bare Israel's illusions of control and calls the community to surrender the whole way it organized life—without caving in to the dominant values and belief systems of its captors. According to Ezekiel, Israel must relinquish such securities so it can recover some semblance of order. Israel must relinquish its stalwart preexilic self to appropriate a more tenuous social and symbolic world.[9] It must relinquish venerable structures and institutions *to belong to God*. A definitive break with its much-loved past is a prerequisite for survival.

Creating Symbolic Order out of Chaos

The book of Ezekiel is a daring textual act of hope. But for hope to resonate, it must thoroughly engage those at risk. This is no easy task, for Ezekiel addresses refugees who were not only homeless but also hopeless. War had devastated their lives. It had shattered dreams, families, overarching systems of value, and the entire way the world was organized. It had thrown into question beloved beliefs, ethical arrangements, ritual practices, and core understandings of community identity. The result was tangible chaos and disorientation.

The force of Ezekiel's articulation of hope lies in its courage to (1) face the abyss, (2) put the destitution into words, and (3) demand an end to precrisis life. This remarkable prophetic performance, however, does even more than confront the real world of human suffering; it organizes the wreckage into manageable shapes and creates a sense of coherence in a world beset by violence. The impetus for such meaning-making is the belief that God is at work *ordering the world in justice* and *holiness*, despite appearances to the contrary. Divine justice, sovereignty, and holiness make sense out of life's nonsense.

When the book of Ezekiel reenacts the events that lead to the fall of Jerusalem in 587 (in chs. 1–24), it not only nails the coffin shut on precrisis life; it also sets the disaster firmly within a morally exacting and symmetrical framework. Ezekiel asserts that Judah's predicament is divine judgment for its idolatry and disobedience to God (see chs. 8–16, 22–24). The tradition is adamant that God's people have deserted God, defiled the temple, and participated in flagrant acts of moral and economic irresponsibility. The Jerusalem crisis is therefore not a consequence of "bad outsiders" with designs toward domination, but an outcome of Judah's own misdeeds.[10] When the prophet declares that everyone will live or die according to his or her own conduct (ch. 18), the reader can hardly escape the conclusion that Judah's dire condition is its own doing: "Yet you say, 'The way of the Lord is unfair.' Hear now, O house of Israel: Is my way unfair? Is it not your ways that are unfair? . . . Therefore I will judge you, O house of Israel, all of you according to your ways, says the Lord GOD" (18:25, 30). The correlation of conduct and condition, couched in priestly garb, serves both to uphold divine justice and to demonstrate that the moral workings of the universe are neither arbitrary nor gratuitous.

It should be noted that Ezekiel's categories of causation are deeply strained. First, they clearly trade in guilt. To hold little Judah responsible for its own predicament is in large measure to blame the victim. Second, to let Babylon off the hook is at best inadequate—historically, theologically, and ethically. While these arrangements serve to uphold a moral structure with meaning, they cannot adequately deal with human brutality.[11]

At the same time, Ezekiel's categories of causation do more than uphold coherent moral structures; they function as survival apparatus for refugees whose world is spiraling out of control. Daniel L. Smith-Christopher observes in this regard that the

> frequency of the motif that "it's all because of our sins" in cross-cultural settings would lead one to reconsider the possibility that it is among the effective coping strategies of a people in crisis. After all, if one's suffering is because of one's own oversights and not because of the power of the emperor and his armies, then this holds out considerably more hope about a future restoration.[12]

Better to live with a degree of guilt—even false guilt—than to lose control of your life. The refugees in Babylon may be laden with guilt (for example, 33:10), but at least they do not have to see themselves as helpless victims, prey to capricious forces. By repentance and obedience they can take back their lives and carry on with a sense of dignity.

At the core of Ezekiel's theological arrangements is a sovereign God who is the author of weal and woe. The prophet contends that this God is ordering the world in and through the contingencies of history. No realm lies outside God's authority, no convergence of raw human power can resist it, and nothing can rival it. YHWH is lord of all. Although other prophetic writings affirm the sovereign lordship of YHWH over nature and world historical forces, Ezekiel is the boldest. As John A. Goldingay observes: "Ezekiel uniquely uses the phrase 'sovereign [YHWH]' [usually translated 'Lord GOD'] as the characteristic title for God."[13] Sovereignty is more than an expression of divine activity; it is a defining attribute of God's character. God *is* the divine ruler, and God *is* sovereign. YHWH's speech, resolve, presence, and work in the world monopolize the textual landscape of the book and tame all life-threatening powers. In response to a world that has seemingly gone mad, Ezekiel affirms that God is still in control. In fact, the prophet is bold enough to attribute "all that happens to [YHWH's] sovereignty."[14] While this theological perspective is beset by interpretive dilemmas, it addresses the most pressing anxieties of a subjugated people.

The imprint of YHWH's reign is evident throughout the prophetic performance. In the initial vision, the heavens are open and Ezekiel encounters YHWH on the chariot throne (1:4-28). The divine king is transcendent, free, and commanding. And YHWH's domain is not limited to any one setting—not even the temple in Jerusalem. The wheels on the divine chariot enable YHWH to rule in all places. And because YHWH's sway is universal, all powers and principalities are subservient. In Ezekiel's culminating vision, YHWH returns to a new and perfectly structured temple to take up residence as king. YHWH's place there is front and center. All life revolves around the One whose glory eventually fills the temple (43:1-9). Not unlike Isaiah's vision of YHWH as divine king or Jeremiah's assertion that YHWH is warrior-king (Jer 50–51), Ezekiel envisages YHWH enthroned on high and "at work in the world, controlling nations and events according to God's own plan."[15] Only once does the tradition refer to a Davidic "king" who will shepherd Israel (Ezek 37:24; cf. 34:23-24). As a rule the prophet disdains Judah's kings for "blatantly [breaking] God's laws and [ravaging] their subjects like lions (chap. 19), for oppressing the very people whose rights they were duty-bound to protect (chap. 22), and finally for rebelling against the pro-Babylonian policy that Ezekiel insisted was [YHWH's] will (chap. 17)."[16] Ezekiel is uncompromising in the claim that YHWH alone reigns.

God's sovereignty is the key to hope. It answers accusations of divine injustice and indifference (for example, 8:12). It functions as an alternative to ordinary power arrangements. It trumps the entire world of Mesopotamian geopolitics. And it interrupts the vicious chain of violence, war, retaliation, and despair. The affirmation that YHWH is sovereign operates as a resistance script in the struggle for community survival. It assures a disheartened people of a promising future. And finally it serves as a claim on Israel. Or as Margaret Odell puts it: Ezekiel "tells the story of God's final attempt as their only legitimate king to claim the loyalty of his subjects, the rebellious and recalcitrant house of Israel."[17]

The only theological assertion that rivals divine justice and sovereignty in the book of Ezekiel is divine holiness. Together the triad—justice, sovereignty, and holiness—stems the tide of chaos produced by war and oppressive human regimes. The Hebrew word for holiness (*qdš*) occurs more than sixty times in Ezekiel—more times than in any other biblical book, with the exception of Exodus, Leviticus, and Numbers. In the first place, holiness defines the character of God.

- YHWH is the Holy One in Israel (39:7).
- YHWH's name or reputation is holy (for example, 20:39; 36:20-22; 39:7).
- YHWH's Sabbaths are holy (20:20; 22:8), as are YHWH's
  - mountain (20:40; 28:14),
  - dwelling place (for example, 41:4; 41:21; 41:23),
  - offerings (42:13; 44:8),
  - priests' clothing (42:14),
  - and the land apportioned to the Levites (48:12, 14).
- YHWH makes the people of Israel holy (20:12).
- YHWH keeps the Sabbath days holy (20:20).
- YHWH promises to display his holiness among the people of Israel (20:41) and in the sight of the nations (28:25).
- YHWH shows concern for his holy name (36:21) and will protect it (36:22; 39:25).
- YHWH resolves to make his great name holy (36:23),
- will display his holy name to all nations (38:23), and
- will make known his holy name among his people of Israel (39:7).

Despite this concentrate of divine awe, God's people insist on defiling God's holiness.

- They desecrate God's temple (8:1–10:22) and holy Sabbaths (20:12-13; 22:8).
- Israel's priests do violence to God's teaching, and they profane God's holy things by not discriminating between the holy and the common (22:26).
- The people of Israel despise or defile God's holy name "with their conduct and their deeds" (36:19-23).

In sum, Ezekiel bears witness to a God who is utterly holy. The places where God dwells are holy, as are the deeds that God does. God's holiness will not tolerate duplicity, disobedience, accommodation, defilement, or moral and economic improprieties.

Such acts have no place in the proximity of this extraordinary and dangerous God (see Ezek 8:1–19:14).

What then does holiness have to do with survival and hope? On the surface, it would seem very little. In the first place, God's holiness transcends utility or expedience. God's holiness is not a means to an end; it is an end in itself. Like God's sovereignty, holiness defines the divine character. Furthermore, holiness creates a huge chasm between God and God's people, which Walter Brueggemann calls a "mismatch." The "disinterested holiness of God and the utilitarian unrighteousness of Israel" is the "overriding truth" of Ezekiel's prophetic ministry.[18] God's holiness poses a grave danger to Israel. It evokes dread and heightens Israel's culpability. It is uncompromising, authoritative, and detached.

Yet holiness, no less than divine justice and sovereignty, is the corridor to hope. Holiness structures life. In the case of Ezekiel, it organizes shattered life; it sets limits and clarifies what God expects. Holiness demands ritual purity as well as a realignment of ethical, economic, and political practices. It insists that the people of God turn from idolatry, greed, and corruption and embrace a life of obedience, justice, and righteousness. Holiness establishes boundaries, spelling out what in God's presence is appropriate or not. It maps out lines of distinction between compliant and noncompliant community members.[19] It keeps community identity intact by reestablishing social roles and ethical standards as well as by insulating the faithful from dangers within and outside the borders. Holiness helps define core values in the face of an ever-present threat of accommodation within the empire. It provides cohesion to a fractured community that is in grave danger of disappearing.[20] Indeed, holiness establishes a new countercultural script in lieu of the old world order. The shift from autonomous state policies and ideologies to "new rules for behavior . . . enable the community to survive and maintain its distinctiveness and cohesion."[21]

Ezekiel's priestly construction of holiness not only provides such values—empowering war-torn refugees to reattach severed parts of their defining narrative—it also lines out a path that leads to worship, which is "at the heart of community building and world formation."[22] Through the lens of worship, God's people can reframe their broken world; they can reenact God's involvement in history; they can recognize God's presence in the painful absences and discern some semblance of meaning in the most inexplicable circumstances. Through the theater of worship, the refugee community can participate in the re-creation of an exquisite world where ethical symmetry, beauty, and justice are present (see especially Ezek 40–48). In all, worship bridges the chasm between sinful Israel and a holy God, and it invites sinful Israel to a renewed relationship with the One who is both dangerous and terrifying. Although it is not readily apparent, holiness is the key to an alternative rendering of life—one that subverts despair, anger, and cynicism.

Unique to Ezekiel, divine holiness is the *foundation* of hope. God's restoration of Israel is rooted in the divine plan to vindicate God's holy reputation:

> Therefore say to the house of Israel, Thus says the Lord GOD: It is not for your sake, O house of Israel, that I am about to act, but for the sake of my holy name, which you have profaned among the nations to which you came. I will sanctify my great name, which has been profaned among the nations, and which you have profaned among them; and the nations shall know that I am the LORD, says the Lord GOD, when through you I display my holiness before their eyes. . . . It is not for your sake that I will act, says the Lord GOD; let that be known to you. Be ashamed and dismayed for your ways, O house of Israel. (Ezek 36:22-23, 32)

Whereas Jeremiah and Second Isaiah emphasize God's unilateral acts of salvation on Israel's behalf, only Ezekiel grounds the divine activity unequivocally in divine holiness. God's great acts of salvation on Israel's behalf are not dependent on the people's obedience or piety. They are not rooted in human initiative, charisma, or even a realignment of values. They are not even motivated by Israel's dire circumstances. The restoration of God's people is anchored firmly in divine inscrutability. And thus survival and newness are as unassailable as the core character of God.

Constructing New Worlds of Hope for the Future

Stark testimonies of trauma and destruction, concerted efforts to sever ties with the old world, and daring attempts to create symbolic order out of the chaos move us closer to Ezekiel's patent language of hope. We encounter the longest meditation on hope in the third section of the book of Ezekiel—following the message of judgment in chapters 1–24 and the Oracles against the Nations in chapters 25–32 (OAN). As we have seen, the first twenty-four chapters are essential to hope. For hope to bloom, Ezekiel must deal a deathblow to the entrenched power arrangements associated with Jerusalem and its temple. The old world must be exposed as a failed system, a stranglehold of injustice and idolatry that can no longer provide security and protection. Although counterintuitive, death and destruction are an integral part of Ezekiel's calculus of hope.

As long recognized, the OAN reflect "provisional hope." The dominant claim of this collection is that the surrounding nations have come under divine judgment for ravishing Israel in its time of need. Consequently, they must pay for their crimes. YHWH takes the Ammonites to task for gloating over Israel's misfortunes

(25:3, 6); YHWH threatens to punish Moab for taunting Judah (25:8); and YHWH indicts Edom for its acts of revenge (25:12) and Philistia for its "unending hostilities" (25:15-17). The king of Tyre is charged with hubris and idolatry ("I am a god" 28:2); Sidon is guilty of contempt (28:24); and Egypt's acts of arrogance and malice do not go unnoticed. In response God will not only act but will act justly and decisively on Israel's behalf. The threatened punishment takes the form of invasion, defeat, humiliation, and devastation: "I will execute great vengeance on them with wrathful punishments" (25:17). And the overriding purpose of the divine action is to vindicate YHWH before Israel and the nations: that they (or you) "shall know that I am [YHWH] GOD" (25:5, 11, 14, 17; 26:6; 28:20, 24, 26; 29:21; 30:8, 19; 32:15). It is of considerable interest that Babylon is not included in the diatribe. Although Babylon is an instrument of divine judgment against Tyre and Egypt (for example, 26:7; 29:17-20; 32:11), Babylon itself is not the target of divine punishment (cf. Jer 50–51).

Divine judgment hurled at Israel's tormenters can only engender hope in Ezekiel's audience. At the least, such scathing language interrupts the invective against Judah/Israel and offers the reading or listening community a momentary reprieve from the rhetoric of violence:

[YHWH] will defend Israel in the face of defeat and humiliation.

[YHWH] will not let the surrounding nations get away with bullying Israel.

[YHWH] promises an end to international contempt.

[YHWH] promises a grand homecoming.

[YHWH] hints at future restoration.

Hence the literary enactment of YHWH's victory over vindictive and self-aggrandizing regimes enables Judean refugees to see beyond their own bleak circumstances to a time when their cries for justice will be heard and their broken lives healed.

Language of hope finally takes center stage in Ezekiel 33–48, but even this grand literary performance bristles with the harsh realities of war (especially in chs. 33–39). The initial chapter (ch. 33) in particular is strangely reminiscent of the judgment oracles in Ezekiel 1–24. While this hinge text paves the way for buoyant expressions of salvation, it still resonates with echoes from the past. It opens with a wartime parable (33:1-6). It reaffirms the prophet's role as battle sentry (33:7-9; cf. 3:16-21). It employs conventional disaster language (for example, "the sword," "blow the siren," "the wicked," "death," "iniquities," "abominations," "blood," "a reckoning," "ruins," "strongholds," "pestilence," and "wasteland"). It calls attention to the hypocrisy of Ezekiel's audience, which listens to his words "but [does] not obey them" (33:31). It revisits the instruction on the way of death and life (33:7-20; cf. 18:5-32). It resumes the question of land rights (33:23-29; cf.11:14-15). And it ends with a confirmation of Ezekiel's status as a prophet (33:33; cf. 2:5). Most significantly, the inaugural chapter of the new epoch bears witness to the fall of Jerusalem. "In the twelfth year of our exile, in the tenth month, on the fifth day of the month, someone who had escaped from Jerusalem came to me and said, 'The city has fallen' " (33:21). The report is terse and almost anticlimatic, and yet it clearly represents a pivotal moment in the prophetic drama. The fugitive's testimony validates Ezekiel's detested predictions of Jerusalem's demise and dashes any hope that the old world will survive.

In addition, the text marks this frightful moment by opening Ezekiel's mouth and enabling him to speak: "So my mouth was opened, and I was no longer unable to speak" (33:22). At the start of his prophetic ministry Ezekiel is struck dumb (3:22-27), and only now does the text reverse this imagery. Joseph Blenkinsopp notes that "the interpretation of Ezekiel's silence is one of the most intractable problems of the book."[23] Taking into consideration the larger literary context, it is at least plausible that the city's collapse frees the prophet to utter words of hope (in chs. 34–39). What follows then is a "virtual plan for restoration."[24] Henceforth Ezekiel will map out God's salvific program for the exilic refugees, which is essentially a sustained response to their tormenting fears and focal concerns.

Three central concerns have already been broached in chapter 33: the question of survival (33:10-16), divine justice (33:17-20), and land rights (33:23-29). All three reveal the people's deep-seated doubts and despair. And all are taken up in detail in subsequent chapters, although anxiety over survival carries the most sustaining force: "Our transgressions and our sins weigh upon us, and we waste away because of them; *how then can we live?*" (33:10; emphasis added). Ezekiel speaks to "his people" (i.e., the exilic community; see "your people" in 33:12, 17, 30; 37:38) about how they can survive the life-threatening wounds of war, hegemony, and displacement. It is no accident that the words *live* or *life* occur ten times in Ezekiel 33 alone. Looming large is the question of life and survival—which, as Donald Gowan notes, may be the governing theme of chapters 33–48.[25] David Petersen likewise suggests, "The driving issue is how *life* [emphasis added] can be possible with the temple in ruins and with many people (and the temple's priests) in exile."[26] As such, the burning query "How can we live and survive?" lays bare the community's fundamental anxiety.

Ezekiel has already done much to deal with this debilitating fear: the prophet has engaged in truth-telling, denial-breaking, testimony, meaning-making, and reestablishing community identity—all attempts at making sense of the senselessness of the national disaster. Now Ezekiel tackles perhaps the most daunting threat to survival: the loss of trust in God. Henceforth the book gives full attention to restoring trust in the face of despair, death, and devastation.

How then can we live and survive? "The most immediate response," Blenkinsopp observes, "is a statement of God's ultimate purpose. . . . I have no pleasure in the death of the wicked. . . . There is always an opening for repentance, for 'turning,' and precisely this is the answer to their question."[27] Pronouncements of death are not irrevocable. God desires no one to perish. "If the wicked restore the pledge, give back what they have taken by robbery, and walk in the statutes of life . . . they shall surely live, they shall not die. None of the sins that they have committed shall be remembered against them; they have done what is lawful and right, they shall surely live" (33:15-16).

A more detailed response to the question of survival is set forth in the remainder of the prophetic performance (chs. 34–48). There Ezekiel makes a number of striking claims that encourage hope for survival: YHWH will defend Israel against predators (34:1-10), restore the divine image (34:11-31), vindicate the divine reputation before Israel and the nations (35:1–36:38; 38:1–39:29), bring Israel back to life (36:24-38; 37:1-28), and come and be present among God's people (40:1–48:35).

First, Ezekiel takes on perpetrators of violence and injustice (34:1-10). Whether the wrongdoers are Israel's own rulers, as long argued, or foreign rulers, as Odell recently suggests,[28] the prophet asserts that malevolent shepherds will not get away with mistreating God's people (34:1-10): "Mortal, prophesy against the shepherds of Israel. . . . Thus says the Lord GOD, I am against the shepherds; and I will demand my sheep at their hand" (34:2a, 10). The new social and symbolic world of Ezekiel demands full accountability of those who place Israel's survival in danger. Their unjust and oppressive policies will be aborted. Their unbridled greed, cruelty, and dereliction of duty will no longer go unchecked. Divine judgment is an integral part of Ezekiel's symmetrical and coherent ethical universe. The tradition cannot imagine it otherwise: survival and hope demand righting wrongs and restoring some semblance of justice (see also Ezek 35:1-15).

Second, after denouncing the shepherd-kings who have ravished Israel, YHWH, the divine shepherd-king, promises to intervene and defend the flock (34:11-31). YHWH pledges to be an entirely different kind of suzerain: one who rules justly, nourishes the flock, defends the weak, and ends oppression. As Israel's good shepherd, YHWH will act unilaterally on behalf of the injured sheep. The long string of first-person-singular statements accentuates God's resolve to create a kingdom of peace in place of the reign of tyranny:

> I myself will search for my sheep.
> I will seek them out.
> I will rescue them.
> I will bring them out . . . and gather them.
> I will bring them into their own land.

174

I will feed them.
I myself will be the shepherd of my sheep.
I will make them lie down.
I will seek the lost.
I will bring back the strayed.
I will bind up the injured.
I will strengthen the weak.
I will destroy the fat and the strong.
I will feed them with justice. (34:11-16)

I will set up over them one shepherd, my servant David. (34:23)

I will defend my flock;
I will make with them a covenant of peace. (34:25)

The surplus of promissory language stresses God's search-and-rescue mission. YHWH vows to take decisive action on behalf of the wounded, and nothing will thwart YHWH's full engagement. Such language is consistent with the claim that God's new program is not for Israel's sake, "but for the sake of my holy name" (36:22). Both the declarative first-person speech and the name formula convey the certainty of God's purposes. God's actions culminate in the establishment of a Davidic prince who will feed and shepherd Israel: "And I, the LORD, will be their God, and my servant David shall be prince among them; I, the LORD, have spoken" (34:24; see also 37:24).

God's saving acts lead to security, peace, and blessing. Although "clouds and thick darkness" encompass the sheep while they are scattered among the nations, the good shepherd will make them "lie down." YHWH will establish "a covenant of peace . . . so that they may live . . . securely" (34:25; emphasis added). "They shall be secure on their soil" (34:27; emphasis added). "They shall live in safety, and no one shall make them afraid" (34:28; emphasis added). The point is this: God's wondrous deeds not only reconfigure social and symbolic realities; they also address the community's emotional needs and concrete fears. YHWH's compassionate kingship restores order and beauty to a world that greed and injustice have brutalized. Or as Odell astutely observes, "Against the imperialist claims of superpowers of his day, Ezekiel asserts that Israel belongs to no other shepherd than [YHWH]."[29]

All told, Ezekiel reconfigures the face of God from that of oppressor-abuser to protector-defender. When the "shepherds of Israel" feed themselves and not the flock, they distort the divine image. When they exploit the flock and rule with an iron fist, they misrepresent the divine shepherd-king who binds up the injured and sustains the weak. Such predatory acts, such betrayals of trust, give rise to emotional suffering, cognitive dissonance, and a myriad of disconcerting questions.[30] In response to this concentration of pain, Ezekiel affirms that YHWH is altogether unlike Israel's unjust and abusive rulers: the true shepherd-king actually pastors the sheep, provides for them, and protects them from dangerous predators. How can we trust again? By reimaging God as the Good Shepherd! "How then can we live and survive?" The Good Shepherd will see to it!

Third, to bolster hope for survival, the divine reputation is vindicated before Israel and the nations (35:1–36:38; 38:1–39:29). In view of the heinous divine caricature, the prophet must *reintroduce* YHWH. Put differently, in light of all that threatens to impugn the divine character, including the destruction of God's residence on earth, YHWH sets out to rehabilitate the divine name. The need for its reestablishment in exile is no less urgent than the revelation of YHWH at the Exodus. At both extremities—at birth and near death—dangerous world historical forces threaten Israel's survival and YHWH's reputation. At Israel's farthest points, imperial policies of superpowers imperil God's people *and* God's character. Survival is thus as much a burning concern in Israel's birth narrative as it is in Israel's near-death narrative in exile.

Both seek to defend God's character before Israel and the nations. The Exodus story *introduces* YHWH to Moses and subsequently to Israel: "I am the God of your father, the God of Abraham, the God of Isaac, and the God of Jacob" (Exod 3:6; 3:13-17). But Moses is concerned that the downtrodden Israelites will not recognize the one who authorizes his mission—that is, they will ask him, "What is his name?" (Exod 3:13). And so God replies, "I AM WHO I AM. . . . Thus you shall say to the Israelites, 'The LORD the God of your ancestors, the God of Abraham, the God of Isaac, and the God of Jacob, has sent me to you'" (Exod 3:14-15). As importantly, the powerful forces of Egypt, embodied in the pharaoh, do not know YHWH: "Who is the LORD that I should heed him and let Israel go? I do not know the LORD, and I will not let Israel go" (Exod 5:2; see also 6:1-8). Only after wondrous displays of unrivaled power do the Egyptians acknowledge YHWH's authority (7:5; see also 7:17; 14:4, 18). So it is, Egypt's ruler eventually accepts YHWH's rule to the point of asking Moses to pray to the God of the enslaved Israelites on his behalf (8:8). Likewise, the Israelites recognize YHWH only after a stunning demonstration of divine power. After crossing the sea, Moses and the people exclaim, "The LORD is a warrior; / the LORD is his name" (15:3, 11). Thus the Exodus event establishes YHWH's name or reputation before Israel and the nations (15:14-18).[31] Now all may come to know that "I am the LORD" (see 5:1-6; 6:2).

In Ezekiel YHWH seeks to *reintroduce* the divine name. The recognition formula, "that you may know YHWH," is almost ubiquitous in this exilic text. Given that military defeat, shame, harsh rulers, and injury have marred the divine reputation, YHWH seeks to restore it before Israel and the nations. Throughout the entire book, YHWH does extensive work to demonstrate that no arena of life lies outside the divine purview. God is involved in every facet of Israel's experience:

> I will stretch out my hand against them, and make the land desolate and waste. . . . Then they shall know that I am the LORD. (6:14)

> You shall fall by the sword; I will judge you at the border of Israel. And you shall know that I am the LORD. (11:10)

> And they shall know that I am the LORD, when I disperse them among the nations and scatter them through the countries. (12:15)

> The inhabited cities shall be laid waste, and the land shall become a desolation; and you shall know that I am the LORD. (12:20)

> I will break down the wall that you have smeared with whitewash, and bring it to the ground, so that its foundation will be laid bare; when it falls, you shall perish within it; and you shall know that I am the LORD. (13:14)

> I will set my face against them; I will make them a sign and a byword and cut them off from the midst of my people; and you shall know that I am the LORD. (14:8)

> I will purge out the rebels among you, and those who transgress against me; I will bring them out of the land where they reside as aliens, but they shall not enter the land of Israel. Then you shall know that I am the LORD. (20:38)

> You shall know that I am the LORD, when I bring you into the land of Israel, the country that I swore to give to your ancestors. (20:42)

Ezekiel insists that Israel's harsh historical circumstances do nothing to blemish YHWH's character. YHWH is indeed present in Israel's experience, even its harsh realities.

Upon arriving at chapter 35 of Ezekiel, we encounter YHWH taking aim at Edom for "harboring an ancient hostility" and exploiting the Israelites in their time of need. When YHWH deals a decisive blow to Israel's adversaries, the Edomites—like the Egyptians (cf. Exod 7:5; 14:4, 18)—will come to recognize: "I am [YHWH]" (Ezek 35:4, 9, 12). In chapters 38 and 39 YHWH confronts menacing Gog and Magog. YHWH crushes these immense forces to reestablish the divine reign on earth. The massive cosmic victory (for example, Ezek 38:17-23; cf. Jer 4:23-28; Ps 46; Heb 12:18-29) not only empowers dejected Jewish refugees; it also parades YHWH's authority as warrior-king. YHWH's triumph over repressive powers and principalities establishes divine "greatness and holiness," ultimately convincing the world that YHWH is the true suzerain (Ezek 38:14-23): "Then they shall know that I am the LORD" (Ezek 38:23). Like the Exodus event, YHWH's victory over hostile hegemonic forces serves to convince all—Israel and the nations—that YHWH is the unrivaled king (39:21-29): "The house of Israel shall know that I am the LORD their God, from that day forward" (Ezek 39:22).

Fourth, once YHWH's reputation is restored, Ezekiel can begin to depict God's redemptive work in greater detail. Interestingly, Israel's birth narrative in the book of Exodus and near-death narrative in Ezekiel once again have much in common. Both celebrate Israel's grand liberation from subjugation. The Exodus story commemorates YHWH's mighty act of deliverance from Israel's first repressive and genocidal ruler. YHWH's defeat of the pharaoh is nothing less than a victory over death and despair. It liberates a broken and conquered people to love and serve the true suzerain, YHWH (Exod 14:30-31; 15:1-2, 21). Similarly, Ezekiel declares that YHWH will punish Israel's oppressors and unshackle Israel from its distressing conditions. Another string of first-person assertions underscores God's resolve to redeem Israel and reverse the conditions of exile (Ezek 36:24-38):

I will take you from all the nations.
I will gather you.
I will bring you into your own land.
I will sprinkle clean water upon you.
I will give you a new heart.
I will put within you a new spirit.
I will remove from your body the heart of stone.
I will give you a heart of flesh.
I will put my spirit within you.
I will make you observe my ordinances.
Then you shall live in the land that I gave to your ancestors; and you shall be my people, and I will be your God.
I will save you from all your uncleannesses.
I will summon the grain. . . .
I will make the fruit of the tree . . . abundant. . . .
Then they shall know that I am [YHWH]. (authors' translation)

God promises a grand homecoming. The land to which the exiles return will be like paradise: "They will say, 'This land that was laid waste has become like the garden of Eden; the cities that were lying in ruins, desolate and destroyed, are now fortified and inhabited.'" (36:35; NIV). God will not only renew the material world but also transform the interior spiritual life of community. God will replace Israel's heart of stone with a heart of flesh, purify Israel, and enable Israel to obey. All Israel must do, it would seem, is follow these instructions: "Do not be afraid, stand firm, and see the deliverance that the LORD will accomplish for you today. . . . The LORD will fight for you, and you have only to keep still" (Exod 14:13, 14). Israel's restoration depends entirely on God.

Like the liberating Passover experience in Exodus, the vision of the valley of dry bones—perhaps the most astounding text in Ezekiel—depicts YHWH's extraordinary acts on behalf of Israel (Ezek 37:1-14). Ezekiel imagines the resurrection of the slain in battle. By the power of the divine word, by the breath of God, the diasporic people of God rise from death as if to break out of a dark dungeon for a world ablaze in hope. Communal renewal is nothing less than an extraordinary act of re-creation. When all hope is seemingly gone—"Our bones are dried up, and our hope is lost"—the God "who gives life to the dead and calls into existence the things that do not exist" (Rom 4:17) raises Israel from the dead and promises to unify the southern and northern kingdoms with David as their shepherd (Ezek 37:15-28). God makes "a covenant of peace with them" and dwells with them forever. At last God reclaims his people: "I will be their God, and they shall be my people" (37:27). Such an astonishing act of imagination breathes life into a disconsolate refugee community; it honors this subject people before the nations (37:28); and it bears out God's unparalleled authority (37:6, 14, 23, 28). Katheryn Pfisterer Darr says it this way: "If [YHWH] can restore desiccated bones and buried bodies to life, then there are absolutely no limits to God's power."[32] Margaret Odell observes: "Having rescued his people from the nations and restored them to their land as a cleansed, united, and covenanted people, [YHWH] thereby indicates to the nations that Israel is off limits."[33]

Finally, after this stunning portrait of God's life-giving activity, Ezekiel (Ezek 40–48), like Moses (Exod 25–31; cf. Lev 18–26), constructs an ideal vision of worship that empowers and ennobles the exiles on their journey through the "wilderness" en route to the "Promised Land." Whereas Moses introduces the divine "pattern of the tabernacle" (Exod 25:9, 40) and concludes the tabernacle instructions with the cloud covering the tent of meeting and the glory of YHWH filling the tabernacle (Exod 40:34), Ezekiel's vision of worship includes a new temple and new gates, and a new world order. The old order has now passed away and all is new (cf. Rev 21:1ff.). This new map of reality restores purity, coherence, and beauty to a world marred by sin, tragedy, and abusive power structures. It is governed by priestly categories and theocratic ideals rather than by the monarchical arrangements: YHWH, not imperial or military figures, enjoys the central place in the life of the new community. Ritual defilement is expunged, as are all forms of violence and oppression (Ezek 45:9). Ancient land boundaries are honored. Economic resources are distributed justly

(45:10-12; 47:14). The stream flowing below the temple—"the river of life"—transforms the desert and brings about fertility and healing (47:1-12).

Altogether Ezekiel has moved from dystopia to utopia, from anger to communion, and from idolatry to doxology. These radical shifts are possible because YHWH returns to the temple to take up residence (43:1-2; cf. 10:1-22). "And the name of the city from that time on shall be, The LORD is There" (48:35). Ezekiel's map of the world imagines God's luminous presence returning to reside among God's people forever. God gets what God has desired all along. And survival is ensured!

Conclusion

Ezekiel is disaster literature. Ezekiel is survival literature. From the outset, this exilic book is torn between extremities. The prophetic text bears witness to deep discontinuities, massive disruptions, and broken lives located on the edges. It also testifies to hope and resilience. Residing in diaspora, it imagines a grand homecoming. Living with excruciating dissonance, it reconstructs an orderly and symmetrical world. Inundated with violence, it anticipates an era of peace (for example, 34:25; 37:26). Tormented by absence, it envisions God's luminous presence. Ezekiel is defined by an array of stark oppositions.

Judgment	—	Salvation
Death	—	Life
Horror	—	Beauty
Earth	—	Heaven
Dystopia	—	Utopia
Defeat	—	Victory
Pollution	—	Holiness
Old Temple	—	New Temple
Hinterlands	—	Homecoming
Trauma	—	Healing
War	—	Peace
Absence	—	Presence

Divides of this sort are not uncommon for cultures in crisis. In the case of Ezekiel they reflect the trauma of war and the audacity of hope. While gratuitous violence and massive cultural disruption, military invasion and occupation, forced deportation and resettlement create gaping rifts in social and symbolic worlds, they do not extinguish the flame of hope and the possibility of newness.

"Can these bones live?" God knows, and in effect so does God's prophet. Ezekiel provides a more detailed response to the question of survival than any other prophetic figure in the Hebrew Bible. Employing priestly categories, Ezekiel asserts that the death of the old world does not represent the death of God or the demise of God's people. The dismantling of long-honored beliefs and institutions does not signal the end of salvation history. And the humiliation of forced relocation does not denote divine abandonment. Indeed, the exilic prophet resolves the conundrum of absence in far-away Babylon: God is not bound to the old city but is present even in the worst of circumstances. God descends from the north—"a great cloud with brightness around it and fire flashing forth continually" (1:4)—and is exiled from the Jerusalem temple to live among refugees in Babylon. Eventually this God returns to the temple to take up residence at the center of Israel's new life. And so Ezekiel can affirm that life's greatest blessings emerge in the most unlikely places. Or as Peter Craigie eloquently notes, Ezekiel "reminds us forcibly that there is no place and no circumstances in which the experience of God may be denied. Perhaps it is even true that God's presence is known [best] at the place and in the circumstances in which it is least expected."[34]

PART FOUR

THE BOOK OF THE TWELVE

AN ANTHOLOGY OF DISPERSION AND DIAGNOSIS (HOSEA–MICAH)

T he book of the twelve prophets (hereafter referred to as "the Twelve") comprises as many as twelve diverse traditions. Yet, at the same time, it reflects a certain unity of concern: in light of the fall of Israel and Judah and the collapse of venerable institutions and beliefs, the question of theodicy organizes the collection as a whole. The arrangement of the Twelve as presented in the MT has been accounted for by various theories. On the one hand, this collection of the Twelve depicts a lack of organization. Any chronological or thematic correlations among the books are too sporadic or random to show evidence of authorial or textual intention. Some scholars have even debated whether the collection originally had eleven or twelve books, because Malachi may have at one point been a part of Zechariah.[1] On the other hand, even though the collection is a loose anthology at best, readers of the final form can detect a certain rationale as to how the compiler(s) or redactor(s) arranged the books. Certain key catchwords and motifs occur somewhat consistently and continually enough to suggest that the Twelve was meant to be read together sequentially and intertextually.[2] The structural order of the manuscripts conveys a thematic unity as revealed by each version's arrangement.[3] In these final chapters we will look at the order of the Masoretic version and explore its conceptual implications as an anthology—especially for the interpretive community, the implied readers in the aftermath of the exile.[4]

Specifically, we will explore how the Twelve functions as a survival text and a definitive meaning-making text, as an anthology of collapse and of rebuilding toward unity and hope against dispersion and despair. The Twelve portrays the abyss as the erosion of unity, moral coherence, and faith in God and in community. The political and religious hegemonies of the two monarchies—northern Israel and southern Judah—are shattered by the upheavals in 722 and 587 B.C.E. Moreover, social ills endemic to both Israel and the dominant empires place the survival of the resultant community in grave danger. It is as if the entire world, including God's people, stands under divine judgment:

> The LORD roars from Zion,
>   and utters his voice from Jerusalem. (Amos 1:2)

185

> Hear, you peoples, all of you;
>> listen, O earth, and all that is in it;
> and let the Lord GOD be a witness against you. (Mic 1:2)

> A jealous and avenging God is the LORD,
>> the LORD is avenging and wrathful;
> the LORD takes vengeance on his adversaries
>> and rages against his enemies. (Nah 1:2)

> I will utterly sweep away everything
>> from the face of the earth, says the LORD. (Zeph 1:2)

At the same time, there are robust constructions of hope. In the first place, almost every chapter of the Twelve ends with expectations for a promising future:

> I will plant them upon their land,
>> and they shall never again be plucked up
>> out of the land that I have given them,
>>> says the LORD your God. (Amos 9:15)

> You will show faithfulness to Jacob
>> and unswerving loyalty to Abraham,
> as you have sworn to our ancestors
>> from the days of old. (Mic 7:20)

> At that time I will bring you home,
>> at the time when I gather you;
> for I will make you renowned and praised
>> among all the peoples of the earth,
> when I restore your fortunes
>> before your eyes, says the LORD. (Zeph 3:20)

Furthermore, the Twelve depicts the possibility of hope for the indomitable, rejuvenated presence of YHWH "on that day." Inspired by the pivotal events of 612 and 540 B.C.E.—the collapse of the empires of Assyria and Babylon, which the people of Israel may have never dared to imagine—the Twelve unashamedly anticipates the dawning of "the day of YHWH." This metaphor is capable of conveying both the salvation and judgment for God's people, as well as the defeat of the arrogant *über*empires:

> Alas for the day!
> For the day of the LORD is near,
>> and as destruction from the Almighty it comes. (Joel 1:15)

> Seek the LORD, all you humble of the land,
>> who do his commands;
> seek righteousness, seek humility;
>> perhaps you may be hidden
>> on the day of the LORD's wrath. (Zeph 2:3)

> And on that day I will seek to destroy
> all the nations that come against Jerusalem. (Zech 12:9)

When listened to in this way, the collection of twelve distinctive voices performs a symphony of diverse yet harmonic expressions of warning and promise, ultimately planting the seeds of hope for the reunification of the twelve tribes, the twelve children of Jacob/Israel returning home to their God.

It is noteworthy that the interpretive community of Sirach identified the Twelve, despite its numerous oracles of judgment, as a source of comfort and hope for Israel: "May the bones of the Twelve Prophets send forth new life from where they lie, for they *comforted* the people of Jacob and delivered them with confident *hope*" (Sir 49:10; emphasis added). We do not know what may have led Sirach to associate this collection with salvation. Perhaps the community recognized in this scroll the candor to critique its own particular circumstances and the audacity to envision a world beyond its deep ruptures. Perhaps it saw language that would help diasporic communities survive the crushing cultural and religious threats that dominant ruling empires imposed. Perhaps it heard language that destabilized but also fostered resistance. Perhaps this community discerned in this anthology a metamorphosis in which harbingers of doom eventually become messengers of hope. In any case, over against the trying colonial settings of the late third century B.C.E., the reading and writing community of Sirach bears witness to the enduring influence of the great prophetic heroes of the past.[5] And in particular, this community gives voice to a literary perspective that interprets the Twelve as "one of consolation and hope."[6] While living under overpowering imperial control, it imagines the ancient promises of salvation ultimately trumping threats of judgment for God's people.

Hosea, Joel, and Amos: (Northern) Israel as an Object Lesson

A key compositional and thematic point of significance resides in the first three books of this anthology: Hosea, Joel, and Amos. The books of Hosea and Amos are intricately related to the settings of the northern kingdom of Israel during the eighth century B.C.E. The book of Joel does not contain any specific indications of its historical setting, thereby making it possible for later readers to consider multiple settings and apply its meanings to their own changing situations.[7] Hence, in the canonical sequence, northern Israel's "shameful past," so vehemently criticized by the prophets, could become an object lesson for the remnants of Judah. Perhaps southern Judah has a lingering rivalry with northern Israel,[8] or perhaps it is too difficult to expose Judah's own sin at the outset. Regardless of these possible rationales, the Twelve begins with reflections on the sins of northern Israel, especially in Hosea and Amos.

At the same time, readers immediately note the kinship of Ephraim and Judah, Samaria and Jerusalem. After all, they are sisters and brothers of the same ancestral family. Thus, the name *Israel* contains a double meaning—the *northern kingdom* of Israel as well as the *entire people* of Israel. The number twelve, as the total number of prophetic books within this collection, may underscore the significance of each prophet's specific identity while also denoting the legitimacy and significance of each of the twelve sons of Jacob in Genesis. Moreover, the people of Judah, like Israel, experience the warnings and sufferings of exile. Ultimately, the shortcomings and fate of northern Israel are intricately entwined with those of southern Judah, much like the book of Joel that links Hosea and Amos. The object lessons recorded in the memoirs about northern Israel also function as a mirror image for the people of Judah. The interpretive community considers how both Israel and Judah, in their collective reflection, repentance, and reformation, eventually fared.

Hosea: An Abusive Prophet of God

The placement of the book of Hosea as the first book of the Twelve both in the MT and in the LXX may be significant in that it suggests a thematic overture for the entire twelve books. It is noteworthy that the name *Hosea* literally means "salvation," implying that the Twelve will somehow address the message of comfort and salvation. In fact, words associated with the verbal root "to save" occur at the initial and closing chapters in the book of Hosea (1:7; 2:12; 13:4, 10; 14:3 [MT 14:4]). Hope for salvation is the dominant theme of this book. YHWH's desire to restore the severed relationship with Israel is portrayed through a number of organizing metaphors.

However, modern readers of Hosea encounter many interpretive difficulties—especially, with the husband-wife-whore metaphor, which functions to depict Israel's religious and political idolatry against YHWH. It should be noted that prophets often employ shocking words and symbolic actions to convey the divine message, with Ezekiel being a prime example (Ezek 4–5; cf. Isa 20). Moreover, one must acknowledge that Hosea 1–3 is a cultural expression of its patriarchal context. Nevertheless, the depiction of the abusive prophet and the abused Gomer creates an unusual hermeneutical challenge because it serves as a metonym for the divine-human relationship. If used or taken improperly, metaphors, like illustrations or analogies, can be damaging to unintended "others," thereby making the purpose of such devices countereffective or even dangerous. How many of today's African American audiences would appreciate the exhortation: "Slaves, obey your earthly masters" (Eph 6:5; Col 3:22)?

Julia M. O'Brien, in a succinct review of various interpretations of the marriage metaphor of Hosea, addresses the importance of the feminist critiques and characterizes scholarly efforts as largely polarized: they often either disparage it or fully embrace it.[9] Bruce C. Birch's caveat is also compelling:

> We must firmly and absolutely reject the appropriateness of abusive actions, physical or emotional, as responses to a broken relationship no matter what the circumstances. The language of a broken relationship as painful and wounding can be preserved. But we must say an absolute no to responses in broken relationships that justify abusive attempts to regain control no matter how painful the brokenness.[10]

Furthermore, Marvin A. Sweeney's trenchant question concerning the silence of Gomer and the implicit negligence of the prophet toward his wife offers, if not a clear answer, at least an alternative perspective:

> In the face of overwhelming Assyrian power, however, YHWH's failure to protect Israel produces a charge of Israel's infidelity to YHWH. Such a charge protects YHWH's reputation, power, and righteousness in the face of charges that YHWH was unwilling, unable, or negligent in seeing to the protection of the nation.[11]

Perhaps this penetrating question rightly curtails modern readers from rigidly defending this biblical text and the God it portrays. Perhaps the text with its "pornographic" metaphors allows the silenced Gomer and the symbolic "Whore Israel" to obliquely accuse her abusive husband and the unreliable God. In the text, Gomer has no voice, and Hosea does not question God as Isaiah does: "How long, O Lord?" (Isa 6:11). God's speech monopolizes the symbolic terrain. Perhaps one can discern faint voices of dissent—from the perspective of the exiles of the devastating debacles in 722 B.C.E. and 587 B.C.E.—drawing attention to "Whore Israel's" unbearable treatment:

> I will strip her naked
>   and expose her as in the day she was born,
> and make her like a wilderness,
>   and turn her into a parched land,
>   and kill her with thirst.
> Upon her children also I will have no pity,
>   because they are children of whoredom. (Hos 2:3-4 [MT 2:5-6])

In doing so, the text depicts the "Whore Israel" as Hagar, her children as Ishmael, and thereby the actor as Abraham, who brutally sent them away (Gen 16; 21). But in Hosea there is no theophany or miraculous rescue because YHWH, not Abraham, is the actor. The text may be alluding not only to the religious or political idolatry of "Whore Israel" but also, cryptically, to the divine mistreatment of exiles who are brutally abandoned. Gomer and her whole children Israel meet Job's wife and her children, except that Job's wife is accorded a defiant voice in the aftermath of calamity (Job 2:10). Perhaps, through silent or silenced dissent, Hosea's metaphors expose the horror and humiliation Israel has to endure.

Hosea: "You are my people"

Hosea's metaphors divulge not only the unbearable abuse of God's people but also the undeniable compassion of God. The marriage metaphor, however problematic or paradoxical, particularly drives home the gratuitous love of YHWH. Katharine Doob Sakenfeld offers an insightful observation that by depicting the covenant relationship in "marriage imagery filled with language of intimacy and emotion," the prophet introduces a new understanding of God, that is, from a fearsome suzerain to a tender partner.[12] The family imagery is also significant because here God becomes a vulnerable family member. In this broken family, God is dependent upon the other members, just as the family members are dependent upon God. Throughout the book of Hosea, the exhortation to "turn back" or "return" occurs quite frequently, as if to express the ongoing yearning of God for reunion and reconciliation: "But as for you, return to your God, / hold fast to love and justice, / and wait continually for your God" (12:6 [MT 12:7]; cf. 5:4; 6:1; 7:10; 14:1-2 [MT 14:2-3]).

Here, the divine pathos is defined and marked out in two paradoxical ways. On the one hand, it encompasses the unveiling of the social and religious ills of God's people. Abraham Heschel expresses this perceptively: "There is an evil which most of us condone and are even guilty of: indifference to evil."[13] The fundamental wrongdoing of Israel and Judah is succinctly summarized: "They have broken my covenant, / and transgressed my law" (8:1). Northern Israel is indicted for covenant violations. Ephraim's evil deeds are condemned in harsh language and depictions in Hosea 9–10. The people should have sowed and reaped righteousness and goodness from seeking YHWH; instead they plowed wickedness and treachery (10:12-13). The conclusion is irrevocable: "At dawn the king of Israel shall be utterly cut off" (10:15). Yet the people of Judah see themselves as if in a mirror, because they too have been faithless to YHWH's Torah. Throughout the book of Hosea, accordingly, Judah is often incorporated into the oracles of divine indictment against northern Israel (1:7; 5:5, 13-14; 6:4; 8:14; 10:11; 12:1, 3). Even the political miscalculation (or "whoredom") of relying immediately on Assyria and Egypt is a tendency of both Israel and Judah (5:13; 7:11; 8:9, 13; 10:6; 12:2). Judah is no better than its rival kindred with regard to the anatomy of sins.

On the other hand, the divine pathos finds expression in God's deep care and longing for return with God's people.[14] From the marriage metaphor (Hosea 1–3) readers would recall the names of the prophet Hosea's illicit children from Gomer: Jezreel, Lo-ruhamah, and Lo-ammi (1:4, 6, 9). *Jezreel* as a pun in Hebrew denotes the people "scattered" or "dispersed," while it may also connote the locale of Jehu's brutal massacre against heirs of Omri and Ahab (2 Kgs 9–10). *Lo-ruhamah* means "not comforted," while *Lo-ammi* means "not my people." Even their existence is denied, and their relationship with God is severed. The exiled, banished "no-people" find themselves rejected by their God. Yet, God's care is noticeable. Divine protection is restricted yet not prohibited, hidden but still present. The concluding section of this initial oracle in Hosea culminates with emphatic signs of YHWH's personal, impassioned resolve to restore the fractured relationship:

> I will sow him for *myself* in the land.
> And I will have pity on Lo-ruhamah,
>   and I will say to Lo-ammi, "You are *my* people";
>   and he shall say, "You are *my* God." (2:23 [MT 2:25]; emphasis added)

One of the most stirring, albeit still troubling, metaphors, the parent-child metaphor, occurs in chapter 11, immediately following the harsh condemnations announced in chapters 9–10. The depth of YHWH's unrequited affection opens the unit: "When Israel was a child, I loved him" (Hos 11:1). The metaphor of God as the loving parent powerfully illustrates the extent and excruciating pain of divine love. Although this is a monologue, God is speaking here as if in a dialogue—as if replying to Abraham's intercessory prayer on behalf of Sodom and Gomorrah (Gen 18:16-33):

> How can I give you up, Ephraim?
>   How can I hand you over, O Israel?
> How can I make you like Admah?
>   How can I treat you like Zeboiim?
> My heart recoils within me;
>   my compassion grows warm and tender. (Hos 11:8; cf. Gen 10:19)

Admittedly, YHWH's deep yearning for Israel to "return" collides with Israel's fleeting loyalty (Hos 6:1-3), resulting in YHWH's lamenting reaction:

> What shall I do with you, O Ephraim?
>   What shall I do with you, O Judah?
> Your love is like a morning cloud,
>   like the *dew* that goes away early. (6:4; emphasis added)

In contrast, the book of Hosea orchestrates another tone—one of hope—which is rooted in YHWH's pathos. Despite the pain of rejection, YHWH will not let Israel go. Parental compassion eclipses anger and exasperation. And so, rejected YHWH, whose heart "recoils within," relents and resolves not to punish wayward Ephraim (11:9). The exiles learn that they are never lost or denied a place in the family of YHWH: "You are my people" (2:23 [MT 2:25])—that is, "You are my family, my beloved." Thus, the exiles hear the good news that divine love transcends the limits of fear, violence, and even acts of betrayal. And God's yearning for God's children (or spouse) testifies to the possibility of a restored relationship. After all, this is the hope implied in the very name of the prophet: Hosea, "salvation."

I will heal their disloyalty;
  I will love them freely,
  for my anger has turned from them.
I will be like the *dew* to Israel;
  he shall blossom like the lily,
  he shall strike root like the forests of Lebanon. (Hos 14:4-6 [MT 14:5-6]; emphasis added)

In a world inundated with violence and fear, and in dire need of love, such a performance of love is quite stunning. Henri Nouwen has suggested that much of life is spent in the "house of fear" or in the "house of love."[15] Although some might dismiss this metaphor as simplistic, Nouwen is no doubt correct in defining love and fear as compelling forces in the world. *Fear*, for one, is pervasive and may be one of the most debilitating diseases of our time. But spending too much time in the house of fear is costly, for fear ravages bodies and minds. It drives us to despair and even to violence against others and ourselves. And if we reside there too long, we run the risk of missing the wondrous gifts that life affords. But how does one sell the house, so to speak, and move out? The book of Hosea might provide some help in that regard, especially in its claim that love is the antidote for fear. *Love* liberates us from oppression and empowers us to take risks; it is love, John reminds us, that "casts out fear" (1 John 4:18), that renders it null and void.

And yet it is strangely difficult to talk about love in our complex world. Love can seem insignificant and naive against the backdrop of impressive power structures and technological achievement. Even so, poets and playwrights, artists and philosophers, and many social scientists and medical professionals have made a most convincing case that nothing is more important than this four-letter word when the dust of life settles. Love, in all its varied forms, gives meaning to the chaos of life.

After years in a concentration camp where he endured the most monstrous acts conceivable, Victor Frankl concluded that "the salvation of [humankind] is through love and in love."[16] Frankl refused to let fear and hatred overcome love. The Jewish psychiatrist was clearly not living in denial: he had encountered firsthand the many distorted postures of evil, the randomness of suffering, and even the deafening silence of God. And yet in a bold act of faith and moral courage, he insisted that love is all-important. Without it—without poetry and beauty, music and imagination; without concrete expressions of caring and compassion—life is reduced to little more than utility, productivity, and achievement.

In 1961, psychologist Carl Rogers made a rather subversive statement, suggesting that if we would invest the price of one or two large rockets in the search for love, the world would be a far safer place.[17] Sadly, we still know far more about military technology than we do about love, and our global and national investment in each is dangerously disproportionate. In other words, we must spend far more time in the house of love than in the house of fear.

In the 1990s, in a university class at Lima Correctional Institution, a high-medium security prison, we were studying the book of Hosea, this ancient prophet of love. Students were informed that this prophetic text is often associated with the Hebrew word חֶסֶד (*ḥesed*) because Hosea insists that true love—divine love—endures all things, including infidelity, rejection, and even betrayal. Hosea embodies such love when he does not throw in the towel despite betrayal and rejection—just as God does not give up on God's people.

At that point students were asked to help define this strange and wondrous word חֶסֶד (*ḥesed*), as used in Hosea. After a rather uncomfortable silence, a student in the back of the class blurted out, "Guts!" He then explained, "It takes guts to hang in there when there is every good reason to quit. That's what I imagine love to be!"

And perhaps he was right: Hosea's dangerous love is bold, dogged, and "gutsy." "It bears all things," as Paul says, "believes all things, hopes all things, endures all things" (1 Cor 13:7).

Joel: Suffering through the Lack of Basic Daily Necessities

War destroys, kills, burns. With war comes devastating loss not only of pride and honor but also of families, houses, cattle, and crops. The book of Joel is well-known for its oracles of apocalyptic visions and dreams as well as its mysterious imagery of locusts. Through this dramatic language, the prophetic text rehearses the loss of land and food yield required for basic daily needs. Joel imagines the collapse of agricultural life as a grave threat to the order of creation as well as to ecological stability and community sustainability. Such a claim is not difficult to understand, especially for a "land community." The destruction of natural and economic resources created hardships more serious than the dispossession of religious and political autonomy, including even the loss of dynasty and temple. And the allocation of a barely arable or inhabitable tract of land in exile would do little to mitigate its sting.[18] That the loss of land was viewed as a sign of divine disfavor would only make the pain more unbearable. For agrarian communities, in the ancient and modern world, the destruction of land— whether through drought, famine, disease, or war—is a disaster of cosmic proportions.

Commentators have long noted that Joel's use of locust imagery is fraught with ambiguity, intentionally juxtaposing and blurring agricultural ruin with military invasion.[19] On the one hand, the agricultural vocabulary and metaphors associated with the locusts allude to the breakdown of the natural systems necessary to sustain human society. The four types of locusts ("cutting locust," "swarming locust," "hopping locust," and "destroying locust," 1:4; cf. 2:25), suggest devastation of farmland. It is likewise possible that "fire" and "flames" (1:19) allude to the scorching heat (NJPS) of barely arable farmland; the same vocabulary recurs in the depiction of the horde of locusts sweeping over the entire region:

> Fire devours in front of them,
>> and behind them a flame burns.
> Before them the land is like the garden of Eden,
>> but after them a desolate wilderness,
> and nothing escapes them. (2:3)

The effects of such forces on community life are dreadful:

> The fields are devastated,
>> the ground mourns;
> for the grain is destroyed,
>> the wine dries up,
>> the oil fails. . . .
> The vine withers,
>> the fig tree droops.
> Pomegranate, palm, and apple—
>> all the trees of the field are dried up;
> surely, joy withers away
>> among the people. (1:10, 12)

On the other hand, the imagery of locusts represents military invasion, as specific terms such as "nation" (1:6), "northern army" (2:20), and "great army" (2:25) suggest. And the metaphors of "fire" and "flames" work as well with the horror of war as they do with natural disaster: "For fire has devoured / the pastures of the wilderness, / and flames have burned / all the trees of the field" (1:19). Broader depictions associated with these terms, moreover, allude expressly to the contexts of military assault. An invading "nation" approaches with "lions' teeth" (1:6). The aggressor appears like "war-horses" leaping

> on the tops of the mountains,
> like the crackling of a flame of fire
>> devouring the stubble,
> like a powerful army
>> drawn up for battle. (2:4-5)

Hence, the attacking army is like locusts, and the locusts strike with the vigor of a military machine.[20] That the book of Joel never identifies the "northern army" further heightens the ambiguity and the resultant dread.

What remains evident is the terrifying poetic expression that gives voice to acute economic, psychological, and social trauma. Whereas Jeremiah speaks of national disaster as cosmic crumbling and a return to primordial chaos (4:19-26), and Ezekiel envisages military defeat and forced deportation as the exile of YHWH (8:1–11:25), Joel imagines the end of social and symbolic structures as horrifying locusts ravaging Israel and striking terror in its people: "Before them peoples are in anguish, / all faces grow pale" (2:6). In a very direct manner, Joel's horrific vision expresses the most profound fears of land communities: the loss of land, regardless of agency. Such a nightmare topples the world; it shatters identity; it destroys faith; it disrupts relationships; and it renders victims helpless and desperate.

Some might recall the excruciating pain farmers across the United States experienced in the early 1980s when interest rates soared to more than 20 percent. Foreclosure and loss of land were so unbearable that many farmers took their lives. The loss of the family farm was tantamount to losing *everything*; it devastated faith and extinguished hope. (In response to the crisis in rural communities across the country, new ministries emerged, especially within Catholic parishes, to address the psychological, emotional, and financial wreckage.) In these "land communities," exile had rendered life unbearable. Although many families eventually recovered from the crisis, others never did; the loss of land and the loss of life were too great a burden to bear.

Joel gives voice to such grief. The prophetic text reimagines the years of violence and scarcity, the deaths of families as well as family markets. It breaks denials and confronts the pain of forced deportation and military defeat, which many no doubt read as the collapse of the world. The flames of war had traumatized the defeated; the empire's shock-and-awe campaigns had successfully created unspeakable horror. These experiences lingered in debilitating silence only to be awakened by Joel's haunting eschatological vision. The intent of this performance, however, is not to induce further terror or to summon up haunting memories, but to "find language that conveys fully and persuasively what one has seen"[21] so that healing and recovery are possible.

Joel's literary reenactment not only imagines the horror of land loss and military defeat; it also calls for collective grief, without which community recovery is all the more difficult:

> Wake up, you drunkards, and weep;
>   and wail, all you wine-drinkers. . . .
> Lament like a virgin dressed in sackcloth
>   for the husband of her youth. . . .
> Be dismayed, you farmers,
>   wail, you vinedressers. . . .
> Put on sackcloth and lament, you priests;
>   wail, you ministers of the altar. . . .
> Sanctify a fast,
>   call a solemn assembly. (1:5, 8, 11, 13, 14)

Most remarkably, the text has the audacity to imagine it otherwise. The prophetic performance will not allow the excruciating pain of invasion and exile to have the last word. Divine promises of recovery, reparation, and restoration emerge in their place. But such prospects, at least initially, depend on the people's response to the prophetic appeal. If God's people are willing to change ("rend") their hearts and "turn" to God, God may be willing to change course (regarding the disaster) and "relent." God's relenting (2:14; cf. Amos 7:3, 6; Jonah 3:9) in mercy is not a guarantee, as the prophet is all too aware, "Who knows whether he will not turn and relent, / and leave a blessing behind him?" And yet, hope is rooted in such a prayerful heart. This is hope for "returning" (Joel 2:12-13; cf. Hos 3:5; 12:6; 14:1; Amos 4:6, 8-11; Jonah 3:8; Hag 2:17) as the prophetic proclamation recounts the divine attributes of the old traditions:

> Rend your hearts and not your clothing.
> Return to the LORD, your God,
>   for he is gracious and merciful,
> slow to anger, and abounding in steadfast love,
>   and relents from punishing.
> Who knows whether he will not turn and relent,
>   and leave a blessing behind him? (Joel 2:13-14)[22]

As the prophetic performance unfolds, the prospect of restoration becomes all the more certain. In response to the people's lament, YHWH pledges to reverse the fortunes of the beleaguered community and the ravaged land (2:15–3:21). YHWH's promise employs four uses of the words for *rain* (2:23), as if countering the four types of *locusts* (1:4), so as to provide abundant harvests (2:19, 22, 24; 4:13, 18). Furthermore, YHWH resolves to "remove the northern army far from you, / and drive it into a parched and desolate land" (2:20). In response to God's great acts, the "soil" is to "be glad and rejoice," "the animals of the field" are not to fear, and the "children of Zion" are to celebrate the LORD their God (2:21-23). Joy will replace mourning, and valor will dislodge fear. And years of plenty will supplant their haunting memories of paucity: "The threshing floors shall be full of grain, / the vats shall overflow with wine and oil" (2:24). Certainly this vision of the future is as breathtaking as the horror of the past: the restoration of creation, deliverance from oppression, economic and agricultural plenty, the outpouring of God's spirit upon *all* God's people, a grand homecoming, and the inimitable presence of God in their midst.

> You shall know that I am in the midst of Israel,
>   and that I, the LORD, am your God and there is no other.
> And my people shall never again be put to shame. (2:27)

Throughout the book of Joel, it is noteworthy that the word or motif of a *king* does not occur (cf. Hos 10:3; Mic 4:9). Instead, the "elders" or "aged" people are mentioned (1:2, 14; 2:16), which is a unique feature within the Twelve. The implied readers would hear these words in settings where Israel's kingship had long ceased. Against such a backdrop, the call to the "elders" would perhaps remind them of the leaders who led the Israelites through the Exodus and wilderness journey in Moses' time (for example, Exod 4:29; 19:7; Num 11:16). So now, though landless and captive, as in the days of old, the exiles could regroup and face the massive challenges before them. Led by their elders, they could tackle the harsh realities of captivity; they could mourn their lost worlds; they could turn to their God and look forward to reversals of their misfortunes. It is also noteworthy that Joel's vision of hope encompasses not only the community elders but also the children, infants, bridegroom, and bride—that is, *all* God's people (2:16). On that day, when YHWH's spirit is poured out, the people tormented by nightmarish swarms of locusts will "dream dreams," "see visions," and "prophesy" (2:28-29). Such blessing will fall upon *all* God's people, including "sons," "daughters," "old men," "young men," and "male and female slaves" (2:28-29 [MT 3:1-2]). And all will recite their stories of despair, repentance, and renewal:

> Tell your children of it,
>> and let your children tell their children,
>> and their children another generation. (Joel 1:3)

Finally, it should be pointed out that while Joel's message of invasion, destruction, and renewal is distinctive in many respects, it is not a literary island. Similar terms and metaphors occur throughout the Twelve with comparable thematic force. For example, the imagery of *fire* in the context of judgment can be found in the Oracles against the Nations (Amos 1–2) and other related texts (Amos 7:4-6; Obad 18; Nah 1:6; 3:13, 15; Zeph 3:8; Zech 2:9; 9:4; 11:1; 12:6; 13:9; Mal 3:2). The *locust* motif recurs elsewhere with a similar intent to highlight destructive forces from far away (Amos 7:1-3; Nah 3:15-17; Mal 3:11). The key phrase, "the day of the LORD," occurs across the Twelve, often denoting impending punishment (Joel 1:15; 2:1-2, 11; 2:31 [MT 3:4]; 3:14 [MT 4:14]; Amos 5:18, 20; Obad 15; Zeph 1:7-8, 14-18; 2:2-3; Mal 4:5 [MT 3:23]) but also salvation (for example, Hos 1:5; 2:16, 18; Joel 3:18; Amos 9:11; Mic 4:6-7; Zeph 3:11, 16). The haunting description of YHWH roaring from Zion and uttering his voice from Jerusalem (Joel 3:16) occurs almost verbatim in the opening oracle of Amos (1:2). Most significantly, the language associated with *crops*—such as the vine, fig tree, pomegranate, olive tree, and the like—occurs throughout numerous texts with pertinent themes of judgment, survival, and restoration (Hos 9:10; 10:1; Amos 8:1-3; Nah 3:12; Hab 3:17; Hag 1:10-11; 2:15, 18, 19; Zech 3:10; 8:12; 9:17; 10:1, 7; Mal 3:10-11).

Amos as Disaster Literature: "Are you not like the Ethiopians to me, O people of Israel?"

The book of Amos is one of the most well-known prophetic writings from the Hebrew Bible. It contains the famous phrase in Martin Luther King, Jr.'s "I Have a

Dream" speech, which he delivered during the Civil Rights movement in the United States: "Let justice roll down like waters, / and righteousness like an ever-flowing stream" (Amos 5:24). This prophetic book, together with the book of Exodus, has also been instrumental in the liberation theology movement in Latin America, South Africa, and other countries of the Third World.

Amos is one of the eighth-century prophets, along with Hosea and Micah. This may explain why the LXX puts Hosea, Amos, and Micah together (presumably chronologically) at the start of the Twelve. We have noted, however, that in the present form of the MT arrangement only Hosea and Amos are among the initial three books, with the common denominator that both Hosea and Amos, along with Joel, address the fate of northern Israel. Although there may be key elements that provide further rationale for the final form (MT) of the Twelve, this sequential reading allows the implied readers to perceive how the book of Amos picks up the motifs of Hosea and Joel and presents them in its own distinctive form while providing a bridging transition to the subsequent books of the Twelve.

First, the concept of Israel's election, which was depicted metaphorically through relationship in Hosea, is delineated at the outset by the Oracles against the Nations (OAN) in Amos 1–2. We have observed that Hosea introduces the spousal and parent-child metaphors as a depiction of the special relationship between YHWH and Israel, which functions as a foundational theme for the entire collection of the Twelve. Amos adopts this motif but presents it through the OAN.

What is noteworthy in the OAN of Amos is the double meaning implied in the concept of Israel's election. On the one hand, the OAN in Amos 1–2 indicate that Israel (which is also an ambiguous term, referring to both unified Israel and northern Israel) is no better or more righteous than any of their neighbors. YHWH will show no favoritism to Israel when it comes to wrongdoing. Though they are YHWH's own people, Israel must accept that they are not exempt from the laws of justice. This is expressed rhetorically as the OAN unfold, starting from the more remote countries (for example, Aram, Philistia, and Phoenicia; 1:3-10), moving toward the closer neighbors (for example, Edom, Ammon, and Moab; 1:11–2:3), and surprisingly culminating with the accusations against Judah (2:4-5) and Israel (2:6-16).[23] It is notable that unlike the OAN in Isaiah, Jeremiah, and Ezekiel, no oppressive superpower such as Assyria or Babylon is directly mentioned in the OAN in Amos 1–2. Unlike the OAN in Isaiah, Jeremiah, or Ezekiel, where the announcement of divine punishment of the nations serves to bring a sense of hope to defeated and humiliated Israel, the OAN in Amos 1–2 function primarily to accuse YHWH's own people. Judah and, even more emphatically, Israel are the very targets of the announcement concerning "three transgressions . . . and for four" (2:4, 6), meaning abundant sins. Interestingly, a similar motif recurs toward the end of Amos, as if forming an inclusio with Amos 1–2:

> Are you not like the Ethiopians to me,
>> O people of Israel? says the LORD.
> Did I not bring Israel up from the land of Egypt,
>> and the Philistines from Caphtor and the Arameans from Kir? (9:7)

YHWH will neither overlook nor condone any transgressions committed by human beings, whether they are Ethiopians, Philistines, Arameans, or Israelites (9:8-10).

On the other hand, the God who is in control of all nations (another motif of the OAN), and thereby can punish them according to their own sins, is portrayed as showing favoritism toward God's own people, Judah and Israel. This divine favoritism is described in a paradoxical statement, both positively and negatively: "You only have I known / of all the families of the earth; / therefore I will punish you / for all your iniquities" (3:2). Readers must wrestle with the concepts of both phrases. The first phrase, "You only have I known of all the families of the earth," implies that, though Israel can be subjected to punishment like other nations, God's care and concern for Israel will not be severed. The notion "to know," which denotes an intimate relationship, also indicates a covenant relationship in which YHWH confirms the divine commitment to YHWH's own people. From the phrase, "You only have I known," readers may hear an implicit confession of YHWH, "You only have I loved." It is an implicit vow that YHWH will not revoke the covenant fidelity toward YHWH's own people. These notions remind the readers of the divine recognition already expressed in Hosea: "You are my people" (2:23 [MT 2:25]), my family, of "all the families of the earth" (Amos 3:2).

The second phrase, "therefore I will punish you / for all your iniquities," describes divine entitlement in the negative, summarizing the preceding OAN in chapters 1–2. YHWH's own people will be held to a more stringent standard. Thus, the inventory of transgressions reported against Judah and Israel (2:4, 6-12) is more detailed and more exacting than those of the nations. The transgressions of Judah and Israel are fundamentally associated with the holders of privileged power, who are also the unmistakable targets of divine anger in Amos. Political and religious leaders are exposed for their abuse of the poor and needy:

> They sell the righteous for silver,
>> and the needy for a pair of sandals—
> they who trample the head of the poor into the dust of the earth,
>> and push the afflicted out of the way. (2:6-7)

Social injustice perpetrated by corrupt and callous leaders has affected the people at the most basic economic level. It is no coincidence that the devastating invasion of the "locusts" (Joel 1:4) recurs in the "locusts'" irrecoverable damage to Israel's gardens and vineyards (Amos 4:9). Ironically, the leaders are depicted as lounging in the "winter house" and "summer house" and on "beds of ivory" (Amos 3:15; 6:4).[24] This irony reaches its climax in the prophet's caustic invitation, "Come to Bethel—and transgress; / to Gilgal—and multiply transgression" (Amos 4:4), echoing a similar admonition in Hosea 4:15 (cf. Amos 5:5). The irony is striking: the self-righteous leaders are cordially invited to the sanctuaries of Bethel and Gilgal for the activity of transgression, as if that is all they are capable of!

In harsh tones, readers encounter the divine accusation against these rulers and leaders. Whereas in Hosea the divine pathos is subtly hinted in agony over YHWH's own children (Hos 11:1-9), Amos presents YHWH's emotion in intense tones:

> I hate, I despise your festivals,
> and I take no delight in your solemn assemblies. . . .
> I abhor the pride of Jacob
> and hate his strongholds. (Amos 5:21; 6:8; cf. Hos 6:6)

Thus, YHWH, who is expected to appear "like a lion" (Hos 5:14; 11:10; 13:7-8; Joel 4:16), finally comes and "roars" (Amos 1:2; 3:4, 8, 12). Even if Israel might have been spared the fate of "Admah" and "Zeboiim"—the neighboring cities of Sodom and Gomorrah (Hos 11:8; cf. Gen 10:19), the verdict becomes eventually irrevocable (Amos 4:11-12). Ultimately, just as Jonah (mercy on Assyria) encounters Nahum (doom on Assyria) in the canonically sequential way, Hosea's warning runs across Amos's death sentence against Israel: "Fallen, no more to rise, / is maiden Israel; / forsaken on her land, / with no one to raise her up" (5:2).[25] The "whore Israel" of Hosea meets the "maiden [literally, 'virgin' or 'young woman'] Israel" of Amos in the dirge song of lamentation at the heart of the book of Amos (Amos 5:1-17; cf. Joel 1:8).

The implied readers hear a most troubling verdict on the fate of Israel. On the surface, this verdict applies only to northern Israel in the sense that the prophetic ministries of Hosea and Amos are understood to have been related to the northern kingdom of Israel. Thus, idolatry, corruption, and the consequent doom of northern Israel provide an object lesson for southern Judah. However, on a deeper level, the ambiguity and double meaning of the term "Israel" can lead readers to identify with the fate of northern Israel in solemn solidarity. The implied readers will recall that just prior to the accusation of northern Israel in the OAN (Amos 2:6-16), Judah too was accused of rejecting YHWH's laws (2:4-5). One of the central woe-oracles against Israel addresses both north and south: "Alas for those who are at ease in Zion, / and for those who feel secure on Mount Samaria" (6:1). Thus, the prophetic judgment against the social ills of the elite leaders eventually encompasses not only Israel but also Judah.

Amos as Survival Literature: "Seek me and live"

In light of such harsh attention to Israel's sins, is there a message of hope in the book of Amos? Unlike Hosea or Joel, Amos appears to lack virtually any trace of hope except in the closing portion of the last chapter (Amos 9:8b, 11-15), which seems to be out of place, redactionally speaking. Nevertheless, even in the severe warnings, readers might hear a hint of hope. For example, the divine accusation, the refrain, "yet you did not return to me, says the LORD" (4:6, 8, 9, 10, 11), implies divine yearning for Israel's repentance. Within the dreary dirges, readers hear a similar note of hope: "Seek me and live. . . . / Seek the LORD and live" (5:4, 6). In a pronouncement of national doom, the statement that they *may* "live" sounds too fragile. Yet, inasmuch as the vow of hope is uttered in the midst of the deepest lamentations (see Lam 3:21-26), these oracles declare the possibility of (new) life in the face of a death sentence. What then does it mean to "seek God"? The same passage expounds: "Seek good and not evil, / that you may live" (5:14). How does a community "seek good"? An answer is hinted: by "hating evil" and, more concretely, by doing "justice and righteousness."

> Hate evil and love good,
>   and establish justice in the gate;
> it may be that the LORD, the God of hosts,
>   will be gracious to the remnant of Joseph. (Amos 5:15; cf. 5:24)

Precisely here lies the affirmation of hope that YHWH is ready to be gracious to the descendants of Joseph. Accordingly, doing justice and righteousness is equated with seeking good, which means seeking God. Then the death sentence can be thwarted and people can live anew. It should be reiterated that this hope is remote and clearly over-shadowed by the threat of doom. That is precisely why readers encounter the word *perhaps* (the literal meaning of "it may be," Amos 5:15), which may echo a similar notion of hope in the possibility of divine mercy: "*Who knows* whether he will not turn and relent, / and leave a blessing behind him?" (Joel 2:14; emphasis added; cf. Jonah 3:19).

In the aftermath of the September 11, 2001 terror attacks, during a community forum a seminary student testified to the effect of the tragedy on her understanding of the world. Originally from western Pennsylvania, this student admitted to having a bias against people from major East Coast cities such as New York or Washington, D.C. For all their political and economic power, the urban elite struck her as pretentious, arrogant, and downright rude. Besides, what could these people possibly have to do with her small town? That was until one of the airplanes crashed near her hometown. Suddenly, the fate of seemingly distant urbanites and her own community became inextricably entwined. She expressed with solemn respect her conviction that the passengers' courageous act of steering the plane away from its intended target, the

White House in Washington, D.C., was an inspiration to both metropolitan and rural citizens who were indeed united in their patriotism and dedication to their nation's safety.

Amos was a southerner from Tekoa, a little town in Judah, who went up to northern Israel and proclaimed his message there (Amos 7:14-15). It seems evident that northern Israel did not heed the oracles of this prophet (or, to be more precise, this cattle breeder), let alone the outcries of the disenfranchised poor in rural parts of Judah. Hope in Amos, then, is possible not only in "loving God," "loving good," and "doing justice," but especially in "hating evil," which includes the community's unyielding self-criticism of its own rulers and leaders. Hope in Amos does not denote a mere wish but a reform in action. Hope becomes possible when the people rediscover the meaning of their election tradition: that their special relationship with God demands they be stringent in their practice of justice as a community. Doing so requires faithful identification with the poor and the needy.

It is precisely here that the issue of solidarity stands not as an abstract idea but as actions and decisions implemented for the sake of justice and righteousness, for the sake of the powerless and afflicted. It is solidarity that YHWH sought from the nobles and leaders of Israel, though they were prone to "push aside the needy in the gate" (5:12). It is solidarity that northern Israel should extend to their southern family member Judah, and vice versa. It is solidarity that will be a key theme in the book of Obadiah, which follows Amos, where Israel's relationship with twin brother and neighbor Edom is at stake (cf. Amos 9:12). In a broader sense, the OAN in Amos 1–2 may function to pave the way to the following six books of the Twelve (especially Obadiah, Jonah, Nahum, and Habakkuk), which repeatedly address the question of solidarity versus oppression, whether the protagonist is Israel, Edom, Assyria, or Babylon.

Obadiah and Jonah: Oracles against the Nations

After reporting the iniquities and subsequent fate of northern Israel, along with subtle signs of divine mercy, the Twelve addresses the fate of the surrounding nations. The underlying concerns at this juncture are the questions of theodicy, justice, and hope. Why have God's people suffered such humiliating losses? Why have guilty nations escaped unpunished? And how is Israel to live as a faithful community in diaspora? The nations' crimes and punishments—their visible corruption and unreported oppression—thus take center stage in the prophetic performance, as does the governing claim that divine sovereignty extends to all places and people. In a way, the texts pertaining to the Oracles against the Nations (OAN) continue through the book of Zephaniah. Arguably, the six books enveloped by Obadiah at the start and Zephaniah at the end form the nexus of the overarching chiastic structure of the Twelve.[26] The structure of the whole can be seen in the following diagram:

Diagram of the Order of the Book of the Twelve (MT)

	Hos	Joel	Amos	Obad	Jonah	Mic	Nah	Hab	Zeph	Hag	Zech	Mal

north Israel

OAN north Israel

OAN vs. Edom

(OAN) vs. Assyria

fate of Judah

OAN vs. Assyria

OAN vs. Babylon

OAN vs. Ammon/ Moab (/more)

fate of Judah

OAN rebuilding of unified Israel

marriage metaphor

light/water

5 visions

attributes of God

8 visions

light/water

marriage imagery

From the literary location of the OAN itself, one could make the theological case that the nations are of paramount importance to YHWH and YHWH's people!

Obadiah: Abandoned and Betrayed Relationship

This central section of the Twelve begins with the book of Obadiah, which solemnly exposes the often forgotten and untold wrongdoing of Israel's closest neighbor, Edom. In Amos 1–2, the OAN starts with the faraway nations and then approaches those nearby. In contrast, the inner OAN within the Twelve starts with the nearest nation. Edom traces its genealogical origin to Esau, the twin brother of Jacob. Hence, even among Ammon, Moab, and Edom, the nation Edom is the closest relative (cf. Deut 23:8-9).

In the aftermath of disaster, people often think first and foremost of their immediate family. Then they gradually begin thinking about neighbors. The Twelve opens with texts that deal with Judah's and Jerusalem's own family and clan—northern Israel. Then it looks at its closest neighbor, Edom, the once brother nation, "for the slaughter and violence done to your brother Jacob" (v. 10). Obadiah rebukes Edom for failing to be a reliable friend and good neighbor in Israel's time of need.

For such a short book—only twenty-one verses long—the book of Obadiah covers many significant themes. First and foremost, it insists that remembering the past, however painful, can lead to hope for the future. Disclosing the painful scars of previous wrongdoings is not primarily about placing blame, but rather about arriving at the truth, making perpetrators of injustice accountable, and finding courage for victims to survive. No doubt Edom was a nation with problems of its own, struggling to survive the massive pressures exerted by neighboring empires. Nevertheless, Edom's betrayal, its human rights violations, and its failure to maintain solidarity with its neighbor could not be easily dismissed. By turning away from its vulnerable and helpless neighbor Judah, it committed the ultimate act of betrayal. Although sibling rivalries no doubt ran deep and in both directions (in Genesis), Obadiah focuses entirely on Edom's acts of treachery.

It is difficult enough for victims of violence to recover from trauma. The impact of victimization, however, is even greater when perpetrators remain silent or deny responsibility. The book of Obadiah vigorously refuses to let this happen. The first section (vv. 1-9) depicts the *present* hubris of Edom in its seemingly safe rock of Sela, the ancient city of Petra: "you that live in the clefts of the rock" (v. 3). The concluding section (vv. 15b-21) points to the *future* reversal of fortune, when the house of Jacob as fire and the house of Joseph as flame together shall devour the house of Esau as straw (v. 18; recall the "fire" and "flame" motif in Joel). Sandwiched between these images

204

of present security and future misfortune lies the central section (vv. 12-15a; cf. vv. 10-11), which uncovers the malicious wrongdoings Edom committed against Israel in the *past*. Edom's failure to preserve solidarity stands as a core of the book.

The central section opens with harsh criticism of Edom's callous actions. Rather than aiding a "brother" in time of need, Edom casts aside any sense of fraternal obligation and colludes with Israel's enemies (vv. 10-11). The force of the condemnation intensifies in the textually ambivalent assertion and interrogative (v. 12). Three different English translations of the first phrase of verse 12 demonstrate the ambiguity and possible meanings of the accusation: "But you should not have gloated over your brother / on the day of his misfortune" (NRSV); "How could you gaze with glee / on your brother that day, / on his day of calamity!" (NJPS); "Do not gloat over your brother's day, / the day of his misfortune" (NASB).[27] The litany in vv. 12-15, moreover, contains nine occurrences of the phrase "the day of . . ." (the fourth, fifth, and sixth phrases are exactly the same, "the day of his calamity"). In this rhetorically and emotionally charged expression, seven occurrences of the phrase are enveloped by the initial, asseverate reminder of kinship, in "the day of your brother" (v. 12), and the culminating counterannouncement of *lex talionis*, in "the day of the LORD" (v. 15, "As you have done, it shall be done to you"; see also Jer 50:15). Furthermore, the development of the verbs depicts the likely actions of Edom's inhumanity—from gloating, rejoicing, and boasting (v. 12) to entering the gate, gloating, and looting (v. 13) to cutting off fugitives and handing over survivors (v. 14).[28] These indictments explicitly portray the cruelty that the exiled, vulnerable people of Israel endured.

The lessons soberly learned from their own kindred, (northern) Israel, and from their closest neighbor and brother, Edom, serve more than didactic objectives; they provide a window into the community's rage and anguish. In response to the trauma of war and captivity, the text suggests that the people of God will not accept their misfortune passively or merely lament their distressing circumstances. They realign their voices to expose the inhumane acts of their tormentors. Though others may not notice or believe, these victims of brutality need to know the truth. And they must confront their oppressors. If their oppressors do not own up (cf. Hab 2:11, "The very stones will cry out from the wall"), the people themselves, even though seemingly powerless, will raise their voices in protest and resistance. And if their voices are silenced or denied, God in the heavens will recognize their cry and the injustice wrought by their betrayers.

The book of Obadiah reminds the implied readers and modern readers that acts of cruelty and injustice must not be forgotten; in fact, they must be unveiled in solemn truth finding. Although such acts are easily dismissed and denied, especially by those who commit them, they will one day be exposed and set right. *In the meantime*, the community of faith participates in a liturgical performance in which the kingdom of

God rectifies moral incoherence and God's will is "done on earth as it is in heaven"; that is to say, through the lenses of worship the community recognizes the reign of God and the purposes of God in and through the contingencies of history. Thus by the end of this short book, (1) Edom's crimes are exposed, (2) the proud nation is brought low, (3) the fortunes of Edom's malevolence are reversed, and (4) moral symmetry is restored. As God's servant, Obadiah, confesses: "Those who have been saved shall go up to Mount Zion / to rule Mount Esau; / and the kingdom shall be the LORD's" (v. 21).

Jonah: To Repent or Not; That Is the Answer

Now Israel looks beyond Edom, their next-door neighbor, toward Assyria, the far-away foe from the north. This sequence adheres to the internal logic of the OAN in the Twelve. In the book of Jonah, readers discover a strange story of a prophet who reluctantly travels to enemy headquarters at Nineveh only to discover God's mercy and sovereignty. Readers also encounter this God, whose justice and compassion reach to the ends of the earth and whose power foils even the most intimidating of empires.

First, Jonah (which literally means the "dove") personifies the collective people of Israel.[29] Jonah takes the stage as a rebellious servant, who flees "from the presence of the LORD" (1:3), in much the same way as the people of Israel are characterized during the monarchical period—at least by the Deuteronomists. En route to Tarshish, Jonah is forced to mingle with sailors of multiethnic origins, much the way Israel is forced to live among the nations in exile. Not unlike vulnerable Israel, Jonah the dove appears naive and insignificant (cf. Hos 7:11). Here, foreigners seek to understand the reason for their adversity, as would Israel regarding its exilic suffering: "Come, let us cast lots, so that we may know on whose account this calamity has come upon us" (Jonah 1:7). Amid unceasing storms, Jonah plays a significant role not only in saving the lives of the sailors but also in "convincing" them to worship YHWH. The sailors, who initially pray to their gods (1:5-6), end up entreating YHWH, fearing YHWH, and offering a sacrifice to YHWH (1:14; cf. Gen 8:20). Here again, the desperate prayers of the non-Israelite sailors echo Israel's exilic theology: "For you, O LORD, have done as it pleased you" (Jonah 1:14).

If readers allow Jonah to function as a symbolic figure for Israel in the exilic and postexilic diaspora, then they might discover that his journey on the rough seas leads to an unexpected place of hope. Like Jonah, the people of Israel find themselves banished from their homeland. Like Jonah, they lament their situation, even pleading, "Pick me up and throw me into the sea" (1:12). They might even identify with a prophet who finds himself vulnerable and at risk, amid seas and storms. And when overwhelmed by a tangible sense of abandonment and disorientation, they hear

Jonah's inspiring testimony of faith: "I worship the LORD, the God of heaven, who made the sea and the dry land" (1:9). Here, as if by happenstance, Jonah meets Second Isaiah (Isa 40:28; 42:5): the reluctant messenger becomes a prophet (though not of deliverance but of punishment, cf. Gen 8:8-12) who ends up saving the people of Nineveh (Jonah 3). This takes place in a most unlikely manner; but, after all, did not Amos also claim, "I am no prophet, nor a prophet's son" (Amos 7:14; cf. Zech 13:5)? Whether reluctantly or coincidentally, Jonah becomes a symbol for Judean refugees who are called to embody the role of a "prophet to the nations" (Jer 1:5) and "a light to the nations" (Isa 42:6; 49:6). Readers find additional meaning in the fish's divine rescue of Jonah (Jonah 2:11) and the second chance divinely granted to Jonah (3:1); they rediscover hope while confessing with Jonah, "Deliverance belongs to the LORD!" (2:9 [MT 2:10]). Hence, Jonah's thanksgiving prayer mirrors the community's experiences of hardship and resilient hope:

> Then I said, "I am driven away
>   from your sight;
> how shall I look again
>   upon your holy temple?" . . .
> I went down to the land
>   whose bars closed upon me forever;
> yet you brought up my life from the Pit,
>   O LORD my God. (2:4, 6 [MT 2:5, 7])

Second, Assyria's repentance and God's pardon carry rich, though troubling, implications for readers. It is intriguing that the interpretive community would give voice to such a scandalous notion within the Twelve. Yet, on one level, readers learn of God's sovereignty in Jonah. After all, this is Israel's story—not the Assyrians'! The exiled people had suffered much humiliation under the repressive power of the giant empires. In ordinary life, the repentance and forgiveness of a superpower would be utterly absurd, yet in Jonah's story it becomes a (textual) reality. And so, through the power of narrative, the interpretive community imagines the world otherwise. In the "really real" world of the text, intimidating tyrants not only repent but also acknowledge the true champion, the divine suzerain. Like the great pharaoh of old who repents of his sins and begs Moses to intercede on his behalf (Exod 9:27-35), the Assyrian king acknowledges God and repents of his cruelty (Jonah 3:6-10). In response to Jonah's call to repentance, he "rose from his throne, removed his robe, covered himself with sackcloth, and sat in ashes" (Jonah 3:6). The story of Jonah thus is a subversive (liturgical) drama that stirs a vision of hope for the community stripped of power and meaning. This vision reimagines abusive power structures: it refuses to accept them as normative, it denies them the last word, and it affirms that the true king ultimately tames them. After all, this God has already calmed the tempestuous sea (1:15) and domesticated the large fish (1:17; 2:10)! How much easier to humble and pardon human rulers, no matter how defiant!

On another level, the divine mercy extended to Nineveh holds out promise for Jerusalem's deliverance. As Phyllis Trible observes: "The author of Jonah teaches 'the restored and still sinful city' that if God can spare Nineveh, there is yet hope for the salvation of Jerusalem."[30] The implied readers are therefore reminded not only of the enormity of divine power but also of the vastness of divine mercy. For those living under enormous pressure and regret, the possibility of mercy and pardon awakens hope. Furthermore, this prospect of divine mercy extends to all nations—even the most wayward. Here contemporary readers discover, if there were ever doubt, that the story of Jonah is no mere children's story but rather a radical subversive vision, beyond restoration and recovery. When the storyteller declares that "the people of Nineveh believed God" (Jonah 3:5), the interpretive community is invited to envisage all peoples and nations righteously governed by YHWH. Such a prophetic vision dares to imagine the end of evil and oppression, both in Israel and in neighboring nations.

Finally, the issue of theodicy still lingers in anticipation of the book of Nahum. The story of Jonah does not end with definitive answers but with open-ended (albeit rhetorical) questions. If readers are willing to imagine a God who saves "non-Hebrew" sailors and penitent Assyrians through God's conflicted messenger, they may also be inclined to entertain the prophet's defiant complaints and challenges. Jonah is not rebellious because of his reluctance to travel to distant Assyria (in much the same way Amos was called to go and prophesy to Samaria). Nor is Jonah angry because his credentials as a prophet might be jeopardized if his oracles go unfulfilled, thereby making him a false prophet (cf. Deut 18:22). Rather, Jonah is distraught that a brutal oppressor might be granted forgiveness. In biting irony, Jonah now meets Abraham the persistent intercessor. Not unlike the great patriarch who stood and "looked down toward Sodom and Gomorrah and toward all the land of the Plain and saw the smoke of the land going up like the smoke of a furnace" (Gen 19:28), Jonah "went out of the city and sat down east of the city, and made a booth for himself there. He sat under it in the shade, waiting to see what would become of the city" (Jonah 4:5). Whereas Abraham pleads for the divine rescue of Sodom and Gomorrah (Gen 18:23-33; cf. Exod 32:11-14) only to see the cities destroyed, Jonah longs for divine punishment only to witness the oppressive city saved (Jonah 3:10). Clearly the vision of the former is far more morally coherent and less problematic. That is to say, in the Genesis story wrongdoers get their just desserts.

The debate between Jonah and YHWH represents a pressing existential concern of the dislocated interpretive community. The implied readers are invited to identify with the perplexed prophet in casting the tormenting question of theodicy. If evildoers and oppressors are granted mercy, if their dastardly and heinous deeds are absolved, then the world is not only unjust but also void of true hope.[31] No wonder Jonah begs for death, a sentiment to which a suffering community could easily relate: "It is better for me to die than to live" (Jonah 4:8). The exiles raise their outcry to God through Jonah's complaint.

At the same time, the question of theodicy is posed in a very distinctive way in this short story. Other prophets unmistakably address the conundrum of innocent suffering and the integrity of God (see, for example, Hab 1:2-17; Jer 12:1-4; 15:10-18; 20:7-18). But they are beset by the seemingly excessive discharge of divine judgment. Isaiah utters, "How long, O LORD?" (Isa 6:11). God's people lament in the book of Jeremiah:

> Have you completely rejected Judah?
> Does your heart loathe Zion?
> Why have you struck us down
>   so that there is no healing for us? (Jer 14:19)

Jeremiah himself complains, "Why is my pain unceasing, / my wound incurable, / refusing to be healed?" (Jer 15:18). Amos implores God,

> O Lord GOD, cease, I beg you!
> How can Jacob stand?
> He is so small! (Amos 7:5; cf. 7:2)

And Habakkuk cries out:

> O LORD, how long shall I cry for help,
>   and you will not listen?
> Or cry to you "Violence!"
>   and you will not save? (Hab 1:2)

Jonah, however, is not concerned about the disproportionate use of divine judgment as much as he is concerned about divine grace! The runaway prophet is upset that God's mercy is seemingly gratuitous: "For I knew that you are a gracious God and merciful, slow to anger, and abounding in steadfast love, and ready to relent from punishing" (4:2). Ironically, Jonah's concern is unfounded. The storyteller does not suggest that divine grace is cheap or even unmerited, but rather that it is dispensed proportionate to human repentance (Jonah 3:1-10): "When God saw what they *did*, how they *turned* from their evil ways, God changed his mind about the calamity that he had said he would bring upon them; and he did not do it" (Jonah 3:10; emphasis added).

Here the storyteller echoes the words of Jeremiah, who insists that God will "change [plans] about the disaster . . . [intended for a nation]" "if that nation . . . turns from its evil" (Jer 18:8). The Jeremianic subtext strikes both fear and hope in readers. It suggests that no one is beyond the possibility of divine mercy, that the future of God's people is open-ended and buoyant. But at the same time, it is adamant that God is not beyond plucking up and breaking down a nation that once was built and planted, if that nation "does evil in [God's] sight, not listening to [God's] voice" (Jer 18:9-10). In either case, God's actions are directly proportionate to human actions. In this way, the storyteller actually maintains a moral universe that is intact, one that pivots on repentance (turning) as a window to hope. Thus Jonah joins the great eighth-century prophets who call for justice and righteousness (for example, Hos 6:5; 10:12-13; Amos 5:24). And Jonah joins Joel in the call for true repentance (Joel 2:12-14), although Jonah extends the plea to all peoples and all nations. In this way, Jonah imagines the possibility of the end of injustice and the coming of the kingdom of God.

As noted earlier, the book of Jonah concludes with a question rather than a definite answer, stressing the point that the issues at hand are complex and will continue into the books of Nahum, Habakkuk, and beyond.[32] In the meantime, the implied readers of the Twelve must sort out the textual (and historical) dissonance: YHWH's mercy is afforded to Nineveh in Jonah (despite Jonah's vehement complaint); YHWH's judgment is enacted against the wicked city in Nahum, and Nineveh actually falls to Babylon in 612 B.C.E.

Micah: The Fate of Zion amid the Nations

The attention of the Twelve shifts from Samaria to Edom, then from Sela (Petra) to Nineveh, and now from Nineveh back to Zion. Though the focus of the collection moves from nation to nation, its core motifs continue in Micah: the call for justice, the need for repentance, and the promise of newness and restoration. These themes only gain in momentum with a sequential reading. Furthermore, the pattern of the OAN established in Amos 1–2 recurs with greater intensity, except now the spotlight is on Jerusalem, not Samaria. Will Jerusalem fall like Samaria, Sela, and Nineveh? Will Zion be granted divine forgiveness? Here the implied readers engage once again in communal reflection and confession: they must think long and hard about their own quality of life; in the midst of their social and symbolic disarray, they can find hope in the God who can pardon Samaria and Nineveh and who is now all the more anxious to embrace Zion. Ultimately, readers of the book of Micah are invited to ponder the character of their incomparable God: the name Micah literally means "Who is like you [God]?" (cf. Mic 1:1 and 7:18).

Micah: The Fall and Rise of Jerusalem

The book of Micah is located at the core of the Twelve. The LXX situates the books of Jonah and Nahum as the central section, thereby juxtaposing two seemingly contradictory voices. But the MT inserts the book of Micah directly between the two. One can only speculate as to the significance (if any) of the position of the book of Micah in this canonical arrangement. But it would seem plausible to suggest, at the very least, that Judah and Jerusalem *literarily* take the center stage of the Twelve.

First, if we take the pattern of the OAN formulated by Amos 1–2, then the Jerusalemites—the intended audience for the book of Micah—are the targets of the prophecy. Read this way, the focus moves from Edom and Assyria to Judah. The accusation previously made against Sela and Nineveh is now directed against Jerusalem. The book of Micah thus directs readers through the agonizing exposure of Edom's cowardly betrayal (Obadiah) to the absurd prospect of Assyria's penance (Jonah) and in due course back to Judah's infectious wounds:

> For her wound is incurable.
> It has come to Judah;
> it has reached to the gate of my people,
> to Jerusalem. (Mic 1:9)

The book of Micah diagnoses the people of Judah with a disease as life-threatening as that afflicting Israel:

> What is the transgression of Jacob?
> Is it not Samaria?
> And what is the high place of Judah?
> Is it not Jerusalem? (Mic 1:5)

In Amos, the descriptions of the sins of Judah lead the audience to harsh accusations against Israel. In Micah, the route is reversed as the disease of the north (Israel) reaches the southern gate (Judah).[33] Throughout the preceding books of the Twelve, accusations have been leveled against Jerusalem, but now they are front and center. Consequently, there is no place for Judah to hide. Nor can the Judean exiles, the readers and the writers, blame others for their present plight. Here at the core of the Twelve, Jerusalem must look in the mirror, even at the lowest point, and conclude that God's people are not without sin. "Maiden Israel" (Amos 5:2) now meets "Daughter Zion" (Mic 1:13) and both must prepare for disaster. Micah's inventory of sins is lengthy: idolatry (1:2-7), dishonesty, deceit, and violence (6:9-12)—actions that lead to the ruin of society (7:1-10). Such wrongdoing, the prophet declares, is reason for regret and lamentation, as the disturbing wordplay suggests:

> In Beth-leaphrah [the house of dust] roll yourselves in the dust;
> Pass over, inhabitants of Shaphir [beauty], in shameful nakedness. . . .
> Surely the inhabitants of Maroth [bitterness] in anguish writhe for good,

but disaster has come down from YHWH to the gate of Jerusalem. . . .
The houses of Achzib [falsehood] shall be a deception to the kings of Israel.
(Mic 1:10-14, authors' translation)[34]

Once again, it must be noted that such language operates not only as a social commentary but also as a theodicy; that is, it serves, in the first place, to uphold divine integrity, especially divine power and justice, in light of devastating historical circumstances and human suffering. To arrive at some rational understanding of its grim conditions, the interpretive community makes full use of the doctrine of retribution, which interprets the national disaster and chaotic historical forces as divine judgment and punishment for sin. When a retributive perspective is deployed consistently, the world makes sense, moral coherence is maintained, and God's power and justice are preserved; *but the cost is high: divine violence and abuse as well as human blame and guilt*. Sensitive to this dilemma for contemporary readers, Daniel J. Simundson notes: "The book of Micah gives an occasion to think about [the doctrine of retribution], to see what is valid and what needs critique, what should be applied personally and communally, and what should be rejected as not filling one's own circumstances."[35]

Second, as the people of Judah look in the mirror, they discover their own corrupt political and religious leaders lurking in the background. Micah's long list of accusations zooms in on the "heads of Jacob and rulers of the house of Israel!" (3:1). As those entrusted with the care of God's people, they should be well aware of their responsibilities to maintain justice: "Should you not know justice?" (3:1). But like Ezekiel's false shepherds (Ezek 34:1-10), Micah's wicked rulers pervert justice, mistreat those who cannot defend themselves, and devour those who depend on their nurture (Mic 3:1-4, 9-12). Judah's self-serving leaders carry huge stones that eventually drown the whole people, "devise wickedness / and evil deeds on their beds" (2:1), and "build Zion with blood / and Jerusalem with wrong" (3:10). Their dossier includes greed, bloodshed, unlawful seizure of property, and oppression (2:2). They demonstrate proficiency in abusing the poor and vulnerable (2:8-10). The leaders of society sit in the driver's seat and lead the entire nation down the road to ruin—yes, those "rulers of the house of Israel" who are utterly corrupt, priests who "teach for a price" (3:11), and the prophets who live in denial and exploit their power and position for their own welfare (3:5). All betray their divine calling and commit crimes against their own people. And all have the audacity to operate in the name of God:

They lean upon the LORD and say,
"Surely the LORD is with us!
No harm shall come upon us." (3:11)

Micah declares that those "who hate the good and love the evil" (3:2; cf. Amos 5:14-15) will not get away with murder. Indeed, the prophet thunders against them:

> Therefore it shall be night to you, without vision,
>   and darkness to you, without revelation. . . .
> But as for me, I am filled with power,
>   with the spirit of the LORD,
>   and with justice and might. (Mic 3:6, 8)

Railing against unjust leaders in our own time, singer and songwriter Leonard Cohen puts it this way:

> I can't run no more
> with that lawless crowd
> while the killers in high places
> say their prayers out loud.
> But they've summoned,
> they've summoned up
> a thundercloud
> and they're going to hear from me.[36]

Third, as is characteristic of the prophetic corpus as a whole, the book of Micah refuses to throw in the towel and relinquish hope. Micah, the champion of social justice, speaks on behalf of the losers and the victims. This is evident in the accusations against the powerful and in the promissory language of hope for the surviving community. While the book bristles with biting judgment, it also expresses buoyant confidence in Jerusalem's future. The concepts of judgment and hope for Zion and her offspring are not mutually exclusive. Together, they depict the eventual restoration of Judah and Israel.[37] In fact, Micah not only vacillates between disaster and hope, it actually juxtaposes the two to create the overall structure of the book:

- 1:2–2:11   Judgment Oracles against Israel and Judah
- 2:12-13   Promise of Survival
- 3:1-12   Judgment Oracles against Judah's Leadership
- 4:1–5:15   Promises of Restoration and Salvation
- 6:1–7:10   Judgment for Widespread Corruption
- 7:11-20   Promises of Restoration and Divine Compassion

This resultant binary arrangement, though likely superimposed by later interpretive communities, reveals a pastoral penchant for comforting and sustaining readers dealing with devastating historical circumstances. Moreover, it imagines prophetic heroes as both harbingers of doom and harbingers of salvation. And it claims that God's people will eventually survive against all odds.

Micah's vision of hope is a textual tapestry that draws upon a variety of prophetic strands to create its own distinctive artistic expression. Inspired by Jeremiah and Ezekiel, the interpretive community of Micah imagines shepherd-king YHWH gathering the scattered flock of Jacob and protecting it from harm (2:12-13; see also Jer 23:3-4; Ezek 34:11-13). Inspired by Isaiah, the interpretive community of Micah imagines the glorious future of Zion (Mic 4:1-5; Isa 2:2-5). In an astute intertextual comparison of Isaiah and Micah, Marvin A. Sweeney points out key conceptual differences:

> The book of Isaiah points to a future when Israel will be restored, but it will stand as part of the larger Persian empire with which YHWH identifies. . . . Micah, however, points to the emergence of an independent state, ruled by a Davidic monarch, that will bring YHWH's punishment to the nations and stand at their center.[38]

This vision of Zion's resurgence is central to the book of Micah and possibly to the entire collection of the Twelve.

The congregation could only revel in the hope that one day ("in days to come . . . in that day") God would exalt lowly Judah and bring down its arrogant oppressors, in accordance with the Torah (Mic 4:2; 5:1-5). The listening congregation could only delight in the prospect that imperial dominance would someday end, and peace and nonviolence would become the *lingua franca* for the nations. Then they would be able to walk, without fear, "in the name of the LORD [their] God" (4:5). Yes, God's people would face hard times and bear deep scars to prove it, but they would endure and even prevail:

> In that day, says the LORD,
> I will assemble the lame
> and gather those who have been driven away,
> and those whom I have afflicted.
> The lame I will make the remnant,
> and those who were cast off, a strong nation;
> and the LORD will reign over them in Mount Zion
> now and forevermore. (4:6-7)

It should be noted that at the center of this vision Micah imagines a new royal messiah ushering in this epoch of peace, justice, and security:

> But you, O Bethlehem of Ephrathah,
> who are one of the little clans of Judah,
> from you shall come forth for me
> one who is to rule in Israel,
> whose origin is from of old,
> from ancient days. . . .

214

And he shall stand and feed his flock in the strength of the LORD,
  in the majesty of the name of the LORD his God.
And they shall live secure, for now he shall be great
  to the ends of the earth;
and he shall be the one of peace. (5:2, 4-5a [MT 5:1, 3-4a])

According to Micah, this ideal Davidic monarch from unremarkable origins will destroy the oppressive nations and save God's people. And as a result of his triumph, the "remnant of Jacob" will no longer need its false securities, especially the "horses . . . and . . . chariots" (i.e., its military hardware) and "sorceries . . . and . . . soothsayers" (idolatrous practices and worship; 5:10-15).

Micah: "Who is a God like You?"

In the interim, before the full realization of God's promises, Micah instructs the community on how to live as God's people. Once again, readers are reminded that YHWH has demands, and burnt offerings or solemn festivals alone do not cut it. According to Micah, even thousands of rams or vessels of choice oil will not be adequate—from "calves a year old" to "thousands of rams" to "ten thousands of rivers of oil" to even his "firstborn" (6:6-7), readers may wonder when God will be satisfied! No, it is not material or carnal sacrifice—perhaps hinting at the syncretistic religious practices of Ahab and Omri (6:16)—that YHWH requires, but an ongoing and ardent commitment to "do justice, and to love kindness, / and to walk humbly with your God" (6:8). In this most rudimentary commandment lies the possibility of hope. The implied readers, fed up with lawlessness, enmity, distrust, and oppression, can now find hope in the clarity of God's unequivocal expectations; to live as God's people requires justice, love, and humility before God and one another.

Finally, the implied readers find hope in the attributes of YHWH. The concluding chapter contains the prophet's own name, which means, "Who is like you?" The focal concern, presented in question-and-answer form, attends not only to what God requires but ultimately to who God is: "Who is a God like you?" (7:18). Here, at the structurally chiastic center of the Twelve, the book of Micah highlights not only Zion's fate but also the divine pathos expressed in the "I-thou" relationship: "O my people . . . / O my people . . . / you may know the saving acts of the LORD" (6:3-5; cf. 2:12; 3:3; 5:9-14; 7:7). Notwithstanding the sins of (northern) Israel, the betrayal of Edom, the oppression of Assyria, and the infections in Judah, readers come face-to-face with YHWH's core character. The confession of the defining attributes of God occurs in Jonah (4:2), Micah (7:18), and Nahum (1:2-3)—again as if forming two pillars with Micah as the central apex.[39] And so the final words of the book of Micah, in response to the lingering question "Who is a God like you?" lead the congregation in a wondrous testimony of faith:

> Who is a God like you, pardoning iniquity
>   and passing over the transgression
>   of the remnant of your possession?
> He does not retain his anger forever,
>   because he delights in showing clemency.
> He will again have compassion upon us;
>   he will tread our iniquities under foot.
> *You* will cast all our sins
>   into the depths of the sea. (Mic 7:18-19; emphasis added)

AN ANTHOLOGY OF DEBATE AND REBUILDING (NAHUM–MALACHI)

Nahum, Habakkuk, and Zephaniah: Debates concerning Israel, Judah, and the Nations

In the larger central section of the Twelve that resembles the OAN, Obadiah and Jonah meet their counterparts in Nahum and Habakkuk, just as Micah meets Zephaniah.[1] Symmetrically, Obadiah deals with Edom the traitor, while Habakkuk addresses Babylon as the new menacing empire. Edom symbolizes Israel's closest neighbor, and Babylon represents the distant but devastating destroyer of the capital, Jerusalem, and its temple. In between stand Jonah and Nahum, both of which center on Assyria, the bygone oppressor of northern Israel. When Jonah and Nahum are read together, one encounters conflicting, even oppositional, voices, and those who seek logical coherence in the Twelve will be disconcerted by the ongoing disputes about YHWH. The book of Jonah suggests that no one is beyond divine mercy, whereas Nahum accentuates the necessity of retribution for wrongdoers. The former affords Assyria a second chance, just as Jonah himself is granted a second chance. The latter, by implication, would consider any form of amnesty for Assyria utterly offensive. Such theological debates are taken up again and expanded by Habakkuk, with regard to the fate of Babylon. The God of justice will repay sins and exonerate Israel and Judah, a theme addressed once again in Zephaniah.

Nahum: One Who Brings Good Tidings, Who Proclaims Peace

Assyria, the empire that destroyed and exiled the people of northern Israel, fell to the emergent superpower Babylon in 612 B.C.E. The implied readers of Nahum would recall the year 722 B.C.E., when Assyria became a *historical* manifestation of evil. The people of Israel had lived through both the brutal attack and the collapse; and these horrific experiences were burned into collective memory, no matter how many years had passed. At the same time, Assyrian oppression in Nahum represents *symbolic* evil, attending to the construction of theodicy rather than a mere delineation of Assyria *per se*. Ultimately, historical *and* symbolic concerns converge in Nahum's representation of the empire.

The book of Nahum as a disaster text is full of rage, acrimony, and pain. It boldly gives voice to outpourings of curse and anger (especially in ch. 3). Moreover, such passions are theologically grounded, first and foremost, in God.[2] The theological rhetoric of Nahum grows out of divine urgency to maintain the just workings of the universe in light of horrific suffering. The core (creedal) character of YHWH is at stake. Whereas Jonah and Micah testify that YHWH is the God who is compassionate and merciful (Jonah 4:2; Mic 7:18; cf. Exod 34:6-7a; Num 14:18; Joel 2:13; Pss 86:15; 103:8; 145:8), Nahum objects vehemently with this counterargument:

> A jealous and avenging God is the LORD,
>   the LORD is avenging and wrathful. . . .
> The LORD is slow to anger but great in power,
>   and the LORD will by no means clear the guilty. (Nah 1:2-3; cf. Exod 34:7b)

The rebuttal presents as evidence those shattered by adversity and loss.

Nahum gives full vent to outcry and vexation, railing against the immense suffering and injustice of a devastated people.[3] God's people have little time for abstract debate or theological speculation. Their debate is to rage; their theology is to cry out in anguish! Yet here in this maelstrom of raw emotion, readers discover signs of tangible hope. Divine pathos confirms that God neither ignores nor tolerates the wrongs done by oppressors:

> Who can stand before his indignation?
>   Who can endure the heat of his anger?
> His wrath is poured out like fire,
>   and by him the rocks are broken in pieces. (1:6)

In short, divine anger attests to divine fidelity to YHWH's people, even when facing defeat and humiliation. And when divine wrath converges with human pain and anger, the prospect of justice becomes all the more viable.

Nahum's initial theological claim that God is "avenging and wrathful" is further delineated by the assertion that "the LORD is good" (1:7). Modern readers who are accustomed to thinking of benevolence as cordiality will be puzzled by this paradox. How can a "vengeful" God be perceived as good? It is noteworthy that the NJPS version includes an addition to this verse (likely to balance and clarify the poetry): "The LORD is good to [those who hope in Him]." The text itself accounts for the benevolence of YHWH by affirming that this God "protects those who take refuge in him" (1:7), even though they may feel that God has forgotten them ("even in a rushing flood"). Likewise, the prophet contrasts this *good* God directly with the *evil* that the oppressor has plotted against YHWH—evil that will be "cut off and pass away" (1:11-12). Thus, the God of vengeance is recognized as *good*—that is, efficient—in matters of justice.

Furthermore, the book of Nahum, as a survival text, invites readers to celebrate divine shalom. The implied readers learn that hope ends not in vengeance or victory but in the prospect of spiritual restoration and peace. The defeat of the empire creates the conditions necessary for the resumption of worship, for festivity, and for freedom. Thus the announcement of promise, which will find full expression in Habakkuk and Zephaniah, incorporates the elements of joy and renewal:

> Look! On the mountains the feet of one
>   who brings good tidings,
>   who proclaims peace!
> Celebrate your festivals, O Judah,
>   fulfill your vows,
> for never again shall the wicked invade you;
>   they are utterly cut off. (1:15 [MT 2:1])

Contemporary readers might again find such notions odd or even morally troubling: should one gain peace at the expense of another's bad fortune? How can Nineveh's fall ever be considered good tidings?[4] Nahum's nationalistic poems, however, must be heard "at the margins," or "from the bottom up"; that is to say, Nahum speaks on behalf of those who have suffered unspeakable cruelty at the hands of an oppressive empire (Assyria, Babylon, or even Persia). Indeed, Nahum speaks on behalf of all victims of cruel and repressive forces: geopolitical, socioeconomic, ecclesiastic, and even familial. Read in this way, the fall of Nineveh—the existential manifestation of evil—is nothing less than a source of joy and vindication.[5] The poetic images of the devastation of the seemingly impregnable city of Nineveh in Nahum 2:1-13 are graphic expressions of triumph, songs chanted by the oppressed: "What became of the lions' den, / the cave of the young lions? . . . / I will burn your chariots in smoke, and the sword shall devour your young lions" (2:11, 13 [MT 2:12, 14]).[6] When the implied readers hear these taunting songs, they are reminded that the outcries of the downtrodden will not be ignored; justice and peace will appear even in the face of foreboding forces.

Nahum's call for the enactment of justice concludes with a question directed to Assyria and perhaps obliquely to YHWH: "For who has ever escaped / your endless cruelty?" (3:19). When the subjugated community read the prophet's account of Nineveh lying in ruins (3:2-3), they would find little evidence of sorrow or regret. Nahum claims that Assyria's brutality led to its complete demise, with "no end to the plunder" (3:1). The phrase used to express the grave condition of Judah on the verge of demise

("For *her wound is incurable.* / It has come to Judah," Mic 1:9; emphasis added) recurs, except now the death sentence is pronounced against Assyria ("There is no assuaging your hurt, / *your wound is mortal,*" Nah 3:19; emphasis added). Whether a wish or a curse, the description of the empire's collapse is striking and powerful.

Deprived of hope and comfort, the people of Israel and Judah could only imagine the enemy oppressor's fall: " 'Nineveh is devastated; who will bemoan her?' / Where shall I seek comforters for you?" (3:7; the name *Nahum* literally means "comforted"). How else could the community endure its seemingly endless years of captivity?[7] Through the lenses of the text and of worship, the implied audience would envision the demise of the enemy and its politics of domination. They would imagine a realignment of power structures, reenacting the victims' wish for vindication and hope, expressed through cries of anguish and plaintive songs. Through the power of theater, the people of God would revel, ridiculing and even defying their tormenters. And so this theological counterpart to the book of Jonah presents an intense reenactment of *comfort*—comfort that celebrates the end of domination and the prospect of justice for the oppressed.

Habakkuk: Debate over Theodicy between the Intercessor and YHWH

The book of Habakkuk picks up the motifs of Nahum and intensifies them. Habakkuk alters the stage, however, with its focus on a debate between the prophet and God. The setting also shifts from Assyria to Babylon, the new and improved terminator. Just as Micah depicts the frailty and hope of Judah at its lowest level, Habakkuk moves the audience to such depths that they become silent witness to the prophet's argument with God. Just as Nahum grapples with *good versus evil,* Habakkuk deals with *crime and punishment.* Habakkuk parallels the actions of Jacob, thereby representing the entire people of Israel in their wrestling with God (see Gen 32:23-33). In this sense, Habakkuk joins Job and Jeremiah (perhaps also Qoheleth) in struggling to formulate a theodicy during seemingly incessant wars and violence imposed by insurmountable empires—once Assyria and now Babylon. Also like Job and Jeremiah, Habakkuk uses dialogue as a forum for presenting these issues. Clear-cut doctrines and conventional testimonies of faith are thus intentionally avoided. Instead, the dialogues invite readers to consider the arguments of both sides and then develop their own understanding. It is the nature of dialogue to resist dogma and push readers into critical engagement, reflection, and even rebuttal.

First, Habakkuk addresses the sins of his own people: Israel and Judah. The prophet becomes a prosecutor in unveiling the wrongs and violence committed by corrupt rulers. Israel and Judah have long witnessed how their own leaders have twisted the Torah and perverted the divine commandments (Hab 1:4).[8] The case for justice is put to God: "O LORD, how long shall I cry for help, / and you will not listen? / Or cry to you 'Violence!' / and you will not save?" (1:2). YHWH's long silence, and perceived indifference to sin and corruption, is soon broken: YHWH will intervene on behalf of the righteous, whistling for the nations and using them as instruments to punish wrongdoers (1:5-11; cf. Amos 4:12, "Prepare to meet your God, O Israel!"). This divine response to Habakkuk's challenge indicates that YHWH will attend to matters of injustice. The moral world of the prophet may appear arbitrary and incoherent, and YHWH may appear inattentive to "wrongdoing" and "trouble," "destruction and violence," as "the wicked surround the righteous . . . [and] judgment comes forth perverted" (Hab 1:3-4). But eventually YHWH will rectify such wrongs and restore moral symmetry—albeit through the instrumentality of Babylon: "For I am rousing the Chaldeans, / that fierce and impetuous nation" (1:6).

Second, the dialogical form enables readers to ponder the issue of theodicy in conjunction with divine interference. *Divine absence* could not satisfy the crying prophet. Now *divine presence* and interference do not satisfy the complaining prophet because YHWH's "eyes are too pure to behold evil" (1:13). Here Habakkuk joins Jonah in complaining about the rise of violence in the empire, now in Babylon and previously witnessed in Assyria:

> I will stand at my watchpost,
>   and station myself on the rampart;
> I will keep watch to see what he will say to me,
>   and what he will answer concerning my complaint. (2:1; cf. Jonah 4:5)

Whereas Jonah is distraught at the deliverance of Nineveh and divine mercy toward the repentant enemy people, Habakkuk is haunted by the idea that God would use an unrepentant nation to bring judgment on God's people (1:12-17). Such a notion flies in the face of divine justice and moral logic.

YHWH's response to the prophet's complaint is open-ended: "Look at the proud! / Their spirit is not right in them, / but the righteous live by their faith" (2:4). Not unlike the divine response to Job (Job 38–41), YHWH does not resolve Habakkuk's dilemma. As the dialogue continues, however, we learn that evil, when unrepentant, will be dealt with by divine indignation. A series of five woe-oracles, or sayings, highlights the crimes of wicked oppressors and their imminent demise (Hab 2:6-20), although the Babylonians are not specifically identified in these speeches. Nonetheless, the diasporic community could find relief in the claim that unwieldy human power—imperial power and tyranny—will come to an end, whether it appears as Assyria, Babylon, Persia, or Greece. As Theodore Hiebert eloquently writes: "Habakkuk claims that there exists, in the common fund of human experience and wisdom, evidence for a principle of justice operative in the world that in the end destroys all tyrannical power and pretension."[9]

Third, notwithstanding the striking affirmation of a moral order, the book concludes not with a definite answer or a simple solution but rather with the prophet's hope, prayer, and testimony. The psalm of Habakkuk invites readers to join in with their own complaints and confessions (3:1-19). The prayer represents the collective testimony of the greater community. It is a response to the many fractures and disjunctions of life; but it is foremost a powerful declaration of trust in YHWH's mysterious ways. Most assuredly, "the righteous live by their faith" (2:4). Habakkuk's prayer becomes a model, exemplifying how to live by faith—a theological thesis in this book—while beset by treacherous and rapacious tyrants (2:5).

Through dialogue, the prophet is both humbled and empowered to establish his own conviction. Clearly not all questions are answered, nor are many complaints resolved (reminiscent of Jonah's unrecorded response to the divine probe). Yet the book of Habakkuk does end with a response from the prophet—a prayer, a vow to hope against hope. And readers are invited to unite with the prophet in that vow of faith. The result is a defiant confession of confidence and joy. In the course of seemingly endless losses and defeats, the strange vision of hope at the end of Nahum, "All who hear the news about you / clap their hands over you" (Nah 3:19), is now transformed into a beautiful song of the prophet and the people:

> Though the fig tree does not blossom,
>   and no fruit is on the vines;
> though the produce of the olive fails,
>   and the fields yield no food;
> though the flock is cut off from the fold,
>   and there is no herd in the stalls,
> yet I will rejoice in the LORD;
>   I will exult in the God of my salvation.
> GOD, the Lord, is my strength;
>   he makes my feet like the feet of a deer,
> and makes me tread upon the heights. (Hab 3:17-19)

Zephaniah: A Transformed City in a New World

The book of Zephaniah is placed as a counterpart to the book of Micah, with its central focus on the fate of Jerusalem vis-à-vis its purging and restoration. It also functions as a culminating work of the internal OAN section of the Twelve (from Obadiah to Zephaniah). Accordingly, as if summarizing the previous books, readers hear the oracles against various nations, including the Philistines (Zeph 2:4-5); the Moabites and Ammonites (2:8-11); the Cushites, Ethiopians, or Egyptians (2:12); the Assyrians (2:13-14); and possibly the Babylonians (2:15; cf. Isa 47:8), though Edom is missing. Interestingly, Edom does occur in Obadiah, as if these two writings— Obadiah and Zephaniah—form bookends for the internal six books of the Twelve. Furthermore, just as Micah functions as a bridge between Jonah and Nahum in the Masoretic canon, so Zephaniah bridges the gap between the preceding books and the last three books.[10] The book of Zephaniah thus recapitulates the messages of the preceding books, in terms of divine punishment and restoration, while at the same time it paves the way to the return and rebuilding motifs in Haggai, Zechariah, and Malachi.

With rhetorical artistry and intertextual echoes,[11] Zephaniah 1 moves skillfully from the threat of cosmic crumbling to the climactic announcement of the impending day of YHWH. The initial subunit (1:2-6) sets the tone for the larger unit: it alludes to YHWH's insurmountable power to "uncreate" the world. This haunting language is reminiscent of Jeremiah 4:23-26, which also reverses motifs in Genesis 1:

> I will utterly sweep away everything
>   from the face of the earth, says the LORD.
> I will sweep away humans and animals;
>   I will sweep away the birds of the air
>   and the fish of the sea. (Zeph 1:2-3; cf. Hos 4:3)

The created order, the prophet asserts, is in grave danger. Once destroyed by a flood because of human wickedness (Gen 6–9), the earth can again be swept away by divine decree. Indeed, when YHWH "stretches out" his hand, destruction is virtually inevitable (for example, Ezek 14:9, 13). This does not bode well for God's people, for now YHWH "stretch[es] out YHWH's hand against Judah, / and against all the inhabitants of Jerusalem" (Zeph 1:4). As in the case in Micah, the object of judgment in Zephaniah is Judah and its capital city. Furthermore, the divine denouncement highlights worshipers of Baal, who will be "*cut off* from this place." Zion is clearly at risk, for the one who "*cut off* humanity from the face of the earth" (1:3; emphasis added) threatens to "*cut off* . . . every remnant of Baal and the name of the idolatrous priests" (1:4; emphasis added). The prophet casts an ominous cloud over Judah's world.

The subsequent subunit (1:7-13) narrows the focus to the "rulers" and "king's sons" (1:8). Zephaniah denounces these seemingly secure and affluent officials for their moral ineptitude. They "rest complacently on their dregs" and say in their hearts, "YHWH will do neither good nor evil" (1:12, authors' translation; cf. Pss 14:1; 53:1). Once again, haughty rulers who practice idolatry and injustice come under divine scrutiny even as the announcement of the "day of the LORD" (1:14-18) reinforces the initial threat of cosmic crumbling (1:2-3):

> That day will be a day of wrath,
>   a day of distress and anguish,
> a day of ruin and devastation,
>   a day of darkness and gloom,
> a day of clouds and thick darkness,
>   a day of trumpet blast and battle cry. (Zeph 1:15-16; cf. Obad 12-14)

Notice that the word *day* occurs seven times as if its rhetorical expression reminds readers of the creation of the world in seven days (Gen 1:1–2:4a), except here the meaning is reversed. Altogether, the implied readers learn that YHWH, who is capable of undoing the created order, can bring down proud and unjust rulers as an essential step toward the transformation of the city and community.

Zephaniah 2–3 employs rhetorical strategies and intertextual allusions that are similar to those found in chapter 1, although the fortunes of God's people begin to appear far brighter: the foreign nations come into judgment (a sign of hope for Judah) and the humble remnants of YHWH's people are saved. First, "the day of the LORD's wrath" (1:18; 2:3) no longer involves total and unequivocal doom for Judah and Jerusalem; now the prophet invites the humble and contrite to seek YHWH's mercy (2:1-3). The exhortation to "seek the LORD" (2:3) echoes comparable pleas in Hosea 3:5; 10:12; and especially Amos 5:4, 6: "Seek me and live. . . . Seek the LORD and live." Just as the call to seek YHWH interrupts massive condemnation in the dirges of Amos 5, so the same appeal in Zephaniah disturbs the continuity between the oracles against Judah and Jerusalem (in ch. 1) and those against the nations (in ch. 2). In humble acknowledgment and repentance, Jerusalem thus learns of the possibility of deliverance and healing. The humble are admonished to practice "justice" as well as to seek "righteousness" and "humility" in the hope that "perhaps you may be hidden on the day of the LORD's wrath" (2:3). The idea that divine mercy is not an entitlement but a possibility, pregnant in the word *perhaps*, is reminiscent of comparable petitions in the preceding books (authors' translations): "*Who knows?* YHWH might turn, relent, and leave a blessing behind him" (Joel 2:14); "*Perhaps* YHWH, the God of hosts, will be gracious to the remnant of Joseph" (Amos 5:15); "*Perhaps* God will reckon us so that we do not perish" (Jonah 1:6); "*Who knows?* God may turn, relent, and return from his fierce anger, so that we do not perish." (Jonah 3:9).

Following the brief but vociferous call for humility and contrition (Zeph 2:1-3), the prophet announces the downfall of the neighboring nations (2:4-15). At first glance, the list of the nations in this OAN section seems random. However, a closer look at the configuration suggests a meaningful structure, though scholars have presented different interpretations. On the one hand, the nations listed may point to key posts of Assyrian occupation, thereby depicting the fall of each military post as progressive steps toward the collapse of the Assyrian empire.[12] On the other hand, these nations roughly mark the four corners of the idealized world of primeval history: Philistia (west), Moab/Ammon (east), Cush (south), and Assyria (north).[13] In either case, the list of nations proceeds toward its rhetorical climax—that is, the announcement of the destruction of Assyria (2:13-15). Just as the culmination of the OAN in Amos 1–2 highlights the condemnation of Judah and especially northern Israel, so the climax of impending doom in Zephaniah 2 arrives at Assyria. With a similar phrase—"*I will stretch out my hand against* Judah; and against all the inhabitants of Jerusalem" (1:4; emphasis added)—the denunciation of Assyria builds an inclusio, "*He will stretch out his hand against* the north, and destroy Assyria" (2:13; emphasis added). Read together, the initial oracle declaring the divine punishment of Judah is countered by the emphatic pronouncement of the divine punishment of Assyria. Now God's people are to take courage and have hope that the oppressive empire will soon be no more.

Here it is noteworthy that in several texts of Zephaniah the addressees, described as a "nation" or "city," are not clearly identified (2:1, 15; 3:1). For example, from the immediately preceding texts (2:13-14), the "exultant city" (2:15) can refer to Nineveh, but it can also, to the implied readers, refer to any oppressive empire that can become a waste and desolation.[14] The phrase, "the one who says in her heart, 'I am, and there is no other'" (2:15, authors' translation), describes the asinine boasting of the king of Assyria while coinciding with the similar phrase depicting that of Daughter Chaldea, "who say in your heart, 'I am, and there is no one besides me'" (Isa 47:8). To the interpretive community, therefore, the OAN in Zephaniah 2 underscore the assured downfall of seemingly impregnable empires, once Assyria and then Babylon and more.

The anonymous "oppressing city" (3:1) likewise conveys subtle ambiguities and multiple meanings. This unidentified city in the woe-oracle of the culminating chapter 3 might refer to Jerusalem or Nineveh. On the one hand, most scholars consider the depictions of wrongdoing to have originally alluded to the turbulent period near the end of Jerusalem's monarchy. Yet, on the other hand, the poetic phrase, "the oppressing city"—which can denote "dove city" and is pronounced exactly the same as the word *Jonah*—can point to various capitals as symbols of corruption and wrongdoing (3:6-10). Throughout the text, the contents of the evil extant in this city point to the past history of the religiopolitical leaders of Judah who have time and again failed to uphold the Torah commands of justice and righteousness. This oracle specifically names each of the power-abusing classes: the "officials," "judges," "prophets," and "priests" (3:2-4). In sharp contrast, the oracle accentuates the faithfulness of YHWH the righteous judge: "The LORD within it is righteous" (3:5).

Consequently, one subtle but crucial function of the book of Zephaniah is to redirect the focus of the Twelve back to Zion, much like the book of Micah does. What is so theologically striking about this interpretive move, and the prophetic heritage as a whole, is the propensity to make harsh accusations against one's own people, especially the leaders. Perhaps here lies the center, or *Mitte*, of the prophetic traditions in the Twelve: the resolve to envisage Jerusalem as a city that would fall and then rise as a transformed place for the whole world. This vision draws upon the ideals of Josiah's reform. According to 2 Kings 22–23 (2 Chr 34–35), King Josiah promulgated a nationwide reform of religious idolatry and social corruptions. This reform also imagined a purified city of Jerusalem that would regain its status as the center of peace and justice for the whole world. Though clear evidence is lacking, scholars have posited the possibility that the prophet Zephaniah may have been related to King Hezekiah (1:1).[15]

In light of these connections, how would the book of Zephaniah inspire its readers? Is not the vision of a transformed city of Jerusalem in a new world order too utopian? Would the exiles not be aware of the failed reforms of Hezekiah and Josiah? Answers to these questions recur throughout the Twelve with the emphatic divine assertion that God will purge evildoers who "[know] no shame" (3:5) and uplift the "humble and lowly" in bringing them to YHWH's "holy mountain" (3:11, 12):

> For I will leave in the midst of you
>   a people humble and lowly.
> They shall seek refuge in the name of the LORD. (3:12)

As indicated by the overdetermined allusion to the "oppressing city" (in 3:1) and the surplus of harsh words uttered against the people of God and the foreign nations, Zephaniah's vision of a glorious era is never detached from the bleak realities of exilic and postexilic life. Immersed in such realities, the readers and writers of the book inhabit two intersecting worlds—one burdened by the strain of captivity and injustice, and the other buoyed by the hope of liberation and renewal. While the text gives voice to both realities, it is insistent that coercive control, violence, and shame will not have the final say for the surviving community. Thus, poetry and counterstory, no doubt uttered under the radar of the empire, enable the interpretive community to imagine a new world:

> At that time I will change the speech of the peoples
>   to a pure speech,
> that all of them may call on the name of the LORD
>   and serve him with one accord. . . .
>   the remnant of Israel;
> they shall do no wrong
>   and utter no lies,

> nor shall a deceitful tongue
> > be found in their mouths.
> Then they will pasture and lie down,
> > and no one shall make them afraid. (Zeph 3:9, 13)

The central section of the Twelve, dealing with the Oracles against the Nations, concludes with full-bloom hope for Israel and Judah (3:14-20). This final utterance is actually a song of joy that readers are invited to sing while in captivity (cf. Acts 16:20-25). This wondrous liturgical piece celebrates YHWH as Israel's true king who dwells in their midst, dispels their fears, and revels in Zion. The prophetic word again leads its readers in worship and reenacts an alternative universe anchored to hope, justice, and love. And so, even though the people of YHWH are only a tiny Levant surrounded by towering superpowers, they are the ones with magnificent hope. No wonder they "clap their hands" (Nah 3:19), "rejoice" (Hab 3:18), and "rejoice and exult" (Zeph 3:14):

> Sing aloud, O daughter Zion;
> > shout, O Israel!
> Rejoice and exult with all your heart,
> > O daughter Jerusalem! . . .
> At that time I will bring you home,
> > at the time when I gather you;
> for I will make you renowned and praised
> > among all the peoples of the earth. (Zeph 3:14, 20; cf. Zech 2:14; 9:9)

Haggai, Zechariah, and Malachi:
Rebuilding in the Present Reality

Oral prophecy (the spoken word) and written prophecy (the written word) no longer inhabit vastly different spheres. Whereas the prophet and the prophetic scroll had long been estranged in time and place, they now begin to share adjacent social and symbolic worlds. More specifically, the implied readers of the last three books of the Twelve encounter texts that are almost contemporary with them, if we suppose that they are situated in the Persian period and beyond. This does not mean that we can pinpoint the exact historical circumstances and literary development of the books of Haggai, Zechariah, and Malachi, even with the precise chronological allusions in Haggai and Zechariah.[16] But now prophetic speech, writing, and reading shift from diaspora *per se* to the daunting challenges of rebuilding, recovery, and restoration. At the same time, the central concerns of the colonized community clearly leave their indelible imprint on these final three books.

What could be worse than the hardships of war and exile? Perhaps returning home to taunts, ridicule, and disappointment! The implied readers who yearn for a glorious future now stand at its threshold only to encounter frustration rather than fanfare. The anticipated, now realized future, the "grand homecoming," too closely resembles the painful past: scarcity, marginality, poverty, and despair. And in response, readers continue to hear voices of protest and cynicism: "How have you loved us?" (Mal 1:2); " 'How have we wearied [God]?' . . . 'Where is the God of justice?' " (Mal 2:17; see also 3:13-15). Put starkly, the reconstruction of life in postexilic Jerusalem, as depicted in these books (see also Ezra and Nehemiah), is far from that envisioned by earlier prophets. Against this dreary background, the prophetic messages of Haggai, Zechariah, and Malachi become ever more forceful. To the community members who shake their heads, "We can't do it," the prophets respond, "Yes, we can!" To those who cry out, "We've had enough," the prophets proclaim, "Don't give up." To those who insist, "The obstacles are too overwhelming," the prophets give confidence, "Take courage . . . says the LORD; work, for I am with you, says the LORD of hosts . . . My spirit abides among you; do not fear" (Hag 2:4-5).

Haggai: To Rebuild the Temple—the Center and Foundation of the Community

For decades after the fall of the city in 587, the temple remained in ruins, although some modest forms of worship likely continued there (Jer 41:5; Ezra 3:1-7). Then, under the auspices of the Persian government (in 539), Judean refugees in Babylon were granted permission to return to their homeland and rebuild the temple. According to the book of Ezra, the temple restoration started in earnest (ca. 537) in response to a decree issued by Cyrus (Ezra 1:1-4; 3:1-13) only to wane and eventually come to a halt partly because of opposition from northern neighbors (Ezra 4:1-5). After the brief hiatus, however, Ezra reports that the construction of the temple resumed:

> Now the prophets, Haggai and Zechariah son of Iddo, prophesied to the Jews who were in Judah and Jerusalem, in the name of the God of Israel who was over them. Then Zerubbabel son of Shealtiel and Jeshua son of Jozadak set out to rebuild the house of God in Jerusalem; and with them were the prophets of God, helping them. (Ezra 5:1-2)

The books of Ezra and Nehemiah along with Haggai and Zechariah depict the social world of the returnees as riddled with conflict on account of their interaction with "indigenous outsiders" (i.e., "noncompliant insiders," identified in Ezra as "the adversaries of Judah and Benjamin" in 4:1 and "the people of the land" in 4:4). As a result of this contact, the literary and social world of the Judean returnees reflects enormous strain and anxiety. Community life is vulnerable and unstable, internal boundaries are blurred, and the survival of the group is in jeopardy. All this suggests a degree of turmoil bordering on anarchy. By *anarchy* we do not mean the absence of civil law or governmental structures. Clearly the Persian Empire imposed its own systems of control on its provinces. Moreover, the so-called benign policies that enabled colonized communities to return to their homelands also provided various forms of support to sustain reconstruction efforts. And under Persian structures the Judean returnees likely enjoyed a limited degree of autonomy, especially in the exercise of commercial and legal rights.[17]

Nonetheless, conditions in the small province of Yehud, at least as described in the text, were still unstable and dangerous. Even though the Yehudites may have benefited from certain "civil liberties" (the term is clearly anachronistic), they were still only a captive people eking out a new life in extremely trying surroundings. They dared not deny the colonizing governance or, worse yet, attempt to create their own government. Daniel L. Smith-Christopher is undoubtedly correct in his observation that

> part of the myth of Persian benevolence is the idea of an end to the exile in 539. But all that ended was Neo-Babylonian hegemony, to be replaced by that of the Persians. Ezra would point out, in his public prayer, that the Jewish people were "slaves in our own land" under the Persians (Neh 9:36-37). "Postexilic" Hebrew writings, like Daniel, would go so far as to reinterpret Jeremiah's predicted "70 years" into 490 years—effectively implying that the people were still in exile in the Persian and Hellenistic periods.[18]

Although Persian power facilitated the return and reconstruction, many Yehudites—leaders and commoners alike—would not regard their experience under Persian hegemony as a time of independence or liberation. The burden of taxation by the empire and the means of collection were only two reminders that the Yehudite community was by no means free.[19] Persistent resistance from opposing internal groups was also a sure sign of dissension and social disruption. Haggai alludes to this postexilic world as inundated with pain and disappointment; it felt cursed rather than blessed (1:7-11; 2:17-19).

Such volatile conditions easily lead to fragmentation, inertia, and even violence.[20] According to Haggai, the daring enthusiasm that initially propelled the Yehudites to return to Jerusalem had all but vanished. *Generativity* (coined by Erik Erikson), that is, the concern for establishing the next generation, had turned into stagnation and self-preservation. This erosion may have prompted Haggai to prophesy: "My house lies in ruins, while all of you hurry off to your own houses" (Hag 1:9).

With these internal and external challenges in mind, the interpretive community organizes the book around five oracles of Haggai, dated from the sixth through the ninth month of the second year of King Darius of Persia (520 B.C.E.).

- 1:1-6: The word of YHWH delivered on the first day of the sixth month
- 1:7-15: The word of YHWH delivered on the twenty-fourth day of the sixth month
- 2:1-9: The word of YHWH delivered on the twenty-first day of the seventh month
- 2:10-19: The word of YHWH delivered on the twenty-fourth day of the ninth month
- 2:20-23: The word of YHWH delivered on the twenty-fourth day of the ninth month

Interestingly, these prophecies neither launch new programs directed at combating exigent social conditions nor attack the menacing oppositional groups. Rather, the oracles of Haggai, first and foremost, focus on inspiring the Judean community and its leaders to complete the reconstruction of the temple in Jerusalem (Hag 1:2, 8; cf. Joel 1:9, 13-16; Jonah 2:5). By presenting a divine vision directed toward the temple, the prophet promotes group solidarity and cohesion. To be sure, the interpretive community of Haggai makes a forceful case for the centrality of space for YHWH, the preeminence of Jerusalem as cohesive symbol of unity, and the restoration of worship—all fundamental concerns of those who returned to Judea and saw themselves as heirs of the cherished divine promises.

In the first oracle of Haggai (1:1-6), the prophet reprimands the community for its flailing efforts at rebuilding the temple. The prophet refutes the naysayers' contention that the time is not right for reconstruction. Indeed, Haggai contends that the time is long overdue! For far too long, Haggai argues, the people have been preoccupied with their own self-interests rather than the work of God: "Is it a time for you yourselves to live in your paneled houses, while this house lies in ruins?" (1:4). Scholars have interpreted the language "paneled houses" in different ways. Some suggest that this language denotes affluent dwelling and thus a developing class distinction in the province. To support this interpretation, the same language is used to describe Solomon's temple and the royal palace (1 Kgs 6:9, 15; 7:7; cf. Jer 22:14). Thus, we have an indictment of the wealthy, not the dispossessed majority. However, the language may merely suggest that the Judeans on the whole have been overly concerned with a roof over their heads when YHWH does not have a house to live in. In either case, Haggai buttresses his argument by insisting that the hardships the community suffers are a sure sign of divine displeasure.

The second oracle (1:7-15) clearly builds upon the first, making use of morally exacting notions from the Deuteronomic tradition to encourage the building efforts: "You have looked for much, and, lo, it came to little; and when you brought it home, I blew it away. Why? says the LORD of hosts. Because my house lies in ruins, while all of you hurry off to your own houses" (1:9). In response to the prophet's prodding, the

leaders Zerubbabel and Joshua and the remnant of the people "obeyed the voice of the
LORD their God . . . and the people feared the LORD" (1:12). It is noteworthy that the
community "obeyed" and "feared" the Lord. First, this is far from the customary
response to prophetic speech. Second, the announcement of divine assurance directly
follows the community response of obedience, fear, and faith.

It is also of interest that the implied readers of Haggai might recall the story of the
twelve spies in their ancestors' wilderness period (Num 13:1-15); only two of the
twelve expressed positive reports (Num 14:6-9). Now, though the circumstances are
vastly different, the interpretive community is similarly summoned to have faith, over
against the majority who do not believe (cf. Hag 1:2). It is no surprise that the vocabulary of the charge to the people, "I am with you. . . . Do not fear," is quite similar to
that earlier story (Hag 1:13; 2:4-5; cf. Num 14:9). It is equally intriguing that one of
the two spies was Joshua, whose name now recurs as that of the current high priest
(Hag 1:1, 12, 14). The leaders and the whole people are, therefore, to come together
with bold faith and unity, and to work on rebuilding the temple and the nation (Hag
1:14).

Furthermore, within the Twelve, sequential readers might recall the divine promise
announced through Joel to pour out the divine spirit on the whole community (Joel
2:28-29 [MT 3:1-2]): "And the LORD stirred up the spirit of Zerubbabel son of Shealtiel,
governor of Judah, and the spirit of Joshua son of Jehozadak, the high priest, and the
spirit of all the remnant of the people" (Hag 1:14).[21] It is important for leaders to be
transformed in collective unity, but YHWH stirs up, inspires, and guides the *entire* community—the spirits of Zerubbabel, Joshua, and the rest of the people: "For I am with
you, says the LORD of hosts, according to the promise that I made you when you came
out of Egypt. My spirit abides among you" (Hag 2:4b-5; cf. Zech 4:6). If the first temple celebrated the great kings of old, especially kings David and Solomon, the second
temple commemorates the work of the whole community, both young and old, both
male and female, both noble and common.

In the third oracle (2:1-9), Haggai again addresses Zerubbabel and Joshua along
with the remnant of the people, especially those demoralized by lingering memories of
the grandiose Solomonic temple. Haggai prophesies that the rebuilt temple is not to
be disparaged in any way (see also Ezra 3:12-13); in fact, the newly constructed temple will be the very centerpiece of the eschatological and political world order to
come. "In a little while" (2:6) YHWH will "shake the heavens and the earth," take
action against the nations, and fill "this house with splendor" (2:7). This vision of a
resplendent temple and an emergent kingdom of God is in effect a reaffirmation of
divine sovereignty. Governing from the temple, YHWH's rule dwarfs every economic
and political powerhouse, and results in peace and prosperity for God's people (2:8).

Hence, the prophet calls the leaders and inspires all of the people to "take courage
... work ... do not fear" (2:4-5). When Zerubbabel, Joshua, and the entire community trust in YHWH, YHWH rouses their spirits and commissions them for the task of
rebuilding the temple (1:12-14). Through mutual trust and in acting out their collective vision, accompanied by firm faith in God, the divine promises become palpable
realities. The name *Haggai* literally means "festival"; in rebuilding the temple and
faithfully transmitting the sacred traditions, the interpretive community will find
hope, expressed here in God's presence and God's shalom: "I am with you, says the
LORD of hosts. . . . My spirit abides among you" (2:5; 1:13); "The latter splendor of this
house shall be greater than the former, says the LORD of hosts; and in this place I will
give prosperity [literally, 'shalom'], says the LORD of hosts" (2:9).

In the fourth oracle (2:10-19), the prophet Haggai explains the significance of two
priestly rulings for the Judean people. The rulings on consecrated meat and corpses,
though arcane to the modern reader, signify that God's people are in fact defiled and
unable in and of themselves to make offerings to God. For them to do so would desecrate the temple. However, this verdict serves not to condemn but to mark the beginning of a new epoch. The consecration of the temple celebrates the end of the
curse—that is, the cessation of want, destitution, and ritual uncleanness—and the
onset of divine blessing and favor: "From this day on I will bless you" (2:19).

In the short final oracle (2:20-23), given on the same day as the preceding message,
Haggai directly addresses Zerubbabel, the Davidic governor of Judah. The prophet
announces that YHWH will soon "shake the heavens and the earth" (2:21; cf. 2:6; Heb
12:25-29) and overturn all human power brokers and their military machines.
Exploiting language from the Exodus tradition (Exod 15:1, 4, 19), Haggai exclaims
that YHWH will put an end to "chariots and their riders . . . horses and their riders"
(Hag 2:22). In this new exodus, indeed on "that day" (the day of the LORD), YHWH
will not only topple oppressive regimes and dismantle instruments of violence but also
make Zerubbabel "like a signet ring" (Hag 2:23; cf. Jer 22:24). Apparently drawing
upon the cherished promise to David (2 Sam 7:16), God's messenger imagines the
imminent restoration of the Davidic dynasty and Judean independence. Reflecting on
this text in its literary setting, Walter Brueggemann notes: "The most important phenomenon of the Haggai tradition is that it holds together a 'realized eschatology' on
the temple that assures prosperity, peace, and blessing in the present time . . . and a
'futuristic eschatology' of Davidic restoration."[22] With respect to Zerubbabel's role in
the new epoch in particular, Klaus Koch affirms that this Davidic heir "will be the
signet ring on the hand of God, the ring which God will use to stamp his will to peace
into the very earth itself (Hag 2:20-23)."[23]

Zechariah: Eight Visions for Renewed Leadership in Zion

Zechariah belongs together with Haggai (much the way that Hosea, Amos, and Micah belong together): they are located next to each other in the present form of the Twelve and are considered contemporaries. Unlike the direct oracles given by the prophet Haggai, however, Zechariah delivers the divine message in the form of eight visions (chs. 1–8). Zechariah shares this *modus operandi* with Amos, who also communicated the "word" through visionary reports (five of them in Amos 7–9). More significantly, Zechariah fulfills the oracle of Joel that God's spirit will be poured out on everyone:

> Your sons and your daughters shall prophesy,
>   your old men shall dream dreams,
>   and your young men *shall see visions*. (Joel 2:28; emphasis added)

Through these visions, the interpretive community discovers that the divine resolve to communicate with God's people has not diminished or weakened. Accordingly, it is no surprise that many motifs and images in Zechariah's visions carry on key traditions of Isaiah, Jeremiah, and Ezekiel.[24]

What function do these visions play for the discouraged and splintered refugees who returned to Judea? The eight visions of Zechariah operate as a catechistic overview of central issues posed by the community. First of all, it should be noted that the eight visions are held together by a sweeping theological reflection on history in chapters 1 and 7 (Zech 1:3-6; 7:8-14): "The LORD of hosts has dealt with us according to our ways and deeds, just as he planned to do. . . . I scattered them with a whirlwind among all the nations that they had not known. Thus the land they left was desolate" (Zech 1:6; 7:14).[25] These thematic bookends echo the long-standing (Deuteronomistic) assertion that (1) God sent God's "servants the prophets" (1:6) or "the former prophets" (1:4; 7:12; see also 7:7) to warn Israel; (2) the people refused to heed the prophetic warning (Zech 7:12 claims that God hardened the hearts of the people of Israel; cf. Isa 6:10); (3) God brought judgment upon them for disobedience (although chapter 1 introduces the claim that God's people eventually "repent" ["turned"] and confess).

Zechariah's visions of future hope and deliverance counter the overview of past failure and disaster. In the first vision (Zech 1:7-17), patrolling horsemen roam the earth and report that the earth is "at peace" (1:11). This peace is more like an eerie silence that symbolizes the long years of the exile and captivity at the hands of imperial nations: "How long will you withhold mercy from Jerusalem and the cities of Judah, with which you have been angry these seventy years?" (1:12; cf. Jer 25:11). To this question posed by an angel (cf. Isa 6:11), the divine assurance is declared: "I have returned to Jerusalem with compassion; my house shall be built in it. . . . My cities shall again overflow with prosperity; the LORD will again comfort Zion" (Zech 1:16-17; cf. 2:16).

In the second vision (1:18-21 [MT 2:1-4]), four horns represent the overwhelming forces of the oppressors, which will soon be broken. One of them clearly refers to Babylon. Yet some commentators posit that the "four horns," which both scatter Judah and find themselves cut down, may also allude to Persia.[26]

In the third vision (2:1-5 [MT 2:5-9]), Zechariah sees a person with a measuring line (cf. Amos 7:7-8). The measurement displays Jerusalem as a city without walls, implying that the city will be rebuilt and repopulated without limit. Armaments will no longer be necessary, for YHWH will be the wall that surrounds and protects the city.

The fourth and fifth visions form a chiastic center of the eight visions, accentuating the dual leadership of Joshua the high priest and Zerubbabel the Davidic heir who will guide the new community through the empowerment of the "spirit" of YHWH.[27] In the fourth vision (3:1-10), the prophet sees the high priest Joshua cleansed from guilt and given a pure diadem (cf. Isa 6:7; 62:3), signifying divine renewal and reconsecrated leadership. This cleansing is significant, as even the priestly leadership, long exiled in a foreign land, must be ritually and morally purified. Moreover, just as Joshua hears, "I have taken your guilt away from you" (Zech 3:4; cf. Isa 6:7), so the entire community must hear, "I will remove the guilt of this land in a single day" (3:9).

In the fifth vision (4:1-14), Zechariah sees a lampstand—a menorah—and two olive trees, depicting the divine installation of the Davidic heir Zerubbabel. The "two anointed ones" (4:14) refer to both Joshua and Zerubbabel, whose model leadership will be instrumental for the future restoration of Israel; they will be led by divine vision and presence: "Not by might, nor by power, but by my spirit" (4:6). Therefore, the most fundamental source in rebuilding the community, as the prophet hears from YHWH, is neither economic growth nor military force. Rather, it is the spirit of YHWH, which has the regenerating power of life, vision, and hope for the community. The leaders and the community are commissioned just as the prophets of old were commissioned: ". . . the law and the words that the LORD of hosts had sent by his *spirit* through the former prophets" (Zech 7:12; emphasis added); "And the LORD stirred up the *spirit* of Zerubbabel . . . and the *spirit* of Joshua . . . and the *spirit* of all the remnant of the people" (Hag 1:14; emphasis added); "My *spirit* abides among you; do not fear" (Hag 2:5; emphasis added; cf. Isa 11:2; 42:1; 61:1; Ezek 2:2; 37:1; Joel 2:28 [MT 3:1]).

In the sixth vision (Zech 5:1-4), the prophet envisions a flying scroll, which symbolizes a curse upon all who would steal and swear falsely. Zechariah imagines here an idyllic world where there is no falsehood, only faithful obedience to the Torah. The seventh vision (5:5-11) speaks of powers and principalities, personified as a woman in a basket, which will be removed from the earth by "two women" with "wind . . . in their wings" (5:9). In the eighth vision (6:1-8), four chariots patrol the earth, executing YHWH's wrath against evildoers and protecting those dispersed to the four corners of the earth.

These eight visions clearly intend to instill hope in the congregation: with breathtaking figures and graphic images they represent various forces outside the human realm but under the control of divine rule. These visions not only authorize Joshua and Zerubbabel as purified and anointed leaders; they also indicate the importance of trusted and enabled leadership for the community of new generations. To be sure, the people of God are to find meaning and hope in both the newly anointed leadership and in the communal practices of their long-inherited commandments: "Render true judgments, show kindness and mercy to one another" (7:9).

> These are the things that you shall do: Speak the truth to one another, render in your gates judgments that are true and make for peace [literally, "shalom"], do not devise evil in your hearts against one another, and love no false oath; for all these are things that I hate, says the LORD. . . . Therefore love truth and peace [literally, "shalom"]. (Zech 8:16-19; cf. 8:8; Hos 10:12; Amos 5:24; Mic 6:8)

The concentration of divine promises (see, for example, Zech 8:1-5), together with seemingly insurmountable obstacles to Zion's reconstruction, could easily lead to skepticism and emotional dissonance. As if to acknowledge such conflict and doubt, YHWH poses a rhetorical question: "Even though it seems impossible to the remnant of this people in these days, should it also seem impossible to me?" (Zech 8:6). Or, as put elsewhere, "Is anything too hard for [YHWH]?" (Jer 32:27; cf. Gen 18:14; Luke 1:37). The answer has been given repeatedly; this time, through the eight visions, the prophet urges trust and obedience to YHWH's words, so that "the curse" will be removed (Zech 5:3; cf. Hag 1:5-6; Deut 27–28). Indeed, the misery that has so long plagued God's people will be transformed into blessing and joy: "Just as you have been a cursing among the nations, O house of Judah and house of Israel, so I will save you and you shall be a blessing" (Zech 8:13). The source of this blessing is none other than YHWH's presence: "In those days ten men from nations of every language shall take hold of a Jew, grasping his garment and saying, 'Let us go with you, for we have heard that God is with you'" (8:23; emphasis added; cf. Hag 1:13; 2:4).

Zechariah: Blueprint of an Ideal Community

The second half of the book of Zechariah (chs. 9–14), sometimes called Second Zechariah, is quite distinct from the first half.[28] However, in the present form of the book, Zechariah 9–14 is intended to be read in sequence, presenting the imaginative and powerful "blueprint" of an ideal community—designs that are only sketched out in the vision reports in chapters 1–8. In the process, Zechariah 9–14 draws upon a rich supply of images and motifs from other texts of the Hebrew Bible as well as from the books of the Twelve, especially Hosea, Joel, and Amos.[29] Together, these intrabiblical allusions illuminate several key themes in the book of Zechariah: (1) the dramatic restoration of the community by YHWH the warrior and redeemer; (2) the stern condemnation of false shepherds by YHWH the true shepherd; (3) the inauguration of a new creation wrought by YHWH the creator and divine king.

YHWH the warrior and redeemer. First, Zechariah 9–14 envisions the ideal community as a dramatic reversal of the world of despair and threat. In particular, the text infuses with hope and joy old words and images that formerly evoked fear and suffering. And it draws upon an understanding of YHWH as divine warrior and redeemer, echoing the Exodus tradition. These intertextual correlations combat inertia, pessimism, and doubt.

In Zechariah 9:1-8, readers find a concise subunit that resembles the Oracles against the Nations (OAN), especially those of Amos. This truncated OAN portrays YHWH as the triumphant warrior marching toward Jerusalem. In the path of the divine warrior are nations that will soon be trounced. Roughly the list of the nations that are to be subdued corresponds to the initial segment of the OAN in Amos 1–2:

Amos 1	Zechariah 9
Damascus (vv. 2-5)	Damascus (vv. 1-2a)
Gaza/Ashdod/Ashkelon/Ekron (vv. 6-8)	Tyre/Sidon (vv. 2b-4)
Tyre (vv. 9-10)	Ashkelon/Gaza/Ekron/Ashdod (vv. 5-7)

Although the nations are not listed in the same order, the names of key powers in Zechariah 9:1-8 resemble those in Amos 1:2-10—that is, Syria, Philistia, and Phoenicia. What rhetorical effect would these echoes of Amos convey if we presume that the implied readers of Zechariah are familiar with Amos,[30] having read the Twelve sequentially? After hearing of the downfall of Damascus, Gaza, and Tyre, they would expect Judah and Israel to receive the culminating blow, at which point they might react, "Oh, not again!" Precisely here, Zechariah presents a rhetorical twist: "Rejoice greatly, O daughter Zion! / Shout aloud, O daughter Jerusalem!" (Zech 9:9), instead of the indictment of Amos 2:

> For three transgressions of Judah,
> and for four, I will not revoke the punishment. . . .

> For three transgressions of Israel,
> and for four, I will not revoke the punishment. (vv. 4, 6)

Read together, the effect is stunning. In Amos 1–2, when the listening community anticipates an announcement of the divine judgment against Israel's surrounding nations, the prophet delivers a climactic blow against Israel. In Zechariah 9, when this community prepares for the upcoming announcement of Israel's downfall, the prophet delivers the divine assurance to protect YHWH's people.

In Zechariah's climactic pronouncement of the OAN, the implied readers assemble for the dawning of YHWH the redeemer and great warrior. Here the language of YHWH's dramatic deliverance and protection echoes motifs in the Exodus tradition, as if the congregation is invited to reenact the victory songs of the sea (see Exod 15:1-21): "No *taskmaster* shall again pass over upon them, because now *I have seen* with my own eyes" (Zech 9:8, authors' translation); "*I have really seen* the affliction of my people who are in Egypt, and I have heard their cry because of their *taskmasters*" (Exod 3:7, authors' translation). The claim that God has seen the people's hardship and taken note of their abusive "taskmasters" (i.e., oppressors) reinforces the promise of a new exodus for the postexilic community.

Furthermore, the portrayal of YHWH as the deliverer of the new exodus coincides with that of YHWH as the great warrior, once again reminiscent of the Exodus accounts:

> Lo, your *king* comes to you;
> triumphant and victorious is he,
> humble and *riding* on a donkey. . . .
> He will cut off the *chariot* from Ephraim
> and the *war-horse* from Jerusalem. . . .
> Because of the blood of my covenant with you,
> I will set your prisoners free from the waterless pit.
> (Zech 9:9-11; emphasis added; cf. Hag 2:22)

> Then Moses and the Israelites sang this song to the LORD:
> "I will sing to the LORD, for he has triumphed gloriously;
> *horse* and *rider* he has thrown into the sea. . . .
> The LORD will *reign* forever and ever." (Exod 15:1, 18; emphasis added; cf. 15:21)

These similarities, developments, and foils are, by all accounts, far from incidental. Attentive to the literary interconnections, Zechariah's allusion to the divine warrior echoes YHWH's overthrow of the horses and chariots of the Egyptian army. YHWH will again defeat the military forces of the dominant empires, be they Persia or Greece. The king's triumphant entry on a donkey sharply contrasts with the pharaoh's pursuit of

237

the Israelites on chariots (or the processional of any geomilitary ruler): "Behold, your king comes to you; righteous and saving is he, afflicted [or weak] but riding on a donkey" (Zech 9:9, authors' translation).[31] Furthermore, whereas YHWH alone fought the battle against Egypt, in the new exodus YHWH will turn "Judah as my bow" and "Ephraim its arrow" to thwart the oppressive powers of "Greece" (9:13) and "put to shame the *riders* on *horses*" (10:5; emphasis added). Therefore, the implied readers are not only witness to the liberation and restoration of Israel but are also urged to participate in the triumphant and glorious new exodus (cf. 10:10-11).

YHWH the true shepherd. Second, Zechariah 9–14 envisions the ideal community where YHWH the true shepherd finally abolishes all false shepherds. Commentators disagree on the identity of these corrupt "shepherds," as to whether they are corrupt leaders of the Yehud community or the foreign rulers of Persia.[32] What *is* clear is the disconcerting presence of oppressive forces in the world of the text (and perhaps in the readers' actual sociopolitical milieu as well). Against this backdrop, the prophet conveys YHWH's solemn intention: "My anger is hot against the shepherds, / and I will punish the leaders" (10:3).

At this juncture readers discover another intertextual connection, which is to Hosea, in sequential reading within the Twelve. If Zechariah 9:1-8 alludes to Amos 1–2, then Zechariah 11:4-17 hints at Hosea 1–3. Note the comparable linguistic expressions, though they are by no means direct citations: "Thus said the LORD my God: Be a shepherd of the flock doomed to slaughter. . . . *For I will no longer have pity on the inhabitants of the earth*, says the LORD. . . . So, on behalf of the sheep merchants, I became the shepherd of the flock doomed to slaughter" (Zech 11:4, 6, 7; emphasis added); "The LORD said to Hosea, 'Go, take for yourself a wife of whoredom and have children of whoredom . . . by forsaking the LORD.' So he went and took Gomer daughter of Diblaim, and she conceived and bore him a son. . . . *for I will no longer have pity on the house of Israel* or forgive them" (Hos 1:2, 3, 6; emphasis added). In comparison, both texts report the divine command to the prophet to take an action, followed by each prophet's compliance and subsequent announcement of the divine intention.

Against leaders who pursue their own gain at the expense of the "Favor" and "Unity" of the entire people (Zech 11:7, 10-16), the prophetic condemnation is solemnly announced (11:17; 13:2-8). Akin to Hosea, Zechariah declares the divine rejection. Through the purging process, only the faithful—that is, those who follow the commandments of God and practice justice and righteousness—shall be authorized to lead God's people. In the end, after the Jerusalemites are cleansed from "sin and impurity," the faithful community will be restored, and they will receive the same divine assurance once promised to the children of Israel:

> I will put this third into the fire,
>> refine them as one refines silver,
>> and test them as gold is tested. . . .
> I *will say, "They are my people"*;
>> *and they will say, "The* LORD *is our God."* (Zech 13:9; emphasis added)

> And I will sow him for myself in the land.
> And I will have pity on Lo-ruhamah,
>> and *I will say to Lo-ammi, "You are my people"*;
>> *and he shall say, "You are my God."* (Hos 2:23; emphasis added [MT 2:25])[33]

Hence, this idealized community shall be governed by the most trustworthy and righteous shepherd of all, YHWH:

> On that day the LORD their God will save them
>> for they are the flock of his people;
>> for like the jewels of a crown
>>> they shall shine on his land. (Zech 9:16)

Under the guidance of the true shepherd, the flock will no longer fear injury, loss, or hunger (11:16); hereafter God's people will enjoy "showers of rain" to provide "vegetation in the field to everyone" (10:1).

YHWH the creator and divine king. Finally, Zechariah 9–14 envisions this ideal community as the center of God's new creation, which is ruled by none other than the divine king. The divine oracle further highlights the theme of creation, echoing the creation accounts in Genesis 1–2: "Thus says the LORD, who stretched out the *heavens* and founded the *earth* and formed the *spirit of Adam* [humankind] in their midst" (Zech 12:1; authors' translation). Moreover, the whole world will acknowledge YHWH as the divine king and confess together: "The LORD will become king over all the earth" (14:9).

Here, similar to the manner in which Zechariah echoes Amos and Hosea, we find intertextual correlations with Joel, as if forming the internal brackets (Joel and Zech 9–14) within the opening (Hos 1–3) and closing (Mal) of the Twelve.[34] For example, the motif of "light" that never darkens (Zech 14:7) echoes motifs in Joel (cf. Joel 2:10; 3:15 [MT 4:15]). Zion shall not weep or suffer anymore but rather will become the center of light and the source of blessings to others (Zech 14:6-8), as if the sequential readers would hear the reversal of the darkness declared in Joel, "The sun and the moon are darkened, / and the stars withdraw their shining" (Joel 2:10). Likewise, "living waters" that "shall flow out from Jerusalem" on that day (Zech 14:8) echo the similar description of Zion sanctified as YHWH's dwelling place where "a fountain shall come forth from the house of the LORD / and water the Wadi Shittim" (Joel 3:18 [MT 4:18]).[35]

Just as YHWH, the good shepherd, will rule the people of Israel as well as the whole earth (Zech 14:9, 16-21), so Jerusalem will be the exemplar in executing true justice to the nations. In this way, Zechariah brings symbolic symmetry to a literary world fraught with incoherence and pain. Jerusalem, once the object of scorn, is now exalted as the true sanctuary for YHWH's joyful servants: "On that day the LORD will shield the inhabitants of Jerusalem so that the feeblest among them on that day shall be like David, and the house of David shall be like God, like the angel of the LORD, at their head" (12:8).

Malachi: Community Matters; Torah Matters

Malachi follows a formula (*maśśā'*) similar to the two oracles of Zechariah 9:1 and 12:1, as if it is the third in the sequence (Mal 1:1). Yet this book has its own unique pattern of disputation in which related questions and counterarguments recur as thesis, antithesis, and synthesis (cf. Mic 6:6-8). This concluding book in the Twelve incorporates the tenor and theme of the preceding books, sometimes negating or inverting them and then transforming them into its own distinctive claims, namely, that community matters and Torah matters.

Malachi follows the outlines of the ideal community as laid down in the diverse visions and oracles of the preceding books.[36] Those esoteric visions and opaque prophecies are now examined as concrete realities within mundane life settings. Malachi reduces the whole symbolic enterprise to matters of covenant and community relationships: for Malachi, the ideal community is a Torah-observant community, one that acknowledges God's justice and sovereignty and in response lives as a reverential covenantal community.

Malachi also picks up and intensifies key metaphors and motifs of the preceding prophetic pronouncements. The forceful illustrations of the divine pathos are expressed in ways similar to those in Amos: "I hate, I despise your festivals" (Amos 5:21); "I hate divorce" (Mal 2:16; cf. Zech 8:17). And the basic elements of the God-human relationship are presented through the lenses of the parent-child and husband-wife metaphors, following the lead of Hosea (Hos 1–3; 11), thereby building a frame for the overarching inclusio of the Twelve.

Community Matters. "I have loved you" (Mal 1:2, authors' translation; cf. Hos 11:1). This affirmation of divine affection and fidelity to the Torah-abiding community is the very first phrase in this last book of the Twelve. And this is not by coincidence. The imagined audience of Malachi has endured more disappointment than encouragement, more dissension than unity. Surely the building of the temple has been realized, a monumental achievement for a subject ("kingless") community.

Evidently the visionary prophets, Haggai and Zechariah, have rekindled the flagging spirits of the people, and the leadership of Joshua the high priest and Zerubbabel the governor of Yehud, the grandson of King Jehoiachin, has sustained them. The rebuilding of Jerusalem has become a source of pride for the people led by Nehemiah and Ezra.[37] However, God's people are still under fire, as six argumentative cases testify; and these disputations betray mounting cynicism as a result of a social world in utter disarray. That the name of Zerubbabel, the Davidic heir, does not appear in the book of Malachi may also be significant: it may indicate that hope for the ideal community is gradually fading away. It is not by chance that the community has lingering questions about divine love (and justice), "How have you loved us?" (Mal 1:2).

Against such conditions the book of Malachi, at the outset, firmly reiterates YHWH's love for the broken community. God's love has not failed or faded but remains strong in affection: "Yet I have loved Jacob but I have hated Esau" (1:2-3; cf. Amos 3:2; Obad; the OAN sections in the Twelve). The reaffirmation of divine affection for Judah is accompanied by a repudiation of Esau/Edom, Jacob's rival twin and nemesis neighbor nation (see Obad). To respond to Jacob's doubts about divine favor, Malachi points to Edom's destruction and, by implication, Judah's survival. When observing the fate of archrival Esau/Edom, the beloved community of Abraham and Sarah, Moses and Miriam, Joseph and Esther shall affirm: "Great is the LORD beyond the borders of Israel!" (Mal 1:5).

Even though God's people have survived the ordeals of national defeat and dispersion, Malachi asserts that they cannot carry on properly without the reformation, or transformation, of their leaders. Hence, just as Zechariah exposes "worthless" shepherds (for example, Zech 10:2-3; 11:15-17), now Malachi targets corrupt priests. The prophet levels harsh accusations against the priests who despise YHWH's name (Mal 1:6)—that is, who engage in practices that impugn the integrity of YHWH and place the entire community in grave danger. Malachi specifically criticizes these priests for violating the cultic regulations: indeed, they pollute food on the altar and offer unacceptable sacrifices to YHWH—sacrifices that their own governor would reject (1:7-14). Readers can hear the stern indictment in the divine lament: "Oh, that someone among you would shut the temple doors" (1:10). The prophetic denunciation of these priests reaches its climax in 2:1-3, where YHWH pledges a charge against them: "And now, O priests, this command is for you. . . . I will send the curse on you and I will curse your blessings. . . . I will rebuke your offspring, and spread dung on your faces." The divine charge is nothing short of passionate censure of these controlling priests. That God would "curse" their "blessings" is a perverse reversal of the Aaronite privilege: "Speak to Aaron and his sons, saying, Thus you shall bless the Israelites" (Num 6:23).[38] Even worse, if that were possible, God threatens to spread "dung" on *their faces* (certainly not an ideal text for a clergy ordination service!), making a stark contrast with the divine countenance promised in the priestly benediction: "The LORD make *his face* to shine upon you, and be gracious to you" (Num 6:25; emphasis added; cf. Mal 1:9).

Malachi moves from accusation (1:6-14) to judgment (2:1-9) and eventually to priestly repentance and restoration (3:1-5). This reformation involves a thorough cleansing and replacement of those holding the priestly offices—presumably the ethical and political leaders of the community.[39] Thus, YHWH's messenger or angel (literally, "Malachi" in Hebrew; 1:1; 2:7; 3:1 [twice]) is commissioned to purge and purify the priests, just as Joshua the high priest is cleansed (Zech 3:4-5; cf. Isa 6:6-8): "For he is like a refiner's fire and like fullers' soap; he will sit as a refiner and purifier of silver, and he will purify the descendants of Levi and refine them like gold and silver, until they present offerings to the LORD in righteousness" (Mal 3:2-3). Through the radical renewal of the priests, the people of God can rebuild their lives together. Malachi emphasizes the importance of the unity of the entire community: "Have we not all *one* father? Has not *one* God created us? Why then are we faithless to one another, profaning the covenant of our ancestors?" (2:10; emphasis added; cf. 2:15). This attention to oneness is further highlighted by the parent-child (1:6; cf. 3:17; 4:6 [MT 3:24]) and spousal imagery (2:11, 14-16; cf. Gen 2:24). Accordingly, Malachi categorically renounces any act of discord or dissension, whether propagated by priestly leaders or community members at large: "You have caused many to stumble by your instruction. . . . You have not kept my ways but have shown partiality in your instruction" (Mal 2:8-9).

Perhaps nothing disrupts unity more than injustice and idolatry: idolatry fractures the image of the deity; injustice shatters the quality of life of the community. And the prophet accuses God's people of both. As Andrew Hill rightly observes:

> Lest the priests become scapegoats, the prophet rebukes the laity in the third oracle for their faithlessness to [YHWH] (2:10-16). Even as the Levites had corrupted the priestly pact of Levi (2:4, 8), so the people of Yehud had transgressed the covenant of the fathers by marrying foreign women and divorcing their Hebrew wives (2:10-11, 14).[40]

Malachi indicts the people for their infidelity to God and to the wives of their youth (2:10-16). The prophet makes the case that marriage to those outside the covenant community (exogamous alliances)—presumably "for economic benefit or for elevation in social status"[41]—threatens the very identity of the community: "Did not one God make her?" (i.e., "your companion and your wife by covenant," 2:14-15). Additionally, Malachi indicts the people for their injustice. One of the most compelling aspects of the disputations in the book of Malachi is the question posed by the people, be it a naive complaint or an existential outcry: "All who do evil are good in the sight of the LORD, and he delights in them. . . . Where is the God of justice?" (2:17). Here again the questions of good versus evil and justice versus oppression come to the fore. Regardless of the people's own misgivings about divine justice, though, Malachi claims that they have been neither good nor just. And when evil masquerades as good, the God of justice appears absent. Clearly the picture drawn here is one not only of blame but also of scarcity. In light of deteriorating circumstances, doubts about God's justice turn into laments, and laments morph into cynicism and disdain for YHWH (3:13-15). In response, Malachi constructs a coherent apology for divine sovereignty (YHWH's uniqueness) and justice, which involves harsh allegations against both priests and people. As is customary in the Twelve, however, such charges do not have the final say. It is to this people and their priestly leaders that YHWH announces a renewal of the covenant on the day of the messenger's advent (in Malachi 3–4).

Covenant matters. Torah matters. According to God's messenger, however, covenant is neither an entitlement nor a blank check: YHWH's covenant demands reverential obedience to the divine commandments and reverential dealings with one another. God's covenant with Levi was intended as "a covenant of life and well-being [shalom]" (2:5), but the priests "corrupted" this covenant (2:4-9). Malachi claims that the community has violated God's covenant by mistreating one another (2:10-16). And using a play on words, the prophet announces that in preparation for YHWH's appearance in the temple, "the messenger of the covenant" (3:1) will refine God's people like "a refiner's fire and like fullers' soap" ("fullers' soap" has the same consonants as the word *covenant*).

Thus, the secret to living as God's covenant people, according to Malachi, is to get "back to basics," that is, preserving and practicing the laws of YHWH. The divine exhortation to God's people echoes the importance of returning to YHWH and YHWH's statutes as announced at the start of Zechariah and elsewhere (emphasis added): "The LORD was very angry with your ancestors. Therefore say to them . . . *Return to me, says the LORD of hosts, and I will return to you, says the LORD of hosts*" (Zech 1:2-3); "Ever since the days of *your ancestors* you have turned aside from my statutes and have not kept them. *Return to me, and I will return to you, says the LORD of hosts*" (Mal 3:7; cf. Hos 2:7; Joel 2:12; Amos 4:6-11; Hag 2:17). Torah obedience is absolutely crucial for the survival and sustenance of the community.[42] No matter how impressive the map of the future may be, such a future is severely deficient without fierce devotion to YHWH, YHWH's teachings, and YHWH's people. Only the community that builds just and equitable relationships can truly honor God and build the ideal community:[43] "I will be swift to bear witness against the sorcerers, against the adulterers, against those who swear falsely, against those who oppress the hired workers in their wages, the widow and the orphan, against those who thrust aside the alien, and do not fear me, says the LORD of hosts" (Mal 3:5).

Here it is intriguing that the emphasis on Torah observance coincides with vocabulary and motifs in Psalm 1. For example, the language of *blessing* occurs frequently in Malachi 2:2; 3:10. The same expression for being "happy" (*'šr*; Mal 3:12, 15) is found in Psalm 1:1: "*Happy* is the one. . . ." (*'šr*, authors' translation). The motif of Judah and the "children of Jacob" (Mal 3:4, 6) who "delight" (*ḥpṣ*) in the covenant (Mal 3:1; cf. 3:12) is reminiscent of the "delight" (*ḥpṣ*) the righteous person has in the law of YHWH (Ps 1:2). Most notably, the stark division between the "righteous" and the "wicked" (Mal 3:18) closely resembles the words and understandings in Psalm 1:5-6. Likewise, the expression of the wicked becoming a mere "stubble" (Mal 4:1 [MT 3:19]) is strikingly similar to the description of the wicked in Psalm 1:4: "The wicked are not so, / but are like chaff." Reading these intertextual allusions together, we discern a common focus on the covenant traditions, that is, "the Torah of Moses" (Mal 4:4 [MT 3:22]) and "the Torah of YHWH" (Ps 1:2, authors' translations).

In the Christian canon, the book of Malachi is the last book of the Old Testament, anticipating the Gospel of Matthew in the New Testament. In the Jewish canon of the Hebrew Bible, however, this book is followed by the book of Psalms. It is true that lament is the most common genre in the psalms, but if we note that the entire book of Psalms begins with the word *happy* (or *blessed*; Ps 1:1) and concludes with the word *hallelujah* (Ps 150:6), then it is significant that the book of the Twelve Prophets concludes with the solemn promise of the divine blessing to those who revere YHWH and practice Torah obedience (Mal 3–4). Here then lies Malachi's crucial message of hope for the interpretive community: hold fast to the Torah and practice its precepts in the life of the whole community. Admittedly, the disheartened people of God have reservations about the legitimacy and practicality of Torah compliance: "It is vain to serve God. What do we profit by keeping his command?" (3:14; cf. 3:15). To them, Malachi conveys God's firm declaration that such fidelity will not be in vain: "The LORD took note and listened, and a book of remembrance was written before him of those who revered the LORD and thought on his name" (3:16; cf. Ps 1:6). Most assuredly, Malachi makes the case that reverential obedience is the true key to blessing, happiness, and shalom.

To the community that would truly "return" and reform, the divine promise is declared to be theirs, ushering in a time when the curses of dissension and fraud will be turned into the blessings of unity and justice. Just as the covenant expectations for the ideal community are stated not as abstractions but in concrete and localized terms, so the promise of blessing and healing is expressed through abundant agricultural provision. Locusts will vanish and new grains, vines, and wine will be plentiful

(Mal 3:10-11; cf. Zech 9:17; 10:7; Joel 1:4-20). The ending of these admonitions and promises likewise reminds the community not to give up but to continue working together. The divine assurance of hope, therefore, serves not only as the conclusion of the book of Malachi but also of the Twelve:

> Remember the teaching of my servant Moses, the statutes and ordinances that I commanded him at Horeb for all Israel.
> Lo, I will send you the prophet Elijah before the great and terrible day of the LORD comes. He will turn the hearts of parents to their children and the hearts of children to their parents, so that I will not come and strike the land with a curse. (Mal 4:4-6 [MT 3:22-24])

Conclusion

> *The eyes of the future are looking back at us and they are praying for us to see beyond our own time.*[44] —*Terry Tempest Williams*

After the collapse of the Judean state and hardships of the exile, the harsh accusations, the robust exhortations, and the resounding notes of hope in the Twelve would no doubt resonate with readers and listeners struggling to survive in colonized settings. The scroll of the Twelve was not only the word of God addressed to those named within the text, it was also the living, dynamic word of God for readers and listeners in synagogues in Jerusalem, Babylon, Alexandria, and elsewhere. For such communities, the scroll's distinctive and common motifs presented unwavering challenges. This literature of the losers—the legacy of captive and colonized survivors—urges God's people to practice justice and righteousness, to raise fearless shouts against the brutal crimes of superpowers, and to fan undying flames of hope to those denied honor, purpose, and the basic means to survive. It calls for Torah obedience, often expressed as compassion for the poor and the disenfranchised. It summons God's people to turn away from pet idols and to work faithfully toward community-building in their local settings.

Not unlike Isaiah, Jeremiah, and Ezekiel, moreover, the Twelve celebrates—likely in liturgical contexts—the counterintuitive claim that YHWH reigns. It rejects oppressive politics as normative; it says no to hopelessness and apathy. The word of God accentuates the centrality of worship, which is itself a subversive act of praise and gratitude (to the divine king and not human power brokers) as well as protest and dissent. This scroll dares to address the realities of war and captivity; it gives speech to disaster; it speaks openly about the deep ruptures in community life, and so moves from candor to critique. By its very composition of twelve distinct though interrelated voices, the collection refuses to flatten the world into rigid and uniform categories. Its diverse expressions encourage engagement rather than resignation. Ultimately the collection provides buoyant scripts of hope for those weighed down by the world.

Although each book of the Twelve contains its own unique voice, together they build a composite whole, albeit atonal or, perhaps more accurately, cacophonic in character. The various prophetic voices project dissonance as well as assonance; they fall apart and reunite; they deconstruct and reemerge. And they stand in opposition to one another even though they belong to the same composition. Of course, the Hebrew Bible is full of such disjunctions and realignments. One prophet declares Jerusalem's invincibility (Isaiah); another predicts its demise (Jeremiah). At one juncture Babylon is YHWH's servant, and at another, within the same prophetic tradition (Jeremiah), Babylon morphs into YHWH's archenemy. One sage argues that we reap what we sow (Prov); another finds it otherwise (Job). One tradition views the monarchy as a disaster from the inception; a countervoice speaks of it as expedient and hopeful (1 Sam 1–15). In the epic literature, Joseph uses his upward mobility harshly to consolidate the empire of Egypt and at the same time to preserve life and the future of his kin (Gen 41–50). Indeed, readers encounter one pharaoh whose "benign" policies save his subjects, juxtaposed with another whose despotic acts result in death (Exod 1–14). These contrasting depictions of royal power no doubt reflect communal ambivalence about human power structures as well as life itself within the empire.

In similar ways, the Twelve presents thematic tensions and complexities—distinctive voices, even divergent and clashing voices—held together by towering motifs that are common to the prophetic corpus as a whole, such as judgment and salvation; divine absence and divine presence; tradition and hope; war and restoration. Thus, within the Twelve, the first three books—Hosea, Joel, and Amos—reenact the ravaging forces of war, to pluck up and pull down, whereas the last three books—Haggai, Zechariah, and Malachi—imagine restoration, to build and plant. In between these pillars, the remaining six books expose the betrayal, abuse, and demise of the nations (OAN), in which Jonah and Nahum as a core depict two conflicting interpretive perspectives. Surrounding these two books, Obadiah, Habakkuk, and Zephaniah take on the complexities of theodicy with regard to the unjust power dynamics between Israel and the invading nations, vis-à-vis the divine absence and divine presence, divine wrath and divine mercy.

Together, the books of the Twelve intersect major historical-theological moments—the crisis and fall of Israel and Judah (for example, 722, 701, and 587 B.C.E.) on the one hand and the demise of the superpowers (for example, 612, 540, and 333 B.C.E.) on the other hand. The former almost singlehandedly created the need for theodicy. The latter pointed to the fact that even seemingly impregnable superpowers fall. The years 587 (the fall of Jerusalem to Babylon) and 540 (the fall of Babylon to

Persia) in particular enjoy symbolic significance far beyond their historical import. These two massive moments represent, respectively, cosmic crumbling—the dismantling of a once stable and blessed world—and unexpected newness, not unlike resurrection. The year 587 shattered the community's long-standing renderings of YHWH, its understandings of the universe, as well as its cherished narrative. The year 540 opened the door to newness and hope when exile and captivity appeared to be normative. Together these pivotal moments organize the Twelve and propel ongoing interpretive communities to ponder the wreckage of war, exile, and colonization, as well as justice, liberation, and hope.

In retrospect, perhaps the prophetic voices betray only the wisdom of the sages who long observed the ebb and flow of time—a time to weep, a time to laugh, a time to make war, a time to make peace—such times as Israel's unbearable collapse and the enemy superpowers' unexpected demise. The readers of the Twelve—and of the prophetic corpus as whole—discover that even as there are occasions of profound suffering and grief, both national and individual, there are also seasons of joy and hope. In the Hebrew Masoretic text, sandwiched between Jonah (mercy) and Nahum (disaster and judgment) is the book of Micah, which focuses on the illness and health of Judah. Although Micah claims that the nation's wound is mortal, the prophet astonishingly imagines its healing. How does healing occur?

First of all, community healing requires nothing less than an extraordinary act by an incomparable God.

> Who is a God like you, pardoning iniquity
> and passing over the transgression
> of the remnant of your possession? (Mic 7:18)

At the same time, community healing is wrought not only by God but also as the outgrowth of community reflection and action (themselves divine gifts). One of the enduring lessons of Micah—and the prophetic corpus as a whole—is the importance of repentance and reform. Throughout human history there is ample evidence of nations and groups that refuse to reflect upon their own actions and the consequences of those actions for others. This long history of failure reveals the urgency for repentance and renewal today—that is, to consider our moral failings, conflicted loyalties, inner hostilities, misuse of power, as well as our acts of acrimony, greed, ingratitude, and self-aggrandizement. No wonder Yom Kippur, Lent, and Ramadan play such central places in the liturgical year of Jews, Christians, and Muslims. The prophetic exhortation to rise above self-interest to compassionate living is never obsolete. Indeed, Micah's admonition summarizes the whole enterprise:

> He has told you, O mortal, what is good;
>> and what does the LORD require of you
> but to do justice, and to love kindness,
>> and to walk humbly with your God? (6:8)

The challenge to act justly, practice kindness, and live with humility is as pertinent to nations, especially superpowers, as it is to contemporary religious communities. The Swahili proverb still rings true: "When elephants jostle, the grass gets hurt."[45] In large measure the wealthiest nations in the world hold the key to the survival of the planet. And thus the practice of social justice, compassion, and humility may be the most pressing need of our time. Indeed, Micah, the centerpiece of the Twelve, beckons us/U.S. to embrace the praxis of justice and righteousness so that all God's children may dine at the table of hope. Then, like the interpretive community of old, we too may grasp the wondrous promise of Micah that

> [God] shall judge between many peoples,
>> and shall arbitrate between strong nations far away;
> they shall beat their swords into plowshares,
>> and their spears into pruning hooks;
> nation shall not lift up sword against nation,
>> neither shall they learn war any more;
> but they shall all sit under their own vines and under their own fig trees,
>> and no one shall make them afraid;
> for the mouth of the LORD of hosts has spoken. (4:3-4)

If the years 587 and 540 both function as crucial moments in Israel's history of disaster and survival, so in today's U.S. narrative 9/11 and 11/4 represent major historic events fraught with import. September 11, 2001, denotes a moment of collective loss and grief. November 4, 2008—the election of the first African American as the forty-fourth president of the United States—represents a time of collective hope and renewal, celebrated beyond political partisanship and national boundaries. In between these pivotal moments, so many have endured and are still suffering the ravages of war, poverty, bigotry, and exploitation. Such devastation will no doubt continue to haunt us in the years to come. However, just as enormous hardship and loss did not extinguish the flame of prophetic hope for ancient communities, so today, despite enormous challenges and frightful prospects, we dare to imagine a future of hope for all God's children. In between 9/11 and 11/4 stands the number 11. In Chinese characters, when the two vertical lines—such as number 11—are joined together, they can form a letter (人), which denotes a "human being" or "people," meaning that people cannot live alone but must live together. A Korean saying reads, "The heart of the people is the heart of God." The tears and outcries of the people most honestly embody the pathos of God. Human solidarity and trust, together with concrete expressions of generosity and kindness, demonstrate most compellingly the presence of God in a world riddled with pain, violence, and death. The prophetic voices of old, which make up a "great . . . cloud of witnesses" (Heb 12:1), together with heroes and visionaries such as Joseph, Esther, and Daniel—known also by their immigrant names of Zaphenath-paneah (Gen 41:45), Hadassah (Esth 2:7), and Belteshazzar (Dan 1:7)—lead us on a pilgrimage in exile toward our home called hope.

Notes

Introduction

1. Walter Brueggemann, *Introduction to the Old Testament. The Canon and Christian Imagination* (Louisville: Westminster John Knox, 2003), xi.

2. Czeslaw Milosz, "Dawn," *Selected Poems 1931–2004* (New York: HarperCollins, 2006), 10.

3. We also use the terms "the reading or listening community," "readers or writers," "the implied or imagined readers," and "the congregation." These terms denote both the earliest recipients of the prophetic message in writing as well as those who actively participated in the production process.

4. Ehud Ben Zvi, *Signs of Jonah: Reading and Rereading in Ancient Yehud* (JSOTSup 367; London: Sheffield Academic Press, 2003), 9: "By far the most important divide is between the monarchic and the postmonarchic period. To state the obvious, there were major political, social and demographic differences between the two polities. . . . Moreover, postmonarchic communities understood the events around 586 BCE as a major tragedy, and as a watershed in their past. Issues associated with the fall of monarchic Judah and its temple and with the possibility of a future restoration and elevation of Israel to its proper place in the divine economy loomed large in the postmonarchic communities. They captivated their imaginations and became central nodes in their theological thinking"; Jill Middlemas, *The Templeless Age: An Introduction to the History, Literature, and Theology of the "Exile"* (Louisville: Westminster John Knox, 2007), 6: "The templeless age (587–515) thus presents us with a clearly defined period of time in which the lack of a temple provided the backdrop against which creative contributions to the history and religion of ancient Israel were made."

5. Christl Maier, "Jeremiah as Teacher of Torah," *Int* 62 (2008): 22–32.

6. Abraham J. Heschel, *The Prophets* (New York: Perennial Classics, 2001 [original publication by Harper and Bros., 1962]), 3–26.

7. *Peter, Paul and Mary: Carry It On—A Musical Legacy*, 80 min., Rhino Entertainment, 2004.

8. Ibid.

9. Our thanks to Kathleen M. O'Connor for this insight.

10. Lawrence Rinder et al., *The American Effect: Global Perspectives on the United States, 1990–2003* (New York: Whitney Museum of Art Books, 2003).

11. Henri Nouwen, *Peacework: Prayer, Resistance, Community* (Maryknoll, N.Y.: Orbis Books, 2005), 53.

12. Robert P. Carroll, "Century's End: Jeremiah Studies at the Beginning of the Third Millennium," *CurBS* 8 (2000): 18–58 (28).

13. Ronald E. Clements, "The Interpretation of Old Testament Prophecy," in *Old Testament Prophecy: From Oracles to Canon* (Louisville: Westminster John Knox, 1996), 12.

14. Carroll, "Century's End," 28.

15. See Brueggemann, *Introduction to the Old Testament*.

16. This explosion is evident, for example, in the generative work done by the Society of Biblical Literature Consultations on Isaiah, the Twelve, Jeremiah, and Ezekiel, and their respective publications, including *Troubling Jeremiah*, edited by A. R. Pete Diamond, Kathleen M. O'Connor, and Louis Stulman (1999); *Reading and Hearing the Book of the Twelve*, edited by James D. Nogalski and Marvin A. Sweeny (2000); *Ezekiel's Hierarchical World*, edited by Stephen L. Cook and Corrine L. Patton (2004); and *The Desert Will Bloom: Poetic Visions in Isaiah*, edited by A. Joseph Everson and Hyun Chul Paul Kim (2009) to name only a few. See Leo G. Perdue, *The Collapse of History: Reconstructing Old Testament Theology* (Minneapolis: Fortress, 1994); and idem, *Reconstructing Old Testament Theology: After the Collapse of History* (OBT; Minneapolis: Fortress, 2005).

17. Ellen F. Davis and Richard B. Hays, eds., *The Art of Reading Scripture* (Grand Rapids: Eerdmans, 2003), xv.

18. Brueggemann, *Introduction to the Old Testament*, xi.

19. See Marvin A. Sweeney, *The Prophetic Literature* (IBT; Nashville: Abingdon, 2005).

20. J. H. Hexter, *The Judaeo-Christian Tradition* (2d ed.; New Haven: Yale University Press, 1995), 2.

1. Reading the Prophets as Meaning-making Literature for Communities under Siege

1. Martti Nissinen, "How Prophecy Became Literature," *SJOT* 19 (2005): 153–72 (153).

2. In its final form, written prophecy in the Hebrew Bible is a monumental literary achievement. As Ronald E. Clements observes in his *Old Testament Prophecy: From Oracle to Canon* (Louisville: Westminster John Knox, 1996): "Although we now have evidence of the recording of prophetic oracles from such ancient Near Eastern cities as Mari and Babylon, no comparative writings survive in which extensive compilations of large numbers of prophetic sayings have been preserved" (p. 7). Clements goes on to say: "A prophetic literature . . . on the scale that the Old Testament has preserved for us . . . remains a wholly unique product of ancient Israel's religious tradition" (p. 203); see also Susan Niditch, *Oral World and Written Word: Ancient Israelite Literature* (Library of Ancient Israel; Louisville: Westminster John Knox, 1996).

3. For a fuller discussion, see Louis Stulman, *Order Amid Chaos: Jeremiah as Symbolic Tapestry* (The Biblical Seminar 57; Sheffield: Sheffield Academic Press, 1998), 99–108.

4. Robert P. Carroll, "Manuscripts Don't Burn—Inscribing the Prophetic Tradition. Reflections on Jeremiah 36," in *Dort ziehen Schiffe dahin. . . . Collected Communications to the XIVth Congress of the International Organization for the Study of the Old Testament, Paris 1992* (ed. M. Augustin and K.-D. Schunck; Berlin: Peter Lang, 1996), 31–42 (31–32).

5. Clements, *Old Testament Prophecy*, 204.

6. See Carroll, "Manuscripts Don't Burn," 40. See also Paul Ricoeur, *Interpretation Theory: Discourse and the Surplus of Meaning* (Fort Worth: Texas Christian University Press, 1976); Martti Nissinen, "What is Prophecy? An Ancient Near Eastern Perspective," in *Inspired Speech: Prophecy in the Ancient Near East: Essays in Honor of Herbert B. Huffmon* (ed. J. Kaltner and L. Stulman; JSOTSup 378; New York: T&T Clark, 2004), 17-37; Karel van der Toorn, "From the Mouth of the Prophet: The Literary Fixation of Jeremiah's Prophecies in the Context of the Ancient Near East," in *Inspired Speech*, 191–202.

7. Regina Schwartz, "Joseph's Bones and the Resurrection of the Text: Remembering in the Bible," in *The Book and the Text: The Bible and Literary Theory* (ed. R. M. Schwartz; Oxford: Basil Blackwell, 1990), 46.

8. Walter Brueggemann, *A Commentary on Jeremiah: Exile and Homecoming* (Grand Rapids: Eerdmans, 1998), 353.

9. For a full delineation of distinctions between oral and written discourse, see Ricoeur, *Interpretation Theory*; "What Is a Text? Explanation and Understanding," in *Hermeneutics and the Human Sciences* (ed. and trans. John B. Thompson; New York: Cambridge University Press, 1981), 145–64; "The Hermeutical Function of Distanciation," in *Hermeneutics and the Human Sciences*, 131–44.

10. Clements, *Old Testament Prophecy*, 191–202. Of course, (preexilic) prophets were capable of speaking words of hope, but they predominantly spoke of coming judgment.

11. For instance, in Jeremiah 25:1-13, twenty-three years of oral proclamation are reduced to a conventional prose indictment of the community's wonted disobedience to the prophetic message. This account concludes, moreover, with an appeal to the written word as a primary source of authority: "I will bring upon that land all the words that I have pronounced against it, all that is written in this scroll, which Jeremiah prophesied against all nations" (authors' translation).

12. As in the case of Jeremiah 26, Clements notes in *Jeremiah* (Atlanta: John Knox, 1988) that "we need hardly doubt that the precise record of Micah's words reported in 26:18 was drawn from such a preserved body of earlier prophecies" (p. 156).

13. Such observations raise rudimentary questions about the essence of biblical prophecy. What *is* written prophecy? Given its transformations, is biblical prophecy still prophecy? What are the distinguishing traits of this literary phenomenon? What are its objectives or overarching aims? Who are its implied readers?

14. Donald E. Gowan, *Theology of Prophetic Books: The Death and Resurrection of Israel* (Louisville: Westminster John Knox, 1998), 9–16. Michael H. Floyd has recently argued that "the prophetic books are concerned with developments that led to exile under the Babylonians and/or developments that followed from the reversal of exile under the Persians. Each book mines Israel's prophetic tradition to interpret theologically some aspect(s) of exile and restoration" ("The Production of Prophetic Books," in *Prophets, Prophecy and Prophetic Texts in Second Temple Judaism* [ed. M. H. Floyd and R. D. Haak; LHBOTS 427; New York: T&T Clark, 2006], 276–97 [277]).

15. See, for example, Lawrence Rinder et al., *The American Effect: Global Perspectives on the United States, 1990–2003* (New York: Whitney Museum Books, 2003).

16. By *eschatological* we refer to prophetic speech that addresses communities on the verge of collapse. It is "end-time" rhetoric, not because it speaks of the end of the world or of two distinct ages, but rather because it intervenes during periods of massive disruption when fierce world-historical forces threaten long-standing cultural institutions and structures.

17. W. G. Sebald, *On the Natural History of Destruction* (New York: Random House, 2003), 41.

18. See Kathleen M. O'Connor, *Lamentations and the Tears of the World* (Maryknoll, N.Y.: Orbis Books, 2002).

19. Victor Frankl, *Man's Search for Meaning* (New York: Washington Square Press, 1985), 11.

20. Nearly sixty years ago and still very much under the dark cloud of World War II, Herbert Butterfield noted that it was no accident that the prophets emerged at a time when the great empires of the ancient Near East were involved in power struggles that victimized "the ancient Hebrews, though so small a people" (p. 2). Butterfield characterized the Old Testament as a whole as "the search for an interpretation of history which would embrace catastrophe itself and transcend the immediate spectacle of tragedy" (*Christianity and History* [New York: Charles Scribner's Sons, 1950], 2).

21. Although introductory rubrics are not always useful for reconstructing the referential world of the prophet or the prophetic text, they do reveal a deeply ingrained penchant for associating written prophecy with specific temporal and spatial categories.

22. Jean-Marie Lemaire, "Disconcerting Humanitarian Interventions, and the Resources for Collective Healing," in *Psychosocial and Trauma Response in War-torn Societies: The Case of Kosovo: Psychosocial Notebook* 1 (November 2000): 71–77. Online: http://www.forcedmigra tion.org/psychosocial/papers/WiderPapers/iom_notebook1.pdf.

23. Abraham J. Heschel, *The Prophets* (New York: Perennial Classics, 2001 [original publication by Harper and Bros., 1962], 4.

24. Wendy Farley uses the term "radical suffering" to refer to suffering that is "destructive of the human spirit and . . . cannot be understood as something deserved." See her *Tragic Vision and Divine Compassion: A Contemporary Theodicy* (Louisville: Westminster John Knox, 1990), 21.

25. Elzbieta M. Gozdziak, "Refugee Women's Psychological Response to Forced Migration: Limitations of the Trauma Concept," 2006, 14. Online: http://isim.georgetown.edu/ Publications/ElzPubs/Refugee%20Women's%20Psychological%20Response.pdf.

26. See, for example, Ibrahim Aref Kira, "Taxonomy of Trauma and Trauma Assessment," *Traumatology* 7, no. 2 (June 2001): 73–86; Daniel L. Smith-Christopher, *A Biblical Theology of Exile* (OBT; Minneapolis: Fortress, 2002), 105–23.

27. A case in point: except for the Oracles against the Nations in chapters 50–51, the book of Jeremiah refuses to condemn Babylon for the devastating geopolitical exploits of the sixth century. For the moral dilemmas involved in prophetic speech that charges victims of violence with sin, see Marvin Sweeney's *Reading the Hebrew Bible after the Shoah: Engaging Holocaust Theology* (Minneapolis: Fortress, 2008).

28. Contra Sigmund Mowinckel who argues that the Jeremiah of the prose sermons is a shallow and dogmatic figure; see his *Zur Komposition des Buches Jeremia* (Kristiania: Jacob Dybwad, 1914), 38–39.

29. Walter Brueggemann, *Theology of the Old Testament: Testimony, Dispute, Advocacy* (Minneapolis: Fortress, 1997).

30. Mark S. Smith, *The Laments of Jeremiah and Their Contexts: A Literary and Redactional Study of Jeremiah 11–20* (SBLMS 42; Atlanta: Scholars Press, 1990), 67.

31. James A. Sanders, "Adaptable to Life: The Nature and Function of Canon," in *Magnalia Dei: The Mighty Acts of God* (ed. F. M. Cross, W. E. Lemke, and P. D. Miller; Garden City, N.Y.: Doubleday, 1976), 551.

32. Brevard S. Childs, *Introduction to the Old Testament as Scripture* (Philadelphia: Fortress, 1979), 60.

33. Clements, *Old Testament Prophecy*, 191–202: "May the bones of the Twelve Prophets / send forth new life from where they lie, / for they comforted the people of Jacob / and delivered them with confident hope" (Sir 49:10; see also 48:17-25; Tob 14:5; 2 Macc 15:9; as well as the plethora of references to the Latter Prophets in the New Testament). In the canonical Gospels, in particular, the prophets are typically depicted as foretellers of messianic salvation.

34. Clements, *Old Testament Prophecy*, 202.

35. Ibid., 200.

36. Walter Brueggemann, *An Introduction to the Old Testament: The Canon and Christian Imagination* (Louisville: Westminster John Knox, 2003), 107.

37. Marvin A. Sweeney, *Isaiah 1–39* (FOTL 16; Grand Rapids: Eerdmans, 1996), 17.

38. See Clements, *Old Testament Prophecy*, 200–202.

39. Walter Brueggemann, *The Word That Redescribes the World: The Bible and Discipleship* (ed. Patrick D. Miller; Minneapolis: Fortress, 2006), 20.

40. Walter Brueggemann makes a similar point regarding the Oracles against the Nations in the book of Jeremiah. He suggests, "The reason that . . . these texts are crucial is that we in the United States do not read the biblical text 'as Israel.' Rather, we read the text 'as Babylonians,' as the last superpower that has been for a time blessed by God" (*Shaking Heaven and Earth: Essays in Honor of Walter Brueggemann and Charles B. Cousar* [ed. C. Roy Yoder et al.; Louisville: Westminster John Knox, 2005], 160).

41. Another caveat: it is not difficult to locate groups in the United States that still relate to being under siege, so to speak, including undocumented immigrants, the urban poor, and nonheterosexuals.

2. Isaiah as Messenger of Faith amid Doubt

1. A poem by Carl B. Westmoreland, inscribed in front of the slave pen in the National Underground Railroad Freedom Center. Image courtesy of the National Underground Railroad Freedom Center, Cincinnati, Ohio.

2. By "First Isaiah" we do not intend to imply independent authorship of this section, separate from the book of Isaiah as a whole. The recent Isaiah scholarship has significantly

contributed to considering the entire book of Isaiah as a whole, which is taken into account in our study. Hence, the division from a synchronic perspective simply implies a first and second part, with the rationale that this twofold division can help us pay closer attention to the thematic development and relationship of the two parts.

3. Concerning the significance of the postexilic diasporic settings of the Persian period in understanding the interpretive community—whether readers or audiences—of the book of Isaiah, see John Barton, *Isaiah 1–39* (Sheffield: Sheffield Academic Press, 1995), 102. See also Rainer Albertz, *A History of Israelite Religion in the Old Testament Period* (vol. 2; trans. J. Bowden; Louisville: Westminster John Knox, 1994), 437.

4. Roy F. Melugin, "Figurative Speech and the Reading of Isaiah 1 as Scripture," in *New Visions of Isaiah* (ed. R. F. Melugin and M. A. Sweeney; JSOTSup 214; Sheffield: Sheffield Academic Press, 1996), 305. Note also Edgar W. Conrad, *Reading Isaiah* (OBT; Minneapolis: Fortress, 1991), 156–57: "I have argued above that the audience of the book is a community of survivors with minority status. That this community is powerless is indicated by the characterization of its opponents as leaders who are corrupt and inept. The community as royal servant is a community that suffers and is threatened by murder and bloodshed."

5. Walter Brueggemann, *Finally Comes the Poet: Daring Speech for Proclamation* (Minneapolis: Fortress, 1989), 18: "The drama of guilt and forgiveness, when engaged in its undiminished power, does not begin with how we feel. *It begins in candor at the throne of God.* It begins with what God notices and how God responds" (authors' emphasis). Concerning the notion of YHWH's resilient relatedness, see idem, *Theology of the Old Testament: Testimony, Dispute, Advocacy* (Minneapolis: Fortress, 1997), 296.

6. Daniel L. Smith-Christopher, *A Biblical Theology of Exile* (OBT; Minneapolis: Fortress, 2002), 161.

7. Abraham J. Heschel, *The Prophets* (New York: Perennial Classics, 2001 [original publication by Harper and Bros., 1962]), 362–63: "The anger of God must not be treated in isolation, but as an aspect of the divine pathos, as one of the modes of God's responsiveness to [humans]."

8. For an extensive survey of this obduracy text in other ancient texts, see Craig A. Evans, *To See and Not Perceive: Isaiah 6.9-10 in Early Jewish and Christian Interpretation* (JSOTSup 64; Sheffield: Sheffield Academic Press, 1989), 53–80.

9. Marvin A. Sweeney, *Reading the Hebrew Bible after the Shoah: Engaging Holocaust Theology* (Minneapolis: Fortress, 2008), 91.

10. According to Thomas Merton, "underneath the apparently logical pattern of a . . . 'well organized' and rational life, there lies an abyss of irrationality, confusion, pointlessness, and indeed of apparent chaos . . . and [it is] only when the apparent absurdity of life is faced in all truth that faith really becomes possible" (*Disputed Questions* [New York: Farrar, Straus, & Cudahy, 1960], 179–80).

11. Norman Whybray, *Job* (Readings: A New Biblical Commentary; Sheffield: Sheffield Academic Press, 1998), 172. Consider also Roland E. Murphy, *The Book of Job: A Short Reading* (New York: Paulist, 1999), 130: "The attempt to defend the 'justice' of a mysterious God is bound to go down in defeat. The friends of Job presented a defense of God in the terms of the biblical understanding at the time, and it is clearly bankrupt."

12. See Brevard S. Childs, *Isaiah* (OTL; Louisville: Westminster John Knox, 2001), 56–57; Tikva Frymer-Kensky, *Reading the Women in the Bible: A New Interpretation of Their Stories* (New York: Schocken Books, 2002), 43: "Exodus tells us that Pharaoh first hardened his own heart; then God hardened it."

13. For a cogent analysis on the place of chapters 28–33 as an intentional extension and reinterpretation of chapter 5, as well as chapters 1–12, see Gary Stansell, "Isaiah 28–33: Blest Be the Tie That Binds (Isaiah Together)," in *New Visions of Isaiah* (ed. R. F. Melugin and M. A. Sweeney; JSOTSup 214; Sheffield: Sheffield Academic Press, 1996), 68–103.

14. On the parallel pattern of the woe-sayings between Isaiah 1–12 and 28–33, see Joseph Blenkinsopp, *Isaiah 1–39* (AB 19; New York: Doubleday, 2000), 380; Conrad, *Reading Isaiah*, 124–30. Concerning another woe-oracle in 10:1-4, see H. G. M. Williamson, *Isaiah 1–27* (vol. 1; ICC; London: T&T Clark, 2006), 345.

15. See Peter R. Ackroyd, "The Biblical Interpretation of the Reigns of Ahaz and Hezekiah," in *In the Shelter of Elyon: Essays on Ancient Palestinian Life and Literature in Honour of G. W. Ahlström* (ed. W. B. Barrick and J. R. Spencer; JSOTSup 31; Sheffield: JSOT Press, 1984), 247–59; see also Blenkinsopp, *Isaiah 1–39*, 459.

16. Elizabeth Achtemeier, "Isaiah of Jerusalem: Themes and Preaching Possibilities," in *Reading and Preaching the Book of Isaiah* (ed. C. R. Seitz; Philadelphia: Fortress, 1988), 37: "On the face of it, it must have seemed like a ridiculous promise to Ahaz—that God was offering him a little babe to bolster his belief. Ahaz did not need a baby then; Ahaz needed an army! And because he would not believe, he was not established."

17. For a summary of the pertinent redactional theory, see Childs, *Isaiah*, 260–66.

18. Christopher R. Seitz, *Zion's Final Destiny: The Development of the Book of Isaiah: A Reassessment of Isaiah 36–39* (Minneapolis: Fortress, 1991): 194, 206.

19. Ulrich Berges keenly observes that, unlike in Jeremiah or Ezekiel, there is no explicit record of the destruction of Zion in Isaiah. This apparent lacuna, according to Berges, highlights the distinctive emphasis on the ultimately inviolable future of Zion in the theology of Isaiah ("Die Zionstheologie des Buches Jesaja," *Estudios Bíblicos* 58 [2000]: 181–84).

20. Blenkinsopp, *Isaiah 1–39*, 483.

21. Rodney R. Hutton, *Fortress Introduction to the Prophets* (Minneapolis: Fortress, 2004), 43.

22. Gerhard von Rad, *Old Testament Theology* (vol. 2; trans. D. M. G. Stalker; New York: Harper & Row, 1965); Marvin A. Sweeney, "Reevaluating Isaiah 1–39 in Recent Critical Research," *CR:BS* 4 (1996): 84–85.

23. On the poetic use of guerrilla warfare, see Walter Brueggemann, *The Prophetic Imagination* (Philadelphia: Fortress, 1978), 75. Similarly, on the notion of guerilla theater, see idem, *Hope within History* (Atlanta: John Knox, 1987), 21.

24. Andrew D. Lester, *Hope in Pastoral Care and Counseling* (Louisville: Westminster John Knox, 1995), 57.

25. Ibid., 125–52.

26. Rolf P. Knierim, *The Task of Old Testament Theology: Substance, Method, and Cases* (Grand Rapids: Eerdmans, 1995), 253.

27. Hans Wildberger, *Isaiah 13–27* (trans. T. H. Trapp; Minneapolis: Fortress, 1997), 587.

28. For insightful notions of God suffering because of, with, and for the people, see Terence E. Fretheim, *The Suffering of God: An Old Testament Perspective* (Philadelphia: Fortress, 1984), 107–48. See also Knierim, *The Task of Old Testament Theology*, 447.

29. David W. Augsburger, *Helping People Forgive* (Louisville: Westminster John Knox, 1996), 68–72.

30. Jeffrey C. Alexander et al., *Cultural Trauma and Collective Identity* (Berkeley: University of California Press, 2004), 5.

31. This parallel idea was inspired by Professor Thomas C. Oden in his lectures at Drew University.

32. Marcelo M. Suárez-Orozco and Antonius C. G. M. Robben, "Interdisciplinary Perspectives on Violence and Trauma," in *Cultures under Siege: Collective Violence and Trauma* (ed. A. C. G. M. Robben and M. M. Suárez-Orozco; Cambridge: Cambridge University Press, 2000), 2.

33. Admittedly, even in the OAN in Isaiah, there is one section (22:1-14; cf. 17:4-6) in which Jerusalem might have been a target, implying that Judah, too, is not exempt from the divine punishment for wrongdoing, especially the wicked rulers "who have gone up . . . to the housetops" (22:16). See Marvin A. Sweeney, *Isaiah 1–39* (FOTL 16; Grand Rapids: Eerdmans, 1996), 213: "The pronouncement concerning the 'Valley of Vision' (i.e., the Kidron Valley along the eastern edge of Jerusalem) in 22:1-14 demonstrates that Jerusalem, too, must be cleansed in preparation for YHWH's sovereignty"; David L. Petersen, *The Prophetic Literature: An Introduction* (Louisville: Westminster John Knox, 2002), 84: "The oracles against the nations, in their narrowest construal (i.e., chaps. 13–23), include oracles directed against or concerning Jerusalem, most notably 22:1-15."

34. Compare the placement of the OAN in the other major prophetic books: MT Jeremiah 46–51; LXX Jeremiah 25–36; Ezekiel 25–32.

35. On the formation of the anti-Babylonian poems (13:1–14:23 and 21:1-10) that roughly frame Isaiah 13–23, see Blenkinsopp, *Isaiah 1–39*, 272.

36. For a redactional analysis, especially of the parallels between 5:25-30 and 11:11-16, see H. G. M. Williamson, *The Book Called Isaiah: Deutero-Isaiah's Role in Composition and Redaction* (Oxford: Clarendon, 1994), 141–43 and 154–55.

37. John F. A. Sawyer, *The Fifth Gospel: Isaiah in the History of Christianity* (Cambridge: Cambridge University Press, 1996), 220–40.

38. Robert A. Bennett, "The Book of Zephaniah," in *The New Interpreter's Bible* (vol. 7; ed. L. E. Keck et al.; Nashville: Abingdon, 1996), 703: "The real reversal of fortune is not located solely in getting back what was lost in the meting out of divine justice, but in changed relationships between the main protagonists. The heavy sentence of judgment has been commuted, thereby making way for a future that is different from the past."

39. On the thematic relationship of chapters 24–27 as an expansion of chapters 13–23, see Blenkinsopp, *Isaiah 1–39*, 272.

40. Wildberger, *Isaiah 13–27*, 533: "The traditio-historical background of 25:6-8 is to be found within the framework of a description of the deity being enthroned after winning the battle against chaos. In Babylon, Marduk, joyously acclaimed as 'king,' has destroyed Tiamat; Baal becomes king because he was victorious over either Yamm or Mot ['death' in Hebrew]."

41. Henri J. M. Nouwen, *The Living Reminder: Service and Prayer in Memory of Jesus Christ* (New York: Seabury, 1977).

42. Knierim, *The Task of Old Testament Theology*, 253: "Hope depends on future fulfillment, but its rationale is grounded in past experience. This experience may be individual or communal, existential, natural, or historical. It is the reason why hope is realistic and not irrational."

43. See Williamson, *The Book Called Isaiah*, 106–7; note also Conrad, *Reading Isaiah*, 130–53.

3. Vision of Homecoming amid Diaspora

1. On considering Isaiah 40–66 as a unified entity rather than a mere collection of two distinct units in 40–55 and 56–66, note Benjamin D. Sommer, *A Prophet Reads Scripture: Allusion in Isaiah 40–66* (Stanford: Stanford University Press, 1998), 4: "Isaiah 40–66 forms a single corpus, probably by one author"; William L. Holladay, "Was Trito-Isaiah Deutero-Isaiah After All?" in *Writing and Reading the Scroll of Isaiah: Studies of an Interpretive Tradition* (vol. 1; ed. C. C. Broyles and C. A. Evans; Leiden: Brill, 1997), 195: "If one subtracts a few redactional additions from chaps. 56–66 one hears in the remainder the same individual that is heard in chaps. 40–55. . . . That is to say, I reject the hypothesis of a Trito-Isaiah"; Rolf Rendtorff, *Canon and Theology: Overtures to an Old Testament Theology* (trans. and ed. M. Kohl; OBT; Minneapolis: Fortress, 1993), 169: "For chaps. 56–66 are so strongly determined by their relations to the two other parts [chs. 1–39 and 40–55] that it seems to me hardly conceivable that this third part ever had an independent existence."

2. Jeffrey C. Alexander et al., *Cultural Trauma and Collective Identity* (Berkeley: University of California Press, 2004), 61.

3. Walter Brueggemann, *Hopeful Imagination: Prophetic Voices in Exile* (Philadelphia: Fortress, 1986), 94: "The *homecoming* metaphor makes sense only where the metaphor of *exile* has been accepted as true" (author's own emphasis).

4. J. M. Wilkie, "Nabonidus and the Later Jewish Exiles," *JTS* 2 (1951): 37; Joseph Blenkinsopp, *Ezra–Nehemiah* (OTL; Philadelphia: Westminster, 1988), 307: "In spite of the pro-Persian sentiments in Isa 40–48 and favorable allusions to the Persians' providential role in Ezra–Nehemiah, there is no reason to believe that their rule was significantly more benign than that of their Semitic predecessors." Note also Edward W. Said's pivotal remark: "To think of exile as beneficial, as a spur to humanism or to creativity, is to belittle its mutilations" ("The Mind of Winter: Reflections on Life in Exile," *Harpers* [September 1983]: 50; quoted in Daniel L. Smith-Christopher, *A Biblical Theology of Exile* [OBT; Minneapolis: Fortress, 2002], 21).

5. For thorough analyses on the metaphors of the vulnerably violated Lady Babylon, see Katheryn Pfisterer Darr, *Isaiah's Vision and the Family of God* (Louisville: Westminster John Knox, 1994), 169–74; Chris A. Franke, *Isaiah 46, 47, and 48: A New Literary-Critical Reading* (Winona Lake, Ind.: Eisenbrauns, 1994).

6. On the impact of "intergenerational transmission" of the memories of calamity, see Yolanda Gampel, "Reflections on the Prevalence of the Uncanny in Social Violence," in *Cultures under Siege: Collective Violence and Trauma* (ed. A. C. G. M. Robben and M. M. Suárez-Orozco; Cambridge: Cambridge University Press, 2000), 61.

7. Albert H. Friedlander, ed., *The Five Scrolls* (New York: CCAR Press, 1984), 251.

8. John Ahn, "Psalm 137: Complex Communal Laments," *JBL* 127 (2008): 280, 283: "For the community in forced migration, beauty was lament; the shade was the shadows in which they lived. Comfort, rest, and peace were altogether absent. . . . In the *Sitz im Leben* of Psalm 137, the soil, the land, and everything around the exiles is foreign, the reason for tears—the primary contrast to Jerusalem."

9. Georges Roux, *Ancient Iraq* (New York: Penguin Books, 1964), 360: "Herodotus, who is believed to have visited [Babylon] *c.* 460 B.C., admiringly proclaimed: 'It surpasses in splendour any city of the known world' "; A. Bernard Knapp, *The History and Culture of Ancient Western Asia and Egypt* (Belmont, Calif.: Wadsworth, 1988), 230–36.

10. Concerning the likelihood that the exiles were forced to settle in deserted places (cf. Ezra 2:59; 3:15), see Carol L. Meyers and Eric M. Meyers, *Haggai, Zechariah 1–8* (AB 25B; Garden City, N.Y.: Doubleday, 1987), xxx.

11. Leo G. Perdue, *Wisdom Literature: A Theological History* (Louisville: Westminster John Knox, 2007), 81.

12. Kenneth R. Mitchell and Herbert Anderson, *All Our Losses, All Our Griefs: Resources for Pastoral Care* (Louisville: Westminster John Knox, 1983), 54–55: "Guilt, shame, loneliness, anxiety, anger, terror, bewilderment, emptiness, profound sadness, despair, helplessness: all are part of grief and all are common to being human. Grief is the clustering of some or all of these emotions in response to loss."

13. Walter Brueggemann, *Theology of the Old Testament: Testimony, Dispute, Advocacy* (Minneapolis: Fortress, 1997), 436; idem, *Hope within History* (Atlanta: John Knox, 1987), 103: "Lingering long and honestly over the loss is foundational for newness. Elie Wiesel has observed how strange it is that the survivors of the Holocaust are precisely the ones who can yet believe in this God of pathos."

14. The powerful illustration of hope exemplified in this film is derived from Brent A. Strawn, "Second Isaiah and the Exilic Imagination," in *Teaching the Bible: Practical Strategies for Classroom Instruction* (ed. M. Roncace and P. Gray; Atlanta: Society of Biblical Literature, 2005), 175–76. *The Shawshank Redemption*, dir. Frank Darabont, Columbia Pictures, 1994.

15. Joseph Barndt, *Dismantling Racism: The Continuing Challenge to White America* (Minneapolis: Augsburg, 1991), 65.

16. Bernhard W. Anderson, "Exodus Typology in Second Isaiah," in *Israel's Prophetic Heritage: Essays in Honor of James Muilenburg* (ed. B. W. Anderson and W. Harrelson; New York: Harper & Brothers, 1962): 177–95; idem, "Exodus and Covenant in Second Isaiah and Prophetic Tradition," in *Magnalia Dei, the Mighty Acts of God: Essays on the Bible and Archaeology in Memory of G. Ernest Wright* (ed. F. M. Cross et al.; Garden City, N.Y.: Doubleday, 1976), 339–60.

17. Ella Noyes, *The Casentino and Its Story* (London: J. M. Dent, 1905), 5–6.

18. Elie Wiesel, *Legends of Our Time* (New York: Holt, Rinehart & Winston, 1968), 123, 128, as cited by Henri J. M. Nouwen, *The Living Reminder: Service and Prayer in Memory of Jesus Christ* (New York: Seabury, 1977), 17–18.

19. Brevard S. Childs, *Isaiah* (OTL; Louisville: Westminster John Knox, 2001), 336–37: "That this prophetic rhetoric is dialogical and not absolute is made clear in the succeeding verses with the exactly opposite admonition."

20. A prime example of the similar type of a reciprocal dialectic can be found in Proverbs: "*Do not answer* fools according to their folly, / or you will be a fool yourself. / *Answer* fools according to their folly, / or they will be wise in their own eyes" (Prov 26:4-5; emphasis added); or consider, "*Remember* your mercies, O YHWH. . . . *Do not remember* the sins of my youth and my transgressions . . . O YHWH" (Ps 25:6-7; authors' translation); see also Hyun Chul Paul Kim, "Interpretative Modes of Yin-Yang Dynamics as an Asian Hermeneutics," *BibInt* 9 (2001): 287–308.

21. Christopher R. Seitz, "The Book of Isaiah 40–66," in *The New Interpreter's Bible* (vol. 6; ed. L. E. Keck et al.; Nashville: Abingdon, 2001), 378.

22. Note Claus Westermann, *Isaiah 40–66* (OTL; trans. D. M. G. Stalker; Philadelphia: Westminster, 1969), 128: "Deutero-Isaiah had not the slightest intention of saying that the old traditions are abrogated. . . . What he wants to say is rather, 'stop mournfully looking back and clinging to the past, and open your minds to the fact that a new, miraculous act of God lies ahead of you!' "

23. Seitz, "The Book of Isaiah 40–66," 378; Brevard S. Childs, *Introduction to the Old Testament as Scripture* (Philadelphia: Fortress, 1979), 328–30.

24. Walter Brueggemann, *Texts That Linger, Words That Explode: Listening to Prophetic Voices* (ed. P. D. Miller; Minneapolis: Fortress, 2000), 31; Beverly J. Shamana, "Letting Go," in *Those Preachin' Women: Sermons by Black Women Preachers* (ed. E. P. Mitchell; Valley Forge: Judson, 1985), 101–5.

25. Nouwen, *The Living Reminder*, 21.

26. For a major survey of the history—and limitations—of biblical theology, see Marvin A. Sweeney, *Reading the Hebrew Bible after the Shoah: Engaging Holocaust Theology* (Minneapolis: Fortress, 2008), 1–22. Note also Brueggemann, *Theology of the Old Testament*, 328.

27. Alexander et al., *Cultural Trauma and Collective Identity*, 154.

28. On the importance of testimony as a "ritual of healing," see Judith Lewis Herman, *Trauma and Recovery* (New York: BasicBooks, 1997), 181; Inger Agger and Soren B. Jensen, "Testimony as Ritual and Evidence in Psychotherapy for Political Refugees," *Journal of Traumatic Stress* 3 (1990): 115–30.

29. Chris Franke, "Reversals of Fortune in the Ancient Near East: A Study of the Babylon Oracles in the Book of Isaiah," in *New Visions of Isaiah* (ed. R. F. Melugin and M. A. Sweeney; JSOTSup 214; Sheffield: Sheffield Academic Press, 1996), 119–20: "Chapter 47 is the key to the reversal of fortune of Daughter Zion. It functions as a pivot for Second Isaiah in that it is the point in the book where Judah/Israel changes places with the oppressor, Babylon. . . . Everything that Judah once was, Babylon becomes; all that Babylon thought she was is given to

Zion"; Rainer Albertz, A History of Israelite Religion in the Old Testament Period (vol. 2; trans. J. Bowden; Louisville: Westminster John Knox, 1994), 416.

30. Brueggemann, Hopeful Imagination, 102.

31. James A. Sanders, From Sacred Story to Sacred Text (Philadelphia: Fortress, 1987), 103: "What seems clear is that the so-called false prophet did not refer, in times of threat, to God as God also of the enemy. Such an affirmation of God the Creator of all peoples is a part of the canonical monotheizing process"; see also Mark S. Smith, The Origins of Biblical Monotheism: Israel's Polytheistic Background and the Ugaritic Texts (New York: Oxford University Press, 2001), 179–94.

32. Herman, Trauma and Recovery, 75.

33. For a detailed analysis of the image of YHWH as an artisan, in a polemical contrast with the vain artisans of idols, see Sarah J. Dille, Mixing Metaphors: God as Mother and Father in Deutero-Isaiah (JSOTSup 398; London: T&T Clark, 2004), 102–15.

34. We should also note that just as Hosea has three children with their symbolic names for the punishment and restoration of northern Israel (Hos 1:4-9; 2:22-23 [MT 2:24-25]), so Isaiah is described as having children with symbolic names (Isa 7:3; 8:3; cf. 7:14).

35. See Gerlinde Baumann, Love and Violence: Marriage as Metaphor for the Relationship between YHWH and Israel in the Prophetic Books (trans. L. M. Maloney; Collegeville, Minn.: Liturgical, 2003), 186.

36. See John F. A. Sawyer, "Daughter of Zion and Servant of the Lord in Isaiah: A Comparison," JSOT 44 (1989): 106; see also Dille, Mixing Metaphors, 149: "The relationship of a mother to her small child is one of the most powerful images of love, care, and compassion available."

37. Christl M. Maier, Daughter Zion, Mother Zion: Gender, Space, and the Sacred in Ancient Israel (Minneapolis: Fortress, 2008).

38. Dille, Mixing Metaphors, 72.

39. Shalom M. Paul, "Literary and Ideological Echoes of Jeremiah in Deutero-Isaiah," in Proceedings of the Fifth World Congress of Jewish Studies (vol. 1; ed. P. Peli; Jerusalem: World Union of Jewish Studies, 1969), 109–21; Sommer, A Prophet Reads Scripture; Hyun Chul Paul Kim, Ambiguity, Tension, and Multiplicity in Deutero-Isaiah (New York: Peter Lang, 2003), 73–88.

40. For an astute analysis on the literary dependence of Isaiah 40:1–52:10 upon Jeremiah 25–51, see Reinhard G. Kratz, "Der Anfang des Zweiten Jesaja in Jes 40,1f. und das Jeremiabuch," ZAW 106 (1994): 243–61; idem, "Der Anfang des Zweiten Jesaja in Jes 40,1f. und seine literarischen Horizonte," ZAW 105 (1993): 400–419.

41. Adolf Neubauer, The Fifty-third Chapter of Isaiah: According to the Jewish Interpreters (New York: Ktav, 1969); William H. Bellinger and William R. Farmer, eds., Jesus and the Suffering Servant: Isaiah 53 and Christian Origins (Harrisburg, Pa.: Trinity Press International, 1998); Bernd Janowski and Peter Stuhlmacher, eds., The Suffering Servant: Isaiah 53 in Jewish and Christian Sources (trans. D. P. Bailey; Grand Rapids: Eerdmans, 2004).

42. See Robert R. Wilson, "The Community of the Second Isaiah," in *Reading and Preaching the Book of Isaiah* (ed. C. R. Seitz; Philadelphia: Fortress, 1988), 68.

43. See Serge Frolov, "Returning the Ticket: God and His Prophet in the Book of Jonah," *JSOT* 86 (1999): 104–5.

44. Sawyer, "Daughter of Zion and Servant of the Lord in Isaiah," 89–107. In this trenchant study, Sawyer compares Isaiah 54:1-10 and 66:7-14—as if forming an inclusio of chapters 55–66—through which the motif of the "Daughter of Zion" conveys key implications both for the suffering, outcry, and restoration of Daughter Zion and for the faithfulness of YHWH depicted with the feminine imagery of maternal protection.

45. Bruegemann, *Hopeful Imagination*, 2.

46. Interestingly, at the end of chapter 39, readers find the similar vocabulary and motif of "peace" linked to King Hezekiah amid his dealings with Babylon vis-à-vis the prophet Isaiah: "For he thought, 'There shall be peace and security in my time'" (39:8; authors' translation).

47. Joseph Blenkinsopp, *Isaiah 56–66* (AB 19B; New York: Doubleday, 2003), 30.

48. Bernhard Duhm, *Das Buch Jesaia* (Göttingen: Vandenhoeck & Ruprecht, 1892).

49. Rendtorff, *Canon and Theology*, 153–54: "Within the complex of chaps. 40–55, there are several mentions of Israel's earlier sins which have now been set aside. . . . In the complex of 56–66, chap. 59 is again dominated by this theme. . . . The same theme turns up once again in chap. 64 in the confession of sin . . . and in the plea."

50. Paul D. Hanson, *The Dawn of Apocalyptic* (Philadelphia: Fortress, 1975). For an alternative thesis on the identity of the dissenting groups, see Brooks Schramm, *The Opponents of Third Isaiah: Reconstructing the Cultic History of the Restoration* (JSOTSup 193; Sheffield: Sheffield Academic Press, 1995), for example, 111: "[Isaiah 56–66] and the Pentateuch would most likely have had a common opponent, namely, traditional pre-exilic Israelite religion, and that in this respect 'the visionary disciples of [Isaiah 40–55]' and the Zadokite temple priests would have been allies."

51. For a noteworthy sociological analysis of the resurgent barrier between the elite returnees and the impoverished natives, see Gale A. Yee, *Poor Banished Children of Eve: Woman as Evil in the Hebrew Bible* (Minneapolis: Fortress, 2003), 141–42.

52. Lester L. Grabbe, *Judaic Religion in the Second Temple Period: Belief and Practice from the Exile to Yavneh* (London: Routledge, 2000.) Note also Tamara C. Eskenazi and Eleanore P. Judd, "Marriage to a Stranger in Ezra 9–10," in *Second Temple Studies 2: Temple Community in the Persian Period* (ed. T. C. Eskenazi and K. H. Richards; JSOTSup 175; Sheffield: JSOT Press, 1994), 269: "The very ambiguity about terminology [whether the women were foreign or Judean] that frustrates scholars may mirror an historical uncertainty about identity and boundaries in the transitions during the post-exilic era."

53. Alexander et al., *Cultural Trauma and Collective Identity*, 1.

54. Michael Fishbane, *Biblical Interpretation in Ancient Israel* (Oxford: Clarendon, 1985), 128; Mark G. Brett, *Genesis: Procreation and the Politics of Identity* (London: Routledge, 2000), 5–23. Note also Smith-Christopher, *A Biblical Theology of Exile*, 77: "But we have seen this view 'of

the top,' that is, from the perspective of the empires, in the previous chapter. In this chapter we approach the question from the perspective of the victims themselves. Such an investigation is deeply enhanced by a reading of modern refugee studies."

55. Roy D. Wells, "'Isaiah' as an Exponent of Torah: Isaiah 56:1-8," in *New Visions of Isaiah* (ed. R. F. Melugin and M. A. Sweeney; JSOTSup 214; Sheffield: Sheffield Academic Press, 1996), 145: "The complaint of the alien (v. 3a) and the complaint of the eunuch (v. 3b) provide the structure for the 'Torah.'"

56. The meaning of this phrase "a hand and a name" as a hendiadys denotes "place of honor" (cf. Jan L. Koole, *Isaiah III/3: Chapters 56–66* [Leuven: Peeters, 2001], 17).

57. It is intriguing to note that the Levites are included in the same consideration for protection and provision with the groups of the aliens, orphans, and widows, as if they are of the same group or rank (Deut 14:29; 26:11, 13; cf. Isa 66:21).

58. Louis Stulman, "Encroachment in Deuteronomy: An Analysis of the Social World of the D Code," *JBL* 109 (1990): 613–32.

59. Brueggemann, *Hope within History*, 43, 58: "I follow Hanson and Achtemeier in seeing it as a poetic, imaginative proposal for a community of the marginal who are able to envision a different shape for life. . . . The makers of history in this understanding include [YHWH] who is the God allied with the poor"; Hanson, *The Dawn of Apocalyptic*; Elizabeth Achtemeier, *The Community and Message of Isaiah 56–66* (Minneapolis: Augsburg, 1982).

60. Joseph Blenkinsopp, *Isaiah 56–66*, 178: "Fasting and mourning as a response to extreme crisis were distinctive features of religious life in the post-disaster period."

61. Walter Brueggemann, *Isaiah 40–66* (Westminster Bible Companion; Louisville: Westminster John Knox, 1998), 189: "The devotion [YHWH] desires is solidarity that troubles with the elemental requirements of economic life for every member of the community."

62. On the Persian policy of heavy taxation, see Albertz, *A History of Israelite Religion*, vol. 2, 504–21.

63. Blenkinsopp, *Isaiah 56–66*, 207–45. Blenkinsopp delineates wonderfully that Isaiah 60–62 shows considerable literary and thematic dependence on Isaiah 40–55 as well as adaptation into evolving contexts and situations: for example, the "highway" motif (40:3) recurs in "Build up, build up" (57:14) and "Go through, go through the gates. . . . Build up the highway" (62:10); likewise, the reversal of fortune motif that foreigners will attend to the offspring of Zion in the repatriation of the diaspora Jews (49:22-26) recurs in a glorified vision that "foreigners shall build up your walls" (60:10; 60:14-16; 61:5-6; and 66:12).

64. Charles E. Carter and Carol L. Meyers, eds., *Community, Identity and Ideology: Social Science Approaches to the Hebrew Bible* (Winona Lake, Ind.: Eisenbrauns, 1996); Bruce J. Malina, *The New Testament World: Insights from Cultural Anthropology* (3d ed.; Louisville: Westminster John Knox, 2001).

4. Jeremiah as a Messenger of Hope in Crisis

1. William Holladay, *Jeremiah: Spokesman Out of Time* (Philadelphia: Pilgrim, 1974), 135.
2. Ibid., 141.

3. When we allude to "Jeremiah" in this chapter, we are referring, for convenience, either to the book of Jeremiah (MT) or to the prophetic persona, that is, to the literary and theological representation of the prophet by the interpretive community (see, however, note 8 below).

4. Miroslav Volf and William H. Katerberg, eds., *The Future of Hope: Christian Tradition amid Modernity and Postmodernity* (Grand Rapids: Eerdmans, 2004), ix.

5. One major disconnect with the biblical text can hardly be ignored: whereas Jeremiah speaks from below, as a citizen of a minor "state" victimized by the formidable neo-Babylonian empire, the vast majority of readers of this volume are likely children of a superpower, with all the attendant rights and privileges. Such a chasm presents interpretive dilemmas that we have only begun to broach.

6. For more on the role of the prose sermons in Jeremiah as colonizing agents, see Louis Stulman, *Jeremiah* (AOTC; Nashville: Abingdon, 2005).

7. Ibid., 11–19.

8. When reading the book of Jeremiah, it is important to keep in mind the distinction between *Jeremiah the prophet* and *Jeremiah the book*. Although the two are obviously interrelated, they represent distinct stages in the development of the tradition. Based on virtually all of the prose sections in the book, it is safe to assume that *Jeremiah the prophet* was most active from the inauguration of Jehoiakim (609) to the fall of Jerusalem (587). During this time, his oracles focused largely on the devastation to come and the lasting impact it would have on the character of the Judean nation. *Jeremiah the book* took shape by and large after the tragic events and addressed the focal concerns of the Judean community in exile and perhaps the repatriates who returned to Judea in the late sixth and fifth centuries B.C.E. In contrast to those who first "heard" Jeremiah prophecies and supposedly had the chance to circumvent disaster, the exiles in Babylon (as well as later communities) could only look back on fallen worlds in hopes that they would not make similar mistakes. These oral and written stages of the tradition are further complicated by the emergence of two textual witnesses of *Jeremiah the book*: the Hebrew *Vorlage* of the Old Greek of the book and the later MT of Jeremiah. For the implications of these lines of text traditions, see Louis Stulman, "The Prose Sermons as Hermeneutical Guide to Jeremiah 1–25: The Deconstruction of Judah's Symbolic World," in *Troubling Jeremiah* (ed. A. R. P. Diamond, K. M. O'Connor, and L. Stulman; JSOTSup 260; Sheffield: Sheffield Academic Press, 1999), 49–146. Also see introduction.

9. The Greek text of Jeremiah (and its Hebrew *Vorlage*) also functions as a meaning-making map, but it does not sustain the same level of hope that is present in Jeremiah MT (see, for example, the role and placement of the Oracles against the Nations in the Hebrew text).

10. The historical reliability of prophetic superscriptions has long been debated. For a recent assessment, see Philip Davies, who argues in *Scribes and Schools: The Canonization of the Hebrew Scriptures* (Louisville: Westminster John Knox, 1998), 118, that the superscriptions introducing the "minor prophets" "are guesswork . . . either composed and transmitted anonymously or attached to a name and not more." Although the referential value of prophetic superscriptions is clearly uneven, their literary and theological import should not be underestimated.

11. Admittedly, the theological claim that God is involved in the world raises troubling existential questions, especially in the face of unbearable physical and emotional wreckage, random suffering, and the seemingly deafening silence of God. Yet, at the same time, it serves as a profound source of strength and encouragement to those who find themselves in ordinary corners of the world, doing quite ordinary things, and lending a helping hand to ordinary people. For ordinary neighborhoods, even if defined by regal categories (Jer 1:1-3), are nothing less than arenas for the extraordinary. And so the "beyond in our midst" engenders hope in the trenches.

12. Marvin A. Sweeney, *Reading the Hebrew Bible after the Shoah: Engaging Holocaust Theology* (Minneapolis: Fortress, 2008).

13. *Smoke*, dir. Wayne Wang, 112 min., Miramax, 1995.

14. If hope is defined as the expectation for a good outcome or the assurance that what one longs for will eventually occur, then Jeremiah is at best marginally hopeful and far more disturbing and attentive to mere survival (see 5:10-19, especially v. 18; 45:1-5; 50:4-5, 33-34; 51:1-10). Although hope in the tradition of Jeremiah involves newness and a resilient script for the future (30:1–33:26), it is never detached from the fissured world of war and exile. In fact, arrangements of hope that do not take these harsh realities seriously are deemed dangerous and ultimately destructive.

15. Linda Centers, "Beyond Denial and Despair: ALS and Our Heroic Potential for Hope," *Journal of Palliative Care* 17 (2001): 260, quoted by ethicist Matthew Stolick, "Fostering True Hopes of Terminally Ill Patients," *BIO Quarterly* 17/2 (Summer 2006): 3.

16. Elzbieta M. Gozdziak, "Refugee Women's Psychological Response to Forced Migration: Limitations of the Trauma Concept," 2006, 14. Online: http://isim.Georgetown.edu/Publications/ElzPubs/Refugee%20Women's%20 Psychological%20Response.pdf.

17. See Ibrahim Aref Kira, "Taxonomy of Trauma and Trauma Assessment," *Traumatology* 7, no. 2 (June 2001): 76. Also note Daniel L. Smith-Christopher, *A Biblical Theology of Exile* (OBT; Minneapolis: Fortress, 2002), 105–23.

18. See the next chapter for a more detailed treatment of this tension.

19. Walter Brueggemann, *The Theology of the Book of Jeremiah* (OTT; Cambridge; Cambridge University Press, 2007), 5, emphasis added.

20. See, for example, the recent work by Carolyn J. Sharp, *Prophecy and Ideology: Struggles for Authority in the Deutero-Jeremianic Prose* (OTS; New York: T&T Clark, 2003).

21. Interpretive problems are made all the more challenging by the fact that the prophetic persona and message are mediated through poetry, prose sermons, and narrative accounts.

22. Henning G. Reventlow, *Liturgie und prophetisches Ich bei Jeremia* (Gütersloh: Gütersloher, 1966); Mark E. Biddle, *Polyphony and Symphony in Prophetic Literature: Rereading Jeremiah 7–20* (Studies in Old Testament Interpretation 2; Macon, Ga.: Mercer University Press, 1996).

23. Mark S. Smith, *The Laments of Jeremiah and Their Contexts: A Literary and Redactional Study of Jeremiah 11–20* (SBLMS 42; Atlanta: Scholars Press, 1990), 67.

24. When considering slavery in the United States, historians have always wondered why there were not massive insurrections in the South, where blacks might have outnumbered whites by as many as ten to one. One explanation given is that slaves counted their own

survival (and that of their family members) as a greater prize than freedom, which was seen as an extremely dangerous and impermanent state.

25. Martin Kessler, *Battle of the Gods: The God of Israel Versus Marduk of Babylon: A Literary/Theological Interpretation of Jeremiah 50–51* (Assen: Van Gorcum, 2003).

26. Walter Brueggemann, *A Commentary on Jeremiah: Exile and Homecoming* (Grand Rapids: Eerdmans, 1998), 418.

27. This observation is supported in chapter 51 where YHWH resolves to reduce Babylon to rubble. In an overwhelming display of combat imagery (51:11-33), Israel's divine warrior resolves to crush Babylon and its gods. Since the "destroying mountain" has devastated the whole earth (51:24-26), YHWH deploys the multitudes against Babylon (51:27-33). They have borne the brunt of Babylon's abuse, and it stands to reason that they must witness and participate in the liturgical drama of Babylon's defeat. Every nation takes a shot at Babylon for the damage it has done—with the exception of the Judean refugees in Babylon. Though Judah has suffered sorely at the hand of Babylon, YHWH does not summon the citizens of Jerusalem to battle. Instead, YHWH, their warrior king, directly and decisively repays Babylon for the wrong it has afflicted on Zion. "Yet a little while / and the time of her harvest will come" (51:33). For the exiles listening, this enactment of divine vengeance flags YHWH's just kingship in the world, and it indirectly serves as a script for nonviolent resistance. Rather than relying on their own strength and ingenuity, they are to trust that YHWH will realign the world as they imagine it in worship.

28. Gozdziak, "Refugee Women's Psychological Response to Forced Migration," 17.

5. Jeremiah as a Complex Response to Suffering

1. Walter Brueggemann, *Hopeful Imagination: Prophetic Voices in Exile* (Philadelphia: Fortress, 1986), 3–7.

2. Kathleen M. O'Connor, "The Book of Jeremiah: Reconstructing Community after Disaster," in *Character Ethics and the Old Testament: Moral Dimensions of Scripture* (ed. M. Daniel Carroll R. and Jacqueline E. Lapsley; Louisville: Westminster John Knox, 2007), 82.

3. Louis Stulman, *Order Amid Chaos: Jeremiah as Symbolic Tapestry* (The Biblical Seminar 57; Sheffield: Sheffield Academic Press, 1998), 54.

4. Kathleen M. O'Connor, "The Tears of God and Divine Character in Jeremiah 2–9," in *God in the Fray: A Tribute to Walter Brueggemann* (ed. T. Linafelt and T. K. Beal; Minneapolis: Fortress, 1998), 172–85.

5. Admittedly, there is a strong tendency in the present form of the book of Jeremiah to use the suffering of Jeremiah and his prayers of protest to reinforce symmetrical moral categories. The Deuteronomic prose tradition exploits the rejection and harsh treatment of Jeremiah to demonstrate the guilt of Judah: Judah rejects YHWH and the words of YHWH's messenger Jeremiah, and therefore deserves divine judgment. In this way Jeremiah's suffering "makes sense." Such an interpretive strategy is only partially successful, for it is unable to silence the force of Jeremiah's cries and those he represents. Thus, both theodicy and antitheodicy strands coexist and create a rich theological tension.

6. Scholars often treat Jeremiah 20:7-18 as the fifth and sixth confessions of Jeremiah. Such issues, however, need not occupy our attention because the same argument can be made whether the unit comprises one or two of Jeremiah's laments. For a discussion of these critical issues, see A. R. Pete Diamond, *The Confessions of Jeremiah in Context: Scenes of Prophetic Drama* (JSOTSup 45; Sheffield: JSOT Press, 1987), 101–25.

7. Stulman, "The Prose Sermons as Hermeneutical Guide to Jeremiah 1–25," 34–63; R. R. Wilson, "Poetry and Prose in the Book of Jeremiah," in *Ki Baruch Hu: Ancient Near Eastern Studies in Honor of Baruch A. Levine* (ed. R. Chazan, W. W. Hallo, and L. H. Schiffman; Winona Lake, Ind.: Eisenbrauns, 1999), 413–27.

8. For a recent examination of the phrase "my servants the prophets" and its implications for the composition of Jeremiah, see Carolyn J. Sharp, *Prophecy and Ideology: Struggles for Authority in the Deutero-Jeremianic Prose* (OTS; New York: T&T Clark, 2003), 41–80.

9. For example, Jeremiah 11:3 equals Deuteronomy 27:26; Jeremiah 11:4 equals Deuteronomy 4:20; Jeremiah 11:5 equals Deuteronomy 7:8; 8:18; 9:5; Jeremiah 11:7 equals Deuteronomy 4:30; 8:20; Jeremiah 11:8 equals Deuteronomy 29:1, 9; Jeremiah 11:10 equals Deuteronomy 8:19; 11:28.

10. Marvin A. Sweeney discusses the difficulties of such a stance in *Reading the Hebrew Bible after the Shoah: Engaging Holocaust Theology* (Minneapolis: Fortress, 2008).

11. See Diamond, *The Confessions of Jeremiah in Context*, 101–13; Abraham J. Heschel, *The Prophets* (New York, Perennial Classics, 2001 [original publication by Harper and Bros., 1962]), 144–46; Kathleen M. O'Connor, *The Confessions of Jeremiah: Their Interpretation and Role in Chapters 1–25* (SBLDS 94; Atlanta: Scholars Press, 1988), 70–75.

12. Gerhard von Rad, "The Confessions of Jeremiah," in *Theodicy in the Old Testament* (ed. J. L. Crenshaw; Philadelphia: Fortress, 1983), 96.

13. Ibid., 95.

14. Henning G. Reventlow, *Liturgie und prophetisches Ich bei Jeremia* (Gütersloh: Gütersloher, 1966).

15. von Rad, "The Confessions of Jeremiah," 96–99.

16. Robert P. Carroll, *The Book of Jeremiah* (OTL; Philadelphia: Westminster, 1986), 701.

17. Critical assessments of the governor's actions are as different as night and day; some commentators consider him a "saint," while others see him as inept, at best.

18. Henri Nouwen, *Reaching Out* (New York: Doubleday, 1975), 65–109.

19. An insight from A. R. Pete Diamond.

20. The story of Josiah's untimely death in 2 Kings reads as a stunning narrative analogy. It should also be noted that the Gedaliah fiasco likely serves the interests of the Judean exiles in Babylon. The failure of Gedaliah and his administration to provide a viable alternative in the land provides further "proof" that the Babylonian exiles are true heirs of the divine promises.

21. From a pastoral point of view, the silence of Job's friends (Job 2:11-13) is surely the smartest thing they do. When they eventually open their mouths, the author transforms Job's friends into enemies. With words as weapons they do violence to the sufferer and to all those crushed by life's injustices.

22. Kathleen M. O'Connor, *Lamentations and the Tears of the World* (Maryknoll, N.Y.: Orbis Books, 2000), 86.

23. Bernhard Duhm, *Das Buch Jeremia* (Tübingen: J. C. B. Mohr, 1901); Sigmund Mowinckel, *Zur Kompositon des Buches Jeremia* (Kristiania: Jacob Dybwad, 1914).

24. Until recently, the poetry of Jeremiah or the so-called A source or tradition was viewed as the authentic witness of the book. This material was read not only as Jeremianic but also as engaging, dynamic, and original. In stark contrast, the C material was interpreted as impoverished, dull, and legalistic (see, for example, Mowinckel, *Zur Kompositon des Buches Jeremia*, 36–39). Following Mowinckel's lead, the majority of scholars have disparaged the prose literature in Jeremiah. For a different view, see Stulman, *Order Amid Chaos*; idem, "The Prose Sermons as Hermeneutical Guide to Jeremiah 1–25," 34–63; see also idem, *Jeremiah* (AOTC; Nashville: Abingdon, 2005).

25. Robert Carroll has made an incisive case for the importance of listening to "something rich and strange" in Jeremiah. See Carroll, *The Book of Jeremiah*, 423–43.

26. Walter Brueggemann, "Meditation upon the Abyss: The Book of Jeremiah," *Word & World* 22 (2002): 350. Kathleen M. O'Conner says it this way: "First and foremost, the book of Jeremiah names the disaster, reveals its contours, and mirrors it back to the audience. It depicts the totality of the destruction, speaks of pain and bitter grief, and articulates the rawness of the world in which the survivors find themselves." See her essay "Surviving Disaster in the Book of Jeremiah," *Word & World* 22 (2002): 370.

27. Brueggemann, "Meditation upon the Abyss: The Book of Jeremiah," 350.

6. Conflicting Paths to Hope in Jeremiah

1. On the importance of "naming the disaster," see Kathleen M. O'Connor, "Surviving Disaster in the Book of Jeremiah," *Word & World* 22 (2002): 369–77.

2. Isaiah 40–55 is the prophetic text usually attributed to helping the Jewish exiles cope with the devastating experiences of Babylonian invasion and deportation.

3. Brevard S. Childs, *Introduction to the Old Testament as Scripture* (Philadelphia: Fortress, 1979), 350–52.

4. Ibid., 351.

5. Ronald E. Clements, *Jeremiah* (Interpretation; Atlanta: John Knox, 1988), 3; note also his earlier article, "Jeremiah: Prophet of Hope," *Review and Expositor* 78 (1981): 345–63.

6. Walter Brueggemann, *A Commentary on Jeremiah: Exile and Homecoming* (Grand Rapids: Eerdmans, 1998); see also idem, *Hopeful Imagination: Prophetic Voices in Exile* (Philadelphia: Fortress, 1986), 29–31.

7. Walter Brueggemann, "Meditation upon the Abyss: The Book of Jeremiah," *Word & World* 22 (2002): 341.

8. O'Connor, "Surviving Disaster."

9. Ibid., 369.

10. Louis Stulman, *Order Amid Chaos: Jeremiah as Symbolic Tapestry* (The Biblical Seminar 57; Sheffield: Sheffield Academic Press, 1998), 56–98, 137–66.

11. Stulman, *Order Amid Chaos*, 23–55.

12. Abraham J. Heschel, *The Prophets* (New York: Perennial Classics, 2001 [original publication by Harper and Bros., 1962]), 3–6.

13. In his notes in *The New Oxford Annotated Bible* (3d ed.; Oxford: Oxford University Press, 2001), Mark E. Biddle describes the failings of the Jewish communities in Judah and Egypt (Jer 40:7–44:30) as a strategy to demonstrate that "hope for the future of God's people lies only with the Babylonian exiles" (1142).

14. Clements, *Jeremiah*, 180.

15. See Brueggemann, *Hopeful Imagination*, esp. 1–7, 10–47.

16. Henri Nouwen, *With Open Hands* (Notre Dame, Ind.: Ave Maria, 1972). This first edition of Nouwen's work includes marvelous photographs by Ron P. Van Den Bosch and Theo Robert.

17. Cf. Henri Nouwen, *The Living Reminder: Service and Prayer in Memory of Jesus Christ* (San Francisco: Harper & Row, 1984), 22.

18. An incisive treatment of the conditions of the diasporic community in Babylon can be found in Daniel L. Smith-Christopher, *A Biblical Theology of Exile* (OBT; Minneapolis: Fortress, 2002).

19. For a provocative anthology on hope in action, see Walter Brueggemann, ed., *Hope for the World: Mission in a Global Context* (Louisville: Westminster John Knox, 2001).

20. For a critical analysis of personal religion, especially as it appears in second-millennium Mesopotamian texts, see Thorkild Jacobsen, *The Treasures of Darkness: A History of Mesopotamian Religion* (New Haven, Conn.: Yale University Press, 1978), 145–64.

21. See T. A. Raitt, *A Theology of Exile: Judgment/Deliverance in Jeremiah and Ezekiel* (Philadelphia: Fortress, 1977).

22. See, for example, Henning G. Reventlow, *Liturgie und prophetisches Ich bei Jeremia* (Gütersloh: Gütersloher, 1966).

23. Mark E. Biddle, *Polyphony and Symphony in Prophetic Literature: Rereading Jeremiah 7–20* (Studies in Old Testament Interpretation 2; Macon, Ga.: Mercer University Press, 1996).

24. Walter Brueggemann, *Ichabod towards Home: The Journey of God's Glory* (Grand Rapids: Eerdmans, 2001); idem, *A Commentary on Jeremiah*, 418–24.

25. John J. Collins is surely correct that "the line between actually killing and verbal, symbolic, or imaginary violence is thin and permeable" (see "The Zeal of Phinehas: The Bible and the Legitimation of Violence," *JBL* 122 [2003]: 4). Collins also observes that in certain instances language of violence gives "hope to the oppressed" (ibid., 18), which is likely the case in the OAN.

7. Ezekiel as Disaster Literature

1. Albert Hourani, *A History of the Arab Peoples* (New York: Warner Books, 1991), 300–301.

2. Margaret S. Odell, *Ezekiel* (Macon, Ga.; Smyth & Helwys, 2005), 10.

3. This is not to say that recent scholarship has ignored Ezekiel. On the contrary, one can even speak of a resurgence of interest during the past decade (see Risa L. Kohn, "Ezekiel at the Turn of the Century," CBR 2 [2003]: 23). See also Andrew Mein, Ezekiel and the Ethics of Exile (Oxford: Oxford University Press, 2001); Margaret S. Odell and John T. Strong, eds., The Book of Ezekiel: Theological and Anthropological Perspectives (SBLSymS 9; Atlanta: Society of Biblical Literature, 2000); John F. Kutsko, Between Heaven and Earth: Divine Presence and Absence in the Book of Ezekiel (Winona Lake, Ind.: Eisenbrauns, 2000); Paul M. Joyce, Ezekiel: A Commentary (LHBOTS 482; New York: T&T Clark, 2007); Daniel L. Smith-Christopher, A Biblical Theology of Exile (OBT; Minneapolis: Fortress, 2002); also note the outstanding commentaries by L. C. Allen, J. Blenkinsopp, W. H. Brownlee, R. E. Clements, M. Greenberg, and of course W. Zimmerli. To some degree, an intense interest in the social realities of exile has fueled recent interpretation.

4. Donald E. Gowan, Theology of the Prophetic Books: The Death and Resurrection of Israel (Louisville: Westminster John Knox, 1998), 122.

5. Ibid.

6. Mein, Ezekiel and the Ethics of Exile, 101–36.

7. Abraham J. Heschel, The Prophets (New York: Perennial Classics, 2001 [original publication by Harper and Bros., 1962]).

8. In a personal correspondence, Carolyn J. Sharp suggested that Ezekiel might in fact support some of Heschel's arguments: for example, that the prophets experience everything much more acutely in this intensely magnified way, which could actually shade over into pathology, or into what the contemporary culture might read as pathology.

9. Walter Brueggemann, Hopeful Imagination: Prophetic Voices in Exile (Philadelphia: Fortress, 1986), 51.

10. See Katheryn Pfisterer Darr, "The Book of Ezekiel," in The New Interpreter's Bible (vol. 6; ed. L. E. Keck et al.; Nashville: Abingdon, 2001), 1101–07.

11. Walter Brueggemann, An Introduction to the Old Testament: The Canon and Christian Imagination (Louisville: Westminster John Knox, 2003), 191.

12. Ibid.

13. See, for example, David G. Garber Jr., "Traumatizing Ezekiel, the Exilic Prophet," in From Genesis to Apocalyptic Vision (vol. 2 of Psychology and the Bible: A New Way to Read the Scriptures; ed. J. H. Ellens and W. G. Rollins; Praeger Perspectives: Psychology, Religion and Spirituality; Westport, Conn.: Praeger, 2004), 215–35; Daniel L. Smith-Christopher, "Reassessing the Historical and Sociological Impact of the Babylonian Exile (597/587–539 B.C.E.)," in Exile: Old Testament, Jewish, and Christian Conceptions (ed. J. M. Scott; Supplements to the Journal for the Study of Judaism 56; Leiden: Brill, 1997), 7–36; idem, "Ezekiel on Fanon's Couch: A Postcolonialist Dialogue with David Halperin's Seeking Ezekiel," in Peace and Justice Shall Embrace: Power and Theopolitics in the Bible (ed. T. Grimsrud and L. L. Johns; Telford, Pa.: Pandora, 1999), 108–44.

14. Walter Brueggemann, The Word Militant: Preaching a Decentered Word (Minneapolis: Fortress, 2007), 133.

15. Mein, *Ezekiel and the Ethics of Exile*, 1–3.

16. Ralph W. Klein, *Israel in Exile: A Theological Interpretation* (OBT: Philadelphia: Fortress, 1979), 2.

17. Smith-Christopher, *A Biblical Theology of Exile*, 104.

18. Oded Lipschits, *The Fall and Rise of Jerusalem* (Winona Lake, Ind.: Eisenbrauns, 2005), xi.

19. Ibid., 367.

20. Judith Herman, *Trauma and Recovery* (New York: Basic Books, 1997), 77.

21. Ibid., 87.

22. Ibid., 94.

23. Ibid., 84.

24. Ibrahim Aref Kira, "Taxonomy of Trauma and Trauma Assessment," *Traumatology* 7, no. 2 (June 2001): 73–86.

25. Henry McKeating, *Ezekiel* (OTG; Sheffield: Sheffield Academic Press, 1993), 75.

26. Robert J. Lifton, *Death in Life: Survivors of Hiroshima* (New York: Random House, 1968), 57; contra Lifton, certain groups apparently maintain a sense of innocence during and after periods of profound loss. In the biblical corpus, those responsible for the complaint or lament psalms are fairly tenacious in their insistence of innocence. Those responsible for the so-called confessions of Jeremiah likewise maintain a clear sense of innocence in the face of profound suffering. And the same is apparently true of the Yahi Native Americans (Mill Creek), about whom we admittedly know very little. From what can be surmised, one of the ways these Native Americans survived unspeakable atrocities and an invisible existence was to maintain their sense of innocence. In an essay first published in March 1967 in *The Catholic Worker*, Thomas Merton notes that "the Yahi found strength in the incontrovertible fact that they were right" (Thomas Merton, *Passion for Peace* [New York: Crossroad, 2006], 122). And quoting Ishi, "the last wild Indian," "*Of very great importance to their psychic health was the circumstance that their suffering and curtailments arose from wrongs done in them by others.* They were not guilt-ridden" (ibid.).

27. Herman, *Trauma and Recovery*, 75.

28. Ibid., 53.

29. Ibid., 53–54.

30. See the splendid dissertation by David G. Garber Jr., "Trauma, History and Survival in Ezekiel 1–24" (Ph.D. diss., Emory University, 2005), especially 24.

31. Smith-Christopher, *A Biblical Theology of Exile*, 6.

32. Ibid., 21.

33. Admittedly the notion of "national consciousness" grew out of the Enlightenment idea of political sovereignty; perhaps the neutral term "self-concept" is a more accurate rendering.

34. Brueggemann, *The Word Militant*, 132–33.

35. Henri Nouwen, *Peacework: Prayer, Resistance, Community* (Maryknoll, N.Y.: Orbis Books, 2005), 110.

36. Mein, *Ezekiel and the Ethics of Exile*, 3. This is not to deny that the book of Ezekiel is a product of multiple communities, audiences, and settings, as noted by R. E. Clements and

others. But this traditioning process, this process of growth and development, is difficult to delineate with any certainty.

37. One might note, in this regard, women in Iran who were doctors, lawyers, and business leaders before the revolution in 1979 and who are now both disenfranchised and disempowered.

38. On complacency in Ezekiel, see Gowan, *Theology of the Prophetic Books*, 123–24.

39. Ibid., 122.

40. Heschel, *The Prophets*, 505–6.

41. For an insightful study of the traumatic impact of exile on Ezekiel, see Garber Jr., "Trauma, History and Survival in Ezekiel 1–24."

42. Social anthropologists and trauma scholars have noted that an acute sense of defilement and stigma is often indicative of psychological trauma.

43. One could think of the world created by Ian McEwan in his much acclaimed book *Atonement* (New York: Doubleday, 2001). Briony, Robbie, and Cecilia experience the devastation of a morally exacting world in which one offense has lingering and haunting consequences.

44. Odell, *Ezekiel*, 13–38.

45. Ibid., 125.

46. Kutsko, *Between Heaven and Earth*, 97.

47. The theme of divine absence and presence in the book of Ezekiel has been treated most thoroughly by Kutsko, *Between Heaven and Earth*, 26.

48. Henri Nouwen with Michael J. Christensen and Rebecca J. Laird, *Spiritual Direction* (San Francisco: HarperSanFrancisco, 2006), 134.

49. Ibid., 135.

8. Ezekiel as Survival Literature

1. Tod Linafelt, *Surviving Lamentations: Catastrophe, Lament, and Protest in the Afterlife of a Biblical Book* (Chicago and London: University of Chicago, 2000), 117.

2. Judith Lewis Herman, *Trauma and Recovery* (New York: Basic Books), 1.

3. Ibid.

4. David G. Garber Jr., "Trauma, History, and Survival in Ezekiel 1–24" (Ph.D. diss., Emory University, 2005), 1.

5. Ibid., 5.

6. Michael H. Floyd, "The Production of Prophetic Books," in *Prophets, Prophecy and Prophetic Texts in Second Temple Judaism* (ed. M. H. Floyd and R. L. Haak; London: T&T Clark, 2006), 285.

7. Yehezkel Kaufmann, *Israelite Religion from Its Beginnings to the Babylonian Exile* (trans. Moshe Greenberg; New York, Schocken Books, 1972), 427.

8. Ibid., 428.

9. The book of Ezekiel's tenuous social world is defined by liminality and hybridity: as a result of war, its implied audience is located on the margins in a distant land and longs for return to its homeland.

10. See Katheryn Pfisterer Darr, "Ezekiel's Justification of God: Teaching Troubling Texts," *JSOT* 55 (1992): 98–117.

11. Ezekiel will not afford Babylon the power of life and death. That authority belongs only to YHWH.

12. Daniel L. Smith-Christopher, *A Biblical Theology of Exile* (OBT; Minneapolis: Fortress, 2002), 81.

13. John A. Goldingay, "Ezekiel," in *Eerdmans Commentary on the Bible* (ed. J. D. G. Dunn and J. W. Rogerson; Grand Rapids; Eerdmans, 2003), 624.

14. Ibid.

15. Katheryn Pfisterer Darr, "The Book of Ezekiel," in *The New Interpreter's Bible* (vol. 6; ed. L. E. Keck et al.; Nashville: Abingdon, 2001), 1085.

16. Ibid., 1084.

17. Margaret S. Odell, *Ezekiel* (Macon, Ga.: Smyth & Helwys, 2005), 1.

18. Walter Brueggemann, *Hopeful Imagination: Prophetic Voices in Exile* (Philadelphia: Fortress, 1986), 57.

19. Andrew Mein, *Ezekiel and the Ethics of Exile* (Oxford: Oxford University Press, 2001), 176.

20. Ibid.

21. Ibid., 216.

22. Samuel E. Balentine, *Leviticus* (Interpretation; Louisville: John Knox, 2002), 14.

23. Joseph Blenkinsopp, *Ezekiel* (Interpretation; Louisville: John Knox, 1990), 150.

24. Donald E. Gowan, *Theology of the Prophetic Books: The Death and Resurrection of Israel* (Louisville: Westminster John Knox, 1998), 134.

25. Ibid., 103.

26. David L. Petersen, *The Prophetic Literature: An Introduction* (Louisville: Westminster John Knox, 2002), 156–57.

27. Blenkinsopp, *Ezekiel*, 148.

28. Odell, *Ezekiel*, 423–34.

29. Ibid., 431.

30. Victims of clergy abuse often deal with lifelong humiliation and pain. And many ask, "How can we reconnect to God when 'God' has wrecked our lives? How can we trust God when God—it would seem—has been our abuser?"

31. Of course, immediately after the Israelites confess that "The LORD will reign forever and ever" (15:18) they call into question YHWH's sovereignty (Exod 16–17; see also 32:1-35).

32. Darr, "The Book of Ezekiel," 1503.

33. Odell, *Ezekiel*, 457–58.

34. Peter C. Craigie, *Ezekiel* (The Daily Study Bible; ed. J. C. L. Gibson; Philadelphia; Westminster, 1983), 13.

9. An Anthology of Dispersion and Diagnosis (Hosea–Micah)

1. David L. Petersen, *The Prophetic Literature: An Introduction* (Louisville: Westminster John Knox, 2002), 209.

2. Paul R. House, *The Unity of the Twelve* (JSOTSup 97; Sheffield: Almond, 1990); James D. Nogalski, *Literary Precursors to the Book of the Twelve* (BZAW 217; Berlin: de Gruyter, 1993); idem, *Redactional Processes in the Book of the Twelve* (BZAW 218; Berlin: de Gruyter, 1993); Barry A. Jones, *The Formation of the Book of the Twelve: A Study in Text and Canon* (SBLDS 149; Atlanta: Scholars Press, 1995); Paul L. Redditt and Aaron Schart, eds., *Thematic Threads in the Book of the Twelve* (BZAW 325; Berlin: de Gruyter, 2003). Note also Paul L. Redditt, "Recent Research on the Book of the Twelve as One Book," *CR:BS* 9 (2001): 48: "Reading the Twelve as a whole supplements usual techniques of reading, and yields insights missed by reading them only in isolation from each other."

3. Marvin A. Sweeney, *The Prophetic Literature* (Nashville: Abingdon, 2005), 168–69; note also Russell Fuller, "The Text of the Twelve Minor Prophets," *CR:BS* 7 (1999): 81–95, especially on the Dead Sea Scrolls.

4. Note Ehud Ben Zvi, *Micah* (FOTL 21B; Grand Rapids: Eerdmans, 2000), 5: "It suffices at this point to mention that these books shaped, reflected, and reinforced: (1) the story of postmonarchic Israel (i.e., the Jerusalemite-centered communities of the Achaemenid period) about itself, (2) those communities' self-understanding, (3) their understanding of the divine economy and their place in it, (4) their understanding of the attributes and past and future actions of YHWH, and (5) hope for a great and glorious future, in opposition to their actual position in worldly terms."

5. James L. Crenshaw, "The Book of Sirach," in *The New Interpreter's Bible* (vol. 5; ed. L. E. Keck et al.; Nashville: Abingdon, 1997), 613. See also pp. 855–56, 860.

6. Patrick W. Skehan, *The Wisdom of Ben Sira* (AB 39; New York: Doubleday, 1987), 544.

7. Marvin A. Sweeney, *Form and Intertextuality in Prophetic and Apocalyptic Literature* (FAT 45; Tübingen: Mohr Siebeck, 2005), 209: "Joel's typological character and the difficulties in establishing its historical setting make it an eminently mobile text within the sequence of the Twelve."

8. Note the ancient traditions of the tension and enmity toward Shechem, Shiloh, Samaria, and so on in the ideology of the Deuteronomistic history (Deut 12:13-14; Judg 21:19; 1 Kgs 12:15, 25-33; cf. Gen 34; Jer 7:12-15; 26:4-9). Even in the Achaemenid period, readers can easily discern tension between "the people of the land," who were left in Palestine during the exilic era and affected by the ethnic mixture of the Assyrian policy, and the community of the exilic returnees (Tamara C. Eskenazi and Eleanore P. Judd, "Marriage to a Stranger in Ezra 9–10," in *Second Temple Studies 2: Temple Community in the Persian Period* [ed. T. C. Eskenazi and K. H. Richards; JSOTSup 175; Sheffield: JSOT Press, 1994], 266–85). The increased antinorthern tradition becomes further noticeable when directed against the Samaritans in the New Testament literature.

9. Julia M. O'Brien, *Challenging Prophetic Metaphor: Theology and Ideology in the Prophets* (Louisville: Westminster John Knox, 2008), 31–48.

10. Bruce C. Birch, *Hosea, Joel, and Amos* (Westminster Bible Companion; Louisville: Westminster John Knox, 1997), 31.

11. Marvin A. Sweeney, *Reading the Hebrew Bible after the Shoah: Engaging Holocaust Theology* (Minneapolis: Fortress, 2008), 154.

12. Katharine Doob Sakenfeld, *Just Wives? Stories of Power and Survival in the Old Testament and Today* (Louisville: Westminster John Knox, 2003), 100.

13. Abraham J. Heschel, *The Prophets* (New York: Perennial Classics, 2001 [original publication by Harper and Bros., 1962]), 364.

14. Martin Buber, *I and Thou* (trans. R. G. Smith; New York: Scribner's, 1970 [original publication, *Ich und Du*, 1937]), vii: "There is, however, one *Thou* which never becomes an *It*, the 'eternal *Thou*,' God. Though we may speak of God in the third person, the reality of His approach is constituted in the fullness of the relation of an *I* with a *Thou*. In truth, God may only be 'addressed, not expressed'" (see also pp. 79–81). For an insightful discussion of the transferability between the individual and the collective in Psalms, which may be applicable to the imagery in Hosea, see Harold Fisch, *Poetry with a Purpose: Biblical Poetics and Interpretation* (Bloomington: Indiana University Press, 1988), 112: "The I/Thou becomes the We/Thou" (see also pp. 104–14).

15. Henri Nouwen, *Life Signs: Intimacy, Fecundity, and Ecstasy in Christian Perspective* (New York: Random House, 1989).

16. Victor Frankl, *Man's Search for Meaning* (4th ed.; Boston: Simon & Schuster, 2000), 49.

17. Carl Rogers, *On Becoming a Person* (Boston: Houghton Mifflin, 1961).

18. Even all the way down to the postexilic settings of the Persian domination, which some scholars consider to have been a period substantially better for the Judeans than the period of Babylonian suppression, some scholars claim that the imperial taxation system may have meant the consistent hardship of colonized Yehud. See Lester L. Grabbe, "The Law of Moses in the Ezra Tradition: More Virtual than Real?" in *Persia and Torah: The Theory of Imperial Authorization of the Pentateuch* (ed. J. W. Watts; Atlanta: Society of Biblical Literature, 2001), 110: "There is no evidence that it was Persian policy to fund and support religious cults and temples in general. On the contrary, they usually taxed temples. . . . There is no reason to think that the Jerusalem temple and priesthood would have had decrees favoring them by tax exemptions under normal circumstances."

19. Marvin A. Sweeney, *The Twelve Prophets* (vol. 1; Berit Olam; Minneapolis: Liturgical, 2000), 151: "Overall, the book of Joel equates the threat posed to Israel by nature, employing a locust plague to symbolize that threat (Joel 1:2-20), and by enemy nations (Joel 2:1-14)."

20. For a discussion of locust imagery in ancient Near Eastern texts, see James L. Crenshaw, *Joel* (AB 24C; New York: Doubleday, 1995), 91–94; Richard Coggins, "Joel," *CBR* 2 (2003): 97.

21. Judith Lewis Herman, *Trauma and Recovery* (New York: Basic Books, 1997), 2.

22. Christopher R. Seitz, *Prophecy and Hermeneutics: Toward a New Introduction to the Prophets* (Grand Rapids: Baker Academic, 2007), 209: "Joel separates Hosea and Amos in order to signal that God is always in a position to relent, if the people turn back. Just as God relents before he utters his sentence of judgment through the speech of Amos reporting what he sees ('fruit,' 'end'), so it belongs to God's character to be 'slow to anger.'"

23. Scholars have observed that the order of these nations in Amos's OAN may have been intended to mirror the geographical route of the Assyrian and Babylonian invasion against Israel. See Shalom M. Paul, *Amos* (Hermeneia; Minneapolis: Fortress, 1991), 76; Robert Martin-Achard, *God's People in Crisis: A Commentary on the Book of Amos* (ITC; Grand Rapids: Eerdmans, 1984), 16; Sweeney, *The Prophetic Literature*, 185.

24. See Philip J. King, *Amos, Hosea, Micah—An Archaeological Commentary* (Philadelphia: Westminster, 1988), 137–61.

25. For a study on Amos's dependence on and adaptation of Hosea, see Jörg Jeremias, "The Interrelationship between Amos and Hosea," in *Forming Prophetic Literature: Essays on Isaiah and the Twelve in Honor of John D. W. Watts* (ed. J. W. Watts and P. R. House; JSOTSup 235; Sheffield: Sheffield Academic Press, 1996), 171–86.

26. Hyun Chul Paul Kim, "Jonah Read Intertextually," *JBL* 126 (2007): 497–518. Interestingly, whether coincidentally or deliberately, whereas Obadiah deals predominantly with the fate of Edom, the Oracles against the Nations in Zephaniah 2 omit Edom in addressing Ammon, Moab, Philistia, and Assyria. Read together, these two books, like bookends, form an internal inclusio on the one hand and single out Edom, which Obadiah highlights for the implicit twin relationship with Jacob/Israel, on the other hand (cf. Isaiah 34).

27. Concerning Obadiah's use of "vetitives" so as to address both the past and present, see Paul R. Raabe, *Obadiah* (AB 24D; New York: Doubleday, 1996), 58.

28. Philip Peter Jenson, *Obadiah, Jonah, Micah: A Theological Commentary* (LHBOTS 496; New York: T&T Clark, 2008), 21: "It evokes the idea of fugitives nearly attaining escape and then being cruelly picked up by neighbours intending the total destruction of the nation. . . . At various times Edom (along with other nations) is criticized for taking part in the slave trade (Amos 1:6, 9; 2 Chr 28:17)."

29. Ehud Ben Zvi, *Signs of Jonah: Reading and Rereading in Ancient Yehud* (JSOTSup 367; Sheffield: Sheffield Academic Press, 2003), 99–100: "The book of Jonah reflects and carries a message of inner reflection, and to some extent critical self-appraisal of the group within which and for which this book was written."

30. Phyllis Trible, "The Book of Jonah," in *The New Interpreter's Bible* (vol. 7; ed. L. E. Keck et al.; Nashville: Abingdon, 1996), 489; see Elias Bickerman, *Four Strange Books of the Bible* (New York: Schocken Books, 1967), 38–45.

31. Serge Frolov, "Returning the Ticket: God and His Prophet in the Book of Jonah," *JSOT* 86 (1999): 85–105.

32. Richard J. Coggins, *Israel among the Nations: A Commentary on the Books of Nahum and Obadiah* (ITC; Grand Rapids: Eerdmans, 1985), 12: "It is noteworthy that Nahum and Jonah are the only two books in the whole Bible which end with a question." Beyond the obvious fact that both Jonah and Nahum address the fate of Assyria, it is noteworthy that in Jonah the phrase *nhm* (נחם), which literally means "to comfort" or "to relent" and is connected to the name "Nahum," occurs in the theologically pivotal texts: "Who knows? God may relent (*nhm*) and change his mind. . . . God changed (*nhm*) his mind about the calamity . . . ready to relent (*nhm*) from punishing" (Jonah 3:9, 10; 4:2).

33. Francis I. Andersen and David Noel Freedman, *Micah* (AB 24E; New York: Doubleday, 2000), 174: "Micah is a Judaean. He would be expected to criticize Samaria as apostate. To turn the same charge back even more explicitly on Jerusalem might be unexpected and unacceptable in southern circles, but its shock value would be great, and Micah's contemporaries used it effectively. The best known case is Amos 1–2."

34. On the wordplay of the cities of Judah, see Andersen and Freedman, *Micah*, 212–49.

35. Daniel J. Simundson, "The Book of Micah," in *The New Interpreter's Bible* (vol. 7; ed. L. E. Keck et al.; Nashville: Abingdon, 1996), 537.

36. Leonard Cohen, "Anthem," from the CD *The Future* (Nashville: Sony/ATV Music Publishing, 1992).

37. Mignon R. Jacobs, *The Conceptual Coherence of the Book of Micah* (JSOTSup 322; Sheffield: Sheffield Academic Press, 2001), 222–23: "What then constitutes the conceptuality of the book of Micah? Is it judgment or hope? The fact of the matter is that it is both. . . . The final word, however, is not the judgment, but the hope that beyond the judgment lies a future in which the existence of Israel is a reality."

38. Marvin A. Sweeney, "Micah's Debate with Isaiah," *JSOT* 93 (2001): 122.

39. Admittedly, compared to Jonah 4:2 and Nahum 1:2-3, the phrase in Micah 7:18 is a less direct allusion to the creedal formula of Exodus 34:6-7. Also, Micah 7:18 may have its primary function as a chain-link catchphrase connected to Nahum 1:2-3, that is, conjoining the ending part of Micah and the beginning part of Nahum. In any case, the threefold occurrence of this formula in these books is striking.

10. An Anthology of Debate and Rebuilding (Nahum–Malachi)

1. Oskar Dangl, "Habakkuk in Recent Research," *CurBS* 9 (2001): 154–55: "[Paul R. House] thus draws the conclusion that several literary elements conjoin this segment of the Twelve Prophets—a dramatic coherence in the group Nahum, Habakkuk and Zephaniah (pp. 206–8)"; Paul R. House, "Dramatic Coherence in Nahum, Habakkuk, and Zephaniah," in *Forming Prophetic Literature: Essays in Isaiah and the Twelve in Honor of John D. W. Watts* (ed. J. W. Watts and P. R. House; JSOTSup 235; Sheffield: Sheffield Academic Press, 1996), 195–208.

2. Elizabeth Achtemeier, *Nahum–Malachi* (Interpretation; Atlanta: John Knox, 1986), 5: "Nahum is not primarily a book about human beings, however—not about human vengeance and hatred and military conquest—but a book about God." For a survey of the theological interpretations on this difficult issue of violence in Nahum, see Julia M. O'Brien, *Nahum, Habakkuk, Zephaniah, Haggai, Zechariah, Malachi* (AOTC; Nashville: Abingdon, 2004), 27–30.

3. Francisco O. García-Treto, "The Book of Nahum," in *The New Interpreter's Bible* (vol. 7; ed. L. E. Keck et al.; Nashville: Abingdon, 1996), 613: "The verse [3:1] is thus not to be read as an expression of grief over the demise of Nineveh, but rather as performative speech that vents anger"; Claus Westermann, *Basic Forms of Prophetic Speech* (Philadelphia: Westminster, 1967), 190–98; Waldemar Janzen, *Mourning Cry and Woe Oracle* (BZAW 125; Berlin: de Gruyter, 1972), 27–39.

4. Concerning the hermeneutical problem of the violence inherent in Nahum, see García-Treto, "The Book of Nahum," 619; see also Richard J. Coggins, *Israel among the Nations: A Commentary on the Books of Nahum and Obadiah* (ITC; Grand Rapids: Eerdmans, 1985), 60.

5. For a profound explication on the "cathartic" effects of the "venomous passages," see Walter Brueggemann, *Praying the Psalms* (Winona, Minn.: St. Mary's Press, 1982), 69–70.

6. Comparatively, in commenting on Psalm 137:9, Robert Alter poses the possibility that Psalm 137 may have been the very song the captives sang in the language of Hebrew, which was not understandable to the Babylonian captors: "No moral justification can be offered for this notorious concluding line. All one can do is to recall the background of outraged feeling that triggers the conclusion: . . . the powerless captives, ordered—perhaps mockingly—to sing their Zion songs, respond instead with a lament that is not really a song and ends with this blood-curdling curse pronounced on their captors, who, fortunately, do not understand the Hebrew in which it is pronounced" (*The Book of Psalms: A Translation with Commentary* [New York: W. W. Norton, 2007], 475).

7. Marvin A. Sweeney, *Reading the Hebrew Bible after the Shoah: Engaging Holocaust Theology* (Minneapolis: Fortress, 2008), 160: "Altogether, the book of Nahum is formulated to celebrate the downfall of an oppressor comparable to the downfall of Nazi Germany or Imperial Japan in World War II; it is not an expression of Judean hatred against Gentiles or a glorification of violence."

8. Commentators disagree on who the "wicked" oppressors are in Habakkuk 1:2-4 and throughout the book of Habakkuk. For example, the possibilities include the ruling class within Judah, the Assyrians, the Babylonians, or another group or country. One thing that seems evident is that other than the one-time occurrence of the word denoting Babylon ("For I am rousing the Chaldeans," 1:6), these poetic texts of Habakkuk do not clearly identify the opponents and oppressors. Even the superscription does not include the target audience (1:1). Interestingly, some of the imagery in the accusations can be applicable to the ruling class within Judah and Yehud rather than to Babylon (for example, 2:5-6, 9-12; but see 2:8). This ambiguity thus heightens the multiple possibilities for readers to identify the "wicked" powers that be. See O'Brien, *Nahum, Habakkuk, Zephaniah, Haggai, Zechariah, Malachi*, 62.

9. Theodore Hiebert, "The Book of Habakkuk," in *The New Interpreter's Bible* (vol. 7; ed. L. E. Keck et al.; Nashville: Abingdon, 1996), 648.

10. On the literary coherence of the Twelve, meticulously proposed by James D. Nogalski, note Marvin A. Sweeney, "Zephaniah: A Paradigm for the Study of the Prophetic Books," *CurBS* 7 (1999): 140: "Zephaniah thereby plays a crucial role in the Book of the Twelve in that it facilitates the transition between the portrayal of Yʜᴡʜ's judgment against Israel/Judah and the nations and Yʜᴡʜ's restoration of Jerusalem at the center of the nations"; James D. Nogalski, *Literary Precursors to the Book of the Twelve* (BZAW 217; Berlin: de Gruyter, 1993), 171–215.

11. Adele Berlin, *Zephaniah* (AB 25A; New York: Doubleday, 1994), 13: "The Book of Zephaniah is a study in intertextuality. A highly literate work, it shares ideas and phraseology with other parts of the Hebrew Bible to such an extent that at times it may appear as nothing more than a pastiche of borrowed verses and allusions."

12. Marvin A. Sweeney, *Zephaniah* (Hermeneia; Minneapolis: Fortress, 2003), 110–55; O'Brien, *Nahum, Habakkuk, Zephaniah, Haggai, Zechariah, Malachi*, 118.

13. Berlin, *Zephaniah*, 120: "Zephaniah, I believe, does this by shaping this prophecy around an older mythopoetic theme. That theme has been preserved in literary form in Genesis 10, and it is Genesis 10, I will argue, that serves as the conceptual undergirding, and to a larger extent the literary model, for Zephaniah 2:5-15"; Michael H. Floyd, *Minor Prophets: Part 2* (FOTL 22; Grand Rapids: Eerdmans, 2000), 211: "The directional categories of the four points of the compass are simultaneously operative. . . . They should also be mapped out in relation to the main contours of 'the face of the earth,' over which primeval humanity was scattered from the central location of Shinar (Gen 11:1-9) as described in the mythical geography of Genesis."

14. This term "exultant city" (*'allîza*) occurs elsewhere denoting Jerusalem (Isa 22:2; 32:13) or Tyre (Isa 23:7). Interestingly, a verb with the same root (*'elôzâ*) occurs in Habakkuk 3:18, "I will *rejoice* in the LORD" (emphasis added), as if alluding to YHWH as the most secure city of joy and hope.

15. Also, we cannot rule out the possibility that this prophet may have had ancestral lineage with Ethiopia, not only because he is described as "son of Cushi" (1:1; cf. Num 12:1; 2 Sam 18:21; Jer 36:14; 38:7) but also because the nation Cushi does occur at thematically significant places throughout the book (2:12; 3:10). See Robert A. Bennett, "The Book of Zephaniah," in *The New Interpreter's Bible* (vol. 7; ed. L. E. Keck et al.; Nashville: Abingdon, 1996), 670–72; Floyd, *Minor Prophets: Part 2*, 211.

16. For instance, for Haggai, key events take place during the sixth, seventh, and ninth months of the second year of Darius (520 B.C.E.). For Zechariah, especially the first half of this book, key events take place during the eighth and eleventh months of the second year of Darius (520 B.C.E.) and the ninth month of the fourth year of Darius (518 B.C.E.).

17. David S. Vanderhooft, "New Evidence Pertaining to the Transition from Neo-Babylonian to Achaemenid Administration in Palestine," in *Yahwism after the Exile: Perspectives on Israelite Religion in the Persian Era* (ed. R. Albertz and B. Becking; Assen: Van Gorcum, 2003), 219–35.

18. Daniel L. Smith-Christopher, *A Biblical Theology of Exile* (OBT; Minneapolis: Fortress, 2002), 65.

19. Note Carol L. Meyers and Eric M. Meyers, *Haggai, Zechariah 1–8* (AB 25B; Garden City, N.Y.: Doubleday, 1987), xxxix: "The people of Yehud, however, were still liable for taxes and subject to the corvée (Ezra 4:12-16). . . . In addition, Darius ordered that once the temple was completed, a daily offering and prayer were to be made for the welfare of the king (Ezra 6:10)."

20. According to Josephus's *Jewish Antiquities*, we even learn about internal dissension within the group of the high priests, which culminated in fraternal murder, during the approximate time of Ezra. Josephus (*Jewish Antiquities* 11.297–301) records the murder Joannes the high priest, or the high priest elect, committed against his brother Jesus. Immediately following this incident, Bagoses, the general of Artaxerxes's army, intervened, resulting in the Persian governance's defilement of the temple. This information was made available by Rainer Albertz, "The Controversy about Judean versus Israelite Identity and the Persian Government: A New

Interpretation of the Bagoses Story (*Antiquitates* IX.297–301)" (paper presented at the annual meeting of the Society of Biblical Literature, Boston, Mass., 23 November 2008).

21. On the ensuing hope and vision toward Zerubbabel as the anointed of YHWH, note Marvin A. Sweeney, *The Twelve Prophets* (vol. 2; Berit Olam; Minneapolis: Liturgical, 2000), 531, 533. Note also Leo G. Perdue, *Wisdom Literature: A Theological History* (Louisville: Westminster John Knox, 2007), 142, 151: "Zealots, inspired perhaps by Haggai and Zechariah as well as other nationalistic prophets, may have attempted to foment rebellion in order to return to establish an independent state under the dynasty of David. . . . The prophets and apocalyptic seers formed a second party that looked to a new messianic age in which the Persian Empire would fall into disarray and a restored Jerusalem would become the center of the new, divine reign."

22. Walter Brueggemann, *An Introduction to the Old Testament: The Canon and Christian Imagination* (Louisville: Westminster John Knox, 2003), 251.

23. Klaus Koch, *The Prophets: The Babylonian and Persian Periods* (Philadelphia: Fortress, 1982), 163.

24. On Zechariah's intertextual dependence on Isaiah, see Sweeney, *The Twelve Prophets*, vol. 2, 563; idem, *Form and Intertextuality in Prophetic and Apocalyptic Literature* (FAT 45; Tübingen: Mohr Siebeck, 2005), 222–35.

25. Note that the detailed chronological information, which replicates the same pattern of Haggai, also functions to frame these eight visions by Zechariah 1:7 (cf. 1:1) and 7:1.

26. See Meyers and Meyers, *Haggai, Zechariah 1–8*, 148.

27. Note that among the eight visions, only the two central visions—fourth and fifth—do not have a typical report phrase by the prophet, for example, "I lifted up my eyes" or "I saw":

1:8   "I saw."

1:18 [MT 2:1]   "I looked up and saw."

2:1 [MT 2:5]   "I looked up and saw."

3:1   "He showed me."

4:1   "The angel . . . wakened me."

5:1   "Again I looked up and saw."

5:5 (5:9)   "Look up and see." ("Then I looked up and saw.")

6:1   "Again I looked up and saw."

28. In addition to the notable distinctions with regard to literary style and content, the second half has two places (9:1 and 12:1) that start with the words "an oracle" (*maśśāʾ*), which signifies that these subunits may have been originally independent compositions. See Carol L. Meyers and Eric M. Meyers, *Zechariah 9–14* (AB 25C; New York: Doubleday, 1993), 30–31; Floyd, *Minor Prophets: Part 2*, 306.

29. Recent scholarship on Zechariah has flourished on the issues of the innerbiblical allusions. For Zechariah's intertextual relationship with Isaiah, see Marvin A. Sweeney, "Zechariah's Debate with Isaiah," in *The Changing Face of Form Criticism for the Twenty-first Century* (ed. M. A. Sweeney and E. Ben Zvi; Grand Rapids; Eerdmans, 2003), 335–50; Risto Nurmela, "The Growth of the Book of Isaiah Illustrated by Allusions in Zechariah," in *Bringing*

out the Treasure: Inner Biblical Allusion in Zechariah 9–14 (ed. M. J. Boda and M. H. Floyd; JSOTSup 370; Sheffield: Sheffield Academic Press, 2003), 245–59.

30. Other more subtle intertextual correlations between Amos and Zechariah 9–14 include, "*I am no prophet, nor a prophet's son; but I am a herdsman, and a dresser of sycamore trees*" (Amos 7:14; emphasis added) // "*I am no prophet, I am a tiller* of the soil; for the land has been my possession since my youth" (Zech 13:5; emphasis added); "He saw concerning Israel in the days of *King Uzziah of Judah* . . . two years before the *earthquake*" (Amos 1:1; emphasis added) // "And you shall flee as you fled from the *earthquake* in the days of *King Uzziah of Judah*" (Zech 14:5; emphasis added).

31. For the royal motif of "riding on a donkey," see David L. Petersen, "Zechariah 9–14: Methodological Reflections," in Boda and Floyd, *Bringing out the Treasure*, 218. Although this phrase in Zech 9:9 does not seem to imply the nuance of humility, it is intriguing that a similar combination of words occurs in Isaiah 53:7, "He was oppressed, and he was afflicted." Note the same root words, "to oppress" (*ngś*) and "afflicted" (*ʿnh*), with Zechariah 9:8-9, "oppressor"/"taskmaster" (*ngś*) and "humble"/"afflicted" (*ʿnh*). Note also that these two root words occur in Exodus 3:7 (cf. Isa 58:3). Furthermore, the word *humble* correlates Zechariah 9:9-11 with the same word in Zephaniah 3:12 (emphasis added), "For I will leave in the midst of you / a people *humble* and lowly. / They shall seek refuge in the name of the LORD." In this correlation, it is interesting that the summons to "sing aloud" also occurs in Zephaniah 3:14 and Zachariah 9:9. In light of these catchwords, it seems these two subunits (i.e., Zeph 3:11-15 and Zech 9:9-11) bracket Haggai and Zechariah 1–8.

32. On the identity of the "official leadership of the Judaism of their time," see Rex Mason, "The Use of Earlier Biblical Material in Zechariah 9–14," in Boda and Floyd, *Bringing out the Treasure*, 204; on the identity of Persia, see Sweeney, *The Twelve Prophets*, vol. 2, 567, 671, and especially 677.

33. On the linguistic and thematic connections between Zech 13:9 and Hos 2:23 (as well as Mal 3:2-3), see Paul L. Redditt, *Introduction to the Prophets* (Grand Rapids: Eerdmans, 2008), 342–44.

34. John D. W. Watts, "A Frame for the Book of the Twelve: Hosea 1–3 and Malachi," in *Reading and Hearing the Book of the Twelve* (ed. J. D. Nogalski and M. A. Sweeney; SBLSymS 15; Atlanta: Society of Biblical Literature, 2000), 210.

35. For further examples of interconnections between Joel and Zechariah 12–14, see Nicholas Ho Fai Tai who proposes that within the frame of the Twelve set by Hosea and Malachi, both Joel and Zechariah 12–14 also construct a symmetrical frame ("The End of the Book of the Twelve: Reading Zechariah 12–14 with Joel," in *Schriftprophetie: FS für Jörg Jeremias zum 65. Geburtstag* [ed. F. Hartenstein, J. Krispenz, and A. Schart; Neukirchen-Vluyn: Neukirchener, 2004], 341–50).

36. Andrew E. Hill, *Malachi* (AB 25D; New York: Doubleday, 1998), 41: "By way of hermeneutic, these Second Temple 'rhetors' appealed authoritatively to other texts of Hebrew Scripture and exhibited a continuity with earlier prophetic tradition in their use of vocabulary."

37. Note that Targum Jonathan, an Aramaic manuscript, even identifies Malachi with Ezra (see Sweeney, *The Twelve Prophets*, vol. 2, 715).

38. See William P. Brown, *Obadiah through Malachi* (Westminster Bible Companion: Louisville: Westminster John Knox, 1996), 197.

39. If this intertextual allusion is legitimate, it is interesting that the divine vow of dismissal echoes the Aaronite priestly circle, whereas Malachi appears to accentuate the priestly groups of the Levites throughout, if not exclusively (Mal 2:4, 8; 3:3); see Paul D. Hanson, *The Dawn of Apocalyptic* (Philadelphia: Fortress, 1975); idem, *The People Called: The Growth of Community in the Bible* (San Francisco: Harper & Row, 1986).

40. Hill, *Malachi*, 43.

41. Eileen M. Schuller, "The Book of Malachi," in *The New Interpreter's Bible* (vol. 7; ed. L. E. Keck et al.; Nashville: Abingdon, 1996), 865.

42. Aaron Schart, "Putting the Eschatological Visions of Zechariah in Their Place: Malachi as a Hermeneutical Guide for the Last Section of the Book of the Twelve," in Boda and Floyd, *Bringing out the Treasure*, 343: "[The redactors] attached the writing of Malachi in order to prevent readers of the eschatological visions from misunderstanding them. . . . There also needs to be a counterbalancing emphasis on not neglecting the everyday practice of Torah, which is the lifelong task of every single person."

43. On the pertinent effect of the tithe for the greater community, see Brown, *Obadiah through Malachi*, 202: "On the giving of a mere portion of one's own livelihood rests the livelihood of the whole of the community."

44. Robert Shetterly, *Americans Who Tell the Truth* (New York: Dutton Children's Books, 2005), 25.

45. The recent global recession is a painful case in point.

BIBLIOGRAPHY

Achtemeier, Elizabeth. "The Book of Joel." Pages 299–336 in *The New Interpreter's Bible*. Vol. 7. Edited by L. E. Keck et al. Nashville: Abingdon, 1996.

———. *The Community and Message of Isaiah 56–66*. Minneapolis: Augsburg, 1982.

———. "Isaiah of Jerusalem: Themes and Preaching Possibilities." Pages 23–37 in *Reading and Preaching the Book of Isaiah*. Edited by C. R. Seitz. Philadelphia: Fortress, 1988.

———. *Nahum–Malachi*. Interpretation. Atlanta: John Knox, 1986.

Ackroyd, Peter R. "The Biblical Interpretation of the Reigns of Ahaz and Hezekiah." Pages 247–59 in *In the Shelter of Elyon: Essays on Ancient Palestinian Life and Literature in Honour of G. W. Ahlström*. Edited by W. B. Barrick and J. R. Spencer. JSOTSup 31. Sheffield: JSOT Press, 1984.

———. *Studies in the Religious Tradition of the Old Testament*. London: SCM, 1987.

Adams, Jim W. *The Performative Nature and Function of Isaiah 40–55*. New York: T&T Clark, 2006.

Agger, Inger and Soren B. Jensen. "Testimony as Ritual and Evidence in Psychotherapy for Political Refugees." *Journal of Traumatic Stress* 3 (1990): 115–30.

Ahn, John. "Psalm 137: Complex Communal Laments." *JBL* 127 (2008): 267–89.

Albertz, Rainer. *A History of Israelite Religion in the Old Testament Period*. Vol. 2. Translated by J. Bowden. Louisville: Westminster John Knox, 1994.

———. *Israel in Exile: An Introduction to the History and Literature of the Sixth Century B.C.E.* Studies in Biblical Literature 3. Atlanta: Society of Biblical Literature, 2003.

Alexander, Jeffrey C. et al. *Cultural Trauma and Collective Identity*. Berkeley: University of California Press, 2004.

Alfaro, Juan I. *Justice and Loyalty: A Commentary on the Book of Micah*. ITC. Grand Rapids: Eerdmans, 1989.

Alter, Robert. *The Book of Psalms: A Translation with Commentary*. New York: W. W. Norton, 2007.

Andersen, Francis I. *Habakkuk*. AB 25. New York: Doubleday, 2001.

Andersen, Francis I. and David Noel Freedman. *Amos*. AB 24A. New York: Doubleday, 1989.

———. *Micah*. AB 24E. New York: Doubleday, 2000.

Anderson, Bernhard W. "Exodus and Covenant in Second Isaiah and Prophetic Tradition." Pages 339–60 in *Magnalia Dei, The Mighty Acts of God: Essays on the Bible and Archaeology in Memory of G. Ernest Wright*. Edited by F. M. Cross et al. Garden City, N.Y.: Doubleday, 1976.

———. "Exodus Typology in Second Isaiah." Pages 177–95 in *Israel's Prophetic Heritage: Essays in Honor of James Muilenburg*. Edited by B. W. Anderson and W. Harrelson. New York: Harper & Brothers, 1962.

Augsburger, David W. *Helping People Forgive*. Louisville: Westminster John Knox, 1996.

Balentine, Samuel E. *Leviticus*. Interpretation. Louisville: John Knox, 2002.

Baltzer, Klaus. *Deutero-Isaiah: A Commentary on Isaiah 40–55*. Translated by M. Kohl. Hermeneia. Minneapolis: Fortress, 2001.

Barndt, Joseph. *Dismantling Racism: The Continuing Challenge to White America*. Minneapolis: Augsburg, 1991.

Barton, J. *Isaiah 1–39*. OTG. Sheffield: Sheffield Academic Press, 1995.

Baumann, Gerlinde. *Love and Violence: Marriage as Metaphor for the Relationship between YHWH and Israel in the Prophetic Books*. Translated by L. M. Maloney. Collegeville, Minn.: Liturgical, 2003.

Becking, Bob and Marjo C. A. Korpel, eds. *The Crisis of Israelite Religion: Transformation of Religious Tradition in Exilic and Post-exilic Times*. OtSt 42. Leiden: Brill, 1999.

Beeby, H. D. *Grace Abounding: A Commentary on the Book of Hosea*. ITC. Grand Rapids: Eerdmans, 1989.

Bellinger, William H. and William R. Farmer, eds. *Jesus and the Suffering Servant: Isaiah 53 and Christian Origins*. Harrisburg, Pa.: Trinity Press International, 1998.

Bennett, Robert A. "The Book of Zephaniah." Pages 657–704 in *The New Interpreter's Bible*. Vol. 7. Edited by L. E. Keck et al. Nashville: Abingdon, 1996.

Ben Zvi, Ehud. *A Historical-Critical Study of the Book of Zephaniah*. BZAW 198. Berlin: de Gruyter, 1991.

———. *Micah*. FOTL 21B. Grand Rapids: Eerdmans, 2000.

———. *Signs of Jonah: Reading and Rereading in Ancient Yehud*. JSOTSup 367. Sheffield: Sheffield Academic Press, 2003.

———. "What is New in Yehud? Some Considerations." Pages 32–48 in *Yahwism after the Exile: Perspectives on Israelite Religion in the Persian Era*. Edited by R. Albertz and B. Becking. Assen: Van Gorcum, 2003.

Berges, Ulrich. *Das Buch Jesaja: Komposition und Endgestalt*. Herders biblische Studien 16. Freiburg: Herder, 1998.

———. "Die Zionstheologie des Buches Jesaja." *Estudios Bíblicos* 58 (2000): 167–98.

———. *Jesaja 40–48*. Vol. 1. HThKAT. Freiburg: Herder, 2008.

Berlin, Adele. *Zephaniah*. AB 25A. New York: Doubleday, 1994.

Beuken, Willem A. M. *Isaiah 28–39*. Translated by B. Doyle. Leuven: Peeters, 2000.

———. "The Main Theme of Trito-Isaiah: The 'Servants of YHWH.' " *JSOT* 47 (1990): 67–87.

Bickerman, Elias. *Four Strange Books of the Bible*. New York: Schocken Books, 1967.

Biddle, Mark E. "Jeremiah." Pages 1073–1166 in *The New Oxford Annotated Bible*. 3d ed. Edited by M. D. Coogan. Oxford: Oxford University Press, 2001.

———. *Polyphony and Symphony in Prophetic Literature: Rereading Jeremiah 7–20*. Studies in Old Testament Interpretation 2. Macon, Ga.: Mercer University Press, 1996.

Birch, Bruce C. *Hosea, Joel, and Amos*. Westminster Bible Companion. Louisville: Westminster John Knox, 1997.

Blenkinsopp, Joseph. *Ezekiel*. Interpretation. Louisville: John Knox, 1990.

———. *Ezra–Nehemiah*. OTL. Philadelphia: Westminster, 1988.

———. *Isaiah 1–39*. AB 19. New York: Doubleday, 2000.

———. *Isaiah 40–55*. AB 19A. New York: Doubleday, 2002.

———. *Isaiah 56–66*. AB 19B. New York: Doubleday, 2003.

———. *Opening the Sealed Book: Interpretations of the Book of Isaiah in Late Antiquity*. Grand Rapids: Eerdmans, 2006.

———. "The Prophetic Biography of Isaiah." Pages 13–26 in *Mincha: Festgabe für Rolf Rendtorff zum 75. Geburtstag*. Edited by E. Blum. Neukirchen-Vluyn: Neukirchener, 2000.

———. "Was the Pentateuch the Civic and Religious Constitution of the Jewish Ethnos in the Persian Period?" Pages 41–62 in *Persia and Torah: The Theory of Imperial Authorization of the Pentateuch*. Edited by J. W. Watts. Atlanta: Society of Biblical Literature, 2001.

Boda, Mark J. "Majoring on the Minors: Recent Research on Haggai and Zechariah." CBR 2 (2003): 33–68.

———. "Zechariah: Master Mason or Penitential Prophet?" Pages 49–69 in *Yahwism after the Exile: Perspectives on Israelite Religion in the Persian Era*. Edited by R. Albertz and B. Becking. Assen: Van Gorcum, 2003.

Boda, Mark J. and Michael Floyd, eds. *Bringing out the Treasure: Inner Biblical Allusion in Zechariah 9–14*. JSOTSup 370. London: Sheffield Academic Press, 2004.

Bosshard-Nepustil, Erich. *Rezeptionen von Jesaja 1–39 im Zwölfprophetenbuch: Untersuchungen zur literarischen Verbindung von Prophetenbüchern in babylonischer und persischer Zeit*. OBO 154. Freiburg: Universitätsverlag, 1997.

Bosshard-Nepustil, Erich and Reinhard G. Kratz. "Maleachi im Zwölfprophetenbuch." *Biblische Notizen* 52 (1990): 27–46.

Brett, Mark G. *Genesis: Procreation and the Politics of Identity*. London: Routledge, 2000.

Brown, William P. *Obadiah through Malachi*. Westminster Bible Companion. Louisville: Westminster John Knox, 1996.

Brueggemann, Walter. *A Commentary on Jeremiah: Exile and Homecoming*. Grand Rapids: Eerdmans, 1998.

———. *Finally Comes the Poet: Daring Speech for Proclamation*. Minneapolis: Fortress, 1989.

———. *Hopeful Imagination: Prophetic Voices in Exile*. Philadelphia: Fortress, 1986.

———. *Ichabod towards Home: The Journey of God's Glory*. Grand Rapids: Eerdmans, 2001.

———. *Introduction to the Old Testament: The Canon and Christian Imagination*. Louisville: Westminster John Knox, 2003.

———. *Isaiah 1–39*. Westminster Bible Companion. Louisville: Westminster John Knox, 1998.

———. *Isaiah 40–66*. Westminster Bible Companion. Louisville: Westminster John Knox, 1998.

———. "Meditation upon the Abyss: The Book of Jeremiah." *Word & World* 22 no. 4 (2002): 340–50.

————. *Praying the Psalms*. Winona, Minn.: St. Mary's Press, 1982.

————. *The Prophetic Imagination*. Philadelphia: Fortress, 1978.

————. *Texts That Linger, Words That Explode: Listening to Prophetic Voices*. Minneapolis: Fortress, 2000.

————. *The Theology of the Book of Jeremiah*. OTT. Cambridge; Cambridge University Press, 2007.

————. *Theology of the Old Testament: Testimony, Dispute, Advocacy*. Minneapolis: Fortress, 1997.

————. *The Word Militant: Preaching a Decentered Word*. Minneapolis: Fortress, 2007.

————. *The Word That Redescribes the World*. The Bible and Discipleship. Minneapolis: Fortress, 2006.

Brueggemann, Walter, ed. *Hope for the World: Mission in a Global Context*. Louisville: Westminster John Knox, 2001.

Buber, Martin. *I and Thou*. Translated by R. G. Smith. New York: Scribner's, 1970 [original publication, *Ich und Du*, in 1923].

Butterfield, H. *Christianity and History*. New York: Charles Scribner's Sons, 1950.

Canetti, Elias. "Excerpt from *The Secret Heart of the Clock* [Die Geheimherz der Uhr]." Pages 25–39 in *Contemporary Jewish Writing in Austria: An Anthology*. Edited by D. C. G. Lorenz. Lincoln: University of Nebraska Press, 1999.

Carroll, Robert P. *The Book of Jeremiah*. OTL. Philadelphia: Westminster, 1986.

————. "Century's End: Jeremiah Studies at the Beginning of the Third Millennium." *CurBS* 8 (2000): 18–58.

————. "Manuscripts Don't Burn—Inscribing the Prophetic Tradition. Reflections on Jeremiah 36." Pages 31–42 in *Dort ziehen Schiffe dahin. . . . Collected Communications to the XIVth Congress of the International Organization for the Study of the Old Testament, Paris 1992*. Edited by M. Augustin and K.-D. Schunck. Berlin: Peter Lang, 1996.

Carter, Charles E. and Carol L. Meyers, eds. *Community, Identity and Ideology: Social Science Approaches to the Hebrew Bible*. Winona Lake, Ind.: Eisenbrauns, 1996.

Centers, Linda. "Beyond Denial and Despair: ALS and Our Heroic Potential for Hope." *Journal of Palliative Care* 17 (2001): 259–64.

Chalmers, R. Scott. *The Struggle of Yahweh and El for Hosea's Israel*. Sheffield: Sheffield Phoenix Press, 2008.

Childs, Brevard S. *Introduction to the Old Testament as Scripture*. Philadelphia: Fortress, 1979.

————. *Isaiah*. OTL. Louisville: Westminster John Knox, 2001.

————. *The Struggle to Understand Isaiah as Christian Scripture*. Grand Rapids: Eerdmans, 2004.

Clements, Ronald E. *Isaiah 1–39*. NCB. Grand Rapids: Eerdmans, 1980.

————. *Jeremiah*. Interpretation. Atlanta: John Knox, 1988.

————. "Jeremiah: Prophet of Hope." *Review and Expositor* 78 (1981): 345–63.

————. *Old Testament Prophecy: From Oracles to Canon*. Louisville: Westminster John Knox, 1996.

Coggins, Richard. *Israel among the Nations: A Commentary on the Books of Nahum and Obadiah.* ITC. Grand Rapids: Eerdmans, 1985.

———. "Joel." *CBR* 2 (2003): 85–103.

Collins, John J. *Encounters with Biblical Theology.* Minneapolis: Fortress, 2005.

———. "The Zeal of Phinehas: The Bible and the Legitimation of Violence." *JBL* 122 (2003): 3–21.

Conrad, Edgar W. *Reading Isaiah.* OBT. Minneapolis: Fortress, 1991.

Cook, Joan E. *Hear, O Heavens and Listen, O Earth: An Introduction to the Prophets.* Collegeville, Minn.: Liturgical, 2006.

Cook, Stephen L. and Corrine L. Patton, eds. *Ezekiel's Hierarchical World: Wrestling with a Tiered Reality.* SBLSymS 31. Atlanta: Society of Biblical Literature, 2004.

Craig, Kenneth M. "Jonah in Recent Research." *CurBS* 7 (1999): 97–118.

Craigie, Peter C. *Ezekiel.* The Daily Study Bible. Edited by John C. L. Gibson. Philadelphia: Westminster, 1983.

Crenshaw, James L. "The Book of Sirach." Pages 601–867 in *The New Interpreter's Bible.* Vol. 5. Edited by L. E. Keck et al. Nashville: Abingdon, 1997.

———. *Joel.* AB 24C. New York: Doubleday, 1995.

Dangl, Oskar. "Habakkuk in Recent Research." *CurBS* 9 (2001): 131–68.

Darr, Katheryn Pfisterer. "The Book of Ezekiel." Pages 1073–1607 in *The New Interpreter's Bible.* Vol. 6. Edited by L. E. Kick et al. Nashville: Abingdon, 2001.

———. "Ezekiel's Justification of God: Teaching Troubling Texts." *JSOT* 55 (1992): 98–117.

———. *Isaiah's Vision and the Family of God.* Louisville: Westminster John Knox, 1994.

Davies, Philip R. *The Origins of Biblical Israel.* LHBOTS 485. New York: T&T Clark, 2007.

———. *Scribes and Schools: The Canonization of the Hebrew Scriptures.* Louisville: Westminster John Knox, 1998.

Davis, Ellen F. and Richard B. Hays, eds. *The Art of Reading Scripture.* Grand Rapids: Eerdmans, 2003.

De Hoop, Raymond. "Delimitation Criticism and Exegesis: Isaiah 56 as an Introduction to the Theme." Pages 1–28 in *The Impact of Delimitation Criticism on Exegesis.* Edited by R. de Hoop et al. Leiden: Brill, 2008.

———. "The Interpretation of Isaiah 56:1-9: Comfort or Criticism?" *JBL* 127 (2008): 671–95.

Diamond, A. R. Pete. *The Confessions of Jeremiah in Context: Scenes of Prophetic Drama.* JSOTSup 45. Sheffield: JSOT Press, 1987.

———. "Playing God: 'Polytheizing' YHWH-Alone in Jeremiah's Metaphorical Spaces." Pages 119–32 in *Metaphor in the Hebrew Bible.* Edited by P. J. P. van Hecke. BETL 187. Leuven: Peeters, 2005.

Dille, Sarah J. *Mixing Metaphors: God as Mother and Father in Deutero-Isaiah.* JSOTSup 398. London: T&T Clark, 2004.

Duhm, Bernhard. *Das Buch Jeremia.* Tübingen: J.C.B. Mohr, 1901.

———. *Das Buch Jesaia.* Göttingen: Vandenhoeck & Ruprecht, 1892.

Emmerson, Grace I. *Isaiah 56–66.* OTG. Sheffield: JSOT Press, 1992.

Eskenazi, Tamara C. and Eleanore P. Judd, "Marriage to a Stranger in Ezra 9–10." Pages 266–85 in *Second Temple Studies 2: Temple Community in the Persian Period*. Edited by T. C. Eskenazi and K. H. Richards. JSOTSup 175. Sheffield: JSOT Press, 1994.

Eszenyei Széles, Mária. *Wrath and Mercy: A Commentary on the Books of Habakkuk and Zephaniah*. ITC. Grand Rapids: Eerdmans, 1987.

Evans, Craig A. *To See and Not Perceive: Isaiah 6.9–10 in Early Jewish and Christian Interpretation*. JSOTSup 64. Sheffield: Sheffield Academic Press, 1989.

Everson, A. Joseph and Hyun Chul Paul Kim, eds. *The Desert Will Bloom: Poetic Visions in Isaiah*. SBLAIIL 4. Atlanta: Society of Biblical Literature, 2009.

Farley, Wendy. *Tragic Vision and Divine Compassion: A Contemporary Theodicy*. Louisville: Westminster John Knox, 1990.

Fisch, Harold. *Poetry with a Purpose: Biblical Poetics and Interpretation*. Bloomington, Ind.: Indiana University Press, 1988.

Fishbane, Michael. *Biblical Interpretation in Ancient Israel*. Oxford: Clarendon, 1985.

Floyd, Michael H. *Minor Prophets: Part 2*. FOTL 22. Grand Rapids: Eerdmans, 2000.

———. "The Production of Prophetic Books." Pages 276–97 in *Prophets, Prophecy and Prophetic Texts in Second Temple Judaism*. Edited by M. H. Floyd and R. D. Haak. LHBOTS 427. New York: T&T Clark, 2006.

Franke, Chris A. "Reversals of Fortune in the Ancient Near East: A Study of the Babylon Oracles in the Book of Isaiah." Pages 104–23 in *New Visions of Isaiah*. Edited by R. F. Melugin and M. A. Sweeney. JSOTSup 214. Sheffield: Sheffield Academic Press, 1996.

Frankl, Victor. *Man's Search for Meaning*. 4th ed. Boston: Beacon, 2000.

Fretheim, Terence E. *The Suffering of God: An Old Testament Perspective*. Philadelphia: Fortress, 1984.

Friedlander, Albert H., ed. *The Five Scrolls*. New York: CCAR Press, 1984.

Frolov, Serge. "Returning the Ticket: God and His Prophet in the Book of Jonah." *JSOT* 86 (1999): 85–105.

Frymer-Kensky, Tikva. *Reading the Women in the Bible: A New Interpretation of Their Stories*. New York: Schocken Books, 2002.

Fuller, Russell. "The Text of the Twelve Minor Prophets." *CurBS* 7 (1999): 81–95.

Gampel, Yolanda. "Reflections on the Prevalence of the Uncanny in Social Violence." Pages 48–69 in *Cultures under Siege: Collective Violence and Trauma*. Edited by A. C. G. M. Robben and M. M. Suárez-Orozco. Cambridge: Cambridge University Press, 2000.

Garber, David G. *Trauma, History, and Survival in Ezekiel 1–24*. Ph.D. diss., Emory University, 2005.

———. "Traumatizing Ezekiel, the Exilic Prophet." Pages 215–35 in *From Genesis to Apocalyptic Vision*. Vol. 2 of *Psychology and the Bible: A New Way to Read the Scriptures*. Edited by J. H. Ellens and W. G. Rollins. Praeger Perspectives: Psychology, Religion and Spirituality. Westport, Conn.: Praeger, 2004.

García-Treto, Francisco O. "The Book of Nahum." Pages 591–619 in *The New Interpreter's Bible*. Vol. 7. Edited by L. E. Keck et al. Nashville: Abingdon, 1996.

Goldingay, John A. "Ezekiel." Pages 623–64 in *Eerdmans Commentary on the Bible*. Edited by J. D. G. Dunn and J. W. Rogerson. Grand Rapids: Eerdmans, 2003.

Gowan, Donald E. *Theology of Prophetic Books: The Death and Resurrection of Israel*. Louisville: Westminster John Knox, 1998.

Gozdziak, Elzbieta M. *Refugee Women's Psychological Response to Forced Migration: Limitations of the Trauma Concept*, 2006. http://isim.georgetown.edu/ Publications/ElzPubs/Refugee%20 Women's%20Psychological%20Response.pdf.

Grabbe, Lester L. *Judaic Religion in the Second Temple Period: Belief and Practice from the Exile to Yavneh*. London: Routledge, 2000.

———. "The Law of Moses in the Ezra Tradition: More Virtual than Real?" Pages 91–113 in *Persia and Torah: The Theory of Imperial Authorization of the Pentateuch*. Edited by J. W. Watts. Atlanta: Society of Biblical Literature, 2001.

Grabbe, Lester L., ed. *Like a Bird in a Cage: The Invasion of Sennacherib in 701 B.C.E.* JSOTSup 363. New York: T&T Clark, 2003.

Graffy, Adrian. *A Prophet Confronts His People: The Disputation Speech in the Prophets*. AnBib 104. Rome: Biblical Institute Press, 1984.

Gruber, Mayer I. "The Motherhood of God in Second Isaiah." *RB* 90 (1983): 351–59.

Hanson, Paul D. *The Dawn of Apocalyptic*. Philadelphia: Fortress, 1975.

———. *The People Called: The Growth of Community in the Bible*. San Francisco: Harper & Row, 1986.

Hasel, Gerhard F. *The Remnant: The History and Theology of the Remnant Idea from Genesis to Isaiah*. Berrien Springs, Mich.: Andrews University Press, 1972.

Hauser, Alan J., ed. *Recent Research on the Major Prophets*. Sheffield: Sheffield Phoenix Press, 2008.

Herman, Judith Lewis. *Trauma and Recovery*. New York: Basic Books, 1997.

Heschel, Abraham J. *The Prophets*. New York: Perennial Classics, 2001 (original publication by Harper & Row, 1962).

Hexter, J. H. *The Judaeo-Christian Tradition*. 2d ed. New Haven: Yale University Press, 1995.

Hiebert, Theodore. "The Book of Habakkuk." Pages 621–55 in *The New Interpreter's Bible*. Vol. 7. Edited by L. E. Keck et al. Nashville: Abingdon, 1996.

Hill, Andrew E. *Malachi*. AB 25D. New York: Doubleday, 1998.

Holladay, William. *Jeremiah: Spokesman out of Time*. Philadelphia: Pilgrim, 1974.

———. "Was Trito-Isaiah Deutero-Isaiah After All?" Pages 193–217 in *Writing and Reading the Scroll of Isaiah: Studies of an Interpretive Tradition*. Vol. 1. Edited by C. C. Broyles and C. A. Evans. Leiden: Brill, 1997.

Horsley, Richard A. *Scribes, Visionaries, and the Politics of Second Temple Judea*. Louisville: Westminster John Knox, 2007.

Horsley, Richard A., ed. *In the Shadow of Empire: Reclaiming the Bible as a History of Faithful Resistance*. Louisville: Westminster John Knox, 2008.

Hourani, Albert. *A History of the Arab Peoples*. New York: Warner Books, 1991.

House, Paul R. "Dramatic Coherence in Nahum, Habakkuk, and Zephaniah." Pages 195–208 in *Forming Prophetic Literature: Essays in Isaiah and the Twelve in Honor of John D. W. Watts*. Edited by J. W. Watts and P. R. House. JSOTSup 235. Sheffield: Sheffield Academic Press, 1996.

———. *The Unity of the Twelve*. JSOTSup 97. Sheffield: Almond, 1990.

———. *Zephaniah: A Prophetic Drama*. Sheffield: Almond, 1988.

Hutton, Rodney R. *Fortress Introduction to the Prophets*. Minneapolis: Fortress, 2004.

Jacobs, Mignon R. "Bridging the Times: Trends in Micah Studies since 1985." CBR 4 (2006): 293–329.

———. *The Conceptual Coherence of the Book of Micah*. JSOTSup 322. Sheffield: Sheffield Academic Press, 2001.

Jacobsen, Thorkild. *The Treasures of Darkness: A History of Mesopotamian Religion*. New Haven: Yale University Press, 1978.

Janowski, Bernd and Peter Stuhlmacher, eds. *The Suffering Servant: Isaiah 53 in Jewish and Christian Sources*. Translated by D. P. Bailey. Grand Rapids: Eerdmans, 2004.

Janzen, Waldemar. *Mourning Cry and Woe Oracle*. BZAW 125. Berlin: de Gruyter, 1972.

Jenson, Philip Peter. *Obadiah, Jonah, Micah: A Theological Commentary*. LHBOTS 496. New York: T&T Clark, 2008.

Jeremias, Jörg. "The Interrelationship between Amos and Hosea." Pages 171–86 in *Forming Prophetic Literature: Essays on Isaiah and the Twelve in Honor of John D. W. Watts*. Edited by J. W. Watts and P. R. House. JSOTSup 235. Sheffield: Sheffield Academic Press, 1996.

Jones, Barry A. *The Formation of the Book of the Twelve: A Study in Text and Canon*. SBLDS 149. Atlanta: Scholars Press, 1995.

Joyce, Paul M. *Ezekiel: A Commentary*. LHBOTS 482. New York: T&T Clark, 2007.

Kaltner, John and Louis Stulman, eds. *Inspired Speech: Prophecy in the Ancient Near East: Essays in Honor of Herbert B. Huffman*. JSOTS 378. New York: T&T Clark, 2004.

Kaufmann, Yehezkel. *Israelite Religion from Its Beginnings to the Babylonian Exile*. Translated by Moshe Greenberg. New York: Schocken Books, 1972.

Kessler, Martin. *Battle of the Gods: The God of Israel versus Marduk of Babylon: A Literary/Theological Interpretation of Jeremiah 50–51*. Assen: Van Gorcum, 2003.

Kessler, Martin, ed. *Reading the Book of Jeremiah: A Search for Coherence*. Winona Lake, Ind.: Eisenbrauns, 2004.

Kim, Hyun Chul Paul. *Ambiguity, Tension, and Multiplicity in Deutero-Isaiah*. New York: Peter Lang, 2003.

———. "Form Criticism in Dialogue with Other Criticism: Building the Multidimensional Structures of Texts and Concepts." Pages 85–104 in *The Changing Face of Form Criticism for the Twenty-first Century*. Edited by M. A. Sweeney and E. Ben Zvi. Grand Rapids: Eerdmans, 2003.

———. "Interpretative Modes of Yin-Yang Dynamics as an Asian Hermeneutics." BibInt 9 (2001): 287–308.

———. "Jonah Read Intertextually." JBL 126 (2007): 497–518.

————. "Recent Scholarship in Isaiah 1–39." Pages 118–41 in *Recent Research on the Major Prophets*. Edited by A. J. Hauser. Recent Research in Biblical Studies 1. Sheffield: Sheffield Phoenix Press, 2008.

————. "Tsunami, Hurricane, and Jeremiah 4:23–28." *BTB* 37 (2007): 54–61.

King, Philip J. *Amos, Hosea, Micah: An Archaeological Commentary*. Philadelphia: Westminster, 1988.

Kira, Ibrahim Aref. "Taxonomy of Trauma and Trauma Assessment." *Traumatology* 7 (2001): 73–86.

Klein, Ralph W. *Israel in Exile: A Theological Interpretation*. OBT. Philadelphia: Fortress, 1979.

Knapp, A. Bernard. *The History and Culture of Ancient Western Asia and Egypt*. Belmont, Calif.: Wadsworth, 1988.

Knierim, Rolf P. *The Task of Old Testament Theology: Substance, Method, and Cases*. Grand Rapids: Eerdmans, 1995.

Knoppers, Gary N. "An Achaemenid Imperial Authorization of Torah in Yehud?" Pages 115–34 in *Persia and Torah: The Theory of Imperial Authorization of the Pentateuch*. Edited by J. W. Watts. Atlanta: Society of Biblical Literature, 2001.

Koch, Klaus. *The Prophets: The Babylonian and Persian Periods*. Philadelphia: Fortress, 1982.

Kohn, Risa Levitt. "Ezekiel at the Turn of the Century." *CBR* 2 (2003): 9–31.

Koole, Jan L. *Isaiah III/1: Chapters 40–48*. Kampen: Kok Pharos, 1997.

————. *Isaiah III/3: Chapters 56–66*. Leuven: Peeters, 2001.

Kratz, Reinhard G. "Der Anfang des Zweiten Jesaja in Jes 40,1f. und das Jeremiabuch." *ZAW* 106 (1994): 243–61.

————. "Der Anfang des Zweiten Jesaja in Jes 40,1 f. und seine literarischen Horizonte." *ZAW* 105 (1993): 400–419.

————. "Israel in the Book of Isaiah." *JSOT* 31 (2006): 103–28.

————. *Kyros im Deuterojesaja-Buch: Redaktionsgeschichtliche Untersuchungen zu Entstehung und Theologie von Jes 40–55*. FAT 1. Tübingen: Mohr Siebeck, 1991.

Kutsko, John F. *Between Heaven and Earth: Divine Presence and Absence in the Book of Ezekiel*. Winona Lake, Ind.: Eisenbrauns, 2000.

Leclerc, Thomas L. *Introduction to the Prophets: Their Stories, Sayings, and Scrolls*. New York: Paulist, 2007.

Lemaire, Jean-Marie. "Disconcerting Humanitarian Interventions, and the Resources for Collective Healing," Pages 71–77 in *Psychosocial and Trauma Response in War-torn Societies: The Case of Kosovo*. Under the direction of Natale Losi. Psychosocial Notebook. Vol. 1. November 2000.

Lester, Andrew D. *Hope in Pastoral Care and Counseling*. Louisville: Westminster John Knox, 1995.

Lifton, Robert J. *Death in Life: Survivors of Hiroshima*. New York: Random House, 1968.

Linafelt, Tod. *Surviving Lamentations: Catastrophe, Lament, and Protest in the Afterlife of a Biblical Book*. Chicago: University of Chicago, 2000.

Lipschits, Oded. *The Fall and Rise of Jerusalem*. Winona Lake, Ind.: Eisenbrauns, 2005.

Maier, Christl M. *Daughter Zion, Mother Zion: Gender, Space, and the Sacred in Ancient Israel.* Minneapolis: Fortress, 2008.

———. "Jeremiah as Teacher of Torah." *Int* 62 (2008): 22–32.

Malina, Bruce J. *The New Testament World: Insights from Cultural Anthropology.* 3d ed. Louisville. Westminster John Knox, 2001.

Martin-Achard, Robert. *God's People in Crisis: A Commentary on the Book of Amos.* ITC. Grand Rapids: Eerdmans, 1984.

Mason, Rex. *Preaching the Tradition: Homily and Hermeneutics after the Exile.* Cambridge: Cambridge University Press, 1990.

———. "The Relation of Zech. 9–14 to Proto-Zechariah." *ZAW* 88 (1976): 227–39.

———. "The Use of Earlier Biblical Material in Zechariah 9–14." Pages 2–208 in *Bringing out the Treasure: Inner Biblical Allusion in Zechariah 9–14.* Edited by M. J. Boda and M. H. Floyd. JSOTSup 370. Sheffield: Sheffield Academic Press, 2003.

Mathews, Claire R. *Defending Zion: Edom's Desolation and Jacob's Restoration (Isaiah 34–35) in Context.* BZAW 236. Berlin: de Gruyter, 1995.

McGinnis, Claire Mathews and Patricia K. Tull, eds. *"As Those Who Are Taught": The Interpretation of Isaiah from the LXX to the SBL.* SBLSymS 27. Atlanta: Society of Biblical Literature, 2006.

McKeating, Henry. *Ezekiel.* OTG. Sheffield: Sheffield Academic Press, 1993.

Mein, Andrew. *Ezekiel and the Ethics of Exile.* Oxford: Oxford University Press, 2001.

Melugin, Roy F. "Amos in Recent Research." *CurBS* 6 (1998): 65–101.

———. *The Formation of Isaiah 40–55.* BZAW 141. Berlin: de Gruyter, 1976.

———. "Isaiah 40–66 in Recent Research: The 'Unity' Movement." Pages 142–94 in *Recent Research on the Major Prophets.* Edited by A. J. Hauser. Recent Research in Biblical Studies 1. Sheffield: Sheffield Phoenix Press, 2008.

Melugin, Roy F. and Marvin A. Sweeney, eds. *New Visions of Isaiah.* JSOTSup 214. Sheffield: Sheffield Academic Press, 1996.

Merton, Thomas. *Disputed Questions.* New York: Farrar, Straus, & Cudahy, 1960.

———. *A Year with Thomas Merton. Daily Meditations from his Journals.* Selected and edited by Jonathan Montaldo. New York: HarperOne, 2004.

Meyers, Carol L. and Eric M. Meyers. *Haggai, Zechariah 1–8.* AB 25B. Garden City, N.Y.: Doubleday, 1987.

———. *Zechariah 9–14.* AB 25C. New York: Doubleday, 1993.

Middlemas, Jill. *The Templeless Age: An Introduction to the History, Literature, and Theology of the "Exile."* Louisville: Westminster John Knox, 2007.

Miller, William R. and Kathleen A. Jackson. *Practical Psychology for Pastors.* Englewood Cliffs, N.J.: Prentice Hall, 1995.

Mills, Mary. *Alterity, Pain, and Suffering in Isaiah, Jeremiah, and Ezekiel.* LHBOTS 479. New York: T&T Clark, 2007.

Milosz, Czeslaw. *Selected Poems 1931–2004.* New York: HarperCollins, 2006.

Miscall, Peter D. *Isaiah 34–35: A Nightmare/A Dream*. JSOTSup 281. Sheffield: Sheffield Academic Press, 1999.

Mitchell, Kenneth R. and Herbert Anderson. *All Our Losses, All Our Griefs: Resources for Pastoral Care*. Louisville: Westminster John Knox, 1983.

Mowinckel, Sigmund. *Zur Komposition des Buches Jeremia*. Kristiania: Jacob Dybwad, 1914.

Murphy, Roland E. *The Book of Job: A Short Reading*. New York: Paulist, 1999.

Neubauer, Adolf. *The Fifty-third Chapter of Isaiah: According to the Jewish Interpreters*. New York: Ktav, 1969.

Niditch, Susan, *Oral World and Written Word: Ancient Israelite Literature*. Library of Ancient Israel. Louisville: Westminster John Knox, 1996.

Nissinen, Martti. "How Prophecy Became Literature." *SJOT* 19 (2005): 153–72.

———. "What Is Prophecy? An Ancient Near Eastern Perspective." Pages 17–37 in *Inspired Speech: Prophecy in the Ancient Near East: Essays in Honor of Herbert B. Huffmon*. Edited by J. Kaltner and L. Stulman. JSOTSup 378. New York: T&T Clark, 2004.

Nogalski, James D. *Literary Precursors to the Book of the Twelve*. BZAW 217. Berlin: de Gruyter, 1993.

———. *Redactional Processes in the Book of the Twelve*. BZAW 218. Berlin: de Gruyter, 1993.

Nouwen, Henri. *Life Signs: Intimacy, Fecundity, and Ecstasy in Christian Perspective*. New York: Random House, 1989.

———. *The Living Reminder: Service and Prayer in Memory of Jesus Christ*. San Francisco: Harper & Row, 1984.

———. *Peacework: Prayer, Resistance, Community*. Maryknoll, N.Y.: Orbis Books, 2005.

———. *Reaching Out*. New York: Doubleday, 1975.

———. *With Open Hands*. Notre Dame, Ind.: Ave Maria, 1972.

Nouwen, Henri with Michael J. Christensen and Rebecca J. Laird. *Spiritual Direction*. San Francisco: HarperSanFrancisco, 2006.

Nurmela, Risto. "The Growth of the Book of Isaiah Illustrated by Allusions in Zechariah." Pages 245–59 in *Bringing out the Treasure: Inner Biblical Allusion in Zechariah 9–14*. Edited by M. J. Boda and M. H. Floyd. JSOTSup 370. Sheffield: Sheffield Academic Press, 2003.

O'Brien, Julia M. *Challenging Prophetic Metaphor: Theology and Ideology in the Prophets*. Louisville: Westminster John Knox, 2008.

———. *Nahum, Habakkuk, Zephaniah, Haggai, Zechariah, Malachi*. AOTC. Nashville: Abingdon, 2004.

O'Connor, Kathleen M. "The Book of Jeremiah: Reconstructing Community after Disaster." Pages 81-92 in *Character Ethics and the Old Testament. Moral Dimensions of Scripture*. Edited by M. Daniel Carroll R. and Jacqueline E. Lapsley. Louisville: Westminster John Knox, 2007.

———. *The Confessions of Jeremiah: Their Interpretation and Role in Chapters 1–25*. SBLDS 94. Atlanta: Scholars Press, 1988.

———. *Lamentations and the Tears of the World*. Maryknoll, N.Y.: Orbis Books, 2002.

———. "Surviving Disaster in the Book of Jeremiah." *Word & World* 22 (2002): 369-77.

Bibliography

Bibliography

———. "The Tears of God and Divine Character in Jeremiah 2–9." Pages 172–85 in *God in the Fray: A Tribute to Walter Brueggemann*. Edited by T. Linafelt and T. K. Beal. Minneapolis: Fortress, 1998.

Odell, Margaret S. *Ezekiel*. Smyth & Helwys Bible Commentary. Macon, Ga.: Smyth & Helwys, 2005.

Odell, Margaret S. and J. T. Strong, eds. *The Book of Ezekiel: Theological and Anthropological Perspectives*. SBLSymS 9. Atlanta: Society of Biblical Literature, 2000.

Ogden, Graham S. *A Promise of Hope—A Call to Obedience: A Commentary on the Book of Joel*. ITC. Grand Rapids: Eerdmans, 1987.

Oswalt, John N. *The Book of Isaiah, Chapters 1–39*. NICOT. Grand Rapids: Eerdmans, 1986.

———. *The Book of Isaiah: Chapters 40–66*. NICOT. Grand Rapids: Eerdmans, 1998.

Pagán, Samuel. "The Book of Obadiah." Pages 433–59 in *The New Interpreter's Bible*. Vol. 7. Edited by L. E. Keck et al. Nashville: Abingdon, 1996.

Paul, Shalom M. *Amos*. Hermeneia. Minneapolis: Fortress, 1991.

———. "Literary and Ideological Echoes of Jeremiah in Deutero-Isaiah." Pages 109–21 in *Proceedings of the Fifth World Congress of Jewish Studies*. Vol. 1. Edited by P. Peli. Jerusalem: World Union of Jewish Studies, 1969.

Perdue, Leo G. *The Collapse of History: Reconstructing Old Testament Theology*. Minneapolis: Fortress, 1994.

———. *Reconstructing Old Testament Theology: After the Collapse of History*. OBT; Minneapolis: Fortress, 2005.

———. *Wisdom Literature: A Theological History*. Louisville: Westminster John Knox, 2007.

Perry, T. Anthony. *The Honeymoon Is Over: Jonah's Argument with God*. Peabody, Mass.: Hendrickson, 2006.

Petersen, David L. *The Prophetic Literature: An Introduction*. Louisville: Westminster John Knox, 2002.

———. *Zechariah 9–14 and Malachi*. OTL. Louisville: Westminster John Knox, 1995.

———. "Zechariah 9–14: Methodological Reflections." Pages 210–24 in *Bringing out the Treasure: Inner Biblical Allusion in Zechariah 9–14*. Edited by M. J. Boda and M. H. Floyd. JSOTSup 370. Sheffield: Sheffield Academic Press, 2003.

Raabe, Paul R. *Obadiah*. AB 24D. New York: Doubleday, 1996.

Rad, Gerhard von. "The Confessions of Jeremiah." Pages 88–99 in *Theodicy in the Old Testament*. Edited by J. L. Crenshaw. Philadelphia: Fortress, 1983.

———. *Old Testament Theology*. Vol. 2. Translated by D. M. G. Stalker. New York: Harper & Row, 1965.

Raitt, T. A. *A Theology of Exile: Judgment/Deliverance in Jeremiah and Ezekiel*. Philadelphia: Fortress, 1977.

Redditt, Paul L. *Introduction to the Prophets*. Grand Rapids: Eerdmans, 2008.

———. "Recent Research on the Book of the Twelve as One Book." *CurBS* 9 (2001): 47–80.

Redditt, Paul L. and Aaron Schart, eds. *Thematic Threads in the Book of the Twelve*. BZAW 325. Berlin: de Gruyter, 2003.

296

Renaud, B. *Michée, Sophonie, Nahum*. Paris: Gabalda, 1987.

Rendtorff, Rolf. *Canon and Theology*. Translated by M. Kohl. OBT. Minneapolis: Fortress, 1993.

Reventlow, Henning G. *Liturgie und prophetisches Ich bei Jeremia*. Gütersloh: Gütersloher, 1966.

Ricoeur, Paul. "The Hermeneutical Function of Distanciation." Pages 131–44 in *Hermeneutics and the Human Sciences*. Edited and translated by J. B. Thompson. New York: Cambridge University Press, 1981.

———. *Interpretation Theory: Discourse and the Surplus of Meaning*. Fort Worth: Texas Christian University Press, 1976.

———. "What Is a Text? Explanation and Understanding." Pages 145–64 in *Hermeneutics and the Human Sciences*. Edited and translated by J. B. Thompson. New York: Cambridge University Press, 1981.

Rinder, Lawrence and Tariq Ali. *The American Effect: Global Perspectives on the United States, 1990–2003*. New York: Whitney Museum of Art Books, 2003.

Roberts, J. J. M. *Nahum, Habakkuk, and Zephaniah*. OTL. Louisville: Westminster John Knox, 1991.

Roux, Georges. *Ancient Iraq*. New York: Penguin Books, 1964.

Sanders, James A. "Adaptable to Life: The Nature and Function of Canon." Pages 531–60 in *Magnalia Dei, The Mighty Acts of God: Essays on the Bible and Archaeology in Memory of G. Ernest Wright*. Edited by F. M. Cross et al. Garden City, N.Y.: Doubleday, 1976.

———. *From Sacred Story to Sacred Text*. Philadelphia: Fortress, 1987.

———. *Torah and Canon*. Philadelphia: Fortress, 1972.

Sasson, Jack M. *Jonah*. AB 24B. New York: Doubleday, 1990.

Sawyer, John F. A. "Daughter of Zion and Servant of the Lord in Isaiah: A Comparison." *JSOT* 44 (1989): 89–107.

———. *The Fifth Gospel: Isaiah in the History of Christianity*. Cambridge: Cambridge University Press, 1996.

Schart, Aaron. *Die Entstehung des Zwölfprophetenbuchs: Neubearbeitungen von Amos im Rahmen schriftenübergreifender Redaktionsprozesse*. BZAW 260. Berlin: de Gruyter, 1998.

———. "Putting the Eschatological Visions of Zechariah in Their Place: Malachi as a Hermeneutical Guide for the Last Section of the Book of the Twelve." Pages 333–43 in *Bringing out the Treasure: Inner Biblical Allusion in Zechariah 9–14*. Edited by M. J. Boda and M. H. Floyd. JSOTSup 370. Sheffield: Sheffield Academic Press, 2003.

Scheuer, Blaženka. *The Return of YHWH: The Tension between Deliverance and Repentance in Isaiah 40–55*. BZAW 377. Berlin: de Gruyter, 2008.

Schramm, Brooks. *The Opponents of Third Isaiah: Reconstructing the Cultic History of the Restoration*. JSOTSup 193. Sheffield: Sheffield Academic Press, 1995.

Schuller, Eileen M. "The Book of Malachi." Pages 841–77 in *The New Interpreter's Bible*. Vol. 7. Edited by L. E. Keck et al. Nashville: Abingdon, 1996.

Schwartz, Regina. "Joseph's Bones and the Resurrection of the Text: Remembering in the Bible." Pages 40–59 in *The Book and the Text: The Bible and Literary Theory*. Edited by R. M. Schwartz. Oxford: Basil Blackwell, 1990.

Sebald, W. G. *On the Natural History of Destruction.* New York: Random House, 2003.

Seitz, Christopher R. "The Book of Isaiah 40–66." Pages 307–552 in *The New Interpreter's Bible.* Vol. 6. Edited by L. E. Keck et al. Nashville: Abingdon, 2001.

———. *Isaiah 1–39.* Interpretation. Louisville: Westminster John Knox, 1993.

———. *Prophecy and Hermeneutics: Toward a New Introduction to the Prophets.* Grand Rapids: Baker Academic, 2007.

———. *Zion's Final Destiny: The Development of the Book of Isaiah: A Reassessment of Isaiah 36–39.* Minneapolis: Fortress, 1991.

Shamana, Beverly J. "Letting Go." Pages 101–5 in *Those Preachin' Women: Sermons by Black Women Preachers.* Edited by E. P. Mitchell. Valley Forge: Judson, 1985.

Sharp, Carolyn J. *Prophecy and Ideology: Struggles for Authority in the Deutero-Jeremianic Prose.* OTS. New York: T&T Clark, 2003.

Shetterly, Robert. *Americans Who Tell the Truth.* New York: Dutton Children's Books, 2005.

Simon, Uriel. *Jonah.* JPS Bible Commentary. Translated by L. J. Schramm. Philadelphia: The Jewish Publication Society, 1999.

Simundson, Daniel J. "The Book of Micah." Pages 531–89 in *The New Interpreter's Bible.* Vol. 7. Edited by L. E. Keck et al. Nashville: Abingdon, 1996.

———. *Hosea, Joel, Amos, Obadiah, Jonah, Micah.* AOTC. Nashville: Abingdon, 2005.

Skehan, Patrick W. *The Wisdom of Ben Sira.* AB 39. New York: Doubleday, 1987.

Smith, Mark S. *The Laments of Jeremiah and Their Contexts: A Literary and Redactional Study of Jeremiah 11–20.* SBLMS 42. Atlanta: Scholars Press, 1990.

———. *The Origins of Biblical Monotheism: Israel's Polytheistic Background and the Ugaritic Texts.* New York: Oxford University Press, 2001.

Smith-Christopher, Daniel L. *A Biblical Theology of Exile.* OBT. Minneapolis: Fortress, 2002.

———. "Ezekiel on Fanon's Couch: A Postcolonialist Dialogue with David Halperin's *Seeking Ezekiel.*" Pages 108–44 in *Peace and Justice Shall Embrace: Power and Theopolitics in the Bible.* Edited by T. Grimsrud and L. L. Johns. Telford, Pa.: Pandora, 1999.

———. "Reassessing the Historical and Sociological Impact of the Babylonian Exile (597/587–539 B.C.E.)." Pages 7–36 in *Exile: Old Testament, Jewish, and Christian Conceptions.* Edited by J. M. Scott. Supplements to the Journal for the Study of Judaism 56. Leiden: Brill, 1997.

Sommer, Benjamin D. *A Prophet Reads Scripture: Allusion in Isaiah 40–66.* Stanford: Stanford University Press, 1998.

Stansell, Gary. "Isaiah 28–33: Blest Be the Tie That Binds (Isaiah Together)." Pages 68–103 in *New Visions of Isaiah.* Edited by R. F. Melugin and M. A. Sweeney. JSOTSup 214. Sheffield: Sheffield Academic Press, 1996.

Steck, Odil Hannes. *Bereitete Heimkehr: Jesaja 35 als redaktionelle Brücke zwischen dem Ersten und dem Zweiten Jesaja.* SBS 121. Stuttgart: Katholisches Bibelwerk, 1985.

Stolick, Matthew. "Fostering True Hopes of Terminally Ill Patients." *BIO Quarterly* 17 no. 2 (2006): 3–10.

Strawn, Brent A. "Second Isaiah and the Exilic Imagination." Pages 175–76 in *Teaching the Bible: Practical Strategies for Classroom Instruction*. Edited by M. Roncace and P. Gray. Atlanta: Society of Biblical Literature, 2005.

Stulman, Louis. "Conflicting Paths to Hope in Jeremiah." Pages 43–57 in *Shaking Heaven and Earth: Essays in Honor of Walter Brueggemann and Charles B. Cousar*. Edited by C. R. Yoder et al. Louisville: Westminster John Knox, 2005.

———. "Encroachment in Deuteronomy: An Analysis of the Social World of the D Code." *JBL* 109 (1990): 613–32.

———. *Jeremiah*. AOTC. Nashville: Abingdon, 2005.

———. "Jeremiah as a Polyphonic Response to Suffering." Pages 302–18 in *Inspired Speech: Prophecy in the Ancient Near East. Essays in Honour of Herbert B. Huffmon*. JSOTSup 378. Edited by J. Kaltner and L. Stulman. New York: T&T Clark, 2004.

———. *Order Amid Chaos: Jeremiah as Symbolic Tapestry*. The Biblical Seminar 57. Sheffield: Sheffield Academic Press, 1998.

———. "The Prose Sermons as Hermeneutical Guide to Jeremiah 1–25: The Deconstruction of Judah's Symbolic World." Pages 34–63 in *Troubling Jeremiah*. Edited by A. R. Diamond, K. M. O'Connor, and L. Stulman. JSOTSup 260. Sheffield: Sheffield Academic Press, 1999.

Suárez-Orozco, Marcelo M. and Antonius C. G. M. Robben. "Interdisciplinary Perspectives on Violence and Trauma." Pages 1–41 in *Cultures under Siege: Collective Violence and Trauma*. Edited by A. C. G. M. Robben and M. M. Suárez-Orozco. Cambridge: Cambridge University Press, 2000.

Sweeney, Marvin A. *Form and Intertextuality in Prophetic and Apocalyptic Literature*. FAT 45. Tübingen: Mohr Siebeck, 2005.

———. *Isaiah 1–39*. FOTL 16. Grand Rapids: Eerdmans, 1996.

———. "Micah's Debate with Isaiah." *JSOT* 93 (2001): 111–24.

———. *The Prophetic Literature*. Nashville: Abingdon, 2005.

———. *Reading the Hebrew Bible after the Shoah: Engaging Holocaust Theology*. Minneapolis: Fortress, 2008.

———. "Reevaluating Isaiah 1–39 in Recent Critical Research." *CurBS* 4 (1996): 84–85.

———. *The Twelve Prophets*. Vols. 1 and 2. Berit Olam. Minneapolis: Liturgical, 2000.

———. "Zechariah's Debate with Isaiah." Pages 335–50 in *The Changing Face of Form Criticism for the Twenty-first Century*. Edited by M. A. Sweeney and E. Ben Zvi. Grand Rapids: Eerdmans, 2003.

———. *Zephaniah*. Hermeneia. Minneapolis: Fortress, 2003.

———. "Zephaniah: A Paradigm for the Study of the Prophetic Books." *CurBS* 7 (1999): 119–45.

Tai, Nicholas Ho Fai. "The End of the Book of the Twelve. Reading Zechariah 12–14 with Joel." Pages 341–50 in *Schriftprophetie: FS für Jörg Jeremias zum 65. Geburtstag*. Edited by F. Hartenstein, J. Krispenz, and A. Schart. Neukirchen-Vluyn: Neukirchener, 2004.

Toorn, Karel van der. "From the Mouth of the Prophet: The Literary Fixation of Jeremiah's Prophecies in the Context of the Ancient Near East." Pages 191–202 in *Inspired Speech:*

Prophecy in the Ancient Near East: Essays in Honor of Herbert B. Huffmon. Edited by J. Kaltner and L. Stulman. JSOTS 378. New York: T&T Clark, 2004.

Trible, Phyllis. "The Book of Jonah." Pages 461–529 in *The New Interpreter's Bible.* Vol. 7. Edited by L. E. Keck et al. Nashville: Abingdon, 1996.

———. *God and the Rhetoric of Sexuality.* OBT. Philadelphia: Fortress, 1978.

Vanderhooft, David S. "New Evidence Pertaining to the Transition from Neo-Babylonian to Achaemenid Administration in Palestine." Pages 219–35 in *Yahwism after the Exile: Perspectives on Israelite Religion in the Persian Era.* Edited by R. Albertz and B. Becking. Assen: Van Gorcum, 2003.

Volf, Miroslav and William H. Katerberg, eds. *The Future of Hope: Christian Tradition amid Modernity and Postmodernity.* Grand Rapids: Eerdmans, 2004.

Waard, Jan de. "The Chiastic Structure of Amos V 1–17." *VT* 27 (1977): 170–77.

Wagner, Thomas. *Gottes Herrschaft: Eine Analyse der Denkschrift (Jes 6,1 – 9,6).* VTSup 108. Leiden: Brill, 2006.

Waltke, Bruce K. *A Commentary on Micah.* Grand Rapids: Eerdmans, 2007.

Watts, John D. W. "A Frame for the Book of the Twelve: Hosea 1–3 and Malachi." Pages 209–17 in *Reading and Hearing the Book of the Twelve.* Edited by J. D. Nogalski and M. A. Sweeney. SBLSymS 15. Atlanta: Society of Biblical Literature, 2000.

———. *Isaiah 1–33.* Rev. ed. WBC. Nashville: Thomas Nelson, 2005.

———. *Isaiah 34–66.* Rev. ed. WBC. Nashville: Thomas Nelson, 2005.

Weigl, Michael. "Current Research on the Book of Nahum: Exegetical Methodologies in Turmoil?" *CurBS* 9 (2001): 81–130.

Weinberg, Joel. *The Citizen-Temple Community.* Translated by D. L. Smith-Christopher. JSOTSup 151. Sheffield: Sheffield Academic Press, 1992.

Wells, Roy D. "'Isaiah' as an Exponent of Torah: Isaiah 56.1-8." Pages 140–55 in *New Visions of Isaiah.* Edited by R. F. Melugin and M. A. Sweeney. JSOTSup 214. Sheffield: Sheffield Academic Press, 1996.

Westermann, Claus. *Basic Forms of Prophetic Speech.* Philadelphia: Westminster, 1967.

———. *Isaiah 40–66.* OTL. Translated by D. M. G. Stalker. Philadelphia: Westminster, 1969.

Whybray, R. Norman. *The Second Isaiah.* OTG. Sheffield: JSOT Press, 1983.

Wildberger, Hans. *Isaiah 1–12.* Translated by T. H. Trapp. Minneapolis: Fortress, 1991.

———. *Isaiah 13–27.* Translated by T. H. Trapp. Minneapolis: Fortress, 1997.

Willey, Patricia K. *Remember the Former Things: The Recollection of Previous Texts in Second Isaiah.* SBLDS 161. Atlanta: Scholars Press, 1997.

Williamson, Hugh G. M. *The Book Called Isaiah: Deutero-Isaiah's Role in Composition and Redaction.* Oxford: Clarendon, 1994.

———. "Hezekiah and the Temple." Pages 47–52 in *Texts, Temples, and Traditions: A Tribute to Menahem Haran.* Edited by M. V. Fox et al. Winona Lake, Ind.: Eisenbrauns, 1996.

———. *Isaiah 1–27.* Vol. 1. ICC. London: T&T Clark, 2006.

———. *Studies in the Persian Period History and Historiography.* FAT 38. Tübingen: Mohr Siebeck, 2004.

Wilson, Robert R. "The Community of the Second Isaiah." Pages 53–70 in *Reading and Preaching the Book of Isaiah*. Edited by C. R. Seitz. Philadelphia: Fortress, 1988.

———. "Poetry and Prose in the Book of Jeremiah." Pages 413–27 in *Ki Baruch Hu: Ancient Near Eastern Studies in Honor of Baruch A. Levine*. Edited by R. Chazan, W. W. Hallo, and L. H. Schiffman; Winona Lake, Ind.: Eisenbrauns, 1999.

Yee, Gale A. "The Book of Hosea." Pages 195–297 in *The New Interpreter's Bible*. Vol. 7. Edited by L. E. Keck et al. Nashville: Abingdon, 1996.

———. *Poor Banished Children of Eve: Woman as Evil in the Hebrew Bible*. Minneapolis: Fortress, 2003.

Zenger, Erich. "Das Buch Nahum." Pages 509–12 in *Einleitung in das Alte Testament*. Edited by E. Zenger et al. Stuttgart: Kohlhammer, 1998.

http://www.forcedmigration.org/psychosocial/papers/WiderPapers/iom_note book1.pdf.

http://isim.georgetown.edu/Publications/ElzPubs/Refugee%20Women's%20Psycho logical%20Response.pdf.

INDEX OF SCRIPTURE REFERENCES

Hebrew Bible

303

Isaiah (continued)

1:2	30, 44, 49	5:22	35
1:3	30, 45, 46	5:25	37, 45
1:4	31	5:25-30	258
1:6	36	6	32, 34, 37, 39
1:9-10	45	6:1-5	70
1:10	31, 37	6:3	32
1:11-14	30	6:5	32, 52
1:15	31	6:6-8	242
1:16	46	6:7	234
1:16-17	31, 43	6:8	32
1:17	51	6:8-12	61
1:18	32	6:9	32, 34, 36
1:18-20	42	6:9-10	30, 36, 57
1:21	30, 72	6:9-12	33
1:21-23	37	6:10	32, 33, 46, 76, 233
1:23	50	6:10-13	76
1:25	46	6:11	33, 34, 52, 189, 209, 233
1:27	30	6:13	33, 43
1:29	37	7	37
2:1	49	7–8	38
2:2	46	7:3	38, 262
2:2-4	39, 46	7:4-9	38
2:2-5	214	7:9	50
2:3	44, 49	7:14	41, 262
2:3-4	47	8:1-2	48
2:4	45, 130	8:3	262
2:5	43, 50	8:8	41
2:6	158	8:10	41
2:11-17	35	8:16	48
2:17	41	8:17	49
2:20	41	8:21	49
3:4	46	9	51, 77
3:12	30	9:1	43, 50
3:14-15	35	9:2	43, 50
3:15	50	9:5	50
3:16-23	50	9:5-6	38
4	28	9:6	50, 51
4:2	41	9:6-7	38
4:4-6	42	9:7	51
5	35, 37, 87, 257	9:8-9	37
5:1-7	35, 45	9:11	37, 45
5:7	30, 35, 37, 46	9:12	37
5:8	35, 36	9:16	37
5:11	35	9:17	37, 45
5:18	35, 36	9:17-20	45
5:20	35, 46	9:20	37, 45, 46
5:20-23	36	9:21	37
5:21	35	10	44
		10:1	46

Deuterocanonical Books

New Testament

9 780687 465651